The Challenge of Soccer

The Challenge of Soccer
A Handbook of Skills, Techniques, and Strategy

Hubert Vogelsinger

Yale University

ALLYN AND BACON, INC.   BOSTON

To my secret (sometimes not so secret) weapon,
companion, and collaborator, my wife Lois.

Library of Congress Catalog Card Number: 73-
82966

Printed in the United States of America

Acknowledgements

I should like to acknowledge the debt I owe to the colleagues and players of many countries for the long hours of discussion about all phases of the game. Through these discussions, the many clinics I have given throughout the United States, and also from close association with the players at Yale and at the All Star Soccer School, I was able to formulate the needs and methods of coaching instruction for this book.

To Herman Masin I owe a special debt for stimulating criticism and sharp editing. That our friendship survived the confrontation of a writer prone to excessive detail and elaborate development of ideas with an editor who delights in crisp, precise phrasing and a direct approach is a testament to our faith in one another and the importance we placed upon the material.

For the outstanding photographs I must thank Sab Frinzi of New Haven, Connecticut (Figs. 2.17, 3.17, 3.19, 4.10, 8.10, 9.7, 9.8, 9.28, 11.2, 11.6, 13.2, 13.3, 13.4, 13.5, 13.6, 13.7, and 13.43); Milton Smith of New Haven, Connecticut (Figs. 2.10, 3.4, 3.11, 3.12, 4.11, 7.10, 7.11, 8.5, 8.12, 13.8, 13.16, and A.2); Lois Vogelsinger; and Horst Müller of Düsseldorf, Germany (opening photographs for Chapters 2, 3, 4, 5, 8, 9, 10, 12, 14, 15, and 16 and Figs. P.2, 1.3, 2.1, 2.2, 2.9, 2.14b, 2.19, 3.1, 3.3, 3.18a, 4.1, 4.2, 4.5, 8.1, 8.2, 8.16, 9.1, 9.4, 9.20, 9.26, and 13.29). Special thanks must go to Gerd Dassler of PUMA, S.A. cf Germany for providing the many fine photographs of international players in action and the permission to use these great shots: from Agfa Gevaert, Mexico City, Figs. P.1 and 13.1; from Bippa, London, Figs. 2.14a, 6.14, and 9.3; from Foto Bert, Barcelona, Fig. 2.7; from General News Agency International, Athens, Fig. 9.19; from D. Green, Manchester, England, Figs. 6.11 and 6.13; from Keystone, London, Fig. 2.3; from London Photo Agency, London, Figs. 2.23, 7.3, and 9.25; from Ian McLennall, Essex, England, Fig. 3.2; from Otto Metelmann, Hamburg, Figs. 4.13, 9.2, 9.6, and 13.21 and opening photograph for Chapter 7; from Press Association Photos, London, Fig. 6.1 and opening photograph for Chapter 11; from Provincial Press Agency, Southport, England, Figs. 3.18b, 6.7, 7.5, 7.13, 7.15, 9.14, and 9.17; from Sven Simon, München, Germany, Figs. 1.2 and 7.2; from Syndication International, London, Figs. 3.16, 4.3, 6.4, 7.1, 7.6, 7.12, 9.12, 9.15, 9.18, 9.23, and 11.7; from United Press International, London, opening photograph for Chapter 6 and Figs. 6.6, 11.3b, and 11.4; from Hans Vincurek, Wien, Austria, Fig. 2.13; and from Wirtschaftswerbung Franker, Nürnberg, Germany, Fig. 1.1. Lee Stock of Sports Beconta, Inc., New York, was also most helpful in getting these photographs for publication.

Graphic photographic sequences were made possible by the demonstrating assistance of my friend and colleague, Ben Brewster, and also Dick Howard and many of my players, especially Steve Greenberg.

I am grateful to Professor Arthur Miller for his confidence in my ability to prepare a manuscript on soccer that would meet the high standards of the coaching series he edits. To be part of his fine project with Allyn and Bacon, Inc., has been a most rewarding experience.

Preface

Baseball, basketball, and football are America's national pastimes. Hockey is the rage in Canada. Rugby is next to godliness in the "Land Down Under." But association football, or soccer, remains the number one sport of the universe—the fun and fever of one hundred forty nations and over sixteen million players.

What makes this basically elementary game so irresistible? Its objective is simple enough: to kick a ball through a goal eight feet high and twenty-four feet wide. But the manner in which this is done is both a science and an art.

The unpredictability of the ball offers a constant challenge. At one moment, it may require just a light touch to be put under control; at the next, it may demand a violent thrust to be slammed into the net.

Fig. P.1 *"The objective is simple enough: to kick a ball through a goal eight feet high and twenty-four feet wide. But the manner in which this is done is both a science and an art."*

The player must be able to coordinate with the ball—to become one with it. He must also have the stamina of a cross-country runner and the mental nimbleness of a chess player to anticipate his opponent's moves and outwit him.

Physical contact? Exquisite technique? Stop-and-go action? Individual and team strategy? Soccer has them all. Its individualism and relevancy make it THE game for the NOW generation. Soccer is "relevant" in that it is dynamic with non-stop action, it can be played by anyone, it is fast and tough, it requires courage and will power, and it frowns upon conformity. It is "individualistic" because, though it is a team game, the player with the ball is always the quarterback, and he must, with his skill and imagination, determine the course to be taken. All players must be resourceful and responsible, for with no time-outs and with such fluid action, the players cannot count on outside help. The game truly becomes theirs rather than the coach's.

The sport requires apostles and organizers whose enthusiasm must be contagious and who can communicate the techniques and strategy of the game. Soccer needs all kinds of communicants—coaches, instructors, reporters, and announcers. Television analysts have done much for golf, baseball, football, and basketball. Their fluent expertise has educated, entertained, and stimulated millions of viewers. They have made the public more knowledgeable and more conscious of the sports being described. Soccer also has a great need for such analysts—experts who can clarify and dramatize the complex action on the pitch. The specific purpose of this book, then, is to communicate the ABC's, as well as the D's through Z's, of the sport—to help the coach teach, the player learn, and the spectator enjoy.

Part I offers a brief review of the game's history and international appeal. Part II presents an overview of the offensive positions. Part III describes the defensive positions; both II and III include the style, techniques, and skills of great players; what the coach should look for in each position; and whom the young player should try to emulate.

The book emphasizes those individuals who embody their particular positions because of their original style or ability to capitalize on natural talent. Pinpointed here are Italian fullback Giacinto Facchetti for his renowned overlapping attacks and thunderous shots; English wing forward Stanley Matthews for his remarkable dribbling along the touchline; and of course the "king" of soccer, the great Pelé (Edson Arantes do Nascimento) for his impeccable technique (there never has been a player quite like him).

The comprehensive analysis of the various positional responsibilities should be especially helpful. For example, the center halfback's duties are outlined first for the offensive system, then for the "stopper" center halfback WM system, and finally for the modern systems such as the 4-2-4, 4-3-3, and even the "sweeper" center halfback. All the basic skills and techniques for each position are thoroughly described and illustrated in game-like situations to enhance their usefulness. For example, the center forward frequently will find himself crowded after receiving a pass from the wing forward. He will not have time to control the ball, so he will have to make a first-touch volley shot.

The book links all the individual positions to their responsibilities in a team structure. First come the general principles of play. Why, for example, is width so essential on attack? (Because it counteracts the basic principle of defense—concentration.) The basic principles are then applied to collective offensive and defensive patterns. The classic diagonal (swivel) pattern of defense is outlined and then adapted to the more modern systems of play (4-2-4 and 4-3-3, for example). The same procedure is observed for the ultimate tactical development —the sweeper center halfback. The book shows how to play it defensively and how to beat it.

Hints are also given for special tactics such as the "shuffle offense" (which exploits the American predilection for set patterns), continuity in attack, and "pressure defense," which provides for a vigorous harassment of the opponents.

In Part IV are the ramifications of the game itself, starting with the special situations and tactics that are applicable to every level of soccer, and then giving a clinical analysis of the systems of play.

Fig. P.2 (a and b) *The "king of soccer," Pelé, shows the enthusiasm the game generates.*

These are historically and practically analyzed (with line drawings) so that they become functional tools rather than mere arrangements of players on the field. Recommendations are given for adapting the system to the available personnel.

Part V comes to grips with the problems of teaching, coaching, and scouting and presents the latest ideas from all over the world, specially adapted for the American game. The underlying philosophy is practicality. The full range of skills, techniques, and strategies can be taught with the international game as the ultimate goal. A progressive teaching unit is included with specific activities in skills and techniques and practical suggestions for teaching and coaching elementary school, junior high school, and high school players.

Particularly valuable is the analysis of general tactics. It starts with the simplest tactical hints for dribbling and feinting, proceeds to technical and tactical tools for the individual duels, and culminates with two-on-one, three-on-two, all the way to eleven-on-eleven (with suggested exercises and line drawings).

Since organization and planning are important in a program, it is essential for the coach to establish both immediate and future goals and to frame a philosophy for team organization, systems of play, and relationships with the players.

The coach must understand that winning is an essential factor but *not* everything; that it cannot be employed as the sole motivating force and sole reward; and that the players must assume responsibility for motivating themselves as well as being motivated by the coach.

The scientific principles of conditioning the body per se are no mystery to the coach and athlete, as long as everything is clear-cut, such as when the distance can be measured, the energy output estimated, the speed timed, and the like. But it becomes more involved (more of an art) when training must be applied to a team sport like soccer. It is further complicated when, particularly on the scholastic level, the time available for practice is limited. We must make use of the time in the most economic way possible. The great contribution of Chapter 15 in Part VI is the presentation of the most well-known, scientifically sound principles of conditioning—such as the interval method and circuit method—and their adaptation to soccer needs. "Economic training" means combined physical, technical, and tactical training, the idea being to reach maximum results in preparation for soccer in the minimum amount of time.

Organization and planning are the life blood of a good program. It is essential to establish immediate and future goals. The essentials of off-season, pre-season, and seasonal programming are identified in Part VI, Chapter 16.

This book offers essentially a distillation of the author's experience around the world as a professional player, coach, and student of the game; the most successful ideas and methods of playing and coaching, adapted to the American soccer scene, are presented.

Foreword

THE ALLYN AND BACON SPORTS EDUCATION SERIES

Sports play a major role in the lives of practically everyone—the players, the coaches, the officials, and the spectators! Interest in sports is the result of several factors.

There is increased emphasis on *personal physical fitness.* Formal exercises or calisthenics, while worthwhile, are not as popular nor as motivating to the promotion of fitness as participation in sports. Through *sports participation,* children and adults gain fitness but also develop skills, group and personal satisfactions, and enjoyment.

Another factor in the growing interest in sports is the increase in television and radio broadcasts of sporting events. Team sports such as baseball, football, basketball, soccer, and hockey are seasonally covered by practically all channels. The lifetime sports including bowling, golf, tennis, and skiing are also receiving more air time. Activities such as gymnastics, swimming, and other aquatic sports have, and will continue to receive, more expanded coverage. The analysis of skills and strategy within each sport by knowledgeable commentators using instant video replay and stop-action techniques, makes the game or activity more interesting to the viewer.

The Allyn and Bacon Sports Education Series has been created to meet the need for players, coaches, and spectators to be informed about the basic and advanced skills, techniques, tactics, and strategies of sports. Each book in the Series is designed to provide an in-depth treatment of a selected sport or activity. Players find the individual skills and accompanying picture sequences very valuable. Coaches gain basic and advanced knowledge of individual and team play along with techniques of coaching. Sports fans are provided information

about the activities and are thus able to become more knowledgeable about and appreciative of the basic and finer aspects of sports.

The authors of the *Sports Education Series* have been carefully selected. They include experienced teachers, coaches, and managers of college and professional teams. Some books represent the combined effort of two or more authors, each with a different background and each contributing particular strengths to the text. For other books, a single author has been selected, whose background offers a breadth of knowledge and experience in the sport being covered.

Among the authors and titles of some of the team sport books is George Allen, successful coach of the Washington Redskins, who collaborated with Don Weiskopf on the information book *Inside Football.* Weiskopf also wrote with Walter Alston, of the Los Angeles Dodgers, the *Complete Baseball Handbook.* The book *Basketball—Concepts and Techniques,* by Bob Cousy, coach of the Royals, and Frank Power, presents the game for men. *Women's Basketball,* by Mildred Barnes of Central Missouri State University, covers the "new" five-player game for girls. Dr. Barnes also wrote the book *Field Hockey. The Challenge of Soccer* is by Hubert Vogelsinger, varsity coach at Yale University, and the book *Winning Volleyball* was written by Allen Scates of UCLA. A group of authors including General Managers Jack Kelley of the New England Whalers, Milt Schmidt of the Washington Hockey Club, and Harry Sinden of the Boston Bruins collaborated on the book *Hockey—Bantam to Professional.*

Individual sports included in the series are: *Racket Work—The Key to Tennis* by Jack Barnaby of Harvard University, *Modern Track and Field for Girls and Women* by Donnis Thompson of the University of Hawaii, and *Golf* by Tom and Don Weiskopf. The book on *Gymnastics* is by Kitty Kjeldsen of the University of Massachusetts.

Tutko and Richards collaborated on the meaningful texts *Psychology of Coaching* and the *Dynamics of Coaching*.

This Sports Series enables readers to experience the thrills of the sport from the point of view of participants and coaches, to learn some of the reasons for success and causes of failure, and to receive basic information about teaching and coaching techniques.

Each volume in the series reflects the philosophy of the authors, but a common theme runs through all: the desire to instill in the reader a knowledge and appreciation of sports and physical activity which will carry over throughout his life as a participant or a spectator. Pictures, drawings, and diagrams are used throughout each book to clarify and illustrate the discussion.

The reader, whether a beginner or one experienced in sports, will gain much from each book in this Allyn and Bacon Sports Education Series.

Arthur G. Miller
Chairman, Department of Human Movement
*   and Health Education*
Boston University

Contents

Symbols

CB	Center Back	RCB	Right Center Back
CF	Center Forward	RFB	Right Fullback
CHB	Center Halfback	RHB	Right Halfback
CMP	Center Midfield Player	RIF	Right Inside Forward
D Sc	Defensive Screen	RMP	Right Midfield Player
G	Goalkeeper	R Str	Right Striker
LCB	Left Center Back	RW	Right Winger
LFB	Left Fullback	SW	Sweeper
LHB	Left Halfback	△	Attackers
LIF	Left Inside Forward	O	Defenders
LMP	Left Midfield Player	----	Movement
L Str	Left Striker	——	Pass
LW	Left Winger		

Introduction

The universal appeal of soccer is evident in its long history in many countries. It was English Association football, however, with its fourteen "Cambridge rules," including the eleven-man team, that ultimately spread around the world. Though these basic rules have changed little in succeeding years, interpretation of play has varied with the increased sophistication of each generation and by the characteristics of different nationalities. World Cup games, held every four years, now pit the winners of the qualifying matches among the one hundred forty member nations of FIFA, the world governing body, in a variety of styles of play.

The United States' involvement with the game has had three high points of international interest. The first was in the 1930 World Cup games when the American team placed third; the second was the 1950 World Cup victory of the U.S. over England, and the third was the formation in 1966 of two professional leagues.

The satisfaction from the game anyone can play is evidenced by the increased number of registered players and the growth of the sport in schools and colleges. In this era of individualism, soccer continues to rise in popularity because of its non-stop action, because it takes courage and will power, because it scorns conformity, and because, though it is a team game, it offers opportunity for the expression of individuality.

The Evolution of Soccer

WORLD SOCCER

The logical question to ask in observing the tremendous popularity of soccer throughout the world is "Where did it all begin?" History redounds with references to a ball being kicked in games or ceremonies. "The fundamentals of the game are so natural and simple that it's scarcely surprising to find early traces of it in many different cultures."[1]

We hear of *Tsu chu* in China 3,000 years B.C.; *Kemari* or *Kernart* fourteen centuries ago in Japan; *Harpaston* in Roman times; *episkiyros* in early Greece; *Calcio* in medieval Florence; *Gomacari* in Mexico; *poltapok* in Yucatan; and so on.

Though a leather sphere, probably stuffed at first with hair, then sand or air (the Chinese had a stuffed leather ball; Egyptians and Babylonians played with one made of bamboo fibers; Romans had a ball inflated with an ox's bladder) always seems to have been the object of play, the field, goals, and rules have differed considerably over the years.

In China, for example, goal posts were thirty feet high and decorated with silk fabrics. In front was a net, also of silk, with an opening of only one foot through which the players had to kick the ball. The

Japanese eight-man teams made quite a ceremony of passing the ball from one to the other on a field sixty feet long with attractive trees planted at each corner. Greeks and Romans tried to pass the ball over a stake that served as a goal. They played with both hands and feet on a field four hundred by one hundred and fifty feet and needed six referees, who conveniently sat in the stands. Colombians in South America were only allowed to hit the ball with their right shoulder, while Huitotos used their knees, and Cubans their hips.

The early Olympic Games in ancient Rome featured twenty-seven men on a side, who competed so vigorously that two-thirds of them had to be hospitalized after a fifty-minute game, and this same sort of violence seems to have marked the early history of the game in the British Isles. Ireland had no limitations on players or field size. City teams would put the ball somewhere out in the open and play without rest and without a goal. They tried to get behind the opposing team, sometimes way out of town. Since they could use their fists, a misdirected punch to the opponent's face often led to altercations.

In King Edward's time in England (1314), a proclamation threatened incarceration to anyone caught playing soccer. This came after about 1,000 years of play, according to some English historians. Legend has it that the English beat the Romans at

---

[1] Brian Glanville, *Soccer,* New York: Crown Publishers (1968).

the game in 217 A.D. at Derby, and since soccer was called derby in England for many years, the story may have credence.

Some thirty-five years later, and again in 1389, the sheriffs of England were ordered to discourage playing of the game as well as other "useless practices." Henry IV and Henry VIII both legislated against it, and Queen Elizabeth I had soccer players jailed for a week, with a follow-up church penance. Quite a change from the more recent Queen Elizabeth, who in 1966 knighted the English national team manager, Alf Ramsay, for winning the world soccer title for England!

In 1681 an English nobleman familiar with Italian soccer introduced a new brand of the game. Because it was different from the savage game inherited from the Romans, and because it now had official sanction, it grew in popularity. Since teams played by their own rules, however, organized games were difficult to arrange. English universities drew up a set of rules for "association football" and in 1848 the fourteen "Cambridge rules," including the eleven-man team, were adopted. These rules, except for minor changes, have remained in international use ever since.

Two features of the rules show the influence of English public school origins. First, substitutes were discouraged and players injured or otherwise unable to play could not be replaced. And although the Sheffield rules provided for umpires, the Football Association assumed that captains would manfully settle all disputes.

Fifty years after the founding of the Football Association, the game had spread to Europe. Scottish and English coaches, notably Jimmy Hogan, traveled around the world, "teaching short passing, defense, and team play. Between 1910 and 1930 Hogan not only improved the quality of German and Dutch play but was recognized as the guiding genius of Austrian and Hungarian football."[2]

The first international contest was played between England and Scotland on November 30, 1872, in Glasgow. The teams offered an interesting contrast in style. Scotland's game was based on short passes and England's on long, forward movements. Scotland put great emphasis on skill and perfect mastery of the ball rather than mere force or speed.

This had a great influence on English soccer, although the English continued to emphasize power.

The British sent their game out into the world with their merchants, navies, and ambassadors to Switzerland, Belgium, France, Spain, and the rest of Europe, and even to America.[3]

England proved its world mastery at the 1908 and 1912 Olympic Games. After World War I it declined to defend its title because of its animus toward the Central Powers—Germany, Austria, Hungary, and Turkey. It relented in 1924, then broke off again in 1928 over a definition of amateurism and broken payments. When it returned in the late 1940's, the world had caught up and the team suffered a humiliating defeat from, of all opponents, the United States in World Cup competition.

Hungary, with its deep-lying center forward, took the lead from England in 1953. Brazil then soared to the top with its 4-2-4 system in the 1958 World Cup, but England came bouncing back in 1966 with a stirring victory over Germany. Brazil finally achieved permanent possession of the World Cup trophy (as a third-time winner) in 1970 with a brilliant display of attacking artistry. (For the tactical evolution of the game, see Chapter 12.)

Although Europe and South America have dominated the game in the last hundred years, North Koreans showed great promise in their defeat of Italy in the 1966 World Cup. Africans also show great potential, and many of them are now playing on European and South American teams. Once they can improve the organization of their leagues, there is no reason why they cannot become a power on the international scene.

In America, aside from the formation of the North American Soccer (professional) League, "there is a vast underground expansion in secondary school and collegiate soccer,"[4] which can only lead to outstanding national teams in the future.

The Federation Internationale de Football Association (FIFA) estimates that there were between sixteen and twenty million active soccer players in the world in 1972, seventy-six percent of whom were registered Europeans. The English Football Association originally consisted of eleven clubs and now has 35,000 members in ninety-two clubs in four divisions, below which are hundreds of minor

[2] *Collier's Encyclopedic Yearbook 1970,* New York: Crowell-Collier, p. 33.

[3] Ibid, p. 35.

[4] Ibid.

Fig. 1.1 *A historic moment—Pelé scoring his thousandth goal.* **Fig. 1.2** *Eusebio of Portugal and Benfica, the scoring king of the 1966 World Cup.* **Fig. 1.3** *Gerhard Müller, a prolific scorer for Germany.*

leagues. The Soviet Union has 3,800,000 registered players. West Germany has 2,300,000 and Holland has 577,690—one out of every twenty-one citizens! One hundred and forty nations are now registered members of FIFA, and the World Cup games can offer many surprises.

Besides the World Cup games and the Olympic matches, every nation sponsors a variety of tournaments. For example, the European Cup brings together the champion league clubs of each member country of the European Union of Football Associations. Initiated in 1956, the European Cup features two matches in each round on a home and away basis. It is an elimination competition, with the winner being decided by an aggregate of goals. Real Madrid won the first five cups and repeated in 1966. Other winners have been Benfica (Portugal), Milan AC and Internazionale Milan (Italy), Glasgow Celtic (Scotland), and Manchester United (England).

The European Cup Winners Cup is for the winners of each national cup competition; the Inter-Cities Fairs Cup is contested among the best European clubs not qualified for the above two; and the unofficial Club Championship of the World was founded in 1960 for home and away contests between winners of the European Cup and the South American Cup in order to fill the gap between World Cups. Winners of this latter cup have been Real Madrid (Spain), Penarol (Uruguay) twice, Santos (Brazil) twice, Internazionale Milan (Italy) twice, and Racing Club Buenos Aires (Argentina). For important dates in the evolution of the game, see Appendix B.

SOCCER IN THE UNITED STATES

Soccer has been played in the United States since the 1840's. In the Boston Common is a memorial plaque to the "first organized football club in the U.S.," the Oneida, which claims that "from 1862 to 1865 their goal was never crossed" and that "they played against all comers."[5] The sixteen players on this team "were placed on the field [in positions] most likely to catch or meet the ball when kicked by our opponent in order that we might return it without delay toward their own goal."[6]

[5]Winthrop Saltonstall Scudder, *An Historical Sketch of the Oneida Football Club of Boston, 1862–1865,* Massachusetts Historical Society, June 4, 1926, p. 13.

[6]Ibid.

The club was organized by a great enthusiast, Gerritt Smith Miller, who learned the game at the Boston Private Latin School. In every period of its history, soccer has had some energetic and enthusiastic apostle to breathe verve and vigor into it. Yet the game showed no consistent or national pattern of growth until the 1960's and 1970's.

Probably the first soccer of any sort was played at Harvard in 1830. It was patterned after the English Association game, but it was very informal and had no specific number of players, field size, or rules. By 1844 it had been taken up by several other colleges, and by 1860 a dozen colleges along the Atlantic coast were playing the game that had now become standardized.

In 1865 Rutgers and Princeton drafted a set of rules that provided for twenty-five men on a side and goal posts twenty-five feet wide. Six goals constituted a game, the ball had to be kicked, and throwing or carrying was barred.[7]

In 1869 Rutgers beat Princeton, 6-4. Princeton retaliated a week later, 6-0. These games induced Columbia to organize a team in 1870, Yale in 1872, Pennsylvania and Harvard in 1874, and then Haverford, Stevens, New York University, and City College of New York.

When Yale and Harvard met in 1875, they (unfortunately for soccer) played "rugby rules" because they liked running with the ball. Their choice influenced other colleges, and the American Intercollegiate Football Association rules were organized along rugby lines, except that games were decided by touchdowns. This changed the destiny of soccer, and it went through some lean times between 1877 and 1905.

In 1913 the United States entered the international soccer scene with the U.S. Football Association. A struggle ensued between the American Football Association, which controlled professional leagues in the Northeast, and the American Amateur Football Association. Each group sought sanction by the world soccer governing body, FIFA. They were told to settle their differences and merge. The professionals walked out of the discussions that followed.

When the eastern amateur clubs came out in support of the U.S. Football Association, FIFA recognized it. The American Football Association ultimately joined, and since 1914 the U.S. Soccer Football Association (USSFA) has controlled both amateur and professional soccer in the U.S.

Records show that sixty candidates showed up for the 1920 Yale team under Coach Ferne, and that soccer was considered a "fast and very interesting game for the spectator."[8]

College and school groups developed their own organizations and became associate members of the USSFA. By 1926 interest had risen markedly and the Intercollegiate Soccer Football Association was formed. The National Collegiate Athletic Association, the Amateur Athletic Union of the U.S., and the National Federation of State High School Athletic Association soon became involved, and finally the National Soccer Coaches Association with its quarterly organ, *Soccer Journal*, appeared on the scene to lend further authority to the sport. By this time, of course, public and private schools were playing the game and local teams were being organized, primarily along ethnic lines.

The National Challenge Cup was instituted in 1913. The championship (Dewar Trophy) was open to both professional and amateur teams, but the entries proliferated so rapidly that the USSFA decided to separate the amateurs from the pros. It inaugurated the National Amateur Cup Competition in 1923 and the National Junior Challenge Cup (for players under age eighteen) in 1934.

The first National Collegiate Soccer Tournament was held at the University of Connecticut in 1959 and was won by St. Louis University, which went on to dominate the championships for many years. Colleges and universities competed for the same title until 1972, when they were separated into two divisions. In that year, Southern Illinois University won the college division title and St. Louis won the university title.

U.S. soccer has had three highwater marks in the international stream. The first was in 1930, when Uncle Sam agreed to participate in the first World Cup soccer games in Uruguay. The USSFA got together a team composed primarily of muscular former European professionals, notably the Scots Alex Wood, Jimmy Gallacher, Andie Auld, Jimmy Brown, and Bart McGhee, and the Englishman George Moorhouse. They played a very modern game with eight men on defense and only three

---

[7] *Encyclopaedia Britannica*, 14th ed., Vol. IX, 1957, Norris D. McWhirter, "Football," p. 473.

[8] J. G. Stovall, "Soccer," *Yale Graphic*, Vol. 3, No. 4, December 1, 1920, p. 150.

on attack, relying on the counterattack to score. Competition that year was organized into four leagues, and the winner and the runner-up in each moved into the semi-finals. The semi-final and the final were decided on an elimination basis. The United States won its first game against Belgium, 3-0, its second against Paraguay, 3-0, then lost to Argentina (the second-place winner), 1-6, to place third in world competition. (They might have done as well in the second World Cup in 1934 with a team composed of several of the same players, but this was a straight elimination affair and the U.S. was unlucky enough to draw the eventual winner, powerful Italy, in the first round and lost 1-7.)

The second outstanding event was the United States' victory over England, 1-0, in the 1950 World Cup in Brazil. This was England's first World Cup competition and it fielded a team of top professionals, including Stanley Matthews, who for some reason did not play against the U.S. The English began confidently, even laughingly. They were in no hurry to score, and the Brazilian crowd began to cheer the underdog U.S. team. About five minutes before the half, the American right wing forward put a good cross into the decisive area in front of the goal, and Joseph Gaetjens jumped high and slammed a perfect header right into the goal. The English tried to rally, but the Americans played an inspired defensive game and eventually were carried off the field victorious.

Since that time, no U.S. team has been able to qualify for the finals. Until the U.S. appoints a qualified national coach and gives him authority, financing, and staff, it is unlikely that Uncle Sam, even with his vast reservoir of athletic talent, ever will be a serious international contender.

An Arthur D. Little research report in 1964 concluded that the USSFA needed greater financing to conduct a program that could establish soccer as a significant sport in the U.S. Money was needed for publicity and educational programs, top-level coaching instruction, and more support for U.S. teams in international competition. "U.S. players need greater opportunity to play together as national teams and greater opportunity for international competition."[9] Nevertheless, soccer has been played continually in the United States since

its introduction, although it has always been over-shadowed by football.

All countries have adapted the game to their individual temperament and national character, and Americans are no exception. They play a more rugged game—definitely more physical, more forthright, less subtle, and with constant movement (the latter being a great asset in the modern game).

International soccer was promoted successfully in the U.S. for many years by Enzo Magnozzi and William Cox. There also were a National League, a German-American League, and a Continental League, with year-round schedules. So the formation of two professional leagues in 1966 really was not a big surprise. It represented the third big stride in Uncle Sam's bid for world recognition.

The mounting of the operation reversed normal procedure. Instead of leagues being formed in answer to a surge of interest, they were formed in the hope of promoting the game from the top down.

The United Soccer Association and the National Professional Soccer League began operations in 1966. The USA had official approval of USSFA and FIFA; the NPSL did not. The USA started with a provisional season of foreign clubs; the NPSL began with teams composed primarily of former professionals from other countries.

The formations of these professional leagues and their rivalry stirred world interest in the American soccer scene. The "experiment," as it was considered by all, was watched with great interest. After taking a bath in red ink the first season, the two leagues merged into the North American Soccer League to eliminate rival teams in the same cities and to coordinate their efforts. After several disappointing seasons, even with TV coverage, the noble experiment expired. Contributing factors were primarily the dearth of Americans on the teams, and secondarily the quality of play, the heat of the summer season (chosen to compete with baseball instead of football), and poor promotion, among others. Most of the teams quietly disbanded and the foreigners returned home.

By 1969 the North American Soccer League was left with five teams (which did not include New York), and it began a low-key operation out of Georgia in the hope of maintaining some semblance of a professional league while a grassroots interest was being developed. The NASL has given

[9]John Allen, *Soccer for Americans*, New York: Grosset and Dunlap, 1967.

support to a developmental program conducted by the USSFA.

In 1970 the central office was moved from Atlanta to New York. A New York team and several others were added as the NASL began to show slow but steady signs of growth. In addition to its playoffs, the NASL conducted an International Cup Tournament with each team adding a match or two to their schedules against foreign teams, and a minimum number of American players on each team became mandatory.

In the meantime, the USSFA was organizing coaching courses, in the hope of getting a U.S. team into Olympic and World Cup finals. The appointment of a national coach was approved, and organized development of the game on all levels was planned.

In 1972 a U.S. team won its qualifying games and was able to compete in the Olympics in Munich.

Though the team did not get beyond its preliminary matches, hope for high calibre of American play on the international level continued.

In 1966 the U.S. had 25,000 registered amateurs, 1,500 professionals, and 10,000 juniors connected with neither the schools nor colleges. By 1972, 2,800 high schools were playing the game (more than doubling the number of seven years before) and three hundred and seventy institutions out of more than seven hundred soccer-playing colleges sponsored soccer on the intercollegiate level and were eligible to participate in the NCAA tournaments, testifying to the truth of a l972 survey of NCAA membership which revealed that "soccer is the fastest growing team sport among the nation's colleges and universities."[10]

[10] *NCAA News,* Vol. 9, No. 15, November 15, 1972, "Inaugural C. D. Soccer Tournament Under Way," p. 3.

II

Individual and Team Offense

Offensive play is concerned with advancing the ball upfield and scoring goals. It is decisive in determining the success of any team.

Part II begins with individual offense (the center forward, wing forward, and inside forward positions) and culminates in team offense. Each position is developed through the playing characteristics of great individual players who personify the position, a comprehensive analysis of the positional responsibilities in various tactical schemes, and the skills and techniques indispensable to these positions. The skills and techniques are described in detail and photographed in skill sequences so that their tactical use in combination with other skills in game situations can be appreciated.

The individual positions are linked with responsibilities in a team structure, and the general principles of offensive play are outlined and applied to collective offensive patterns of play.

2

The Center Forward

Whether we call him center forward, striker, or front runner, at least one player must have the prerequisites to spearhead the attack. Although it does not matter who scores goals, the preference is for an aggressive center forward who is a goal-hunter rather than a deep-lying playmaker.

Center forward is a sensitive, dangerous, and exciting position. It is also a tremendously demanding one. The center forward is expected to convert all the team skill and team effort into the hard currency of goals. Putting all these elements together, one can understand why the great center forwards become legends.

There is no doubt about it: The thrill of banging the ball into the net far surpasses any other pleasure in soccer.

NATURAL QUALIFICATIONS

Determination and Confidence

Great center forwards are born, not made. They have courage, will-power, and the determination to penetrate the opposite team, exploiting the slightest error by the goalkeeper or his defenders. They also have a shakeless confidence in themselves. They cannot afford self-doubts or fears. The slightest lack of confidence can make them indecisive, and hesitation can cost valuable goals. Confidence, courage, and aggressiveness will prepare them to accept failures against the highly disci-

plined modern defenses and go right back to attack.

Attacking Sense

Whatever the formation, the center forward is expected by the very nature of his position to look for scoring opportunities. He must possess an awareness that enables him to be at the right spot at the right time. Openings close as fast as they appear, and he must have the lightning reflexes and coolness to make the most out of half-chances.

Strength and Size

Though the center forward does not necessarily have to be big and powerful, it is a great asset to be built along "blockbuster" lines, provided he has the quickness of mind and foot to go with it.

The center forward must be able to produce the brilliant exchange of short passes in the penalty area and to put himself in the clear with the ball at his feet. He must possess the electric finishing power, the first-touch crash volley, the leaping header, or the quick shot out of nowhere.

STYLE OF GREAT CENTER FORWARDS

The center forward's style of play depends largely on his physique, skill, and tactical maturity. Only a few players have everything, and some manage very well on just one outstanding talent. The screening for such natural assets must be intelligent, as the player's natural endowments will determine the type of striker—center forward—he should concentrate on becoming.

Blockbusting Spearhead

This is the physical, forceful center forward who follows the traditional concept of the center forward being the orthodox leader of the attack.

One immediately thinks of Nat Lofthouse, an English Internationalist who was called "Lionheart" for his abundant courage and "Lofty" for his superb heading ability. Any ball dropping into the goal area was likely to be flashed into the net by him.

Bobby Smith, another English Internationalist, was a strong player with great determination and courage. He had a thunderous shot with either foot and was a fine header as well. He was one of the most thrustful center forwards of the WM era—it was impossible to knock him off the ball, and when he started to run with it, the opposing defenses quivered as he burst through them.

This type of center forward is mostly respected for his courage and determination. He plays a bone-crushing, hustling game and is absolutely fearless in going in hard for the half-chances. He must, necessarily, have a tall, robust frame to stand up to all the hard knocks he takes when shielding the ball with his body or bearing in on the target swiftly and determinedly.

Since the spearhead type of center forward must be able to out-head his immediate opponent,

height is a great advantage. A few extra inches will enable him to take the ball a fraction of a second sooner than the average player.

The "blockbuster" is still an invaluable type of center forward, and the team that is lucky enough to have him should make it a policy to feed him. He should be permitted to scheme the openings, race through for the ball, or flash the ball into the net with an acrobatic header.

Lurking Opportunist

This is the striker who lives off the mistakes of others, who always seems to get to the half-clearance first, who is always there when the goalkeeper fumbles, and who, thanks to his great reflexes, can bury the ball into the net while everyone around him is still trying to make up his mind about what to do next!

This kind of center forward does not have to be as tall and strong or good in the air. Uwe Seeler, the inspiring German star, is a short, sturdily built fellow who has many of the attributes generally claimed for the typical English center forward: strength, courage, determination, playmaking skill, and shooting ability. Above all, he is a superb header. It is exciting to see Seeler leap high above the opposition and, with perfect timing, head a ball home as hard as many players can shoot (Fig. 2.1). He never seems to need the time and space that other players demand. His chunky build, short legs, lack of back (leg) swing at the ball, cool brain, and stabbing shot, plus his ability to exploit half-chances, make him a world-class striker.

Gerhard Müller, another German Internationalist who was the scoring king of the 1970 World Cup, is another chunky spearhead forward cast in the contemporary German mold: less tall than his English counterparts, adequate in the air, and particularly adept at controlling the ball in tight situations and shooting for goal (Fig. 2.2). This type of center forward relies on exceptional positional sense to be at the right spot at the right time. He is an opportunist, very elusive, and goes about his job very single-mindedly.

Deep-Lying Schemer

Alfredo di Stefano, the most complete soccer player of his age, was called "the golden arrow" at the start of his career and "the divine bald one" when he retired at age forty-one. The Real Madrid

Fig. 2.1 *Uwe Seeler making a spectacular overhead shot.*

immortal was more than a goal scorer. He could dominate the midfield, particularly around the center circle, with needle passes through gaps unseen by others. He punished loose play unmercifully and was so fast and elusive that he seldom ever was marked out of the game.

The versatile di Stefano also could set up a brilliant exchange of short passes against the tightest defense in the penalty area, and his electric finishing power made him one of the greatest center forwards (Fig. 2.3). Like Nandor Hidegkuti of the great Hungarian team of the early fifties, di Stefano was the hub of his team's entire attacking strategy. But di Stefano could do more than Hidegkuti. He could head the ball off his own goal line one moment and into the opposition's goal a few moments later. Blessed with tremendous stamina, he often would go back into his own penalty area for the ball.

POSITIONAL PLAY

Offense

There was a time when the center forward stayed in the middle of the field and waited for the ball to be served to him. That day is gone. In these days of the stopper center halfback—sweeper—the center forward is the most closely marked man on the field.

He must seek scoring opportunities by every means in his power. The modern fluid tactical formations have considerably altered his role. The center forward must hold his forward line together by serving as the pivot of the attack, by linking up with his wing forwards, or by receiving passes from his defense and laying the ball back to his inside forwards.

A fundamental problem for all center forwards is taking up the right position—the one that yields the most direct route to a goal. Since he is the most closely covered of all the forwards, this never is simple.

The chief objective of the center forward is to penetrate—to run for "through" balls. But he has to use discretion and deceit to outwit the opposing stopper center halfback. He must be prepared to vary his approach by running off the ball diagonally and laterally, as well as through, and by employing sudden dashes into any momentary gaps, frequently working with a "give and go."

Fig. 2.2 *Gerhard Müller smashing home a winning goal.*

Fig. 2.3 *Alfredo di Stefano displays his artistry as he eludes two opponents.*

The timing of these runs, particularly running on to a through ball, is particularly vital. A premature start will cause an offside call; a late start will allow a defender to get there first.

Many center forwards like to slip away from the covering defender toward a wing in the hope of drawing the stopper center halfback with him, thus creating a vacant space for another forward to exploit. If the stopper refuses to follow, the center forward can work himself open for a pass.

Should the stopper center halfback follow the center forward and thus open up the middle of the field, or should he stay at home and face a fluid forward movement? Actually, this dilemma is more fancied than real, for in these days of defensive blocs and sweepers, this sort of play is too simple to cause much trouble unless it is executed with exceptional speed and timing.

Any deep-lying attack leader can cause havoc in the opposing defense. Whenever he goes back to organize his initial attack and wanders all over the field, he is creating problems for the opposing team. A move to the wing also can be unsettling to a fullback and can give the wing forward the room in which to beat his immediate defender.

Halfbacks, and midfield players in particular, can use the center forward for a wall pass to come through on an overlap for a strike at goal.

The center forward must have a thorough understanding with his forwards, as the interchanges of positions are only effective when executed at the right time with clockwork precision.

Defense

Traditionally, the center forward was strictly an attacking player whose mission ended the moment his team lost the ball. Today the center forward is an integral part of the overall team play. He is expected to tackle back after losing the ball, and he must harass the defender and try to get the ball away from him in critical situations. Even if he does not succeed in getting the ball, he may force the defender into a hurried clearance. He also must keep his eye on the overlapping stopper-sweeper, as he often is the only forward up front. It is his responsibility to keep as many defenders occupied as possible to prevent them from taking part in attack. Equally important, he must be prepared to counterattack.

SPECIAL SKILLS AND TECHNIQUES

Since the center forward is playing in the most vulnerable area of the field, the central path to the goal, he is the most closely marked player on the field. Shooting skill is by far the most important single requisite. The center forward's motto must be "Shoot hard at sight of the goal!" He must be hungry for goals, and he must have confidence in his ability to score them.

The average player should imitate the game's power shooters. They have developed the technique of planting the non-kicking foot out ahead of the ball and "squeezing" the ball away on a low trajectory, which is particularly effective on wet grass. It keeps the ball low for a maximum distance.

Constant practice is demanded, as it takes immense power to shoot from, say, forty yards out, and keep the ball low enough to have a chance of scoring. Obviously, the forward also must be able to shoot quickly and accurately under pressure. That means he must learn to adjust his body rapidly and restrict the back-swing of his kicking leg.

Low Drive with Full Instep

This represents the most efficient shot in the game, as the instep is the most powerful part of the foot and the approach and follow through are in line with the intended direction of the shot (Fig. 2.4). This assures maximum power and control.

a

Fig. 2.4 *Classic shot with the full instep firm from a straight approach.*

b

c

d

e

Approach

The player accelerates as he nears the ball, while calculating the proper timing and positioning of the supporting foot. He also shoots a glance at the goal to size up his target, the position of the goalkeeper, and a placement for the shot.

He then concentrates on the ball and the timing of the last stride. The last step is somewhat accentuated and places the supporting foot, heel first, comfortably alongside the ball. Instinctive adjustments must be made when the ball is moving, which is usually the case in match play.

Positioning of Supporting Foot

As the heel of the supporting foot hits the ground, the center of gravity is immediately shifted to this foot. The player leans slightly backward and sideward to check his momentum and maintain good balance, and extends his arms for stability and body control. This assures a free leg action.

The momentum of the approach run causes the player to rock heel to toe on the supporting foot and bend the knee considerably. He points his toes in the intended direction of the shot and comes nearly vertical over the ball. The body is well-arched, with the head down and eyes fixed on the ball.

Leg Swing

As the balance leg rocks forward, the kicking leg swings back in a naturally synchronized (though slightly exaggerated) action. The back knee is completely flexed so that the heel of the foot comes back nearly to the buttocks. This deeply flexed foreleg is essentially the sole source of power. When extended fully and dynamically, it allows for a very explosive action—the secret of effective shooting. The uncoiling action of the knee joint, lower leg is delayed until the knee comes almost over the ball. Then the lower leg snaps forward explosively.

Impact

The leg extends fully, with the foot locked at the ankle and the toes pointed downward and braced against the sole of the shoe. This enables the player to drive the firmly braced instep forcefully through the dead center of the ball.

The relationship of the knee to the ball at the moment of impact is important. Ideally, the knee should be over the ball to help keep the shot low.

Where the knee is brought too far forward, the instep will be forced down and will drive the ball into the ground, dissipating its force. Where the knee is brought too far behind the ball, the instep will have to be brought upward, causing the shot to be skyed.

Follow Through

As the ball is driven away, the leg continues its extension forward and upward. The supporting leg also extends as the player rises to the toes. The momentum and leg swing may cause the player to take a gliding hop with the supporting foot to stay on balance. The entire action must be executed smoothly and fluidly to furnish pace and power at the precise moment of contact. The head must be kept down throughout the action. Young players, anxious to see the result of the shot, tend to look up too soon.

Getting the Shot Off Quickly

The center forward must be ready to seize any half-chance to get off a shot. He cannot wait for perfect openings. They rarely come, and when they do they quickly disappear. So the player must be prepared to react instantly to any opportunity. Indeed, some of the greatest goals have been scored from seemingly hopeless positions.

It follows that shooting quickly is more important than shooting hard. But this does not mean that a forward should rush his shots: there is nothing sadder than the sight of a center forward trying to play faster than he is equipped to do. Nevertheless it is important for him to get his shot in without delay; once a player tries too hard to make certain of his shot, you can bet he will take too long to do it.

Economic Method of Shooting

Goalkeepers can be surprised by a sudden shot. When there appears to be no room for maneuvering, an experienced center forward can, with a very short back-lift, strike the ball with a short, vicious "stab" shot from the knee.

When time is of the essence in front of the goal, the wise player will avoid a big back-swing. He will never or hardly ever be able to get the shot off otherwise. If his leg does not get entangled with a defender coming in from behind, the ball surely will be whipped away before he can bring his leg through or he will be jostled off-balance before he can shoot.

Shooting the Volley or Half-Volley

The center forward must be able to shoot accurately in situations where the ball bounces awkwardly to him from various heights and angles. The vital point to remember in hitting a first-touch volley is to observe the basic principles of shooting. The knee must be over the ball at the moment of impact to keep the ball low (Fig. 2.5).

If given the choice, the player should allow the ball to fall "through" and strike it at the lowest point possible, thus assuring a natural and powerful leg swing. The higher the contact point, the more difficult the shot.

a

b

c

d

Fig. 2.5 *Volley shot from a front approach with the full instep. The height of the ball limits the player's leg action.*

The "secret" of good contact is leaning to the side opposite the kicking foot. This enables the player to pivot on the supporting foot and swing the kicking leg in an arc that brings it horizontally or downward into the ball. Most players use this technique because it allows them to hit the ball early and with a maximum amount of power (Figs. 2.6 and 2.7).

The half-volley requires perfect timing. Just as the ball hits the ground, the player must meet it with the full instep or outside of the foot and drive through the dead center of it. The principles are identical to those for the low drive with the full instep (Fig. 2.8).

Screening the Ball

Being the closest marked player on the field, the center forward seldom is given the luxury of space-time to receive the ball. He will invariably be immediately challenged by a defender. So it is not surprising to find him facing the wrong way (back to the goal under attack) upon receiving passes from his midfield players (Fig. 2.9).

a   *b*   *c*

d   *e*   *f*

Fig. 2.6 *A flying side-volley shot.*

Fig. 2.7 *Action shot of a flying side-volley shot.*

a

b

c

d

e

Fig. 2.8 *Half-volley shot. Total concentration must be given to timing in order to have the knee hovering over the ball and to strike it at the moment of rebound to keep it low.*

Fig. 2.9 *Screening the ball.*

If the ball is not returned to him but is slung out to one of the wing forwards, he should again move into the best possible (unmarked) position for a pass from the wing. His laying off of the ball and his movement into open space not only will give the receiver someone to pass to, it will confuse the defense and possibly create panic at the back.

The defender has a right to expect a "front man" to be a goal scorer. So when the latter begins to lay off as well as shoot, the defender is in for a long, difficult match.

Meeting the Ball to Take It Early

More often than not, the center forward is going to be closely challenged for the ball by the center halfback. The wise center forward would not wait for the ball, but would run to meet it, take it early, and then play if off first-touch or gain sufficient space and time to control it in the air.

It is fascinating to see a crack center forward outrace his defender to meet a high cross with the chest, semi-control it, and set himself up for a crack at goal, and then, only moments later, see him control the ball against a defender breathing down his neck by screening him off with the full width of his body, and making the play.

Killing the Ball with the Chest

This skill is effective only when the defender's challenge is coming from behind and the center forward has enough space to move off in the direction he is facing to ensure possession (Fig. 2.11).

It is essential to gauge the ball's flight carefully. The player must get right behind and across the ball as he runs to meet it. He assumes a well-balanced lunging position, with the chest fully expanded and the shoulders and elbows pulled well-back. He tries to have the ball drop on top of the chest, right below the chin or sternum area, depending upon the particular trajectory.

At the moment of impact, the chest collapses and the shoulders roll forward simultaneously, forming a concave cushion for the impact. As the ball strikes the chest, the knees straighten with a sudden flexion of the hip, and the player rises on his toes or may even leave the ground momentarily, allowing him to ride back and bend forward over the ball, forcing the ball to drop to his feet. He then checks it once more with his feet and takes off without delay.

He must learn to receive the ball or play it first-touch despite a defender breathing down his neck. This calls for the skillful use of the body to protect or screen the ball from the opponent. Every player must master this most basic element of sound ball-control. It requires good balance, instinctive awareness of the opponent's whereabouts, and the courage and confidence to face up to an aggressive tackle from the rear.

Laying Off Passes First-Touch

A long ball coming out of the defense often will catch the center forward standing with his back to the opponents' goal, with one or two defenders marking him. If he gathers the ball and tries to turn with it, his better positioned markers will quickly dispossess him.

His alternative is simple—and effective. As the ball reaches him, he should, without pausing to control it, pass it to the nearest unmarked advancing teammate. He should then immediately turn and move into an open space, away from his markers, ready to take a return pass (Fig. 2.10).

a   b

c   d

Fig. 2.10 *Laying the ball off with the outside of the foot (flick volley).*

Semi-Controlling the Ball with the Chest

The center forward often may prefer to keep the ball in the air. In a crowd of players, for example, it would be suicide to take the time to get the ball down to his feet. He is better off trying for a controlled rebound by "riding" it off the upper part of his chest. Then, by playing the ball off on the volley or turning with it and screening off the defender at the same time, he can crash the ball home (Fig. 2.12). Though a very spectacular movement, this is a risky one. Any temporary loss of body-control will give the defender a fighting chance for the ball.

The approach—meeting the ball with both feet on the ground or receiving it after a running jump—has little bearing on actual skill. The main thing is the timing of the jump.

a   b   c   d

Fig. 2.11 *Controlling the ball in midair with the chest to make the play on the second-touch.*

a   b   c

Fig. 2.12 *Meeting the ball to control it in midair with the chest, allowing for a controlled rebound to carry the ball through a turn to make the play.*

22

The chest is expanded by pulling both the shoulders and elbows well-backward. The hips are thrust vigorously forward and the trunk is allowed to sink well-backward and downward underneath the ball where it can ride with it.

The ball is taken just below the chin, which has been tucked in to enable the player to keep his eyes on the ball, and the body is in a perfect arch position. Perfect timing and coordination are the essence of the controlled rebound.

Heading at Goal

The secret of good heading is the timing of the run or jump to get to the ball first to meet it squarely with the front of the forehead. Some of the best headers will, however, flick the head sideward at the last moment to gain extra impetus.

It is essential to get on top of the ball when trying to head goals. In most instances it is wise to head the ball down: first, to avoid skying the ball over the goal, and second, to give the goalkeeper a more difficult angle to deal with (Fig. 2.13).

Most players can execute very nicely when they are standing firmly on the ground, healthily isolated from the opponent. They just have to brace themselves and concentrate on meeting the ball cleanly with the forehead and punching straight through the dead center of the ball.

Timing the Approach Run

The real test of heading at goal is to win the race to the goalmouth in time to meet a hard cross from the wing forward or to meet a cross at the near post and merely steer it into the far corner of the goal.

Nine times out of ten, the run to meet the cross from the wing forward is made too early. Forwards are usually too eager or anxious to get into the goalmouth. They must be taught to delay and time their runs according to the trajectory of the ball. This is particularly true of young and inexperienced forwards, who frequently are caught waiting for high crosses to head into the goal. They often wind up helplessly out of position watching the ball sail over their heads.

Double-Leg Takeoff

In assuming the proper lunging position for a stationary double-leg takeoff, the player should bend his legs slightly at the ankle, knee, and hip, bend

Fig. 2.13 *When heading for goal, it is advisable to head the ball down.*

the trunk forward, shift the center of gravity over the balls of the feet, and extend the arms sideward and downward, ready for a double-arm lift.

The vertical drive is effected by a vigorous extension of the body, a straightening of the trunk, and a forceful double-arm lift. While on the rise, the player must cock his trunk, head, and neck, and simultaneously bring his legs backward to "hang in the air" in a perfectly arched position.

Single-Leg Takeoff

The player must time his approach in a way that will enable him to convert horizontal momentum into maximum vertical lift for a powerful header at goal.

The approach run should be effected in the same manner as a lay-up in basketball—rhythmically, with gathering speed, and with progressively longer last steps. The final push-off stride must be well-exaggerated. The takeoff foot should be driven heel first into the ground, well-ahead of the body, enabling the trunk and hip to sink back and lower the center of gravity. This is the critical posi-

a   b

Fig. 2.14 *Attacker demonstrates excellent technique as he unleashes a powerful header.*

tion that enables the player to check horizontal momentum and convert it to vertical drive.

The momentum of the approach will cause the player to rock over the well-bent takeoff leg, heel to toe, and thrust him upward. The other leg, which is well-bent at the knee, will simultaneously drive up forcefully. This, together with the double-arm swing, will add considerably to the vertical lift.

Heading Forward

While still rising, the player arches his body like a bow, with head and legs well-back and braced. At the peak of his jump, he is in a perfectly cocked position, almost suspended in air.

Ideal timing and coordination will enable him to head the ball in this position. He watches the ball right onto his forehead and unleashes his body at it in jackknife fashion. He pulls his arms vigorously down and back and, with his forehead inclined downward, punches fiercely through the dead center of the ball. The trunk and leg continue the jackknife action and follow through in the direction of the header (Fig. 2.14).

It is important to maintain perfect body control

in order to land in a normal running stride, preferably making contact with the takeoff foot. This will absorb the impact of the landing and enable the player to follow up the ball (Fig. 2.15).

Heading Sideward

The most reliable method of heading sideward follows the classic pattern of heading forward. Since the player usually faces the ball as he braces himself in bow-like fashion, he adjusts his trunk and hips to permit use of the same body mechanics as heading forward. The timing becomes more difficult when the player must run to jump and meet a high cross coming from the wing. He must then coordinate the jump and the rotation of his body (Figs. 2.16–2.19).

Another rather common but complex method of heading sideward consists of bending the trunk and thrusting the hip well-sideward. A proper head adjustment will then enable the player to use the full surface or, more likely, the side of his forehead to meet the ball.

The technique is similar to that of throwing a football or even shot put. In fact, many players find

a

b

c

d

e

Fig. 2.15 *Heading forward.*

this technique more natural for their bodies to perform than the classic method of heading the ball. It is easier for most people to bend sideward than backward, and the peculiar sideward action of the trunk permits an extremely hard hit.

Some players add force to the header through a twisting action of the trunk and swivel of the head.

25

a

b

c

d

Fig. 2.16 *The center forward meets a cross to head for goal.*

a   b   c   d

Fig. 2.17 *Heading sideward.*

Fig. 2.18 *Player demonstrates the technique and timing essential to meet a cross at the far or near post.*

Fig. 2.19 *The center forward meets a cross at the near post and allows it to glance off his forehead in order to head it into the far corner of the goal.*

Slipping or Deflecting the Ball with the Head at Goal

Many goals have been scored from apparently hopeless situations by letting a well-placed cross glance off the forehead into the far corner of the goal. This is a highly individualized skill. Some players will suddenly turn their head and let the ball glance off the full surface of the forehead. No attempt is made to "punch" the ball. They simply angle the ball off, with the forehead serving as a mere gliding surface.

Other players prefer a flicking technique, using more of the side of the forehead combined with a sideward flexion and twisting of the trunk. Although highly advanced, this technique is extremely effective because it is difficult to anticipate.

Diving Header

Often the only way to cash in on a scoring opportunity is with a dive. The takeoff—single- or double-leg—will depend on the available time and the distance to be covered.

a   b   c

Fig. 2.20 *Torpedo header. "The player throws himself headfirst into a complete layout."*

Fig. 2.21 *The center forward scores with a sensational torpedo header.*

Torpedo Header

The approach and dive coincide with the direction of the header. The player throws himself headfirst into a complete layout, cocking his head and kicking his heels to assure heaving power. From this well-braced prone position, identical to the classic heading position, the player snaps his forehead at the ball (Figs. 2.20 and 2.21).

Salamander Dive Header

This technique is used for a sideward header. It is identical to the regular technique (previously described), except that the bending and sideward twisting is coordinated with a horizontal rather than a vertical leap, ergo, the label "salamander" dive header. To ensure a soft landing, the player must absorb the impact of the fall with his hands (Figs. 2.22 and 2.23).

REALISTIC PRACTICES

As previously mentioned, the center forward cannot pick and choose his scoring opportunities. He cannot wait for perfect openings but must be ready to seize upon any half-chance to get in his shot. He may be blocked by the center halfback and the ball may arrive at a difficult height, but he must be able to hook the ball on the volley and shoot at goal.

In certain situations he may have to fling himself into a slide to beat a tackling foot or throw himself forward into a dive header to deflect a fast center into goal.

The ability to score goals from seemingly hopeless situations calls for mastery of the basic skills and techniques. It requires a powerful shot, the

a   b   c

Fig. 2.22 *Salamander dive header. "The bending and sideward twisting is coordinated with a horizontal rather than a vertical leap."*

ability to know when to shoot, the intuition to be in the right place, and the determination and eagerness to score goals. The most successful method of developing the ability is through realistic practices that simulate match play.

Shooting and Heading at Goal from Cross Centers

A wing forward centers the ball to the center forward, who is being challenged by the center halfback. The center forward must meet the ball quickly and shoot or head at goal or lay off a pass to the inside forward.

In this two-on-one situation, the center forward is expected to create an opening to receive the cross and to seize any opportunity to shoot or head at goal if close enough or to lay the ball off for the inside forward and reposition himself immediately for a return pass and shot.

Running at the Goal with a Defender in Pursuit

The center forward must be able to break through the last line of defense with a quick burst of speed either with the ball at his feet or on the receiving end of a through pass.

Fig. 2.23 *The center forward uses a salamander dive header to meet a cross and head it into the far corner of the goal.*

Typical attacking patterns that can be used as bases for practice drills are:

1. The center forward must be able to sense a through pass behind the defenders. He must avoid being caught offside and must prevent an easy interception by the center halfback.

The blind-side run is a good tactic in this situation. Instead of running directly forward, as the inside approaches with the ball, the center forward darts to the left so that the center halfback cannot watch both him and

29

the ball. This is the moment for the right inside forward to deliver a lead pass that the center forward can convert into a shot.

2. When the center halfback is the only player obstructing the path to the goal or is pursuing from behind, the center forward should elude him with a quick change of pace or dribble, driving into the penalty area and getting off his shot before another defender can close in on him.

3. The center forward dribbles by the center halfback in midfield or darts by him for a through pass. He tries to get a good lead on the opponent so that he will not be caught from behind when he has to slow down either to dodge the advancing goalkeeper or to slip the ball past him. There is nothing worse than seeing a center forward hurried into a poor play.

The center halfback and the goalkeeper may vary their play to provide the center forward with different situations.

Dealing with High Services

The center forward must always be ready and willing to fight for the high ball, especially in awkward situations like clearances from his own defenders. He also must be able to initiate an attack from these high clearances. Since he will be facing the wrong way nine out of ten times, and have the center halfback breathing down his neck, he obviously will not have the percentages going for him. Practice is the only way of learning how to deal with high services.

The goalkeeper or fullback clears the ball high upfield, and the center forward tries to make a play from around midfield. Flanked by two wing forwards who are tightly marked by their respective fullbacks, and supported by an inside forward, the center forward may be asked to do one of several things:

1. Head the ball back to the feet of the supporting inside forward or sideward behind and between the center halfback and the wing forward, where the latter can take it on the run and shoot at goal.

2. Go meet the ball, control it, turn while screening it from the challenging center halfback, and start an attack. The quicker he turns with the ball under control and starts the attack, the less time he will give the defense to organize.

3. Run for a well-placed clearance between the center halfback and the fullback and have

a go at the goal or pass off to a wing forward after beating the fullback or center halfback.

If an initial move fails, the attack should be continued with the help of the wing forwards, and the support of the spare inside forward. This creates a four-on-three situation (against the three defenders plus a goalkeeper).

To ensure continuity, the defenders should be instructed to counterattack. The spare inside forward receives the ball and immediately plays it to the goalkeeper to restart the activity.

The main objective of the drill is to give the center forward practice in dealing with high clearances and starting a quick attack. In the early stages, the center halfback should not challenge the center forward very actively. Once the latter acquires a degree of skill, the defensive man can go at him hard. The center forward will then learn how to adjust his play according to the manner of challenge.

Timing the Run to Coincide with the Cross (Center)

The center forward must have a firm grasp of the timing and orientation required to meet a center and head or shoot at goal. The essentials include:

1. When to go to the far post. A wing forward who crosses the ball usually aims for the far post, in classic English fashion. The center forward should take up a position somewhere around the edge of the goal area at the far side enabling him to run up to meet the ball.

2. When to go to the near post. On a fast, low cross to the near post, the center forward may run quickly across the face of the goalmouth to meet the ball. A mere deflection with the head may be sufficient to score, provided the ball has been centered hard enough.

3. When to lay back. Whenever a wing forward or inside forward can reach the goal line well inside the penalty area, he sets up perhaps the best attacking situation in the game. Being in position to shoot at goal, he forces the goalkeeper to set up at the near post and should now lay back around the penalty spot. A well-angled backward pass to his feet or head will set him up beautifully. He will have the full face of the goal to shoot at, the goalkeeper out of position, and the whole defense on the wrong foot.

The greatest problem for the center forward is

patience. He must learn to discipline himself: delay his final run and stay away from the immediate goal area. Common faults are going in too early, over-running a well-angled pass, and being caught underneath the center.

Coordinating with the Inside Forward

The forwards must spend a great deal of time together to learn each other's style of play. Numerous interpassing situations between the center forward and the inside forwards can be used to test and develop their tactical skill.

A four-on-three situation can be created with the center forward and the inside forwards marked closely by their respective opponents, and a midfield player (halfback) serving as a trailing playmaker.

The objective of this drill is to pass the ball around while moving about freely in an effort to shake off the defenders and make a successful attack at goal. Only forwards may score.

For example, the midfield player may lay the ball right to the feet of the center forward, who comes to meet the setup. The center forward has two main courses of action, depending on the action of the defender. First is a "turn" situation. If the center halfback does not follow him, the midfield player shouts "Turn!", whereupon the center forward quickly uses the inside of his foot to receive the ball and turns to face the center halfback.

Meantime, both inside forwards try to shake off their defenders by speeding toward the goal. The center forward delivers the ball to the more open man.

Second is the man-on situation. If the center halfback does follow the center forward and is ready to tackle him, the midfield player shouts "Man on!" The center forward then returns the ball to the midfield player or lays it off for an inside forward. The latter now has the choice of passing to the other inside forward who is racing across and behind the center halfback toward goal, or passing it back to the midfield player for the pass to the cutting inside forward. The center forward must, in either case, get downfield quickly to put pressure on the goalkeeper in case of a shot or to assist the inside forward if the initial attack at goal fails.

At first the coach may ask the players to run the drill at half or three-quarter speed in order to develop a feeling for the move. Once this is achieved, the players should be encouraged to improvise, make each situation realistic, and force the forwards to respond to the defensive counteraction.

The attack is continued until a goal is made. Then, to save time re-forming at midfield, an attack is immediately launched at the other goal. The goalkeeper throws the ball to the midfield player, while the forwards race upfield to take their positions and the defenders scurry back to get on the goal side of their respective forwards.

3

The Inside Forward

Inside forwards come in various guises: (1) the traditional inside forwards, whose prime function is to create openings for other players; (2) the master schemers and tacticians, better known as midfield players; and (3) the modern strikers, whose principal function is to score goals, pretty much in the old-fashioned style of the center forward. The ideal inside forward should combine the best of all three types.

NATURAL QUALIFICATIONS

Positional Sense

The need for outstanding positional sense is evident. Anyone who is expected to create opportunities for those around him has to understand the principles of time and space. Great inside forwards like "Didi" (Waldir Pereira) are able to deploy in the best position to set up the attack and dictate the rhythm and pace of the game.

Good positioning is at least sixty percent "play intelligence," or the natural gift for reading the flow of the game. It enables the player to instantly interpret the movements of both the ball-handler and his nearby teammates and to automatically correlate them with the styles of the players concerned.

Only a computer can do this sort of calculation, but to the gifted inside forward it is second nature. It has to be, for that is the only way he can think

or see two or three moves ahead, defensively as well as offensively, and make the correct decision about when to go right up in attack and when to take a more cautious position.

Stamina-Hustle

Every inside forward will be caught out of position once in a while. That is when stamina and hustle become essential. In fact, these are the first qualifications to look for in choosing a player for this position. The inside forward must be able to cover a lot of ground purposively—never aimlessly—and he must have the mobility to set up intelligent positions in his continual search for the ball. His constant movement and alertness will minimize the effects of any errors he might make.

Improvisation

Another vital consideration is the ability to improvise. The most ingenious maneuver becomes useless when employed too often, just as a player with a set of stock moves can become an easy mark for a good defender.

The inside forward must vary his pattern of distribution. He must pass left or right, forward or backward, long or short, high or low, according to the specific circumstances. Whenever he has the ball, the opposition should have only the vaguest idea of what he is likely to do. He must always use misdirection to keep them off-balance.

The inside forward also needs a built-in safety valve—imagination with a touch of conservatism. He should never be caught unprepared when he has the ball. As the player who feeds and sparks those around him, he must be prepared to inspire them with an imaginative play or to play a safe ball in impossible situations in order to maintain possession.

STYLE OF GREAT INSIDE FORWARDS

Forwards come in different shapes: some are short and stocky; some are willowy and graceful; some are big and burly; others are quite slightly built. Though physical characteristics influence their style of play, they can be divided into two broad categories: those whose prime function is to scheme and create openings for other players and those whose principal contribution is to strike.

Of course, the schemers should be able to finish off the play when required and the strikers should be able to do some constructive, creative playmaking when the situation demands it. Nevertheless, their priorities are undeniably different.

Schemer-Tactician

The inside forward who is a master schemer and tactician, capable of dictating the run of play from midfield, is the backbone of the attack. His role demands the greatest amount of skill in the manipulating the ball, which is why players like Luis Suarez of Inter-Milan and Spain, Giovanni Rivera of AC Milan and Italy, the great Johnny Haynes of Fulham and England, and Waldir Pereira ("Didi") of Santos and Brazil, the exemplars of the South American style of soccer, are legends in their own right and command such huge transfer fees.

Their outstanding characteristic is a graceful, easy style in handling the most difficult situations. They have the kind of inspired positional awareness that stems from an uncanny ability to read the game instantly and truly. It is like second nature for them to know when to part with the ball, which kind of pass is "on," and which position to take next. They always seem to be in the right place at the right time, and they apparently do it with minimum effort. They are artists at making the ball do the work.

This is not to imply that their work rate is not very high. They cover enormous areas. They need a lot of stamina for this, but they do not have to have unusual speed. In fact, most midfield players usually lack something in speed.

Strikers

The striker type of inside forward must, like the center forward, have a single-minded desire to score goals. Whether he achieves this through dazzling individualism or physical dominance and hustle makes no difference, as long as he keeps on scoring.

Individualists

These are the players who are full of exuberance and add a dynamic touch to their game. They are able to fasten on to the ball anywhere from thirty yards out, and are fast and deceptive enough to burst through quickly to score.

Soccer is richer for inside forwards like Ferenc Puskas, the galloping major from Hungary and Real Madrid. His flashes of razor-sharp passing and cannonball shooting with his legendary left foot have made him world famous.

And the incredible Pelé of Brazil! Pelé has the unique ability to "make" a soccer team. With him, Brazil is always dangerous. Without him, they are mere mortals, capable of being beaten (Fig. 3.1).

Pelé's fantastic ability to beat three or even four men in a very small area is just one of his many facets. He has tremendous ball-control. He can receive, control, and dispatch the ball from any angle. And he specializes in dribbling at great speed. His ability to accelerate from a walking pace always takes defenders by surprise.

Cool and insulated, he seems to operate in a private world of space and time. He can curl (bend) a free kick with absolute accuracy, squeezing the ball home between gaps that seem impenetrable. When he shoots straight for the target, his shot zeroes in like a cannonball.

Edson Arantes do Nascimento is a colorful name in itself, but no less colorful than its owner. Just say the word "Pelé" and practically everyone in the world will know whom you mean!

Thrusting Runners

Geoff Hurst of West Ham United and England is the most famous of the thrusting runner type (Fig. 3.2). He is the only player ever to pull the hat trick (three goals in one game) in a World Cup final (1966).

The thrusting runner striker relies on his timing to put him into the goalmouth at the precise moment the ball arrives. His physical strength and courage enable him to stand up to the physical punishment involved in a dive header or a flying crash volley shot at goal.

A striker of this kind is seldom seen around the immediate goalmouth until the time comes to meet the cross at the far or near post to knock it in. The striker who waits around the goalmouth is sure to be marked tightly and thus rendered useless. Men like Geoff Hurst have the knack of flying in at the right moment, scoring, and wheeling away before the defenders can spot the danger. He is an invaluable type of player, as he can often crack the tightest defense for a bid at the goal.

POSITIONAL PLAY

Offense

Traditionally, the inside forward is considered the team's general, capable of dictating the rhythm of play. Both inside forwards should ideally be effective both as goal schemers and goal getters. Unfortunately, the fluidity and pace of the game make this nearly impossible. It would require a superman to do equal justice to both phases of the game; that is, to provide the link between defense and attack to ensure a smooth transition and control of midfield, to drop back when the team is on defense in order to forage for the ball and initiate the counterattack, and in the next moment to join in the final assault on the goal.

Only the best of teams are fortunate enough to possess inside forwards of such caliber—players who can alternate the roles of schemer and striker between them and thus give their team great tactical flexibility.

More common in this era of specialization and paucity of talent is a division of labor. The team will have a scheming inside forward to playmake for his teammates up front, and a goal-getting inside forward farther upfield to carry on the good work and supply the finishing touch.

The wise coach will not play the same type of players side-by-side. There can be only one "general." When two try to do the same job, they often lose effectiveness, and, equally important, any

Fig. 3.1 *"King" Pelé, master of the ball in any situation, shows his incredible balance as he eludes a defender.*

Fig. 3.2 *Thrusting runner Geoff Hurst (in black).*

power struggle can affect the morale of the team. Twin spearhead attackers of the identical mold look for the same scoring opportunities and tend to get into each other's way. If nothing else, this makes it easier for the opposing defenders to cover them.

In the WM system of play (see p. 257), it is possible to have two "general" inside forwards, provided, of course, they can alternate and complement one another in finishing the attack and preparing it from midfield. Basically, however, the inside forward must support the attack by serving as a trailer, following up the direct thrusts of the two wingmen and center forward, ready to come from behind and shoot at goal.

Whenever two central attackers are used as spearheads, they can provide close support for one another. Two central strikers are better able to create space for themselves than any lone center forward can ever hope to do.

This formation calls for inside forwards of different styles. One must play upfield as a thrusting front runner, creating openings through intelligent running off the ball, and also looking for a shot himself. The forward alongside him must be a strong individualist who has flair and imagination with the ball. Brazil's Eduardo Goncales Andrade Tostao and Pelé are the ideal duo.

The more traditional inside forward of the WM era must emphasize attack—creating openings for the strikers, the center forward, and wing forwards.

Defense

Although the inside forward is very much part of the attack, he also has a defensive responsibility: He must check raids by the opposing halfback. Since many attacks stem from the probing runs of the halfback, the inside forward must, as soon as the attack breaks down, be prepared to challenge the halfback. As soon as the ball changes hands, he should quickly move into position in front of the opponent with the ball. He should delay him and obstruct his passing angles, constantly worrying him or forcing him into a hurried pass.

SPECIAL SKILLS AND TECHNIQUES

Complete mastery of the ball is vital: first, because the inside forward is expected to determine the rhythm and pace of the game; second, because he will frequently have to create openings by taking the ball around an opponent.

The inside forward must be able to control the ball at all speeds, coming from any angle or height, and in the face of challenge. The forward who cannot do this smoothly and easily will always be struggling, regardless of his other assets.

Watching Opponent while Receiving Ball

The inside forward should never be caught unprepared with the ball. He must always be aware of what is going on around him, habitually looking around, thinking ahead, and evaluating the circumstances (Fig. 3.3). This will enable him to instantly react upon receiving the ball.

He must constantly be alert for a tackle from the blind side. A defender on his back spells trouble. It becomes difficult to watch the opponent and the ball at the same time. The inside forward will have to glance over his shoulder first and control the ball second. And even then he can never be sure of what the defender is going to do.

By standing or moving sideward toward the defender or the goal, the inside forward will be able to watch the opponent and the ball at the same time. If the opponent is closing in to tackle, the forward can screen the ball from him. If the opponent allows enough space, the forward can simply take the pace off the ball while turning at the same time. It takes experience and practice to be able to receive the ball under close challenge and react instantly and properly.

Ball-Control—Feinting and Turning

The real test of the inside forward lies in his ability to turn with the ball. Skillful players can adapt to any situation. The inside forward often will receive the ball while facing the wrong way (i.e., with his back to the goal under attack). That is when he must be able to lay off a pass to a teammate in a better position to go forward (Fig. 3.4).

The maxim, "play the way you are facing," still holds true, as many players cannot turn with the ball, many more should not, and of course the defenders are not going to allow the forward to do so. When given any sort of space-time, however, the inside forward should be able to control the ball and turn to face his opponent in the same movement. Time after time, a quick counterattack will break down because several defenders will be allowed to get back in the game instead of being left behind by a swift skillful turn with the ball.

The experienced player seems to have his body already partly turned before he meets the ball. He gets right on top of the situation, adjusts his body *before* the ball arrives, stays loose and well-poised, gives with the ball, and remembers that the angle of impact corresponds closely with the angle of the controlled rebound.

Turning without Immediate Challenge

The inside forward will find that he can facilitate his move by dropping back to meet the ball. This will give him the space-time to turn without immediate challenge (Fig. 3.5).

Knowing that he has enough space behind him, the player may elect to turn and let the ball roll past him, move after it, and collect it in full stride. The player must judge the pace of the pass carefully, as the ball could get too far away from him and lead to an easy interception.

Many coaches demand that the player never let a ball go by without checking its pace. They want him to check its pace by letting the foot ride back with the ball, bring it under control, and simultaneously complete the turn by pivoting on the ball on the supporting foot. This will assure the player of complete control of the ball and situation within minimum space. He will be ready to face the challenging defender face on, beat him, or make a pass.

The same technique is recommended for receiving and turning a ball in the air, so long as the feet are used to control the ball. Where the thigh or chest is used, the player must make sure to give with the ball to absorb its pace. At the same time he must allow for a strong enough rebound to enable him to turn and collect the ball in full stride.

Turning with a Man on Tight

It is difficult enough for an inside forward to turn with the ball, but waiting for the ball with a defender breathing down his neck is asking for trou-

Fig. 3.3 *Watching the opponent while receiving the ball.*

| a | b | c | d |

Fig. 3.4 *Semi-controlling the ball in midair with the outside of the foot to lob it over the defender's head and go after it.*

Fig. 3.5 *The forward drops back to meet the ball, shaking the defender temporarily to get space-time to turn without immediate challenge.*

ble, as he is offering the defender a dead target. The smart inside forward makes it a habit to keep moving while receiving and turning with a tight-marking defender on his back.

In meeting a pass from a defensive teammate, the inside forward may take advantage of an eagerly pursuing defender by pretending to control and turn with the ball. At the last second, he lets the ball pass unchecked through his legs, then instantly turns and accelerates to collect the ball behind the beaten defender (Fig. 3.6).

The next time he may pretend to receive the ball and turn to his right. Actually, he lets the ball pass on the right while he turns to his left and accelerates to collect the ball behind the defender. The surprise element and the defender's momentum in committing himself for the tackle will leave him helplessly stranded.

Fig. 3.6 *Turning with a man on tight.*

In tight situations, there is usually not enough space behind the defender. This forces the forward to control and turn with the ball to beat the tight-marking defender. He employs basically the same technique as described, but he must also screen and roll off the defender as he turns with the ball. A preliminary feint—to the opposite side, for example—can be used to get the defender to commit himself (Fig. 3.7).

The player should always try to turn toward the same side as the controlling foot. This facilitates the movement. Yet many players, even on the professional level, will turn to the opposite side. For example, they will use the inside of their right foot to sweep the ball around to their left, seemingly unaware of the time wasted in turning in a semicircle.

Controlling the ball in the air, particularly with the thigh, chest, or even head, is more complicated. The forward must always fight for a position where

a   b   c   d

Fig. 3.7 *The inside forward meets the ball to take it early with the chest, allowing for a controlled rebound. Then he feints to one side to commit the defender. He pivot-traps the ball to go to the other side and accelerate past the defender.*

e

he can stand or move sideward toward the defender or the goal he is attacking.

When receiving a high ball from the wing, he should give just enough to take the pace off the ball and allow for a strong enough rebound. He must let the ball "ride" off his well-angled thigh, chest, or head and collect the rebound behind the tight-marking defender (Fig. 3.8).

This sort of stunt requires sufficient space behind the defender (to follow up the rebound). The forward usually will not find such space, particularly within goal range. While the ball is in the air, he should glance over his shoulder and put a move on the defender. He should then screen off the defender, allowing for a well-controlled vertical rebound off his chest or thigh. He then instantly rolls off the defender, picks up the rebound, and sweeps it along with the inside of his foot in half-

volley fashion or takes a thunderous volley shot at the goal.

Drawing and Committing an Opponent

A clever inside forward knows intuitively when to draw a defender out of position to make a decisive pass or when to provoke him into committing himself.

As artful as his passing and positional play may be, the inside forward will eventually fall into predicaments where his only means of advancing will be by taking the ball around the opponent.

The well-schooled inside forward always will meet—attack—the ball and take off while securing possession or immediately afterward. This will force the defender to chase after him. A sudden stop or turn will then usually create enough space for a play. For example, the inside forward may run

a   b   c   d

Fig. 3.8 *Controlling a ball in midair with the chest to play it off or check again immediately on the ground.*

to his right for a pass while the opponent comes in to challenge from the left. The forward can then check the ball with the outside of the right foot, accelerate, stop abruptly, check the ball with the sole of the foot, and turn to make the play while the opponent is still trying to recover.

Experienced defenders will refuse to commit themselves when the odds are against them. When confronted by a very clever and fast forward or when momentarily outnumbered, for example, they will stall until other defenders provide cover at their backs. That means a forward with the ball must have the ability to force the defender to commit himself.

Overpowering the defender with pure speed offers the simplest method of forcing a commitment. Pelé's tremendous ball-control and ability to accelerate upon spotting an opening continually catches his defenders by surprise. In tight situations, he is so artful and daring that he can kick the ball against the defender's shins and beat him to the rebound.

The complex maneuvers called "showing the ball" bait the defender into tackling. The moment the defender commits, the forward quickly drags the ball out of reach. Combined with a swift body movement and sudden acceleration, this move can leave the defender helplessly stranded.

The forward can start the play by taking the ball to the defender. He fakes a shot or pass, then checks the ball with the sole of the foot. The

defender, ninety-nine times out of a hundred, will instinctively commit himself to a block. The forward then pulls the ball out of reach with the sole of his foot and makes his play.

Some variations are:

1. The forward allows the ball to pass behind his supporting foot, flick passes the ball with the inside of the foot diagonally forward, then instantly accelerates past the defender to pick up the ball (Fig. 3.9).

2. The forward again shows the ball while going straight at the defender. He pretends to pass the ball with the inside of the right foot. As the defender commits himself, the forward drags the ball diagonally sideward out of the lunging defender's foot, quickly pushes the ball past the opponent with the inside of the left foot, and accelerates to collect the ball at the defender's back (Fig. 3.10).

When a forward drops back to meet the ball, he will often have to cope with a defender tight at his back. The forward may deliberately refrain from screening the ball fully. As the defender lunges at the ball, the forward evades the tackle by flicking the ball with the outside of his foot, propelling it diagonally backward through the spread legs of the defender. He then turns and accelerates to collect the ball at the back of the defender.

Close Interpassing

Every team must strive to obtain a numerical advantage in every phase of the game. Once estab-

41

Fig. 3.9 *Flick pass with the inside of the foot behind the supporting foot.*

Fig. 3.10 *The forward commits the defender to tackle by pretending a push pass. Instead he uses a roll over to drag the ball out of the tackle. Then he has the option to quickly push the ball with the inside of the other foot to go past the defender on either the left or right.*

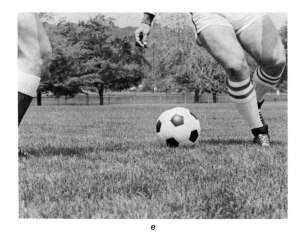

e

f

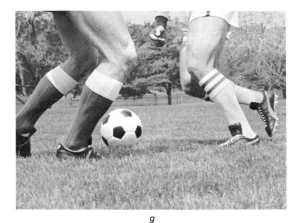

g

lished, its exploitation depends upon one thing—speedy, accurate interpassing.

First-class inside forwards frequently run toward the man in possession of the ball. They run away from him only when he is a decoy to pull the defense out of position. Inexperienced forwards carry the ball too long or else part with it too quickly.

The forward must have the ability to pinpoint a pass with a delicate and quick touch, with just enough spin or swerve, and within limited space and time.

Passing with Outside of Foot

The South American players often do their passing with the outside of the foot. It is most effective when passing diagonally forward, especially on the first pass in a double-pass combination in a tight situation.

The pass with the outside of the foot may be delivered without breaking stride and without elaborate preparatory movement, assuring the element of surprise and deception. This makes it difficult for the opponent to anticipate. The attacker can commit his defender, flick the ball away, and dart off to collect the return pass or the one after it.

The basic technique is rather simple and quite natural. The soccer player's pigeon-toed running style is made for it. By rolling the leg slightly inward, foot extended and well-braced, toes pointing inward and down, the player can contact the ball with the whole outside of the foot.

Pass and Go

The player delivers this pass as part of his natural running stride. By exaggerating the lower-leg action, he can deliver the pass with the necessary pace. The outside of the foot is driven squarely through the dead center of the ball, as the player completes his stride and immediately continues on. It is a very effective technique when used to screen off a challenging defender while passing diagonally forward or sideward.

Flick Pass

In tight situations, the forward can get the defender to commit himself, then play the ball off to one side and run around the defender on the other. The player passes the ball with a crisp flick-like action

Fig. 3.11 *Flick pass with the outside of the foot. "In tight situations the forward can get the defender to commit himself, then play the ball off to one side and run around the defender on the other. The player passes the ball with a crisp flick-like action of the lower leg. The minimal follow through prevents the foot from being jammed in the tackle and enables the passer to beat the defender," in expectation of a return pass.*

of the lower leg. The minimal follow through prevents the foot from being jammed in the tackle and enables the passer to beat the defender (Fig. 3.11).

Passing on Turn—Reverse Pass

The inside forward is often forced by his defender to turn his back to the goal under attack or the direction in which he intends to pass, in order to screen the ball from the attempted tackle (Fig. 3.12).

At other times, the inside forward may choose to dribble across rather than down the field in order to draw the defender's attention away from the actual final thrust at the goal. At the right moment, he can suddenly turn and reverse the play, in the hope of catching the defenders on the wrong foot.

In a very tight situation, the inside forward may succeed in creating space by drawing the defender out of position with a dribble, while shooting a glance backward for a teammate in a better position. If he finds a man, he may set him up for a perfect kill by suddenly passing the ball back with the heel. This sort of quick, accurate back-heel pass will deceive the defense (Figs. 3.13–3.15). But great care should be taken to see that it does not also catch the open teammate by surprise!

Finesse and Artistry of Scoring

Volleying on Turn

Crashing crosses from the wing into goal is a spectacular feat (Fig. 3.16). A great time-saver, it can produce goals that would be lost if the player had to take the time to kill—steady—the ball for a careful shot.

The height of the ball at the moment of impact multiplies the degree of difficulty. To keep the ball

Fig. 3.12 *Flick pass with the outside of the foot with preliminary feint. The forward meets the ball, flicks it off, immediately turns and sprints behind the defender in expectation of a return pass.*

low, it is essential to have the knee above or at least level with the ball at the moment of impact. This normally would greatly reduce the leg swing. So, in order to swing the leg high with sufficient power, the player must make the volley with a sideward approach. The "secret" is to lean toward the off-foot in order to get up to the ball above waist height and hit it hard.

Where the player has the time to use the foot opposite the approaching ball—to lean into the ball and strike it with the full, well-braced instep—he will also be able to capitalize on the velocity of the ball. The main power will come from the fast straightening of the knee.

More often than not, however, the forward will be forced to use the nearer foot to take a ball coming squarely at him. Most players prefer to use the outside of the foot in such situations, as it provides a somewhat larger area of impact. Many forwards will turn their back to the goal just before

shooting in order to get a full body turn into the shot (Fig. 3.17).

The pivot is initiated by stepping around toward the goal with the supporting foot and simultaneously leaning the body away. This produces a very effective semicircular leg swing.

The player must drive the well-braced and firm instep or outside of the foot horizontally through the dead center of the ball and let the hip swing around, allowing a natural follow through of the leg across the body for maximum control and power. To counterbalance the pivot and circular leg action, the player must counterrotate the trunk and swing the off-arm across the body, keeping the shot on target, not pulling it into the pivot.

Many players actually fall away from the ball as they shoot in this position. First-class players, in fact, develop extraordinary techniques in trying to drive a ball home in full flight. They will fly through the air or slide on the ground.

Fig. 3.13 *Back-heel pass. The forward reverses the play by striding over the ball without immediately transferring weight, back-heeling the ball with a quick flexion of the lower leg, and continuing.*

Fig. 3.14 *Heel-kick option. Heel flick: the forward steps over the ball, puts the weight on his kicking leg, and then reverses the play by a stutter flick step.*

Fig. 3.15 *The player pretends a back-heel pass but instead swings the leg over or beside the ball to push it forward with the inside of the foot and accelerates in order to shake the defender.*

Fig. 3.16 *"Crashing into goal on the volley crosses from the wing is a spectacular feat."*

The player should be taught to concentrate, to control his foot in the air while maintaining good balance, and to focus on his timing. Sometimes the final striking action will have to be suspended, to avoid wildly slashing at the ball. The point to remember is that brute force is useless without perfect timing, particularly when the shot is taken on the volley.

Overhead Scissors Volley Shot

One of the game's most acrobatic skills, strongly favored by South American and Latin players, the overhead scissors volley is self-explanatory. The attacker, caught with his back to the goal, simply plays the ball over his head or shoulder (Fig. 3.18).

He flings himself into the air, feet first, and, while in midair, executes a quick scissors movement. He pretends to strike the ball with one foot, then quickly reverses and plays the ball with the other. It is a dramatic exposition of the art of achieving height, balance, and power, though timing remains the critical factor.

Ideally, the player should drive his heavily pronated instep through the center of the ball just as the ball comes above him, around the hip region. This will ensure the player of a low enough shot to get below the crossbar. The player also must make sure to reach well-back with both hands, palms down, and to keep his head forward with his chin pressed against the chest, and his back well-arched to ensure a comfortable landing.

Some players prefer a slightly different technique. They swing the leg obliquely across the body, playing the ball over the opposite shoulder rather than straight back over the head. Since the player must dip sideward in midair, he brings the hip around to partly face the direction of the intended shot. This technique offers a longer, more natural leg swing, and thus produces a more powerful and accurate shot. It also enables the player to anticipate the landing more readily. All he has to do is glance over his shoulder. He can avoid landing flat on his back by breaking the fall with his nearer hand and rolling over onto a shoulder.

Second-Touch Shot

An inside forward must be able to shoot first-touch. But equally important, he must develop a skill series—second-touch shots. Often it is the fastest way possible to get a shot off in difficult circumstances (Fig. 3.19).

The secret to this skill sequence lies in the initial control of the ball. The player must decide early how to semi-control the ball. He must make sure to angle the thigh or chest or deflect a well-controlled rebound and set himself up for an instant shot at the goal. Perfect timing and body control will enable him to get the shot off before the ball hits the ground or before the defender gets in a tackle.

REALISTIC PRACTICES

Interpassing in Crowded Conditions

The inside forward must have the ability in heavy traffic to control and pass the ball quickly and accurately. He must have the quick acceleration to escape his immediate opponent, and the ability to come to a quick stop and then instantly change direction, and, most of all, the intelligence to move at the right time. His running, with or without the ball, always must have a purpose. He must always think two or three moves ahead of the play.

These are the basic moves of the inside forward, and should be practiced until they become automatic. Game-like conditions are provided by breaking down the team into small groups for play within limited areas. The size of these areas

a   b   c

d   e

Fig. 3.17 *Side volley shot. The secret is to lean away from the ball in order to gain freedom for a circular leg swing down on the ball.*

a   b

Fig. 3.18 *Overhead scissors volley shot, one of the game's most acrobatic skills.*

a   b   c

Fig. 3.19 *Second-touch volley shot. The forward semi-controls the ball with the thigh, allowing for a controlled rebound which he smashes at goal with a side volley.*

d

("grids") depends upon the skill level and number of players involved.

For example, two sets of inside forwards, each supported by a halfback, play each other within a grid approximately forty by twenty yards that has a goal three yards wide at each end. The halfback on offense attacks with his two inside forwards while the other halfback drops back to serve temporarily as goalkeeper. This provides very effective three-on-two practice, ensuring a game-like continuity. The inside forwards are forced to work hard to move the ball, shake free on offense, and convert to defense instantly upon losing possession.

Exploiting the Three-on-Two Situation

Forwards often are unable to exploit the three-on-two situation because they have never been versed in the ways and means of quickly overrunning the two defenders. Speed is important, especially in running directly forward, but the players must be particularly careful to avoid being offside.

The previous activity can be made more realistic by working up and down the field between the two penalty areas. Here again two pairs of inside forwards play against each other. To keep the activity continuous, two fullbacks are positioned at either side of each penalty area, with the defending halfback always dropping back between them. The objective of the inside forwards is to get the ball downfield quickly and to pass the ball to the fullback who is better positioned to receive the ball. The defending halfback, of course, makes every effort to cut off the pass. To give the inside forwards time to recover, the fullback, on receiving the ball, controls it and tries to make an accurate floating pass across the penalty box to the fullback at the other side of the penalty area.

The forwards also can test and improve their skills in the following ways:

1. Two-touch soccer: control pass.

2. Short, long: every other pass must be over thirty yards.

3. Draw a man before passing: the ball handler allows a defender to challenge him, while he holds and screens the ball to slow down the game before making the play.

4. Dribble toward a defender and make him commit himself before making your play.

5. Give and go: a "wall pass" combination.

4

The Wing Forward

Stand by for a soccer revolution: Wingers are coming back!

Remember the wizardry of Sir Stanley Matthews? The poetry in motion of Tom Finney? The power and pace of Helmut Rahn? That was the heyday of the wing forwards. Then came the drought: except for an occasional Garrincha (Manoel Francisco dos Santos) or George Best, wing play deteriorated and began to mean less and less to the attack. One formation followed another and the "safety first" bolting of the back door replaced the flair and enterprise of earlier years.

It had to happen, of course, but, just as the 1950's required greater cerebration, depth, and mobility on defense, the 1970's cry out for wing forwards of vision, courage, and skill.

Most modern defenses have closed the middle of the field to all but the swiftest or most subtle of assaults. That means the offense must get back to using the whole width of the field. Like an army, every defense is vulnerable on its flanks. Even when there seems to be no way through, there is always a way around. It is the winger's job to find that way and to exploit it to the fullest.

With the defense so vulnerable along the touchline, the intelligent offense will force it to spread by attacking on a wide front, with a real wing forward on each flank. In addition to turning the defense, the offense can create big spaces between the central striker and the wing forward,

which either of them or a midfield player can effectively exploit.

NATURAL QUALIFICATIONS

Speed-Quickness

Great speed is the number one prerequisite of the winger. Speed can take various forms. It may be the short, devastating spurt that Sir Stanley Matthews and Garrincha (Brazil) employed to break eight-ten yards clear of their defenders; or it may be the sustained, powerful running that took flyers like Francisco Gento (Spain) and "Jairzinho" Ventura Filho (Brazil) from their own half into the enemy penalty area with the helpless defenders in pursuit.

The essential point is for the winger to be able to outrun his opponent one way or another. The winger without speed is a liability. Even if he can work the ball brilliantly, he will seldom get sufficiently clear to do real damage. His slowness will invariably enable a good fullback to recover and get in another tackle.

Confidence and Initiative

The wing forward must have an abundance of courage and the confidence to take on anyone. The demands of every player are constantly increasing, and this particularly applies to wing forwards. Not only do they have to contend with the frustrations of attacking the highly scientific defensive systems—like getting clear of the fullback only to find the sweeper has come across to intercept—but they also have to carry a far greater work load than ever before.

Garrincha exhibited the ideal kind of confidence and initiative needed by a wing forward (see photo, p. 52). His teammates often would give him the ball and sprint toward the goal instead of lending support. They had confidence in his ability to carve his way through the defense and create openings for others in front of the goal.

The confidence that such players as Garrincha radiate with their daring and ability can calm a team, strengthening its spirit and morale—provided, of course, that the individualism enhances the team's effort rather than merely shows off the individual.

The wing forward must be courageous enough to endure the many knocks and upsets from opponents bent on dispossessing him of the ball. He must take these tackles without losing his temper or resorting to vengeful play. Like Sir Stanley Matthews, he must refuse to be provoked and should use his skill along the touchline to counter brute force and close-marking attention.

Flair for the Unpredictable

The wing forward also must be able to take on a fullback and turn him inside out. A flair for the unexpected marks the great individualist. He is the sort of player who, on a good day, can cause confusion and chaos in the best-organized defense by his skill, daring, and courage.

The danger of becoming stereotyped and entirely predictable is enhanced by the fact that the wing forward is somewhat boxed in by the touchline. There are wings who have only one trick—perhaps a habit of bearing inside and then suddenly swerving to the outside in the hope of sprinting past the fullback and down the touchline.

The winger should never approach a defender with a preconceived plan for eluding him. The only way he can hope to pass his opponent consistently is through "working off the cuff" with a wide assortment of maneuvers. He must determine which trick can best embarrass the defender and then use it mercilessly.

Some wing forwards, even when they break clear, can think of nothing more imaginative than

a hectic dash to the by-line and an orthodox high cross into the goalmouth. Other wingers always want the ball played to their feet when they get in front of the fullback (rather than a lead pass into the space behind the fullback), and then merely try to beat him on their own.

The wing forward must vary his use of the ball to extract the maximum advantage from any given situation. This entails knowing when to hold it to draw a defender and then lay off a pass; or when to beat him down the touchline and settle for a standard high cross to the far post. This usually is the option when the winger is under pressure and has no time to do anything more imaginative. At times a more ambitious alternative will present itself, such as a direct run on goal or a sprint to the by-line (the closer to the goal, the more effective), followed by a sharp turn of the ball right back to the feet of an advancing teammate.

STYLES OF GREAT WING FORWARDS

Raiding-Thrusting

The traditional style of play for the wing forward calls for sustained powerful running à la Helmut Rahn, the 1954 German World Cup hero. Rahn had the ability to take a game by the scruff of the neck and change its course single-handed. It was just about impossible to knock him off the ball. When he started his thrusting raids down the sideline or straight at goal, the defenders literally bounced off him.

The flyer type is exemplified by Francisco Gento of famed Real Madrid of Spain, one of the fastest wing forwards ever to play the game. Or "Jairzinho," a strong, lightning-fast Brazilian with a bullet-like shot, who was the outstanding winger of the 1970 World Cup games in Mexico.

The flyer moves the ball from his own half of the field into the enemy penalty area, usually with a string of helpless defenders in pursuit. The quick, thrusting raid down a flank offers one of the most successful means of infiltrating or turning the last line of defense. It is a style of wing play, relatively simple, that relies on two basic plays:

1. Sometimes the wing forward will dribble the ball up to the fullback and overpower him with pure speed. Or he will use a preliminary body-feint, push the ball ten to twenty yards by the man, and then take off after it like a grey-

hound. The main object is to get to the goal line, pull a defender with him, then cut the ball back across the goalmouth, the most dangerous and productive pass a wing forward can make.

2. At other times, the winger may use a simple "give-and-go" passing combination with a nearby teammate, who sends the ball into the space behind the fullback. The wing forward then simply outraces the fullback to the ball. This lead pass may take the form of a lob from a halfback, or a quick return wall pass from the inside forward.

Talented Individualist

Since the average fullback is a rather speedy, quick-turning, intelligent player, it is very difficult for the wing forward to beat him simply through speed. The winger also must be able to work the ball effectively.

Sir Stanley Matthews' "magic" along the touch-lines was the product of imaginative application (Fig. 4.1). He could do the "impossible"—beat the best fullback in the world from a standing start. The Matthews' dalliance, the shuffling, itchy-twitchy wiggle, the sudden acceleration outside the fullback, the blinding burst of speed to the ball, and the telling strike before the defenders could reach him, were pure artistry.

He was a master at crossing the ball from the wing. His floating, curling centers were devastating. Other times he would drive and cut the ball back after beating the fullback, just out of the reach of the goalkeeper, in a perfect setup for a forward.

Talk of Matthews inevitably leads to Tom Finney—they were so alike in style and their impact on the game. Finney could follow through an attack, switch the ball from one foot to the other with magical dexterity, and finish with a powerful shot. His goal-scoring ability was a heavy plus in his favor over Matthews, but Matthews probably had a little more of that indefinable something that can only be described as "soccer magic." So great was their influence that every wing forward today has a little of either Matthews or Finney in his makeup.

Brazil's elusive "little bird," Garrincha, had such a devastating burst that it made his blue and yellow uniform stripe flash like a strange bird of paradise winging through a dark forest. A short, powerfully built mulatto with a right knee strangely twisted from birth, Garrincha might have been described as a supercharged Matthews. He had all of

Fig. 4.1 *Sir Stanley Matthews.*

Matthews' astonishing ability to accelerate from a standing position and to swerve outside the back. His ball-control was excellent, and like so many Brazilian forwards he delighted in playing with the ball. There was a "jungle cat" quality to his game, a feline waiting and pouncing. He achieved his peak in Sweden in 1958, and in his day he was *the* right wing forward of the world.

George Best is the youngest of that breed. He is the most glamorous and electrifying player in the British Isles. His movements are quick, light, balletic. He sidesteps the charges of defenders, who often triple-team him, as gracefully as a matador. He does it with speed, deception, an uncanny knack of controlling the ball while warding off tackles, and an utter disregard for danger (Fig. 4.2).

Withdrawn Schemer

Mario Jorge Lobo Zagallo played the role of a deep-lying wing forward the way Nandor Hidegkuti had played a withdrawn center forward in Hungary's attack. With his phenomenal stamina, Zagallo was capable of running long after the average player would have dropped. His great skill and tactical maturity were put to great use in the Brazilian midfield. But his real effectiveness lay in the

Fig. 4.2 *George Best: "the most glamorous and electrifying" contemporary wing forward, warding off a tackle to get in a shot at goal.*

fact that he never ceased to be a true winger when the need arose to carry the hostility to the opponent.

The lesson to be learned from such great wing forwards is that it is often wise to pull back the wingers and allow them to play on the touchline from a deeper position. Sometimes it is the only way the winger can free himself from his immediate opponent's stranglehold and get himself into the game in midfield. It is sometimes also the only way he can create space in front of him that can be exploited by his teammates or even himself.

POSITIONAL PLAY

Offense

The play of the wing forward has undergone a dramatic change. A few years ago he paced the touchline, participating in the game by invitation only. It came in the form of a pass from his inside forward or halfback. If they did not get the ball to him, the winger had a quiet day, and he would receive sympathy rather than blame. It provided the winger with a wonderful excuse for an "off" day.

The wing forward now must be an all-purpose player capable of playing in midfield and raiding along the touchline. He is expected to work as hard as any other member of the team. If he is not getting the ball, he is expected to go after it. Once in possession, he must be able to use the ball like the most skillful inside forward or score with the ruthlessness of a center forward.

Basically, the wing forward should hug the touchline, spreading the defense, and creating gaps for the inside forward. Staying wide also helps the winger, as it makes it easier to get the ball to him.

It may seem relatively simple to play the wing forward. With the touchline at his back, he can rarely be caught from the blind side by a defender. He can easily oversee the whole field in front of him. The touchline, however, remains an advantage only until the ball is delivered to the wing; then it becomes a heavy liability. Most fullbacks try to jockey the winger out to the touchline, where his options with the ball are severely limited. An intelligent defender, knowing that he is well-covered in back, will overplay toward the touchline and force the winger to beat him on the inside.

The wing forward's primary duty is to turn the enemy flank and carry the attack right into the goalmouth. It does not matter how he gets past the fullback, as long as he beats him cleanly while retaining possession of the ball. What does matter is how he uses the ball. Most inexperienced wingers tend to bang the ball into the middle as quickly as possible. They think that is all there is to their job and that they cannot be blamed if no goal results from their pass.

The well-coached team will eschew the high hopeful centers from the touchline. This classic style of wing forward play, culminating in the high cross, produces very few goals. The modern highly organized and defensively oriented team rarely will leave a front player uncovered and unchallenged.

Certainly there are times, particularly on a quick, sudden breakaway, when the winger can and must cross the ball quickly from the touchline to a teammate in position to score. As a rule, however, it is vital for the winger to cut in for goal once he has beaten the fullback.

The angle at which he attacks the goal depends upon the disposition of the defenders. The objective is to draw defender(s) out of the crowded goalmouth, as well as turn the defense in the hope of catching them going the wrong way. Another important value of cutting for the goal: the shorter the pass, the less time the defenders will have to reposition themselves. When the ball is crossed from the touchline, the defenders have time to go meet it.

Once the wing forward beats the fullback, whether on the inside or outside, he must move in quickly for goal and do one of the following things:

1. Continue to the by-line and draw a defender across, but, just before he can block the pass, cut the ball back along the ground into the middle for a teammate running in at speed. It is a goal all the way!

The winger should not worry too much about placing the ball right to a teammate's feet. He should just get it back low and hard, aiming between the six-yard line and the penalty spot. The odds are that some teammate will be able to meet it, as he will be taking it in stride while the defenders will be either trying to turn or will be facing the wrong way to make a clearance. Cool thinking and an accurate, well-timed pass will do the trick.

If the middle is blocked, the answer is a swift center beyond the far post that drops behind the defender and out of the goalkeeper's reach. This sets up a handsome opportunity for the other wing forward. He can come running in on the blind side of the fullback for a shot or a header for goal, or he can head the ball back into the goalmouth for an oncoming forward or midfield player to have a crack at goal. The winger also can cross the ball to the near post for a cutting forward to run in on and deflect either into the goal or back into the goalmouth.

2. The other possibility (after passing the fullback) is to cut straight toward goal and try an unorthodox cross shot. Most wing forwards have their own style. The most common and most effective style for a right winger, for example, is to feint, continuing on the outside right to the by-line, then, at the last moment, cut the ball sharply back to the inside and take the shot immediately with his left foot. This will open a much wider angle of the goal to shoot at and momentarily (at least) throw off the defender, particularly the goalkeeper.

Most wing forwards are given the responsibility for all corner kicks. There are a great many ploys for corner kicks, which will be covered in a later chapter, but most of the successful ones hinge on simplicity and the winger's ability to place the ball exactly where it is wanted.

Interchanging Positions

The presence of wing forwards helps add width to the attack and this prevents the defenders from concentrating. The wingers must always be ready to interchange positions with other players. The game demands a fluid interchange of positions, and every player must be familiar with each other's roles and responsibilities.

Since the chief objective is to create defensive confusion, the wing forward may cut across the field to exchange positions with the inside forward or even center forward. This is a well-known scissors move. The most common way that wingers score is after a quick switch of positions that puts them directly in front of the goal, or with a snappy header or shot while running in to meet a sharp pass from the opposite winger.

The winger can create space on the flanks by cutting laterally across the field. This creates an opportunity for players to come from behind on an *overlap*. The use of overlapping runs offers an excellent way to obtain extra men in tight-playing situations. At the same time it adds a high degree of mobility to the attack.

Defense

The wing forward always must remember that he has a defensive as well as an attacking function. Any winger who imagines that he can make a few runs and then spend the rest of the match standing on his touchline calling for passes is not going to last very long with a good team.

Whenever the winger loses possession to the opposing fullback, he must attempt to recover quickly and challenge back for the ball, or else deploy in front of the fullback and restrict his passing angles. This relentless effort to contain the opposing defenders is essential. It gives the defense valuable time to retreat, tighten up the defense, and pounce on the pass when it is made.

The winger is responsible for picking up the opposing fullback on his attempt to come through on an overlap run. He also must go deep into his own half ready to link up with the defense, though he may not be involved in his team's initial defensive play. He should take up a position where he can initiate the immediate counterattack, where he can be reached with a quick outlet pass from his defense.

SPECIAL SKILLS AND TECHNIQUES

How to Beat the Fullback

One of the soccer's most thrilling sights is a player like George Best (Manchester United) and Jairzinho (Santos) running at full speed with the ball. Few players have the talent and confidence to go all out with the ball, however. The ability to do so is erroneously assumed to be a natural gift or is frowned upon as dangerous and destructive to team play. As a result, "running with the ball" is often thought valuable only as a type of dribbling attempt to beat a defender.

Coaches want to keep the ball moving through clever interpassing rather than "running," as the ball can be moved much faster this way. Each move of the ball (pass) forces the defense to change or adjust, whereas the one-man sally gives the defenders time to weigh the situation, pick up their man, and even anticipate the next move.

Of course, great individuals like Matthews or Garrincha can change the defensive picture half a dozen times during a two-yard run with the ball. They instinctively look around for openings while changing pace or direction, feinting, and faking a pass. They force the defense to keep thinking and moving, and thus confuse them. This sort of cat and mouse game requires a great deal of maturity. The player must be able to read the situation and react almost simultaneously.

Running with Ball

The ability to run with the ball underlies the complex technique of beating a man. The wing forward must be able to run at top speed with the ball under close control. The secret is staccato—quick, small steps. This enables him to stop and go, change direction, and feint while sizing up the situation at the same time. Speed can be obtained by playing the ball with the *outside* of the controlling foot each time this foot comes forward, without altering the natural running style. The outside of the foot is commonly used to push the ball quickly past a defender to suddenly dart past him after feinting to go the other way.

The *inside* of the foot is generally used to work the ball, and the *inner edge of the instep* is most effective for sudden changes of direction. In evading a tackle, the winger often has to cut the ball sharply and obliquely backward while in full stride.

The wing forward must be able to stop abruptly in full stride. He may use the *sole of the foot* to stop the ball quickly, and he must be ready to play it again immediately. He can tap the ball forward again and then break into another sprint, or he can even pull the ball around the supporting foot while turning for a dash in the opposite direction.

Using Pure Speed

When the ball is at one's feet, the crux of beating a defender is knowing how far ahead to play the ball. Many players just kick the ball ahead and chase after it. Many others fail to push the ball out far enough, so they are forced to replay the ball before they can accelerate to top speed. This gives the defender an opportunity to get in some sort of tackle.

Tremendously fast wingers like Spain's Francisco Gento can push the ball far forward into space behind the fullback and then get to the ball first. In fact, the first thing most topflight wingers will do in a match is kick the ball past their fullback and sprint after it to see how fast he is on the turn (Fig. 4.3).

Another method of exploiting pure speed can be effected immediately upon the arrival of the ball. The player kicks the ball forward past the defender (first-touch) and then instantly sprints

Fig. 4.3 *Using pure speed, the wing forward pushes the ball past the defender and outraces him to the ball.*

after it (Figs. 4.4 and 4.5). It is surprising how often this play catches the defender flat-footed.

Change of Pace

There are many individual ruses for beating a man, but all are predicated on changing direction, sharply or subtly, or feinting the defender off-balance and then suddenly accelerating (Figs. 4.6 and 4.7).

This explosive acceleration, calling for lightning reflexes, enables the outstanding players to leave their opponents struggling. Of course, they also have balance, timing, and ball-control. But it is their devastating speed off the mark that produces the decisive five or ten yards between them and

their victims. The player who fails to sprint after putting a move on the defender can have his advantage easily cancelled by an alert opponent.

The winger should move the ball up as close as possible to the defender before making his surge. The longer he can delay his burst, the less chance the defender will have to recover and the greater the space and time the winger will gain for himself. It is pointless to feint a man who is six yards away.

The winger also must have the flexibility to change his mind in midfeint. If, for example, he feints a cut to the inside, but the fullback fails to take the bait, the winger should realize that he has failed to throw the fullback off-balance, and that

a

b

c

d

Fig. 4.4 *The wing forward uses a preliminary feint to mislead the defender. Instead of receiving the ball, he allows it to pass through his legs, turns, and sprints after it.*

Fig. 4.5 *Using speed, "the forward kicks the ball forward past the defender (first-touch) and then instantly sprints after it."*

the smart move now is to make a positive action out of the feint—that is, to instantly cut past the fullback on the inside (Fig. 4.8).

The Stanley Matthews "Magic"

The wing forward must always remember that his "tricks" are restrained by the touchline. He has little room to maneuver with the touchline on one side and a clever fullback on the other. A good fullback will overplay toward the touchline and force the winger to beat him on the inside, knowing that he is covered in the back and that the winger prefers to beat him on the outside. If the winger still tries to go outside, the fullback can run him out of play.

a

b

c

d

Fig. 4.6 *Sudden reverse in direction: The forward pretends to continue straight forward by using a feint kick; instead he stops the ball with the sole of the foot, reverses direction, and accelerates.*

a

b

c

d

Fig. 4.7 *Option to reverse in direction: The forward pretends by way of a feint kick to accelerate; instead he stops the ball with the sole of the foot, pushes it forward, and accelerates.*

It was in just such situations that the classic Matthews "dribble" worked like magic (Fig. 4.9). Time and again the fullback knew what Matthews was going to do, but he did not know *when,* and that was what made him helpless. Matthews would take the ball right up to the fullback, knowing full well that the fullback had him pinned to the touchline and that the fullback was confident that he could not be beaten on the outside—that Matthews had to go inside. As Matthews jockeyed the ball up to the fullback at little more than walking pace, he would patiently wait until the fullback committed himself. One could almost imagine him whispering, "Not yet," touch, "Not yet," touch, "Not yet," touch, as he brushed the ball gently each time with the inside of the right foot, making believe that he was going to beat the fullback on the inside. With every touch, however, he moved the fullback a little farther into the field, creating space between the fullback and the touchline, thus setting the fullback up for an outside move.

"Now!" Matthews would brush the ball with the inside of his right foot for the last time, moving

a *b* *c*

d *e* *f*

Fig. 4.8 *The forward quickly protects the ball by turning on it to screen it from the challenging defender. In so doing, he quickly changes feet in order to draw the ball back and use a flick pass with the inside of the foot to pass the ball behind his supporting foot as well as the defender's back, turns quickly to accelerate, and collects the ball.*

a   b   c

d   e

Fig. 4.9 *The Stanley Matthews dribble.*

the ball just enough to lend credence to his inside move. Usually the fullback would instinctively follow. Then Matthews instantly would slide off the ball, check and push it with the outside of the foot past the fullback, and cut back to the outside. Sometimes he even would flip the ball with the outside of his foot over the extended tackling foot of the fullback. Matthews' incredible acceleration,

virtually from a standing start, often stranded the most alert defender.

Opponents who rushed in were easy customers for Matthews and those who countered by backpedaling or jockeying for position also were bilked. Matthews' answer to the retreating fullback was simple. He took the ball up to him faster, still using the same trick of not now . . . touch. If the fullback still refused to commit himself to the tackle, Matthews forced him to do so by adding a magnificent *body swerve*. He would lean—sway—so far over to one side (usually the inside) that it seemed impossible for him to go any other way. Once the fullback swallowed the bait, Matthews would check and cut back on the other side.

His perfect balance always permitted him to drive either way, although he preferred the outside, and his reflexes gave him the split second he needed to evade the tackle.

His secret lay in his ability to retain the initiative. It then simply became a matter of throwing his opponent off-balance. He was always master of the situation, and as often as not the fullback landed up flat on his back without having touched the ball or Matthews, who, by this time, was speeding off down the wing!

Deceptive Ball-Control

The wing forward must be able to control the ball in every possible situation, often in very restricted conditions and in the face of a challenge. The real trademark of the outstanding winger is the swiftness with which he can collect a pass, screen off, beat the challenging fullback, and go downfield in a sweeping attack.

Control with Outside of Foot

Most wing forwards naturally prefer to control the ball with their strong foot. The right winger, for example, would rather reach across his supporting left leg to control a square pass between the outside of his right foot and the ground. He can then pin the ball to the turf and simultaneously sweep it around to his right in a half-volley movement. This allows him to maintain control with his strong foot while pivoting on his supporting foot to turn and take off downfield (Fig. 4.10).

This is a fluid, economic, relatively easy technique—as long as the winger is not facing an immediate challenge. Once a challenging fullback is added, the technique has limitations. Not only will the ball be in full view of the fullback as the winger sweeps it around, but the slightest lack of control will cause him to run straight into the attacking fullback and be swept off his feet.

A skillful winger can still use the sweeping trap with the outside of the foot against a challenging fullback by employing a preliminary feint and a sharper sweep. To throw the fullback off-balance, he starts by feigning control of the ball with the inside of the right foot. He then traps and sweeps the ball sharply to the outside along the touchline. He tries to get into motion forward before the fullback can brace himself for a challenge.

Control with Inside of Foot

The right winger would be wiser, however, to control the ball with the inside of his *left* foot. This is particularly effective whenever he wants to come inside the fullback to gather the ball. It means that his body will be between the fullback and the ball (Figs. 4.11 and 4.12).

The technique is both economic and fluid. It enables the winger to kill the ball while standing still, to sweep it along in a half-volley movement while in full stride, or even change direction in the same movement. It is extremely effective in controlling the ball against a challenge and lends itself naturally to a screen. The player turns sideward and leans, pointing the right shoulder to the inside, where he intends to take the ball. With his back to the opponent, the winger now can trap the ball directly underneath his body (between the inside of the foot and the ground) by placing the inside of his foot above the ball and across its path. The fullback cannot get at the ball as the winger screens it and sweeps it along in moving inside with the ball on his left foot.

If the fullback comes across to get in front of the winger and prevent him from going to the inside, the winger may still control the ball with the inside of the left foot. But, instead of sweeping it along, he can kill the ball, turn sharply to the outside, and sweep the ball along with his right foot to beat the fullback to the outside. Or he may fake ball-control with his left foot as if to cut to the inside, then assume control with the inside of the *right* foot to cut back to the outside. Since such elaborate turns give the fullback ample time to move in for a tackle, however, the winger would more often be better off passing the ball back.

Shooting from an Acute Angle

Although most of the wing forward's runs will end in some kind of pass, he will still get plenty of opportunities to shoot. More often than not, he will have to shoot from a very sharp angle. So he must develop a sense of judgment and orientation.

Fig. 4.10 *Controlling, trapping with a preliminary feint (body-swerve) with the outside of the foot to sweep the ball along as the player moves off.*

Fig. 4.11 *Controlling, trapping with a preliminary feint (body-swerve) with the inside of the foot to sweep the ball along as the player moves off.*

a   *b*   *c*

d   *e*

Fig. 4.12 *The forward pivot-traps with the inside of the foot in order to take off in the direction opposite to that which he is facing and screen the ball from the challenging defender.*

Most inexperienced wingers tend to drive the ball persistently into the near side of the netting. When cutting obliquely toward the goal, they should aim for the far post. Since one of a goalkeeper's cardinal sins is getting beaten at the near post, he tends to overcommit to the near side, and

thus becomes more vulnerable at the far corner (Figs. 4.13 and 4.14).

Most wingers naturally prefer to shoot with their strong foot. Many score spectacular goals by using the outside of the foot to bend the ball around the goalkeeper into the far corner, or to slice it off

65

Fig. 4.13 *The wing forward cuts in toward goal to take the shot first-touch on the volley or half-volley.*

Fig. 4.14 *The wing forward cuts in to head the cross at goal from the opposite wing.*

into the near corner. The technique must become automatic to the winger, so that he will be able to hit the ball in full stride while cutting in toward goal to meet a lead pass on the ground or upon taking a cross in midair from the opposite wing. This is a hard shot to stop because it is powerful and difficult to anticipate.

"Banana" Shot

This delicate shot was perfected by Brazilian Internationalist "Didi" (Waldir Pereira), who called it the "falling leaf." It is effected with the outside of the foot in a way that causes the ball to bend and dip in the air (Fig. 4.15).

Its main objective is deception—to lure the goalkeeper into going the wrong way. The spin that causes the ball to bend and dip will also cause it to kick away in the opposite direction when it bounces. Most players find it more natural to approach the ball at a slight angle. Rather than come straight on, they angle slightly toward the intended direction of the shot on the same side as the kicking foot. This is a natural approach for a winger cutting in toward goal.

The supporting foot is planted heel first, about a foot's length to the side and slightly behind the ball. This enables the player to use a natural, economic, semicircular leg swing. The kicking leg is

rolled slightly inward, with the foot well-braced and firm, toes pointed in and down. The player strikes the ball diagonally across and above dead center, rather than straight through it, with the full surface of the outside of the foot. The lower leg must follow through high across the body, while the trunk and arms counteract naturally for balance.

The faster the foot action at the moment of impact, the more the ball will bend and dip in the direction of the spin. And the more the shot bends, the less powerful it will be. The reason for this is the brief impact between foot and ball.

Shooting on the Turn

The wing forward must be able easily to beat the fullback to the inside and cut in for goal. All wingers have their own way of doing this. The most common method consists of feinting a direct drive to the by-line with the ball, and, at the last moment, cutting the ball back to the inside for a shot right out of the turn (Fig. 4.16).

Since he has the element of surprise on his side, the winger can create a quick opening by taking the shot with his off-foot. A right winger can, by cutting to the inside and shooting with his left foot, immediately widen the angle of the goal.

The inside of the instep lends itself naturally

a   b   c   d

Fig. 4.15 *Banana shot with the outside of the foot.*

a   b   c   d

Fig. 4.16 *Shooting from an angle approach with the inside of the instep.*

whenever the player approaches the ball or goal from an acute angle and has to shoot on the turn to get off the shot. The last stride is greatly accentuated. It looks more like a "jump in," but it helps produce the long leg swing and particularly high back-lift of the foot that is essential for power.

The supporting foot is planted heel first about even with the ball, but slightly farther away from it than usual. By leaning toward the side away from the ball, the player can check his approach and maintain control as he pivots into the ball for the shot. The lean and pivot enable him to bring the hip around in a most effective semicircular leg swing. The vigorous extension of the lower leg is delayed until the knee comes over the ball. The well-braced firm inside of the instep, toes pointed outward, is then driven forcefully through the dead center of the ball.

The momentum will carry the player into the final stage of the pivot—onto the toes of the completely extended supporting leg. The shooting leg naturally follows through across the body.

This means that a shot taken with the right foot has a natural tendency to travel from right to left. The most common problem, then, is pulling the shot too much. The player can offset any excessive leg swing by allowing the trunk to counterrotate naturally and flinging the off-arm across the body as the arm on the shooting side swings back.

Obviously, then, the action of the left side and arm is essential in controlling the direction of the shot. The more a player opens up toward goal before striking the ball, the more likely the shot will be pulled from right to left.

Centering on the Run

The wing forward must be able to center the ball precisely and fluidly while running at top speed down the sideline. The most common technique in centering the ball is the chip pass with the inner edge of the instep. This pass has great versatility. The winger may lob the ball delicately into the goalmouth, or drive it hard and low across the goalmouth (Fig. 4.17).

Once past the fullback, the winger must take a brief look at the defensive situation and the position and movement of his teammates. Usually this will be all the time he will have to deliver a good pass.

The Chip Pass

Whether the winger takes the ball down the touchline or sprints after a lead pass to cross the ball, he must veer out in his final approach stride. Just like a baseball player turning a base, he is faced with the problem of turning the corner (Fig. 4.18).

The final stride, although still made from a rather acute angle, allows him to turn into the ball and initiate the pivot that will enable him to get the cross around into the goalmouth. This stride is greatly accentuated—in fact, it looks more like a jump—but it is essential in producing a long leg swing with a particularly high back-lift of the foot.

The player plants the heel of the supporting foot comfortably alongside (about one foot) and even with or slightly behind the ball, and checks his forward momentum by leaning back and away from the ball. Trunk and hip are held at an acute angle from the ball.

The player must maintain perfect balance on the well-bent supporting leg and provide a stable hinge throughout the pivot that will bring his hip around. He also must counteract the angled, circular leg swing that enables the foot to slide underneath the ball.

Although the player must keep his head down and eyes nearly over the ball, he should feel that he has plenty of room for a free and smooth leg swing. The fact that he can observe his leg swing should help him control the path of his foot.

The leg is applied to the ball like a golf club, with the hip being the center of rotation. As the hip comes around, the player initiates the leg swing with a forceful thigh action. The crisp lower-leg action is delayed until the knee comes almost level with the ball.

The foot strikes the ball sharply, with semi-extended firm toes pointing outward and the inner edge of the instep and top of the big toe squarely under the ball. The boot hardly clears the ground. Quite often in fact the heel carves the turf.

The trunk and arms counteract naturally to control the pivot as well as the circular leg swing in the follow through across the body. The trunk counterrotates, while the near arm swings back and the opposite arm swings across the body.

The winger's most common error is putting the ball behind the goal while trying to cross it in full stride. He is usually unable to check and control his speed and lacks balance as he pivots into the ball, therefore becoming incapable of bringing his hip and foot around quick enough to keep the ball in play.

Sometimes the only way the winger can reach the ball and keep it in play before it crosses the end line is by allowing the momentum of his run and leg swing to carry him through and around, causing him to fall backward. This enables him to get the ball and keep it in play in the shortest way possible.

REALISTIC PRACTICES

"Running" at the Fullback

The wing forward is often left to himself. With the nearest supporting attacker a long way off, it is vital for him to be able to hold the ball against a challenging opponent and to have the confidence to use his dribbling and feinting skill to elude the fullback.

Mark out three squares along the touchline, each ten yards long and ten yards wide, and separated from the others by a two-yard safety zone. Each square is defended by a fullback. The idea is for the winger to get past the fullback within the limited grid and reach the safety zone, where he cannot be challenged, then continue to the next. The winger must keep going until he eludes all three fullbacks, reaches the final safety zone, and crosses the ball into the goalmouth.

The winger may choose or be asked to try to succeed in beating the fullbacks in rapid succession. The fullback is eager to tackle and merely

a

b

c

d

Fig. 4.17 *Centering on the run.*

e

a   b   c   d

Fig. 4.18 *The chip pass with the inner edge of the instep.*

takes advantage of the safety zone to gain perfect control of the ball. The obvious stress is on the essential physical skill and speed of a winger, involving change of pace, quick stopping and starting, and dodging and swerving. The winger also can use the safety zone to slow up or stop completely and then try to beat the retreating fullback from a near standing start, emphasizing slick ball-control and cleverness.

Quick Interpassing with Inside Forward

There are, of course, many ways of getting past the fullback. Those which require a great deal of coordination must be worked on regularly. The idea is to develop a thorough understanding between the wing forward and the inside forward, so that even the greatest of fullbacks will find it difficult to prevent a breakthrough.

The winger and inside forwards must act quickly and decisively to exploit the two-on-one situation against the fullback. They must always keep in mind that, first, a smart fullback, when faced with two forwards, will always try to delay his approach until he is assured of support and cover by his teammates. Second, the fullback will always try to shepherd the winger down the touchline—again delaying his approach, but also trying to trap the winger in the corner of the field while his teammates are checking back to cover the area in front of the goal.

The winger with the ball must therefore run at the fullback, attack him, and force him to react immediately. A "grid" may be used down the touchline ten yards wide and fifteen yards long, ending at the goal line. The objective for the wing forward and the inside forward is to work their way downfield within this restricted area and pass the fullback in the quickest way possible. Then the winger crosses the ball immediately to the wing forward on the opposite side, who is coming in to head or shoot at goal. If he delays his center, the fullback who is chasing him may get in a tackle.

The classic "give-and-go" and "wall pass" combination may also be worked on in three stages:

1. The fullback moves in to tackle the winger and the latter quickly passes to the feet of the inside forward and dashes past the fullback down the touchline. If the pass is delivered with good timing and accuracy, meaning slightly in front of him, the inside forward simply wall passes the ball diagonally behind the fullback for the winger to run onto and cross.

2. The fullback, sensing the possibility of a wall pass, quickly back-pedals as the winger delivers the ball to the inside forward, thus preventing the diagonal pass. The inside forward, instead of wall passing, holds the ball momentarily, just long enough to commit the fullback, and then delivers a through pass. This allows the winger to cut in behind the fullback, collect the ball, and cross it immediately.

3. The wing forward attacks the fullback, using the inside forward merely as a decoy. The fullback, anticipating the square pass, attempts

70

to shut it off by overplaying the winger to the inside. The latter feints as though to make the pass, then flicks the ball with the outside of his foot past the fullback (to his outside) and goes down the wing to the by-line to center the ball.

Each move is practiced separately at first, with the left fullback providing an early and obvious idea of his intention. Then the practice is intensified, with the left fullback doing as he pleases in making a determined effort to stop the play.

Ball-Control–Crossing–Shooting

A perfect lead pass will mean nothing if the winger has difficulty collecting the ball in full stride, cutting in for a shot, or immediately centering it delicately into the goalmouth.

The wing forward must practice all of this in game-simulated conditions. An inside forward in midfield can deliver all sorts of lead passes high and low for the wing forward to run onto from a position about twenty yards below the center line. The covering fullback should give him about a five-yard lead, but still keep sufficient pressure on him. A center forward and a second wing forward also should take up their respective positions, while the serving inside forward, after delivering the initial pass, can act as a trailer.

Depending on the lead pass and the fullback pressure, the wing forward may:

1. Dash down the wing to the corner flag and center the ball to the far post for the opposite winger to head or shoot at goal.

2. Cut in toward goal and center the ball to the near post for the center forward to deflect into goal.

3. Cut in and go down as close as possible to the goal and either pull the ball back to the feet of the trailing inside forward or chip the ball across the goalmouth, out of the goalkeeper's reach, to the far post for a shot by the other wing forward.

4. Cut in and continue to the goal for a shot, aiming for the far post. The next time he can pretend a shot with the right foot, cut the ball back to improve shooting angle, and then shoot with the left foot.

5

Team Offense

METHODS

Soccer offense is predicated on the creation and exploitation of open areas. The defense is aware of this and constantly seeks to deny space (and time) to the offense. It cannot hope to deny all space, of course, but it can restrict the vital areas in relation to the ball and goal—the *decisive space* in front of the goalmouth. That is why so many teams are content to play a waiting game and resort to retreating and funneling tactics, concentrating on the edge of the penalty box to prevent any penetration into the decisive space. They will concede the *important space* on the flanks and immediately in front of the last wall of defenders to gain time to retreat and concentrate, but they will not permit the opponents to turn them or get behind them. Penetration in midfield may, consequently, mean very little. All that interpassing may appear to be intelligent and constructive, but it is pointless. The test of the offense lies in the way it penetrates the heavily guarded decisive space.

The issue has to be settled around the midfield line. The attack must get the defense to commit in midfield, create space behind them, and drive in for the attack on the goal (Diag. 5.1).

Looking for Space

It is often very difficult to create openings for the front players, but it can be done. Whenever there is movement, the defenders must concede space. They must yield it to the moving man or leave it behind when they follow their opponent. Either way, definite advantages accrue to the attacking team. It can exploit these open areas with players who are not tightly marked—the midfield players and/or defensive men.

When coming from behind on an overlap, the defensive players and midfield players assume the

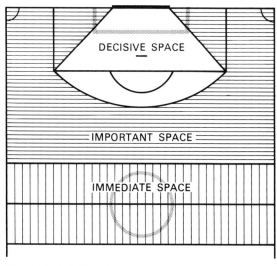

Diag. 5.1 *Definition of space.*

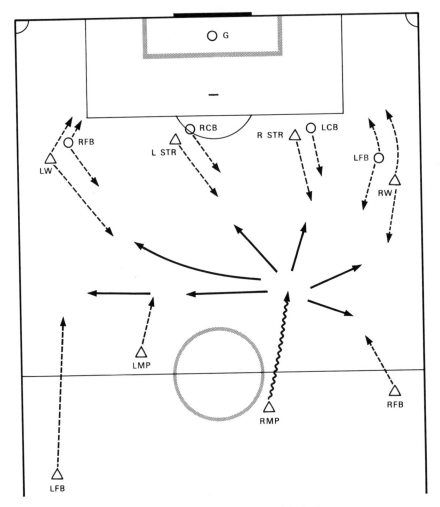

Diag. 5.2 *Depth and support—numerical superiority around the ball.*

tasks of the front players. In modern soccer, each player always must be ready to race forward and exploit space, temporarily assuming the role of a front player. The players generally best suited to exploit the open area are those immediately behind it. A fullback, for example, can use the space created by a wing forward. The players must be trained to look for the man coming from behind on the overlap and to run square to create the space he needs.

PRINCIPLES

Depth

The first principle of team attack is depth. This assures the player in possession of numerous passing opportunities and support (Diag. 5.2).

The minimum number of players that can produce depth is three. They can assume a triangular formation, for example, by keeping the inside forwards somewhat back or by operating with withdrawn wing forwards. (This will be discussed more thoroughly in Patterns, p. 80.)

Players engaging in a concerted attack tend to flatten out across the field as they approach the penalty area. They are restrained by the danger of offside or by having to stop to collect the ball, while those coming from behind are too eager to rush toward the goal to score.

A straight line of attack greatly increases the danger of losing the ball. It reduces the passing possibilities and encourages square passing. The more square passing a team does, the greater the danger of interceptions. Square passing is always risky. It requires great timing and accuracy. The defenders can easily step into the open spaces to intercept, and the attack will then have little chance of retrieving the ball. The passing side also can be easily lured offside.

Support

Depth presumes positive running (moving without the ball). Though the attack may establish depth by having players run away from the ball, it will lack the necessary support, which must come from behind, to establish the important numerical superiority around the ball.

Whether on attack or defense, a team must try to get that extra man advantage. On attack this will mean that no matter how tight the marking, one man will be free to support or press home the advantage. The numerical superiority may produce a brief moment and a small space in which two attackers can interpass during a full-scale movement supported from a deep defensive position. A fullback, for example, may suddenly join an advanced attacking movement through a timely overlap.

Penetration

The initial aim after gaining possession is to advance the ball accurately and quickly, assuming that scoring is the immediate objective. At times a team may interpass without attempting to strike directly at the goal (Diag. 5.3).

Penetration should, however, be the normal objective of play, not only in passing but in getting a man "in" from behind to shoot at the goal. The

great teams effect this with a series of penetrating passes from deep inside their own half.

A team should not necessarily base its approach play on long passes. Obviously the quickest way to the goal is through the long through pass right up the middle, but this is the type of pass and area of the field of which the opponent is most wary. The attack must, therefore, often use evasive or indirect methods to penetrate the defense.

Caution: The more a team passes across the field, the less effective will be its penetration. Ideally, every other pass should be penetrative, or if there are two passing possibilities the one that can achieve greater penetration should be attempted.

Attackers should bear in mind that a forward pass through or behind two or more opponents is more of a threat, as it forces the defenders to turn more than they would with a square pass, of which they can stay in front.

In the last thirty-five to forty yards, the midfield players create the decisive holes between and behind the midfield defenders and try to penetrate with a pass as soon as possible. They do not go in for any interpassing in midfield, as all that would do is give the opponents time to organize their defense and break up the attack.

Even teams that are adept at creating and finding open areas do not always use them to best advantage. Many attacks fizzle out because no one can produce an effective final pass. It is extremely difficult to short pass through the modern pattern of tight marking, zoning, and double cover. Only a handful of players have the ability to dribble through a packed defense. If a team can break through before the wall is formed, so much the better, but the wall remains permanently intact in many games.

The real test of the attack is to sustain its buildup and penetrate, particularly into the decisive gaps between and behind the defenders. Penetration becomes more difficult the nearer a player gets to the goal, as time and space severely restrict control.

Hastiness often causes a breakdown in penetration. Penetration can be achieved only with perfect timing, particularly of the final thrust, and such timing can be developed only through experience. Strict direction from the coach is advisable in the

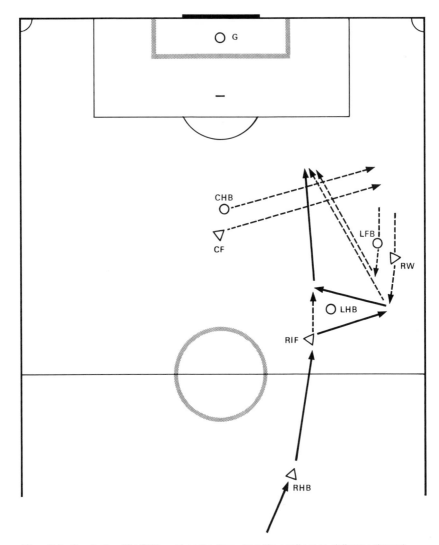

Diag. 5.3 *Penetration: The RHB receives the throw from the goalkeeper, delivers a through ball to the RIF. The RIF and RW use a quick wall pass combination to beat the LHB. In the meantime, the CF cuts to the wing to create attacking space for the RIF to deliver the through pass in and for the RW to collect.*

early going. Alert observation and quick thinking are the keys. The player must have a quick eye for an opening followed by a spontaneous reaction.

Width

The modern trend in defense is retreating and funneling, concentrating on the edge of the penalty area to clutter the goalmouth and keep a mobile,

close-knit unit between the ball and the goal. As a result, the attackers must make every effort to spread the defenders and lure them away from their concentrated positions. This can only be achieved through intelligent passing over the whole width of the field (Diag. 5.4).

Impetuousness is a common cause for the loss of width—attackers rushing toward the goal in

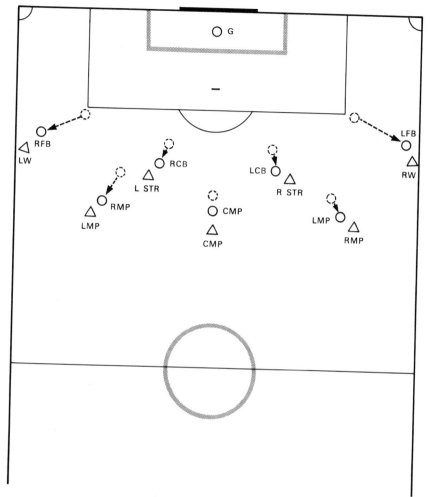

Diag. 5.4 *Width in attack.*

their eagerness to score, while the defenders deliberately give ground in order to concentrate their forces. Many wing forwards cannot resist this temptation. Instead of holding their wide positions and luring the defenders away from their central positions, they play into the defense's hands by following them into the space outside the penalty area, thus creating great congestion in the area and enabling the defenders to keep close to one another and provide cover for each other whenever the need arises.

The dilemma of the modern attack is that with three fulltime attackers (at most) positioned up front for most of the game, width may not seem so essential. When the ball is released to them, it seems far more important to provide them with immediate support. In their attempt to provide whatever support in depth is possible, the offensive team will either concentrate around the central attacker, vacating the flanks, or concentrate on one flank, leaving the other wide open.

The defense is encouraged to concentrate at the central path to the goal, leaving its flanks exposed, or to concentrate on one side of the field, exposing the other. The attack can now reestablish width by coming in from behind. In other words, by loading up on one side, the attack can possibly effect a breakthrough on that side and also set up the opportunity to assume effective wide positions on the far side. The same principle applies to attacks through the central path. While the middle area congests, the wings become open.

It is not necessary for the same player to maintain width. The team that adheres to strict position play, where each man has a specific area to cover, becomes stereotyped and presents the defense with only the problem of ball movement. The wise team will have its players interchange positions freely and thus confuse the defense. However, those not directly concerned with the play should maintain field balance and create width by always being in position for a switch.

What is the answer? By spreading the three front players across the field, one can immediately force the defense to spread its resources. No longer will the defenders be close enough to support each other should the need arise.

Attacking on a wide front creates big gaps—attacking space—between the central striker and the wing forwards, providing much unrestricted operating room for them. Equally important, the wide gaps are ideal for midfield players to come through.

This generalization on width is most applicable to the preparation or building-up phase of the attack. When a team attempts to strike at goal, chances must be taken and decisions made quickly. As a rule, however, the attack should maintain width and reestablish it as quickly as possible whenever it is lost.

Mobility

Creating space and using it require perpetual movement (Diag. 5.5). It means linking with the ball-handler in a collective effort to sustain the attack. The mark of a team playing well is evidenced by the number of players who want the ball and who can receive it at any moment. There is need for constant movement without the ball to achieve a mobile and fluid attack—as in basketball.

Mobility poses a considerable tactical problem for the defenders, who already have their hands full following the ball. Players continually interchanging positions on the attack can often disorganize or imbalance the defense.

Mobility around the penalty area thrusts great pressure on the defenders; they are forced to decide whether to stay home or follow their immediate opponent. Whatever they decide, the movement off the ball—mobility—puts them in trouble. If they stay home, they give the opponent room to run free. If they follow the opponent, they leave room behind them.

Mobility is not simply a matter of sprinting down the field, leaving the ball-handler on his own. The timing of the run is vital; it must be made at the propitious time, neither too soon nor too late.

Another important aspect of movement is direction. No good defense will allow an attacking player to run unopposed toward the goal. Many attackers, particularly beginners, are inclined to run toward the goal in a straight line instead of at an angle. This makes them a difficult target to hit because it is a rather delicate pass to deliver with any consistency. The more long through passes are attempted, the more the defense will fall back. The attackers will soon find themselves running into the welcoming arms of the opponents.

When moving toward the goal away from the ball, the attacker usually isolates himself from support and also risks an offside. Moving toward the ball is not always an improvement. Although it eliminates the danger of offside, it often isolates the front player; if he drops back too far he will cease to be a front player (unless, of course, teammates are coming up from behind on an overlap).

Front attackers should thus do their "positive running" (without the ball) laterally or diagonally. Its purpose is to force the defenders to react across the field. It establishes better passing angles for the player with the ball and creates gaps through which he can pass. At the same time it discourages the defenders from retreating to reduce the space behind them. Only when the front players move across the face of the defenders can they change places with teammates or create openings for players coming from behind.

Intelligent players versed in the art of switching will be able to read the situation and exploit the space immediately. The ideal pass to a player coming from behind is one that gives him the opportunity to head straight for the goal. Stopping or changing direction will tend to slow the attack.

If one can imagine the midfield players and the fullbacks going straight for the goal from their

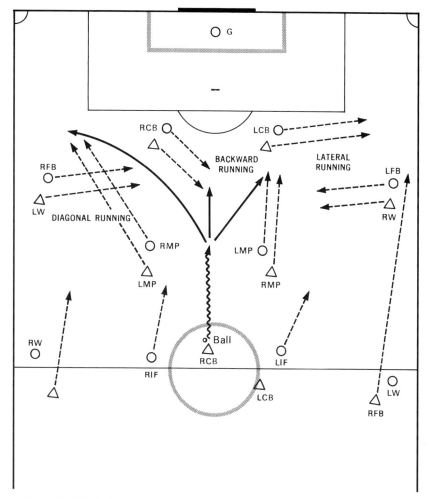

Diag. 5.5 *Mobility in attack—positive running: Players create space, of which other team-mates take advantage, while at the same time there is an ebb to and away from the player with the ball.*

general positions, it can readily be seen that the fullbacks are best placed for a wing attack while the midfield men are generally better placed for a sprint through the center. This ensures that (1) the attacker coming from a defensive position can press the offense with minimum delay, and (2) if the attack breaks down, the defender caught out of position has to cover only the minimum amount of ground (that is, a straight line) back to his defensive position.

Moving without the ball can be developed into

a fine art. The consummate "positive runner" can make himself a multiple threat. He can move into a position that can both threaten the goal and open up a pass to someone just as dangerously placed. A good rule is that the closer the attack draws to the opponents' final defensive positions, the flatter the angle of the run must be.

Mobility demands constant physical and moral determination. Forward running requires special effort and courage. It takes players into positions where they will be tightly marked and subjected to strong physical challenge. But it is essential; without it, the attack has little or no chance of effecting penetration.

Improvisation

No matter how organized the attack, the player must be given some freedom to improvise. This is essential in coping with changing conditions or meeting a challenge. A ball-handler must decide for himself how to beat the defender.

Improvisation is exceedingly complex. A great deal of movement and fluidity is essential in beating the modern defense and creating good scoring opportunities. With the entire team continually changing positions, the players literally are forced to improvise.

Improvisation necessarily demands complete team unity. The players must have a good understanding of each position so they will not be lost when required to operate at some other position. This can be achieved only through long hours of practice and training. The players must get to know each other so well that they will be able to anticipate what their teammates are about to do and can thus be prepared for what will happen next.

Who knows but the team of the future may play without regard to position, merely improvising according to the needs of the situation. This is the ultimate in improvisation. The seeds for it can be found in the movement called overlapping. The overlapping run offers an excellent way of achieving a numerical advantage (getting an extra man) in critical situations and attaining more mobility on attack. (See pp. 82 and 125.)

Though the great improvisers seem to have been born with a gift for it, it can be taught. If the player thinks, and is able to improvise, the coach has made a great contribution to the game.

PATTERNS

The attacking pattern expresses the coach's technical and strategical knowledge. He must try to adapt the collective principles of attack to his players' talents, emphasizing their strengths and exploiting the opponents' weaknesses.

Philosophy

The pattern does not have to be rigidly maintained throughout the game. The manner in which it de-

velops will alter the relative positioning of the players to some extent. The pattern generally must enable the team to make an instant transition from defense to attack. For example, it must provide enough players in midfield to initiate the counterattack and enough players up front to pounce on a through ball and strike at goal.

Most teams have three fulltime attackers at most up front. This may or may not include one or both wing forwards.

The casual observer might think it is pointless to have two players wide on the touchlines when you are operating with three forwards for most of the game. When the ball is sent up the field to the front line, is it not more important to furnish the receiver with immediate support? However, the use of wing forwards offers a great initial advantage. Their mere presence pulls defenders out to the flanks. Equally important, by spreading the three front players across the field, you immediately force the defense to spread. No longer can the defenders stay close enough to support—cover—each other should the need arise.

Attacking on a wide front creates big gaps—attacking space—between the central striker and the wing forwards, providing a lot of unrestricted operating room for them. Equally important, the wide gaps are ideal for midfield ballplayers to come through. Since this pattern of attack cannot be defensed with a collective effort, it gives the attackers the confidence to take on the defenders, knowing that any individual offensive effort has slim chance of success.

From the defensive point of view, the opponents have to be aware that they can be turned along the touchlines. When forced to spread across the field rather than concentrate at the point of attack, the defense requires the midfield players and immediate defenders to cover much greater distances.

Speed is essential in denying the opposing midfield players the opportunity to get back and reinforce their defense in time. When forced to quickly play the ball out of the defense, the team without wing forwards has no option but to launch their attack up the center, which is always the most heavily guarded area.

With two wing forwards up front, the attack more than doubles the task of the defending team. Until the pass to a front player is made, the defense cannot be sure from which point the attack will be initiated. The attackers are able to create openings on the flanks any time they want. This opportunity is granted to all tightly marked front players.

By moving laterally, the wing forwards can create space on the flanks and thus enable any players coming from behind on an overlap to reestablish width. Space can also be created in the center, where it usually is at a premium, and the opening

there will now be of greater importance because the other defenders are less able to cover.

Though the link between defense and attack has always been vital, it never has been more so than in the modern game. The major consideration must be the adequacy of the midfield players in screening their defensive teammates when possession is lost, and in supporting their attacking teammates when the defenders regain possession so that as

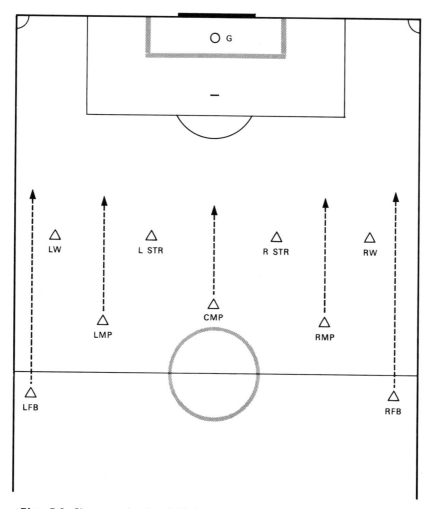

Diag. 5.6 *Players coming from behind on an overlap: If the positioning of the midfield players and the fullbacks is considered if they are going straight for the opponent's goal, it is clear that the fullbacks are best placed for a wing attack while the midfield players are well-placed to sprint through the middle. In this way the attacking player coming from a defensive position will be able to press the attack with minimum delay. If the attack breaks down, the defender caught out of position has only to cover the minimum amount of ground (that is, a straight line) back to his defensive position.*

many players as possible can have the opportunity of coming from behind. Exploiting openings in the defense by moving without the ball makes great demands on midfield players.

Coming from behind on an overlap has become a widely used strategem against the modern concentrated defense. Its great advantage lies in the defensive tendency to relax against supporting players who are behind the player with the ball (Diag. 5.6).

A player with a powerful shot will probably find more opportunities coming from behind than he would if permanently positioned up front. As a front player, the potential scorer will attract the personal attention of a defender. Coming from midfield, he will be much harder to mark (guard). It also will enable him to gather speed over a longer distance, and, of course, the surprise element will be on his side if his timing is right.

The disadvantages of developing the attack slowly are obvious. Time is always the ally of defense. The best kind of offense is the quick, direct attack that relieves defensive pressure through long clearances. That is where the topnotch front man comes in handy.

Many teams deploy a forward upfield who can be easily hit with long passes from almost anywhere on the field. He serves as a relay station: he does not necessarily try to control the passes; he merely plays the ball off to another attacker. It is often easier than his traditional role as a striking center forward. Of course, both roles are still within his scope.

A big man is an advantage in this role. It makes him easier to find by a defender who has to clear the ball under pressure, and he can do a better job of winning the battles in the air. Obviously the players alongside him must be able to anticipate what he is going to do and help him by constantly searching for space between him (front player) and the defense. The front player is not limited to the center of the field, although this area will give him the most operating room.

The essence of modern attack is having the mobility and flexibility to contract and expand in offsetting the defense. But the attack, to be effective, must have a constant threat from the wing forwards and players coming from behind on overlaps.

Ideal Player Combinations

Each player's specific type of scoring skill must be taken into account in organizing a team. If, for example, your two leading scorers are both "lurkers," men who are adept at punishing every error around the goal, you would not want to play them side-by-side. Unless you also had someone who could keep the pressure on the defense and challenge for the centers, the defense would be unlikely to make mistakes that could be punished. So you would end up with two marksmen wandering about looking vainly for their special kind of openings.

The ideal attacking combination should have a representation of every sort of scoring talent. It needs a runner to get there fast and first, when crosses can be pumped into a defense before it has time to get set. It needs a dribbler who can size up the situation when the defense has packed around the goal and has the nerve to unravel the crowd man after man. It needs a lurking marksman with an eye for where the half-chances are likely to come, ready to capitalize upon the hesitation that others might have forced on the defenders. It needs at least one man who can give the defense an extra worry by his ability to snipe at the goal at long range just as the defense has convinced itself that it can stop any intrusion into its area.

Given a man of each type, the attack can take advantage of all the breaks that come its way. And if one adds one or two of the new breed of midfield men, like England's Martin Peters or Bobby Charlton and Germany's Franz Beckenbauer, who can come up and do a bit in any scoring situation, then such a team is not likely to go begging for goals.

The "W"

The classic attacking wing forward type of game is based on the "W" formation (Diag. 5.7). The primary job of the classic wingers is to form flying columns of attack. They must take advantage of their skills and speed to break past their immediate defenders and open up the center with a stream of high passes into the penalty area for the central strikers to head into goal.

Unfortunately, this is easier said than done against a well-organized and well-drilled defense. The modern wing forward has to assume a much greater attacking role than his classic counterpart. He must increase his work rate—cover a greater amount of ground—help forage, and be in position to press home the attack.

The halfbacks and the playmaking inside forwards must effect a smooth transition from defense to attack, engineer the approach play, and support the attack. Their major responsibility is ensuring compactness and continuity. If they fail to move up enough to support the attack, or if the inside forwards neglect to fall back far enough to support the defense, the team will lose its compactness. This will split the attacking and defending units and leave a big gap in midfield (Diag. 5.8). The team will then be unable to effect the necessary buildup and continuity of attack, a common occurrence on lower levels of play.

"Irregular W"

Coaches like to vary the "W" by placing one inside forward considerably deeper than the other (Diag.

5.9). This gives both forwards more space and encourages them to specialize on the strongest part of their game. Thus the shallow inside forward can concentrate on supporting his three striking forwards and linking with the other inside forward, while the deep-lying inside forward can attempt to link with the defense and set up the attack.

Some coaches believe this "irregular W" offers a stronger formation than the orthodox "W." Caution: The inside forwards must swap positions throughout the game as the deep-lying role can be extremely tiring.

The "M"

Also praiseworthy is the way the Hungarians in the 1950's used the wing forwards to turn the attack upside down. On occasion they pulled the wing forwards Zoltan Czibor and Mihaly Toth back in order to allow the inside forwards, Ferenc Puskas and Sandor Kocsis, to play well-upfield. As center forward Hidegkuti also favored a foraging style, the

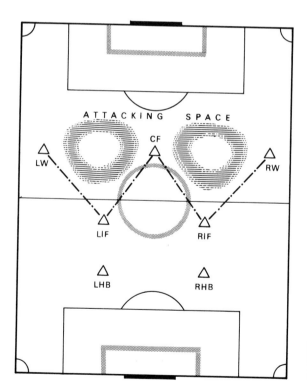

Diag. 5.7 *W formation of attack.*

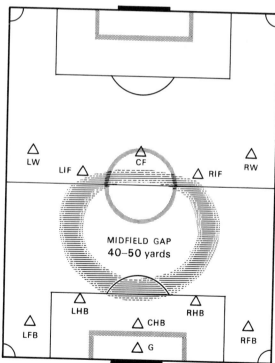

Diag. 5.8 *Midfield gap.*

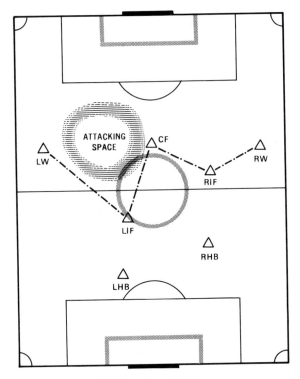

Diag. 5.9 *Irregular W formation of attack.*

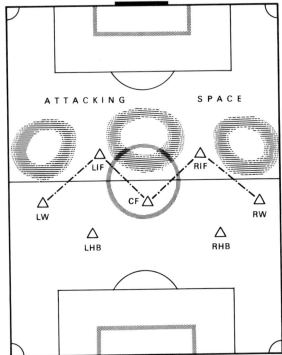

Diag. 5.10 *The "deep center forward" or M formation of attack.*

link took an *M shape*—reversing the familiar W formation (Diag. 5.10). Once again the strategy achieved the element of surprise without damaging the attack's scoring threat.

The Spearhead or Arrowhead Formation

The center forward in the role of the spearhead, assisted by the two inside forwards, is often used to foil the four-back defense (Diag. 5.11). It is especially effective when the inside forwards and the center forward are skilled in interpassing closely down the middle, assisted by two fine attacking halfbacks. The wing forwards serve as the strategists and initiators of the attack and try to draw the opposing fullbacks as far away from goal as possible. This enables the attack to capitalize upon the opening left behind the fullbacks.

The two inside forwards remain in a fairly central but also slightly withdrawn position, allowing the spearhead center forward to move across the

field in search of an opening behind the fullback, and making him an ideal target to lay off passes for the inside forwards.

The spearhead really is a natural formation. The forward line will often find itself in this shape without being aware of it. It enables a deep-playing wing forward to exploit his speed or serve as a playmaker.

The Echelon Formation

A variation of the spearhead, the echelon formation deploys one wing forward in a very deep position and has been used effectively against the three-back diagonal pattern of defense (Diag. 5.12). It allows the attack to flood one side of the field while still retaining effective wide positions on the other side.

The deep wing forward is frequently the focus of defensive clearances, and is supported by the halfback, inside forward, and, if necessary, the fullback. When the opposing fullback is drawn into

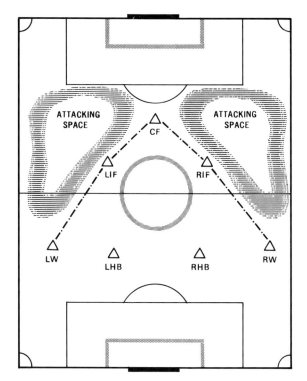

Diag. 5.11 *The spearhead or arrow formation of attack.*

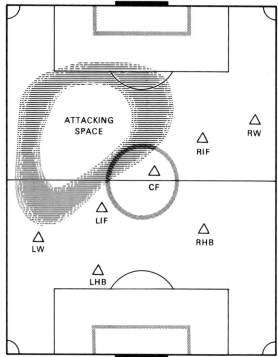

Diag. 5.12 *The echelon formation of attack.*

an advanced position and his center halfback and fullback rotate behind him (the principle of diagonal collective defense), a considerable opening is left behind the right fullback and center halfback.

The attack plays the ball into this area, and one or more of the three advance forwards moves in to upset the defensive balance. The attack also may be built up on the right side of the field through long crossfield passes. Although the defense can be counted on for numerical equality—it will mark each attacker man-for-man—the echelon can produce results as long as one attacker can beat his immediate defender.

Brazil used the echelon with considerable success in the 1950 World Cup. It was perfectly suited to their star player, Jair Ventura. A typical striking inside forward with a lethal shot, he was played up to make greater use of his assets. Ademir de Menezes, a very speedy and intelligent player with a tremendous zest for scoring, also was played somewhat deeper than normal, mainly to distract

the opposing center halfback. The inside right and right wing forwards did much of the playmaking, supported the three main attackers, and helped form the vital link between defense and attack.

Free Lance

A number of experts claim that a soundly grounded team has no need for set plays. They believe that the attack should be natural and spontaneous rather than predetermined and that the players should allow their instinct to tell them where to go. Granted this is an ideal way of playing the game and that teams with above-average talent may be able to permit more individual initiative, but how many teams have *that* sort of talent? Practically no school, college, or amateur team can afford to play this way. The lower down on the soccer ladder the team, the more organization is essential, particularly in light of the heavy trend toward defense.

Too much organization *can* be restrictive. It can reduce the opportunities for initiative and spontaneity. The player must be allowed to exercise his ingenuity in tough defensive situations. He can follow a basic attacking plan, set plays, and still be free, even encouraged, to react naturally and intelligently to new problems. This combination of fixed play and free lance promises to reestablish the balance between attack and defense.

The idea hardly is unique. In 1956 Willy Meisl of Germany predicted that soccer would become more and more defensive and would ultimately lead to the "Whirl." He claimed that the style of the future would be completely fluid. The positions would cease to have real meaning, and the players would continually position themselves as they judged best according to the circumstances. "To execute the Whirl as it were non-stop, every man must be able to tackle anyone else's job temporarily. . . ."[11] The Whirl is a non-stop affair involving all ten players running in all directions and constantly switching responsibilities.

The organized approach is so vastly superior to the instinctive one that it seems impossible to regard "good" soccer as a simple game that anyone can play.

Continuity is essential, and all movement must have purpose. Each motion of the players and the ball must develop a play situation. One or two play options do not constitute continuity. When a team can proceed from one play situation to another without allowing the defense to reorganize, it can gain an advantage. This naturally demands an almost psychic understanding among the players, which can be achieved only by linking the players in a logical, specific pattern of play. With practice, habitizing, the style can become a "natural" game.

Shuffle Offense

The real problem on attack lies in its lack of continuity *after* reaching the opponent's penalty area, where, due to the lack of space, the attack usually slackens off. It is here that the players must show greater imagination.

The shuffle theory, from basketball—constant, purposeful team movement—may be adopted around the penalty box after the initial attack has slacked off. It will ensure greater mobility at the most crucial stage of the attacking movement.

[11]Willy Meisl, *Soccer Revolution*, London: Phoenix Sports Books, 1956, p. 186.

As soon as the attack slacks off, the attackers may deliberately pause while the midfield men contain the ball and probe for an opening in the space in front of the defenders. Note that numerical superiority around the ball is essential to ensure superiority and ball-possession.

The midfield players probe with highly skillful ball-control and interpassing. To create or expose defensive weaknesses, they must be able to shift from a very deliberate pace to top speed. The attackers meanwhile are in constant motion, running a figure eight pattern that ensures both constant superiority around the ball in midfield and an ebb of players away from the ball. The players weave through defenders into the decisive areas in the hope of shaking loose momentarily or creating a gap that can be exploited with a timely pass. They ensure good field balance at the same time, and always are open for a timely surprise overlap by a player coming from behind.

The essence of the shuffle is to ensure continuity and create a good scoring opportunity through constant movement. This is enhanced by:

1. Linking the players mentally, molding them into a unit, though still leaving ample room for individual expression and spontaneity.

2. Lending great confidence to the player in possession by letting him know what is expected of him and his teammates at all times.

3. Providing a great morale booster to the players moving without the ball, because they always know they are making a contribution, though indirect at times, to the final thrust; this, consequently, ensures mobility.

4. Enabling the fullbacks and midfield players to look automatically for exploitable space ahead of them. When it appears, they can move forward confidently and naturally.

BEATING THE ULTRA SWEEPER

Until the sweeper defense came along, the responsibility for depth cover was shared collectively. Each defender had three primary duties: (1) to mark a particular opponent, (2) to provide cover support for his teammates, and (3) to cover an area, primarily his own zone.

As soccer grew more sophisticated it became apparent that the defenders could not be asked to fulfill this triple role. And thus was born the *ne plus ultra* in defense—the sweeper. In modern defense, the fullbacks and center halfback(s) can thus concentrate on their individual opponents. This poses a huge problem to the offense. Against tighter marking and quicker tackling, the front players become considerably less effective and find it much more difficult to score. How can the offense beat this defense?

Counterattack the Immediate Answer

Whenever a team is heavily committed to attack, it is most vulnerable to a counteroffense. Being spread across the field, it leaves maximum space between and behind the rearmost defenders. The more men it commits to attack, the easier will be the counterattack when possession is gained. The philosophy underlying the counterattack is to beat the defense before it packs (Diag. 5.13).

The measure of the attack's success will largely depend on how well it breaks out. To initiate a purposeful counterattack, the team defense must provide a springboard for an instantaneous transition to attack.

The players must observe the following pattern: immediately look for and rush into the open area, pass into the open area, follow the ball on short cuts, dribble self-confidently, use quick-passing combinations (wall passing), center the ball, and strike instantly at the goal.

The attack actually must be prepared *before* possession is gained. Players no longer involved in regaining the ball must put themselves into position to initiate the counterattack. The defenders must habitually observe the whereabouts of their teammates so that they will be able to use the ball constructively.

Time is vital—so vital that the front players must be asked to gain a few precious seconds by challenging. It is a mistake to exchange square passes or dribble in midfield. These are time-killers, and any delay in either the midfield buildup or the final thrust must favor the defending team. Time is always the ally of defense.

Advantage must be taken of the defensive tendency to be caught upfield or spread across the field. Since this leaves maximum gaps between and behind the defenders, it makes them less competent and unified in front of the goalmouth.

Passing out of defense or midfield must be well-timed and penetrating, and the receivers must

shake free or create openings (through intelligent, determined running) for players coming from behind. The attackers must be able to exploit the opportunity as quickly as possible.

The success of a counterattack depends almost entirely on two factors: first, an immediate transition to the constructive use of the ball; and, second, the ability of the key midfield players to deliver the decisive pass to the attacker with the best chance at the goal.

Perhaps the most extreme way to loosen up the ultra defense is by withdrawing to the penalty area and playing a waiting game. In short, giving the ball to the opponents and letting them attack. This usually will bring them out of their tight defense and make them risk some players in attack. The withdrawing tactics lend them a false sense of security and superiority in midfield, which is conceded in order to draw them out.

By knowing exactly what to do as soon as their attack slacks off, a player may be able to beat the defense with an immediate and well-timed counterattack. Since, obviously, such tactics may backfire, they should be adopted only by mature teams.

Committing Defenders in Midfield

As soon as the immediate counterattack has failed or is obviously out of the question, the attackers must resist the natural urge to run toward the goal and check, hold their ground, make diagonal or lateral runs across the field, or even drop back toward their own goal.

The wing forwards should be asked to keep out on the touchline or even drop back into their own half in order to entice defenders out of position. The opposing fullbacks surely will try to mark the wingers tightly, and once they follow the wingers they become vulnerable and isolated. This also forces the defenders to disperse their strength along a broad front and make it difficult to provide close cover and support.

The defenders will be forced to hold their position and thus will be unable to break off the action and withdraw in an orderly fashion. They must be forced to commit on or above the halfway line and to challenge in midfield. Though they will naturally avoid this if possible, they must be made to stand and fight on ground of the attackers' choosing.

Easy passes must be avoided to unmarked men in midfield, as these will give the opponents time

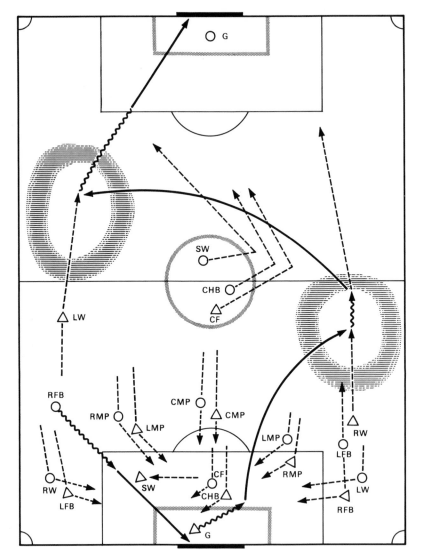

Diag. 5.13 *Counterattack—the immediate answer to beat the sweeper.*

to retreat and settle on the edge of the penalty area—ground of their choosing—where they are most likely to escape defeat.

If the attempt to break through is made deep in the opponents' territory, the space between and behind defenders will become extremely limited. The defenders will now be in close support of each other, and the sweeper will be close at hand to provide immediate cover support and a quick second challenge.

No sweeper wants to be drawn too far from home, and home for him is behind the last line of defenders. To beat him, a player must aim at the inherent weaknesses in this apparently impregnable collective defensive pattern. These weaknesses may be summed up as follows:

1. The midfield players or first line of defenders, in an attempt to establish numerical superiority, concentrate in the area around the ball. This leaves large gaps in other areas.

Whether asked to cover zone or establish numerical superiority around the ball, the front-line defenders have to concede space somewhere.

2. The hard core of the second line of defenders, consisting of centerback(s) and fullbacks, are usually asked to mark their immediate opponent skintight. Hence they can be forced to commit themselves. Intelligent, unselfish running can force the defenders to concede space behind them. If the defender is covering zone, he will have to let the attacker run loose, at least temporarily.

3. If the sweeper is giving a pressured teammate close cover support behind the immediate point of attack, he cannot possibly pick up an unmarked opponent coming from behind on the other flank.

In order to exploit these weaknesses in the sweeper defense, one must understand the theory behind this collective pattern of defense. This can be broken down into three segments:

The first line consists of a host of midfield players operating in front of a hard core of close-marking "backs" who are backed up by the sweeper. Their major defensive role is to challenge any opponent who tries to carry the ball up to the second line of close-marking defenders.

Whenever an opponent succeeds in breaking through the midfield barrier, either one of the backs must leave his immediate man or the sweeper must come forward to challenge. That is why the midfield players prefer to force the opponent to part with the ball by putting pressure on him; they would rather play for an interception than risk an unsuccessful tackle and expose the backs or sweeper. The midfield players tend, therefore, to concentrate on the area around the ball. They must deploy in close support of each other and operate as a mobile unit between the wall of defenders and the ball.

Inevitably, they will have to concede space somewhere. If, for example, the center midfield man has possession, the defense will have to concede space on the flanks in midfield. These gaps become weaknesses, as they enable the offense to spread at will. The open area is known as immediate space, and it is from here that most scoring chances are launched (Diag. 5.14). It can be exploited by having either the midfield men or players coming from behind assume positions very close to their front men on the wings.

The second line of defenders consists of a hard core of either four backs (two center halfbacks and two fullbacks) or three backs (a center halfback and two fullbacks), whose sole job is to mark their respective opponents skintight to prevent them from getting even one touch of the ball. Whenever a front player is in the act of receiving a pass, the defender must be close enough to pounce on him, offering an immediate challenge.

It is obvious that the second line of defenders must follow their opponents wherever they go. Man-to-man marking has become so rigid that the players are almost unconcerned with the ball; their whole concentration is on covering their man.

It should be apparent by now that while the front players will find it extremely difficult to clear an area for themselves, they can do it for a teammate any time they choose. If the front players are intelligent and mobile enough, their markers must either concede space, which can be exploited by another attacker, or allow their men to go free.

If it is assumed that the central midfield player has the ball, both wing forwards make lateral runs and one striker drops back to show himself for a pass. This will force the attack to converge on the central path to the goal. At first glance this does not seem to make sense. Are not the attackers practically playing into the sweeper's hands by converging on the middle?

The front attackers, knowing it is almost impossible to shake loose or create space for themselves, open the area for the players coming from behind by forcing the defenders to commit themselves (Diag. 5.15).

The sweeper, when first introduced, was little more than an extra cover for the old center halfback stopper, who could be beaten by a top-class center forward. Once the pattern of collective defense became better understood, however, it became more flexible.

The present role of the sweeper is quite complex. His responsibilities have evolved to the point where his primary duties are (1) to cover space behind the second line of defenders, providing cover and close support to each teammate who is drawn into a duel for the ball, as well as to intercept any pass that filters through; (2) with the innovation of attackers coming from behind in an overlap, to watch for such a player and challenge him; and (3) to attack by timely overlapping.

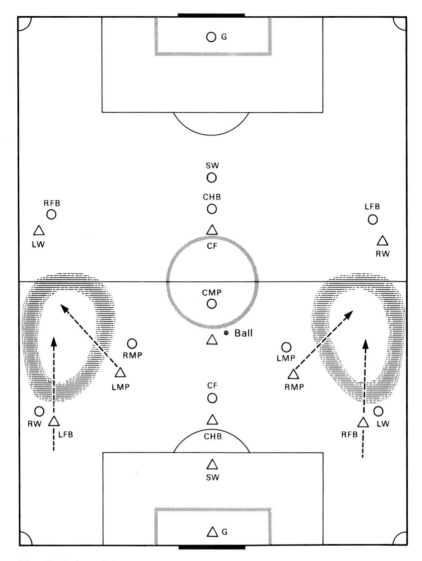

Diag. 5.14 *Immediate space.*

Which of the attacking trio will be in the most threatening position if he can receive a pass and slip by his close-marking opponent? It is up to the sweeper to determine the answer and position himself accordingly.

Probably the sweeper's best choice is assuming a central position and providing cover to all three of his defenders. He can now fulfill the first of his primary duties—covering the decisive area behind the last line of defense. But he still cannot fulfill his second obligation—picking up any unmarked opponent coming from behind.

As the situation develops, there is a chance that two players, one on either flank, could come from behind to join in the attack. The easiest solution would be for one of the midfield players to dispossess the ball-handler while the nearly uncommitted sweeper sags back in anticipation of the next move.

The attackers will have an advantage if the ball-

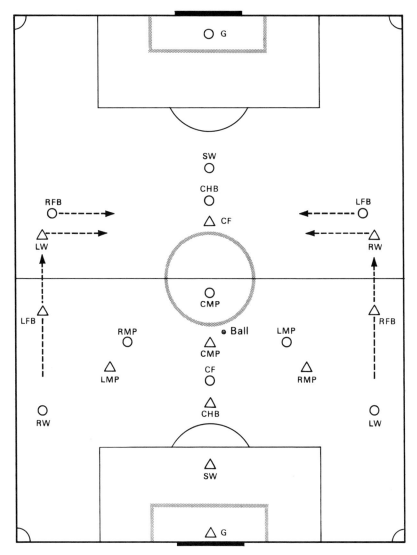

Diag. 5.15 *Forcing the defenders to commit themselves.*

handler can get off a perfect pass into the area created by a wing forward for an overlapping teammate. The sweeper will not only be neutralized (meaning there will be as many attackers as defenders) but, more important, he will have been drawn away from the decisive area behind the last line of defenders in front of the goalmouth, and the defenders will be back-pedaling. This advantage must be instantly exploited, as time always favors the defense (Diag. 5.16).

One could argue for having the midfield players cover definite zones rather than closely supporting each other between the last line of defenders and the ball. This would enable them to pick up any opponent who attempted to outflank the sweeper, but it would mean that the defense would lose numerical superiority in the area around the ball, giving away valuable space for attackers moving without the ball. The attackers could take the initiative and establish numerical superiority in mid-

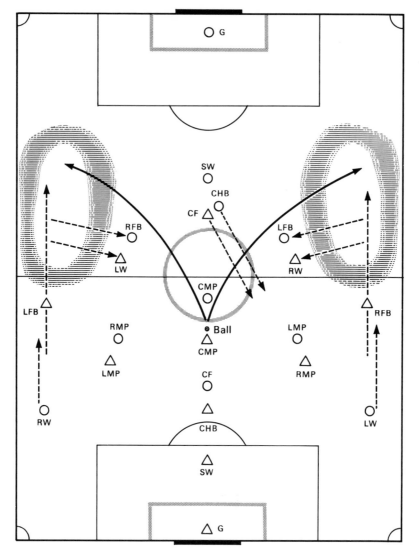

Diag. 5.16 *"The attackers will have an advantage if the ball-handler can get off a perfect pass into the area created by a wing forward for an overlapping teammate."*

field, from which they could create good scoring chances.

The midfield players usually are not beaten in one-on-one situations. Whenever an attacker can beat a midfield player, he will automatically draw the challenge of either the sweeper or one of the tight-marking defenders. Challenging the ball-handler would now mean either neglecting depth cover or, of course, letting an opposing attacker go

free. Neither decision is desirable, as it would neutralize the sweeper. For this reason, it is not advisable to restrict midfield players to defined zones.

It is also the reason why tight-marking defenders should not be asked to accept the additional responsibility of covering their zones. This is very difficult, if not impossible, because the defender is always caught in a dilemma: Should he cover his man and neglect his zone, or should he cover his

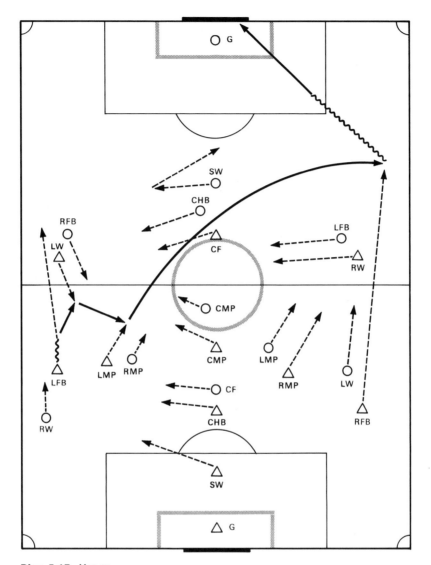

Diag. 5.17 *Man on.*

zone and let his immediate opponent run loose?

If the midfield players and tight-marking defenders are going to be continually pressed by an opponent who knows how to commit them and create space through intelligent and unselfish running without the ball, the sweeper is going to have a problem. In order to furnish close cover support to his pressured defenders, he cannot possibly pick up an unmarked opponent coming from behind.

To commit defenders and open an area for an overlap, the attack can combine the classic English style—the long ball from midfield to the wings—with intelligent and unselfish running by front attackers.

If the left fullback gains possession, his main objective is to launch a counterattack before the defense has time to withdraw, collect its forces, and pack in at the edge of the penalty area. To prevent

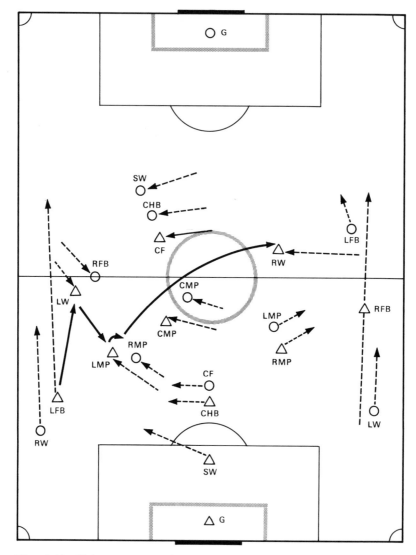

Diag. 5.18 *"If the sweeper commits himself to the overlapping left fullback, the left midfield player in possession must instantly change the direction of the attack."*

this, the attackers must occupy the defenders in midfield. As time is vital, they must avoid any wasteful "easy" pass in midfield that does not create an advantage. The fullback can draw a defensive reaction by delivering the ball quickly to the feet of the left wing forward and following up instantly to overlap the receiver.

This give-and-go pattern must always be accompanied by a shout from the fullback, either "Turn!" or "Man on!" The wing forward must be urged to

drop back toward the ball and make every attempt to screen it from his opponent.

If the opposing fullback stays tight with the wing forward, the fullback must call "Man on!" This means that the wing forward is going to play the ball back to the left midfield player first-touch, while the left fullback instantly overlaps the left wing forward. At the same time, all other players must show themselves for a pass (Diag. 5.17).

The key to success lies in the attacker's instant

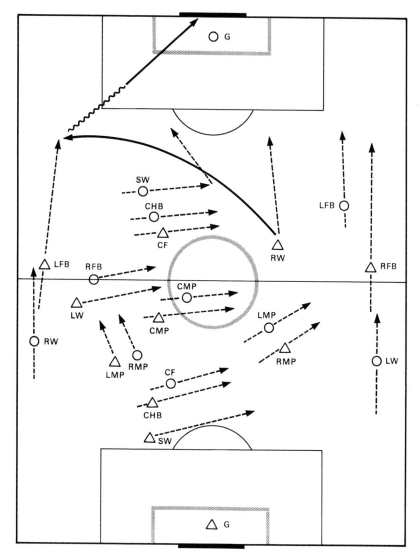

Diag. 5.19 *"The right winger . . . should either send a long diagonal pass for the overlapping left fullback or hit the left wing forward."*

reaction to the response of the sweeper. The attack should be prepared to swiftly change sides—luring the sweeper to the ball side and then switching suddenly to the other side.

If the sweeper commits himself to the overlapping left fullback, the left midfield player in possession must instantly change the direction of the attack (Diag. 5.18). Feinting as though to make the pass to the overlapping left fullback, he controls the ball and turns. This is the sign for the right

wing forward to make his lateral cut to clear out the wing and pose a threat as a receiver.

As the right fullback simultaneously overlaps along the touchline, the opposing left fullback has two choices: to tight-mark his personal opponent (right wing forward) or to cover his zone on the left flank and let the right winger go free. If the left fullback stays with the right winger on his lateral cut, the left midfield player can deliver a long diagonal pass for the overlapping right fullback.

An intelligent left fullback will realize the proximity of the right fullback's overlap run. Instead of following his immediate opponent (the right winger), he will withdraw and cover his zone. The midfield player in possession must respond by passing to the winger, who must instantly turn with the ball. These two players, if skillful enough, can create a highly favorable two-on-one situation. The defender will logically stand off and attempt to delay the attack, hoping for help from the sweeper who is rushing to reposition himself to face this new threat.

The left wing forward makes his diagonal cut at the same time, looking for a pass. The right winger's response will again depend upon the reaction of the right fullback. He should either send a long diagonal pass for the overlapping left fullback or hit the left wing forward (Diag. 5.19).

A well-organized and disciplined attack has an unlimited range. It can probe swiftly for the weak point and press it until it cracks wide open; it can also shift gears smoothly and skillfully whenever it finds an avenue blocked.

Countering the Sweeper by Marking Him

So far it has been assumed that the freeback will be prepared to provide close cover and support for any defender challenging for the ball. Many coaches insist that the place for a freeback is at the edge of the penalty box, and observation confirms that the sweeper will often decline the opportunity to intervene in midfield.

The conservative coach is one who wants his sweeper to stay back, concentrates on the ultra defensive game, and who feels there is no direct relationship between the midfield play and the vital matter of scoring. Such a coach says that only when a failure to intervene can immediately lead to a shot by the opposition can the freeback be allowed to commit himself. Otherwise he must stay firmly entrenched behind the defense, in position to challenge anyone breaking through for an open shot.

A spearhead attacker must be sent against the sweeper and instructed to run right, left, or back to keep the sweeper busy. The extremely conservative sweeper can be "marked." The moment the attack develops, a striker will assume a position alongside the sweeper and stick with him. This

should blunt the sweeper's effectiveness. By keeping him constantly covered, even though on attack, he is forced into positive action (Diag. 5.20).

There is also the possibility that the defender marking the striker will go with him, so that one striker will be occupying two defenders. If the attack can breach the last wall, the ball can be played to the "marking striker." This will be extremely difficult. The passing will have to be very accurate and the front striker will have to be immediately supported as he will be able to do little more than set up plays for attackers coming from behind.

The wall will now be almost completely ineffective, as the tactic will open up the flanks behind the defenders for attackers moving without the ball. The big danger lies in the defenders setting an offside trap on the marking attacker.

Countering the Sweeper via the Wing Forwards

Both wing forwards must keep to the touchlines to ensure the essential width. If the wing forwards come in too early, the attack is bound to fail. A player attacking through the middle has a number of options when confronted by a mass of defenders about thirty yards out:

1. He may dribble and beat one or two defenders, but it is unlikely that even the greatest of strikers could beat four or five defenders, sometimes in as many yards.

2. He may elect to take the ball just another few steps, with or without beating an opponent, and let fly at the goal. The goalie, not expecting a shot from so far out, could be screened, but not many strikers can hit from thirty yards with reasonable consistency.

3. He may play the ball to the feet of a front striker and then run in quickly for a return pass and take a shot first-touch. This give-and-go is a long chance at best, however.

4. He may look for an opportunity to pass into the vital area behind the defensive wall. This calls for near perfection in delivering the pass and timing the run. The modern defense is so tight at the point of attack that the defenders in close cover and support of each other can nearly join hands.

In this concentration at the point of attack, however, lies the clue to beating it. As has been seen, the defenders must concede space somewhere whenever they concentrate. When they

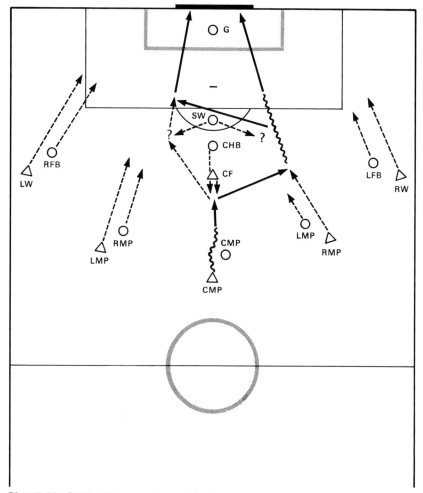

Diag. 5.20 *Beating the sweeper by marking him.*

mass to block the central path to the goal, they leave the flanks wide open.

The indirect way to the goal (over the wings), then, becomes the most effective move. Even statistics bear this out: Three out of four goals stem from assists from the wing forwards. Although it is highly unusual to play the ball out to the wings when so near the goal, the good coaches teach it.

An obvious advantage lies in the fact that this play to the wings forces the defense to spread. It should not be followed by a classic stream of crosses from out near the corner flag, as that would be playing into the defense's hands. It would give

them a fifty-fifty chance of connecting with the ball, and even the average goalkeeper could pick off high crosses close to the goal.

The essence of this move to the wing lies in creating an opening *in front of* the defenders around the edge of the penalty area, in direct contrast to the normal attacking objective. The wing forward must be skillful and intelligent enough to make his way to the goal line as close to the goal as possible and then pull the ball back at the perfect time and angle. Ideally the ball should be slid back swiftly from about the junction of the by-line and the boundary of the six-yard box.

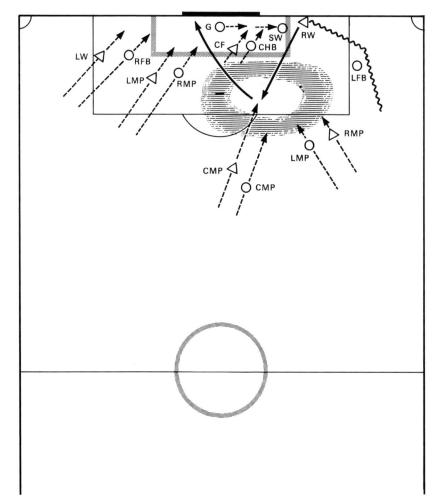

Diag. 5.21 *Shooting first-touch after a backward pass from close to the goal line.*

Three main objectives are achieved: (1) the play draws—commits—and consequently eliminates defenders; (2) it succeeds in jarring the defenders' close-knit unity between ball and goal by moving them into the goal area, creating the vital space in front of them to lay the ball for a player coming from behind; and (3) it catches the defense going the wrong way, making it extremely difficult for them to reposition themselves for the newly created situation.

Several advantages are afforded by shooting first-touch following a backward pass from close to the goal line. The goalkeeper must quickly re-

deploy after moving to the near post to cover the shot and he may fail to orient himself in time. The wing forward also can receive considerable aid from the fact that the area between the goalkeeper and the shooting position is relatively crowded and that everyone there helps screen the goalkeeper (Diag. 5.21).

Power Play

When the match has yet to be won or at least tied, one more possibility remains: the "power play," an all-out attack to keep the opponents under constant pressure and prevent them from breaking out of their defensive positions. With the right kind of personnel, this style often pays dividends. It also can be dangerous. But an all-out attack can be the best defense, and often the only way out of a predicament.

The power play relies on a human frailty: no matter how well-organized a defense may be, and no matter how well-disciplined the defenders are, they will tend to become anxious when subjected to the physical and psychological pressure of a constant attack. A defense can relax only when it regains possession in a reasonable period of time, and the longer they have to wait to get the ball the less relaxed and confident they become—and the less confident they become, the greater the risks they will be tempted to take. Psychological pressure is thus a factor that must be allowed for in all tactical planning.

BEATING THE OFFSIDE TRAP

In previous references to the offside trap, it has been made clear that such tactics are not advocated. Some coaches feel differently, however.

Countering the offside trap requires a thorough understanding of the offside law, as the escapes are naturally based on it. The most obvious method is for the ball-handler to beat the defense by dribbling through. But deception is essential: the dribbler must approach the defensive line at a jogging pace to keep the defenders off-balance and guessing. He may fake a pass to a teammate to lure the defender into a false move and then instantly push the ball through, accelerate, and take the shot himself or turn the ball back to an oncoming teammate.

For variation, the attacker can dribble to one side, drawing his man with him and then suddenly shoot a reverse pass into the vacated area for a second attacker who is dashing through to make the kill.

A third method utilizes a lead pass behind the defender, with a forward dashing through to make the vital play before the defenders can reverse. This is the through pass, either a chip directly over the defender's head, or the ground-hugging defense-splitting type.

The most effective method is the give-and-go—wall pass pattern—that lays the ball behind the defender into the decisive space for a forward drive. Timing is of vital importance since the forward has to move at top speed to beat the defense. Any delay in putting the ball through could catch the forward offside.

The give-and-go wall pass is most effective when the attackers are close together. If too far apart, they give the defenders too much time to counter and force the player running through to go a longer way. Any play that puts the ball behind the defenders can be effective, provided the attacker can beat the opponents to the ball and coordinate his breakaway with the pass. Breakdowns in timing produce offsides: the passer often delays so long that by the time he hits the ball the receiver is already offside.

Although these tactics look quite simple, they actually require a great deal of practice. The players must know when to pass or when to delay, how to pace the pass just perfectly, and precisely when to cut. The well-drilled team members will be able to "read" each other almost automatically.

III

Individual and Team Defense

Defense is concerned with preventing the opposition from scoring and with transferring defensive play into offensive play.

Part III analyzes the individual defensive positions: center halfback, halfback, fullback, and goalkeeper. Each position is developed through the playing characteristics of great individual players who personify the position, a comprehensive analysis of the positional responsibilities in various tactical schemes, and the skills and techniques indispensable to these positions. The skills and techniques are described in detail and photographed in skill sequences so that their tactical use in combination with other skills in game situations can be appreciated.

The individual positions are linked with responsibilities in a team structure, and the general principles of defensive play are outlined and applied to collective defensive patterns of play.

6

The Center Halfback

Down through the years, the center halfback has always been a key player. The typical offensive center half serves as the schemer of the team, whereas the orthodox defensive center halfback "stopper" serves as the kingpin of defense. In the more recent tactical development, he can be found as centerback or sweeper. A forward may fluff a chance and it will be forgotten in a minute. A center halfback who commits a lapse may cost his team the game.

NATURAL QUALIFICATIONS

Confidence

This is essential, as the slightest hesitation can prove fatal. The poised center halfback who quickly jabs the ball out of touch or briskly calls for tight marking can infect the entire defense with his assurance, whereas the center half who rushes around like a tornado and bawls incoherent advice can cause the most confident team to panic.

A confident player with little ability is usually more effective than a talented player who lacks confidence. At the same time, the player should not be overconfident or too clever. The center halfback generally can serve his teammates best by playing the ball off at the earliest opportunity.

The right balance between overconfidence and confidence must be sought, along with a power of command. The only way to develop this ability is

through long hours of practice and practical experience.

Physical Dominance

Many coaches will not have a short player try out for center halfback. Their reasoning is simple: A tall center half is needed to dominate the aerial challenges in front of his goal (Fig. 6.1). His counterpart, the center forward, is almost always a tall and physically strong player. Another asset is long legs, as the extra reach comes in handy in intercepting passes and blunting the attack.

The center halfback must be aggressive to meet force with force and strength with strength in combating the opposing center forward.

Mobility-Agility

The ability to run fast is indispensable, but it is not everything. The center half must also have the mobility and agility to adjust to any situation as rapidly as possible. This embodies mental quickness and quick reactions, as well as pure speed, quick acceleration, and effective stopping, turning, and lateral actions. The vital thing is quickness over the first few all-important yards. "Get there first!" is a good motto for the center halfback.

The center halfback must be mobile enough to:

1. Quickly recover after a missed tackle and go after the attacker.

2. Stand off and delay a clever center forward

who is trying to get past him the shortest possible way.

3. Slide quickly in front of the center forward to intercept the ball or at least pounce on the man the instant he receives the ball, and then dispossess him in the act of turning or shepherd him away from the route to goal by good positioning and powerful tackling.

Concentration-Restraint

Intelligent deployment necessitates a high degree of concentration and an awareness of the risks and priorities whenever the opponents are attacking.

Soccer is, in many respects, a test of patience. The defender who knows exactly when to challenge will stand a very good chance of getting the ball himself or setting it up for his teammates. A smart attacking team will test the patience of the defenders by tempting them to make badly timed challenges. The nearer the play comes to the penalty area, the greater the concentration and restraint that must be exercised by the defenders.

This requires a diagnosis of the opponent's abili-

Fig. 6.1 *"A tall center half is needed to dominate the aerial challenges in front of his goal."*

ties—speed, cleverness, and weaknesses—in order to contain him. Consider, for example, the opposing center forward who dribbles toward the center halfback, swerving, faking, trying to coax him into a desperate lunge. The center half must restrain himself, delay the opponent, until that split second when the ball drifts just a little out of the man's control, or the center half is sure that he (center half) is covered by his teammates.

It is suicide to charge a center forward who is in perfect control of the ball within goal range. The challenge may be spectacular, but if the center half is beaten he may expose the entire defense.

The higher the caliber of competition, the more likely the team with the ball will be able to exploit such weaknesses. Young, inexperienced players have a magnetic attraction for the ball and can be easily led astray by a smart-moving attacker.

Talking It Up

The center halfback is usually in the best position to marshall the defense. Since he can see everything around him, either directly or peripherally, he must help his less fortunate teammates by talking it up. He can help prevent errors by yelling simple terms such as "Time!", "Switch!", and "Cover!" Every defender, particularly the center half, must alert his teammates that he is going for the ball or that he is there to back them up or make sure that the whole defense clears out quickly after an opposing attack has slacked off.

It is also the center halfback's duty to continuously apprise his teammates of the offensive action in areas that they cannot observe.

STYLE OF GREAT CENTER HALFBACKS

Classic Pivot

Herbert Roberts, a giant of a man, was the first great "stopper." His genius helped Arsenal of England chop forty-four goals off its defensive record in one year! The Gunners established a record low of forty-two goals that season (1930–1931).

Roberts provided the perfect example of why center halfback is called the least glamorous position. He rarely received credit for his contribution to Arsenal. But his fame as a great pivot is secure not only because of his genius as a field general with tremendous power of concentration, but because he did not allow himself to be restricted by the "stopper" philosophy. He carried over something of the old attacking center halfback into his game.

Albert Chesternev, of Army Moscow and the Soviet Union, is one of the finest center halfbacks today. This Russian is a big man, six feet tall, weighing almost two hundred pounds. A former track and field athlete, he is very mobile and graceful, calm and dominating, good in the air, decisive on the tackle, and quick to sense danger. He is like the English center halfbacks in the old third-back game, where the stopper center halfback was the pivot, the solid pillar of defense.

Jose Santamaria, of Nacional of Montevideo and later Real Madrid of Spain, gained international fame playing for Uruguay in the 1954 World Cup in Switzerland. A tall, powerful player, excellent in the air and a robust tackler, Santamaria has been described as the perfect type of center halfback: authoritative and fearless. Even though he was an excellent header, he preferred to bring the ball down when he had the time and to use it constructively. He was fast and mobile, cunning in his anticipation of the opponents' moves.

Lurking Tactician

Billy Wright of Wolverhampton achieved immortality by setting a record of seventy consecutive appearances and a total of one hundred and five appearances for England in international play. He was the first player to top the one hundred mark.

Wright was not tall enough according to traditional qualifications. He was well under six feet, but he never came up short when it came to jumping for the ball. He was a prodigious jumper, a powerful header, and a sharp challenger, who tackled tenaciously and with excellent timing and great consistency. He also exhibited an extraordinary control, economy of forward movement, and a flair for making a simple, positive pass to ignite an attack.

Willi Schulz of Hamburg SV is one of the finest and most consistent of modern center halfback sweepers. He played in all six of West Germany's World Championship matches in 1966, has played for FIFA World XI's, and by the end of 1969 had made sixty-one appearances for West Germany in international play.

He played an important part in West Germany's advance to the World Cup final in 1966, and his role as a sweeper-up suited him and the team to perfection. Schulz was always there, ready to cover, ready to step in and swiftly blunt the thrust of the opposing attack.

His attitude toward the game is by no means flamboyant, but he brings with him the resolve and competitive flair that typify the top German players.

POSITIONAL PLAY

Roving Center Halfback

The roving, or offensive, center halfback usually is the best all-round player on the team. He must be able to dominate the midfield—roam all over the center of the field, dictating the pattern of play. On attack, he must advance well into enemy territory to strongly support his forwards. On defense, he must fall back to mark his opponent, the center forward, and furnish as much help as possible to the defense.

The junior or high school coach with one outstanding player would do well to adopt the supposedly old-fashioned "offensive system." By using the star as an offensive center halfback in the offensive system, the coach can get the most out of him.

On the more advanced levels of play, few coaches can afford the luxury of having a brilliant offensive center halfback going on attacking excursions. One bad pass or loss of possession would expose the whole middle of the field, leaving the opposing center forward uncovered for an effective counterattack.

Stopper Center Halfback

The difference between the roving and the stopper center halfbacks is enormous. Whereas the rover is encouraged to follow the ball, the stopper must be content with one basic objective—to seal the vulnerable central path to his goal by marking and, if possible, subjugating the opposing center forward.

Policing or shadowing an opponent may appear to be a negative strategy, but it is essential in any game plan that seeks to eliminate at least one key opposing player. Otherwise the defense will find itself giving away easy goals.

The stopper center halfback should always try

to avoid being drawn out of position. Most goals are scored from the center of the field (the inside or center forward position), and the center half who blocks this route will make it extremely difficult for the attack to break through.

The stopper center halfback is continually confronted with situations calling for quick decisions, particularly when he has to choose between (1) staying with the center forward and marking him tight, and (2) covering the central path to his goal and letting the center forward run free. Specifically: How far should he follow an opponent who wanders to the wings or withdraws into midfield? Of course, the answer depends in part upon the team's basic method of defense. If it is playing strict man-to-man defense, the stopper must follow the center forward wherever he goes. If the defense is applying the more flexible zonal principle, the center halfback must refuse to be drawn out of position. He cannot afford to expose the vital area in front of the goal and, equally important, he must supply the essential cover to his teammates.

The center halfback should leave his position only when he is certain that he can blunt the attack by pouncing on the center forward or dashing to cover for someone else. Even then he must make sure that one of his teammates is covering for him.

Whenever the left fullback is drawn into a duel with the wing forward, the center halfback must cover him (fullback). The center half must be prepared to challenge anyone who eludes a defender, as well as intercept any pass that filters through.

The weakness here is obvious. The stopper can fulfill his double role only for as long as the opposing center forward remains static in the center of the attack. Whenever the center forward moves away from the middle, as a skillful, intelligent center forward will, the stopper will be in trouble.

He must then decide which of his two tasks to perform. If he follows the center forward, he will not be able to cover the direct approach to goal. If he remains in position, the opponent will be free to roam at will.

Since the center halfback alone guards the middle route to the goal, the position calls for a strong tackling type, with experience and patience.

Twin Center (Half) Backs

Everything up to this point has been intended for a center halfback in the normal "stopper" role.

Little change is needed for fitting him into one of the modern defensive systems.

In the 4-2-4, 4-3-3, or one of its variants, two center (half) backs are required to double-blockade the central path to the goal. The center halfback who has been playing the normal "stopper" game, can, with minor adjustments, easily play one of the two central defenders, probably the more static of the two.

The defenders' task is to prevent the opposition from scoring, especially by bursting through the middle of the field. The players have a right to expect considerable assistance from the midfield players in front of them and from the fullbacks flanking them. But it is their responsibility to destroy every attempt to break through the center.

When a single opponent moves toward them, generally one center halfback will tackle him while the other covers. When two or more opponents attack down the middle, the twin center (half) backs will try to retreat slowly until they reach the danger area—the edge of their own penalty area. One of them must then go in for the tackle, and hope that his colleague will cover if he is beaten by a dribble or a pass. This slow retreat usually will give one of the fullbacks or midfield players time to get back and help in the defense.

Sweeper Center Halfback

The ultimate and most destructive defensive formation has one player set up permanently behind the other defenders, who are marking tightly. Known as the free defender, libero, or sweeper center halfback, he is not responsible for marking any one opponent. He is totally responsible for all cover across the width of the field and the central path to the goal, and he provides the defense with the necessary depth.

What happens when the sweeper is drawn out of position? The basic rule of covering must apply. The modern sweeper is not bound by the rigid rules that hamstrung his predecessors. Now that the flexible defenders are constantly switching and providing two or three times as much cover, the sweeper center halfback does not have to feel uneasy about momentarily or periodically vacating the central path to his goal by moving laterally toward the wings or by sprinting up and through the middle in a surprise counterattack. (See also the discussion of sweepers in Chapter 10.).

Offense

Though the day of the attacking center halfback is over, it does not mean that he should never venture up among his forwards. When, after breaking up an attack, he suddenly sees an open lane ahead, he can catch the opposition unaware with a quick counterthrust. As long as he has an understanding with his fellow defenders, there is no reason why he should not go in and attack. Such opportunities may be rare, but they should be exploited whenever they do occur.

The modern center halfback will also be occasionally called upfield to add height and weight to such special-situation attacks as corner and free kicks. And even though he is primarily a defensive player, he should always be on the lookout for a teammate who is open for a well-placed pass.

SPECIAL SKILLS AND TECHNIQUES

Collecting Ball with Body

The more skillful a center halfback's control of the ball, the better are his chances for capitalizing on interceptions. The half who can anticipate the direction of a pass or center often can get to the ball before the opponent can come within challenging distance. If he can bring the ball down to the ground, he will be able to make a good pass.

The center halfback, operating as he does in the crowded goalmouth, must be prepared to deal with delicate situations. The most common of these is beating an opposing forward to the ball. Safety must be the rule, as any error in judgment, timing, or balance while manipulating the ball can spell disaster. The ball may end up right at the opponent's feet.

The larger the surface used to control the ball, the safer. The use of the body has a great advantage in that it enables the player to keep both feet on the ground. He thus can avoid being caught lunging awkwardly at the ball. Putting the body behind the ball also enables the defender to safeguard against possible error, for even the most skillful players make mistakes, especially under pressure or poor field conditions.

Collecting the ball with the full frontal surface of the body may not be spectacular, but it is the safest and most economic technique (Fig. 6.2). The relatively soft and large surface will absorb the pace of the ball. It affords one of the most effective methods of beating the opponent to the ball and then taking it out of danger without slowing down.

As mentioned before, the center half must try

| a | b | c |

Fig. 6.2 *Intercepting the ball by controlling it with the chest.*

to thrust his body across the ball's path whenever possible as he moves in. This should not be too difficult, as he is usually facing the ball. When trying to beat an attacker to the ball, however, he must exercise anticipation, judgment, timing, and a fair amount of aggressiveness.

Collecting Ball in Midair

When the ball is in midair, the center halfback must be able to meet it at full speed and collect it with the middle or lower part of his chest. He must beat the forward to the ball or intercept it by moving quickly in front of him.

The chest collapses at the moment of impact, and the shoulders simultaneously roll forward. The concave chest thus formed produces the necessary cushioning effect. At the same time, the player bends slightly forward to allow his chest to deflect the ball to his feet, where it must be checked again.

Depending upon the situation, the center halfback may take possession by killing the ball so that it drops dead at his feet, or he may play it off second-touch. The next time he may choose to semi-control the ball, effect a controlled rebound, and follow up at top speed while advancing upfield.

Collecting a Bouncing Ball

Quite often the only way the center halfback will be able to gain possession will be by taking the ball on the bounce. It now becomes essential to get on top of the ball, close enough to lean over it, and play it on the rise.

The player runs at top speed to the ball and times his stride so his legs come together at impact. This prevents the ball from slipping through and enables him to arch his body by hyperextending his hips while leaning forward, thus presenting his entire trunk over the rising ball (Fig. 6.3).

The player will feel that he is falling forward at the moment he blocks the ball. He must then instantly recover balance and follow up the controlled rebound at top speed. Ergo the teaching expression, "Run through the ball and carry it with you." The eyes should be kept on the ball at all times, and the arms should be flung wide to ensure better balance and avoid touching the ball.

Intercepting

Coaches tend to deploy the defense deep enough to permit the center halfback to risk trying for an interception rather than playing it cautiously and waiting for a tackle.

A quick center half can often pounce on a loose ball, or even intercept a good pass by jumping ahead of the center forward and heading or kicking the ball away or taking possession of it (Fig. 6.4).

The success of the move depends on the center halfback's quickness and agility. He also needs courage to stretch forward in leaping for the ball, knowing the center forward will be barrelling in. Also vitally essential is a sense of timing, knowing precisely when to go forward and pounce on the ball and when to wait.

Charging

Charging must be effected prudently, but firmly, without restraint or fear of fouling. It offers an essential defensive weapon for the center halfback. It enables him to meet strength with strength and establish physical dominance over his immediate opponent. A good charge can disconcert the center forward and force him to rush his move.

Any part of the shoulder or upper arm can be used against the opponent (Fig. 6.5). The opponent may also be charged from behind if he is obstructing (shielding) the ball. The contact may now be shoulder against shoulder blade. Any other body contact (for example, with the chest or against the chest, or against the spine, or hip against hip) is illegal.

The charge also must be made within playing distance of the ball, that is, against an opponent who has possession or is about to receive the ball, or when both players are struggling for possession. Both men must have at least one foot on the ground, with the elbow kept tightly against the body. An opponent cannot be charged when both his feet are off the ground as he is trying to head the ball (Fig. 6.6). Lastly, both men must be playing the ball and not the opponent.

Charging must not be violent or dangerous. It must be a nudging or riding action in which the body weight is used to upset the opponent's balance, causing him to break stride or momentarily lose control of the ball.

The shoulder charge is most commonly used to

a   b   c

d   e

Fig. 6.3 *Collecting the ball with the thigh.*

obtain an advantageous position or secure possession when running alongside an opponent after a loose ball. It is also used to ride an opponent off the play or move in for a tackle after catching up with him.

Timing is more vital than brute force. Sometimes a well-timed brush is all that will be necessary to tip the opponent off-balance and beat him to the ball or make him lose momentary control of it.

An experienced player will sense when a charge is about to be made and will brace himself by leaning toward the tackler, meeting charge with charge. The intelligent center halfback has two choices: he can fake a charge and withhold it at the last instant, causing the opponent to stumble off-balance; or he can overpower the opponent with a well-timed, forceful shoulder charge.

While running alongside or catching up with the

109

Fig. 6.4 *The center halfback intercepts the ball by reaching across the center forward to make a volley clearance.*

Fig. 6.6 *"An opponent cannot be charged when both his feet are off the ground as he is trying to head the ball."*

Fig. 6.5 *Shoulder charge.*

opponent, the center halfback should try to adjust his rhythm to that of the opponent and, almost simultaneously, lean against him to avoid being called for pushing.

This is also vital in the timing of the final thrust, which should be applied as the player's weight comes over his outside foot. This permits a strong push-off and prevents the opponent from making a quick recovery. If the attempt fizzles, either because the center halfback fails to contact the opponent or because the opponent is able to meet the charge, the center half should be able to use his inside leg to prevent himself from stumbling off-balance.

The center half should launch his charge from a well-bent outside leg, thus enabling him to lower his center of gravity and maintain better balance. Equally important, it will furnish additional force through the vigorous extension of the push-off leg.

Tackling

The center halfback will have numerous opportunities to go in and try to take the ball away from an attacker. He must never give a forward an unchallenged chance to play the ball, whether it is on the ground or in the air. He must be able to tackle cleanly and competently, because just about

Fig. 6.7 *An uncompromising tackle the moment the forward tries to control the ball.*

a

b

Fig. 6.8 *Sole-of-foot tackle.*

any violation in the penalty box can incur a penalty shot.

The best time to tackle the center forward is just at the moment he tries to gain control of the ball (Fig. 6.7). That is the moment he can be caught off-balance. The center halfback must stride into the tackle without delay. This will force the center forward to concentrate on controlling the ball while trying to evade the tackle. The advantage clearly lies with the center halfback.

A clever center forward likes nothing better than a center halfback who continually overcommits in his tackling. A quick sidestep, especially on a wet day, will catch the tackler flat-footed. On the other hand, every center forward dislikes the smart, patient center halfback who will allow a dribbler to bring the ball up close as he slowly retreats—watching and waiting for the most propitious moment to launch his tackle.

The instant the dribbler pushes the ball forward, when it is momentarily out of his direct control, the center halfback should flash in for the tackle. He must concentrate on the ball and avoid being suckered by the forward. A smart halfback will pretend taking the ball and fake the tackle, then pounce on the forward when he tries to move the ball.

Sole-of-Foot Tackle

This tackle necessitates a head-on confrontation. Let us assume the center forward is about to take

Fig. 6.9 *Double-block tackle: "The center halfback goes for the ball with one foot and almost simultaneously comes in with the other. In short, if the initial attempt fails, the second usually will be successful."*

a powerful shot and the center halfback must prevent him from getting the shot off. The sole-of-the-foot tackle offers probably the safest way to do this, as the force of the kick is directed against the bottom of the foot (Fig. 6.8).

Slightly bending the knee will insure it against injury, but care must be taken not to go over the top of the ball. This can cause a serious injury to the forward's shins.

Timing is essential. The center halfback must place the sole of his foot against the thrust of the ball just as the ball clears the opponent's instep. By keeping his toes up and heel down, the halfback can wedge the ball between the sole of his foot and the ground.

The knee of the tackling foot should be bent to serve as a shock absorber, and the supporting foot should be firmly planted within comfortable reach of the ball. A well-bent knee will assure good balance and enable the center halfback to put his

whole body behind his thrust. By immediately drawing back with the sole of his foot, the center halfback can often take the ball out of the forward's reach.

Double-Block Tackle

The center halfback goes for the ball with one foot and almost simultaneously comes in with the other. In short, if the initial attempt fails, the second usually will be successful (Fig. 6.9). Skillful center halfbacks add a little calculation to the technique. By making the initial move with their weak foot, they force the center forward toward their strong foot, and this facilitates the tackle.

Though it sounds rather simple, it actually is a tricky move. The inexperienced player would do well to master it in practice before trying it in a match. The player who lacks balance and timing will often finish on the seat of his pants without any recourse whatever.

a   *b*

c   *d*

Fig. 6.10 *Split tackle: Often the only thing a defender can do to break up the play is to push the ball out of the attacker's reach with the sole of the foot by using the split-slide technique.*

Split Tackle

This is most frequently employed by the center halfback just as the center forward is about to get past him. Around the edge of the penalty box, for example, retreat is no longer possible. The halfback must hold his ground and tackle to prevent the opponent from getting too close to the goal (Figs. 6.10 and 6.11).

The center forward with the ball at his feet obviously has an advantage. Since he has the initiative and is looking for a quick tackle, he will probably dodge it. The center halfback will always be a split second behind.

The clever center halfback can resort to a little strategy. He can pretend to go into the tackle and thus force the center forward to push the ball beyond his immediate control. As the dribbler tries to go past him, the center halfback can turn with the play and simultaneously push off the far foot. This will enable him to make a quick, forceful, long stride into a tackle just before the center forward gets completely past him. He blocks the ball by extending the inside of the near foot across the front of the ball just as the center forward attempts to play it.

Whenever the opponent succeeds in getting by the center halfback and the halfback is required

113

Fig. 6.11 *The center halfback blocks the ball by extending the inside of the near foot across the front of the ball just as the center forward attempts to play it.*

to run him down, he can gain valuable time by using the outside of the near foot to block the ball.

The center halfback must make sure to catch up with the opponent just enough to make the tackle from the side rather than behind. He must avoid illegal charging (hip against hip) or tripping the center forward by reaching across the ball and the player's path.

More often than not, the center halfback will not come out of the tackle with the ball. But at least he will be able to prevent the opponent from getting off a successful shot by deflecting the ball or knocking it out of his control. This usually will be enough to give another defender or the goal-keeper a chance at an interception.

Goal Kick

The goal kick is usually taken by the center half-back, who is almost always the best long-ball kicker. It is usually a long, lofted, carefully placed drive to a wing forward. Since the central path to the goal is usually more congested than the flanks, the wing forward has a better chance than the center forward of gaining possession. The kick to the wing is also less dangerous. An interception near the touchline can seldom be exploited as effectively as one in the center of the field.

In the final analysis, of course, the kick will depend on the relative abilities of the players involved. If the center forward is good enough to wrest the ball from the air and lay it off to a team-mate, the kick should go down the center. If the wing forward can shake his fullback to receive the ball, then that is where it should go.

Lofted Drive

Most players find it easier to approach the ball from an angle rather than from directly behind. A right-footed player, for example, will find that an angled approach run from the left will lend itself naturally to a long, powerful, circular leg swing. The angle should not exceed forty-five degrees, however (Fig. 6.12).

The approach run should be of reasonable length, about seven to nine strides, and it should always be initiated from the same spot and with the same foot. Most players prefer to begin with the non-kicking foot, starting easily and then going into top gear as they near the ball.

The run must have a pronounced rhythm, and the final stride, which ends in the planting of the supporting foot, must be accentuated like a hop-step. This will ensure a long swing of the kicking leg. A poor back-swing will cause a weak kick.

The supporting leg should be planted some ten to twelve inches to the side and behind the ball, with the left hip serving as the fulcrum for the leg swing.

As the supporting foot hits the ground, heel first, the center of gravity is immediately shifted to this leg. The momentum of the approach run and the well-bent knee (acting as a shock absorber) allow the player to ride forward so that his complete weight comes over the supporting leg.

The correct placement of the supporting leg ensures a full extension of the kicking leg. This guarantees maximum velocity at impact and an upward movement of the kicking foot.

The angled approach run puts the player in an obliquely inclined arch position to the side away from the ball. This position is essential for checking the momentum of the approach run and providing a stable hinge for the hip pivot. The player can now make an economic, circular leg swing of maximum length and draw on all sources of power. The head is down, the eyes glued to the ball, and the arms flung wide to counteract the leg swing.

The kicking leg is cocked, with the knee completely flexed so that the heel comes back nearly to the buttocks—this deeply flexed foreleg being essential for power.

a
b
c

d
e

Fig. 6.12 *Lofted drive (goal kick).*

The leg swing is initiated with a forward thrust of the hip. The foreleg action is momentarily delayed and then driven dynamically forward. As the knee uncoils, the foot literally tries to catch up with the knee and does so just before impact. The foot thus achieves maximum velocity at the precise mo-

ment of impact. The distance-power of the kick is directly proportionate to the velocity of the foot at impact.

Contact is made with the well-braced and firm inner edge of the instep, toes pointing outward. A striking action diagonally through the dead cen-

115

ter of the ball produces a powerful, lofted drive. The kicking leg should be fully extended at impact with the instep facing upward. The foot is thus beginning its upward swing.

To counterbalance the free, full upward leg swing, the player leans backward naturally with his arms outspread. The supporting leg adds to the drive by straightening out and bringing the player to his toes. The forward momentum forces the player to take a gliding hop with the supporting foot in order to stay on balance and facilitate the follow through. The trunk and arms counter-rotate naturally in an effort to offset the circular leg swing.

The entire action must be executed smoothly and fluidly to furnish pace and power at the precise moment of contact, and the head must be kept down throughout the action.

Defensive Volleying

Though it is sensible to pass whenever possible, there are still times when it is necessary to clear the ball out of danger, as, for example, when opponents are close by. A sure-footed center halfback who can make volley and half-volley clearances from all angles will be able to quickly repel attacks.

Getting to the ball first sometimes requires daring as well as quickness. The center halfback must develop extraordinary ways of doing this. He should be able to clear the ball while sliding on the ground or flinging himself in the air. He must

Fig. 6.13 *Defensive volley clearance.*

116

take care, however, to avoid hitting anyone with his high-flying feet (Fig. 6.13).

The more power that is required, the greater the need for a long leg swing. The full volley clearance becomes relatively easy when the center halfback is facing a ball that is not coming in too high and he wishes to return it in the same direction.

The lower the ball at the moment of impact, the stronger the volley clearance drive. If the ball is high at impact, the swing will lose power and the foot will lift the ball high but not forward. The player may still be able to gain fair distance by accentuating his lower-leg action from the knee, but he must concentrate on a well-braced, firm instep.

Time permitting, most center halfbacks will choose to allow the ball to drop. At the same time they will step to one side to make the volley clearance as a side approach allows them to develop a free leg swing in much the same way that it does for the lofted clearance drive from ground level. Since the ball is off the ground, they have to compensate by leaning slightly away from it in both a backward and sideward direction as they swing their leg.

Naturally, the higher the ball, the more the player must lean away from it. This will permit the center halfback to clear the ball with a relatively low trajectory.

He may use the full or outer side of the instep, but the most important thing is to drive the firm foot clearly through the dead center of the lower half of the ball. Judgment, coordination, timing, and "eyes on the ball" are essential. Timing is more important than force or wild slashing at the ball. A firm foot at impact is often all that is needed to clear the ball out of immediate danger.

Defensive Heading

When confronted by a clever center around the goal, the center halfback must be able to quickly diagnose the danger and be prepared to deftly head the ball clear of the goal. The cutting off of high crosses is particularly important. The center halfback must be able to get up high and head the ball powerfully, even against aggressive opponents.

The first principle of the defensive head is safety. The farther the center halfback can move the ball away from his goal, the better. If he can be accurate as well, so much the better.

When heading, the center half is almost always in the happy position of facing the ball. This is one of the reasons why center forwards, no matter how good they are in the air, should rarely be able to beat the center half for the high ball.

Since the center half is often forced to back-pedal while watching the attack advance, he must be able to get enough lift and power to clear the ball while running backward or sideward.

Heading with Feet on Ground

Power is predicated upon timing: getting as much body force as possible behind the blow. Like a good puncher, the center half should start with his feet flat on the ground. He should let the heading action start well-down in the legs, and then drive up through the whole body.

He should always fight to get into a stride position that will permit him to shift his trunk backward and forward without danger of imbalance. While judging the flight and speed of the ball, he should keep his eyes on the ball, his trunk bent well-back, and the forehead drawn back fully and squarely facing the ball.

He initiates the heading action by driving off his back foot and throwing his forehead at the ball, straightening his body at the same time. The leg drive causes the hips, trunk, and head to move forward. Since the head moves last, the action resembles the cracking of a whip. The upper forehead (at the hair line) strikes through the lower half of the ball to ensure a high trajectory that will clear the ball out of danger.

Heading with Feet off Ground

The acid test for the defensive header is doing it when both feet are off the ground and he is being crowded. The vital factors become timing and the determination to meet the ball and strike it firmly.

To get any power into his header, the center halfback must never wait for the ball or draw his head down between his shoulders. He must beat the opponent to the ball and go right up for it. If he permits the opponent to jump first, he may find himself blocked from the ball (Fig. 6.14).

The center halfback will seldom have the time or room for more than a two- or three-step run-up. The last stride should be rather long, with the body gathering for the jump. The player should rock over

the well-bent takeoff foot and drive forcefully forward.

Now comes the difficult part. To get into the essential cocked position, the player should kick both heels well-backward and upward. This will arch the body backward and put the player into the classic position for a powerful header. As the ball arrives just above the chest, the player should jackknife forward and drive his upper forehead (at hair line) through the lower half of the ball. The angle and power of the thrust will ensure height and distance.

REALISTIC PRACTICES

Dealing with High Ball

Several players, scattered around midfield, serve balls to the center halfback at the edge of the penalty box, who clears them first-touch. The coach can regulate the pressure through the frequency and difficulty of the serves. The feeders must vary their serves and force the center halfback to go all out to reach the ball before it bounces.

Fig. 6.14 *Defensive heading with feet off the ground.*

Variations are:

1. The center halfback must use only his head to clear the ball back to the initial server.

2. The center halfback must volley or half-volley to clear the ball back to the initial server.

Developing Understanding with Goalkeeper

Same exercise as above, but adding a center forward and a goalkeeper to create a more realistic condition. The choice is now left to the center halfback, who also tries to develop an understanding with the goalkeeper. He must judge the situation correctly—know when to allow the goalie to take the ball and when to challenge for it.

Depending upon the service and the way the center forward challenges him for the ball, the center half may:

1. Head, volley, or half-volley the ball up-field, back to the initial server.

2. Cooperate with the goalie by pretending to play the ball and then allowing it to go through untouched.

3. Play the ball back to the goalie first-touch or after controlling it and turning.

4. Control the ball as he moves toward the touchline and clear it by passing back to the initial server.

5. Evade the center forward's attempt to intercept the ball and quickly pass back to the initial server.

Whenever the goalie gets the ball, he should quickly throw or volley it back to the initial server.

Developing Coordination in Defense

When forced back to the goal area, the defense must react coolly and determinedly, and the center halfback must sense how the defenders around him will react.

The situation can be simulated in practice. The defense can consist of goalkeeper, center halfback, two fullbacks, and two halfbacks. The offense will be their respective opponents: center forward, wing forwards, and inside forwards. The more players in the penalty area, the greater the confusion.

Several other players can be scattered around midfield to act as servers—lobbing or driving balls into the goal area. As one ball is cleared, the next is sent over. Two more players, preferably substitute goalies, can set up behind the goal to retrieve

the balls. The emphasis in this practice could be on several things:

1. The defenders simply clearing the ball first-touch and, if possible, back to the initial server. If the attempted clearance fails, they clear out of the penalty area. The attackers are permitted to shoot at goal, but they are allowed only two touches. This means a lay-off pass followed by a shot.

2. Same as above, but the defenders are asked to clear the penalty area quickly. Any attacker caught in the area after the defenders have cleared it is called offside.

3. Practicing dead-ball situations, such as free kicks, corner kicks, and long throw-ins.

Realistic practice of this kind helps the center halfback develop the necessary experience and confidence to dominate the goalmouth and helps the defense acquire a sense of team play.

Reacting to Critical Situations

The coach must frequently expose the center halfback to situations where the odds are against him. To develop his judgment, reaction, and daring in seemingly hopeless situations, the coach can set up such realistic conditions as:

1. Defending against two or three attackers—two inside forwards and the center forward—who are stationed around midfield. The attackers start to interpass one-touch at the halfway mark, and the center halfback confronts them around midfield. The offside rule is in effect. The attackers must try to bypass the center halfback as quickly as possible and shoot at a goal defended by a keeper. The center halfback must try to stave off the attack through clever maneuvering, retreating, or trying to tackle or intercept a pass.

2. Same as above, except that a right fullback is added. The center halfback now sets up in midfield some twenty yards from the edge of the penalty box. The right fullback deploys nearer the left wing forward, but about five yards deep in the opposing half. This gives the left wing forward a head start, creating the situation wherein the fullback is momentarily caught out of position.

The center forward starts the drill from the halfway mark by driving a long pass toward the left corner flag. The center halfback must now decide whether the fullback can beat the left wing to the ball or whether to go after the interception himself.

Any indecision or misunderstanding will leave the right wing forward (who is cutting for the goal) uncovered and in ideal position to receive a cross and then shoot. Any time the center halfback leaves his position, the fullback must immediately react by cutting toward his goal to cover up for him.

3. The center halfback must try to stop the center forward from getting a shot. The latter sets up somewhere around the edge of the penalty box, and the center halfback covers him tight. The right and left wing forwards act as feeders, serving the ball to the center forward, who tries to beat the center halfback for a shot at the goal. If the center halfback successfully tackles and gets the ball, he plays it back to the server.

The server tries to help the center forward by sending a through or lofted pass for him to take on the run. The center halfback must run down the center forward and prevent him from reaching the ball, either through tackling him or by playing the ball back to the goalkeeper.

By alternating two or even three center forwards, the coach can put the center halfback under great pressure. As soon as he deals with one center forward, another attack can be started with another ball.

4. Four-on-three practices are extremely effective: two wing forwards, a center forward, and one inside forward behind them versus the right and left fullbacks, plus the center halfback. The attacking side interchanges positions freely, and the inside forward adds to the pressure by coming through himself to attack. This puts a great strain on man-to-man marking.

The defenders must be alert for any breakthrough, and each may have to leave his immediate opponent to stop an attacker. All defenders, but particularly the center halfback, must decide whether to stay with their man or cover the central path to the goal.

The center halfback must move quickly to challenge the center forward for possession, but he must not be drawn too far out of position to allow the other attackers to create a scoring opportunity.

7

The Fullback

The role of the fullback has changed appreciably over the years—not in any striking fashion perhaps, but certainly in the levying of more exacting demands. Traditionally the fullback has always had to be strong, quick, and decisive; a sharp, incisive kicker; and a good diagnostician who knows exactly what is expected of him on defense.

The modern game has imposed a new demand—sound ball-control. The fullback must be able to initiate the counterattack out of the defensive zone, join in interpassing moves in midfield, and be ready to move smartly upfield whenever the opposition leaves a gap on his flank.

NATURAL QUALIFICATIONS

Balance

The defender must assume a well-balanced stance, with the body slightly crouched, legs comfortably spread, and knees bent. This gives him a low center of gravity, which allows for the equal distribution of weight over the balls of the feet. It also enables the player to shift instantly into a dynamic stance, primarily through lateral, gliding, or retreating actions, and to stay in perfect balance through sound defensive footwork.

Whether running, jumping, or diving, the fullback must always be able to regain his balance as quickly as possible.

Footwork

No matter how much speed he possesses, the fullback still has to concentrate on his footwork. When confronting and containing an attacker, the fullback must adjust continually to the opponent's movement. His primary emphasis is on lateral and reverse movements. Fortunately, this fundamental footwork can be improved considerably through proper instruction.

In covering the wing forward, the fullback must employ every type of footwork at his command. Fullbacks should back-pedal while facing the receiver. They must be able to shuffle their feet, slide laterally, crossover, and then square up again. At times they even have to turn their back on the play and recover in this manner.

Speed-Quickness

Since fullbacks generally must cope with fast and tricky wing forwards, they must be able to think fast, run fast, and turn or recover fast (Fig. 7.1). A slow fullback cannot afford to lose a tackle, as he will have little chance to recover in time to tackle back or restore the numerical balance on defense.

Sheer speed enables the fullback to run down or outrun a wing forward with or for the ball. It also allows him to recover from defensive mistakes and assume new defensive positions with little overall team danger.

Fig. 7.1 *Once beaten, the fullback must recover quickly to tackle back.*

Quick feet enable the fullback to harass the attacker and neutralize his superior skill. Wing forwards can be disconcerted and demoralized by a fullback who refuses to be shaken off.

Alertness

The player must react immediately to shifts from offense to defense. A lightning reaction will put him in position to cover unguarded opponents, prevent the surprise maneuver, and place the offense at a disadvantage. Such mental alertness, coupled with defensive aggressiveness and faking, can actually force the opponent into a defensive posture while he is in control of the ball.

Ability does not mean anything without a high level of alertness. The fullback must be able to quickly size up his immediate opponents and then immediately capitalize upon this knowledge.

A diagnosis of the opponent's abilities should include his speed, cleverness, and general strengths and weaknesses. Whenever the wing forward advances with the ball—swerving, teasing, trying to coax the fullback into a desperate lunge—the full-

back must restrain himself. He should never charge blindly at the opponent while he is in control of the ball. It would be suicide. He should wait until the split second that the ball drifts a little out of the opponent's control, then pounce on the ball. If the defender thinks fast and acts fast, he may intercept.

It is a cat and mouse game, with the fullback reading the opponent's thoughts and watching the way he shapes up to pass. With great concentration, the fullback can, in time, develop a soccer sixth sense.

Mental alertness on defense also includes an awareness of the ball, a knowledge of the positions of the other defenders, and an understanding of the alignment of other teammates. The unwary fullback pays a double penalty. First, he will have to delay his first move until the attacker makes his move. Second, he will not be ready to react when the attacker does begin his action.

Determination

This is highly essential in every phase of the game, but it is probably more of a requirement for defense. It has been described as self-confidence, the will to win, and the desire to outplay every opponent. It is wanting to beat one's opponent all the time and going after him time and again; it is hanging in there and looking for the ball even when you are being beaten again and again.

STYLE OF GREAT FULLBACKS

Classic Fullback

Djalma Santos of Peleiras and Brazil was one of the first fullbacks from the classic school who had the skill of a modern fullback (see photo, p. 120). This enabled him in the late 1950's to adapt to the modern style of the 4-2-4 system of play. Santos set the Brazilian record for national appearances (100) and participated in four successive World Cup finals, winning gold medals in 1958 and 1962.

At 5'7" Santos was rather small for a fullback, but he had great speed and quickness. His positional sense was uncanny; his playmaking masterful. These outstanding qualities, along with his thorough knowledge of the game, enabled him to organize the defense from the fullback position. In later years he used his enormous experience to compensate for his lack of speed and quickness in outplaying wing forwards nearly half his age.

Modern Fullback

Giacinto Facchetti of Internationale Milan and Italy is very tall and strongly built and comes closest to being the ultimate fullback. He is immensely experienced and has supreme confidence in his ability. He dominates in the air, and, despite his long legs, he is one of the best back-pedalers (containers) in the game, seldom being forced to commit himself to a hasty tackle.

Facchetti was one of the first to exploit wing space in an attacking role on an overlap. He has the strength and imagination to move forward with the attack and bring his left foot thunderously into the firing line. He is renowned as a surprise scorer.

Berti Hans-Hubert Vogts of Borussia Mönchengladbach and West Germany is an outstanding fullback. Quite short (around 5'7") and weighing not more than one hundred and forty pounds, Vogts is nonetheless a strong, determined tackler, is very fast in recovering and intercepting, and is an excellent playmaker. He turns quickly from defense to attack once he has possession (Fig. 7.2). He is also a master at forcing a wing forward away from the goal.

He is a keen play reader. He often will be seen popping up from nowhere to extricate his side from a difficult and dangerous situation. His quickness in recovering is another asset. Once beaten, he can turn smartly and get in another tackle.

POSITIONAL PLAY

Defense

Offensive System

The fullbacks operate on the zone principle, covering the area between the wing and inside forwards, keeping an eye on both, while protecting the central path to the goal. From staggered positions, they try to delay the opposing attack in midfield. They seek to give their halfbacks, particularly the offensive center half, enough time to get back and, equally important, to cover each other.

WM System

The defense now marks man-to-man. The shorter the distance to the ball, the tighter this marking

Fig. 7.2 *Berti Hans-Hubert Vogts turns quickly from defense to attack once he has possession.*

must be; the farther the distance, the looser the marking may be.

Both fullbacks are directly responsible for their wing forwards, as well as for providing the necessary cover and depth in defense. The defense is flexibly organized, shifting between man-to-man marking and covering the center halfback. If the right fullback attacks the left wing forward, the center halfback must provide cover for him, while the left fullback must sag to the inside, behind the center halfback, to provide the necessary cover depth for him.

4-2-4 System

The two backs flanking the two center backs are expected to blanket the opposing wing forwards, to assist the attack in midfield, and to use the ball to penetrate for a center or a shot. Speed is essential.

4-3-3 System

In this system or any of its variations, such as the sweeper, it is difficult to determine who is a wing forward or fullback because of all the leapfrogging going on, the wingers coming back deep, and the fullbacks charging upfield. It would appear that all the positions eventually will become even less departmentalized. But, while the fullback's job has become more sophisticated, his main responsibility still must be to shut out the opposing wing forward.

Marking an Opponent

If the fullback is marking his opponent closely, he must maintain a position:

1. Between the opponent and the goal.
2. Where he can see the opponent and the ball at all times without having to turn his head.
3. Near enough to the opponent so that if the ball is passed to him he can intercept it or tackle instantly for it.

When to Mark Tight and When to Cover

This is the most important judgment the fullback has to make, and he must make it very quickly. He must never allow the field to open up behind him for any kind of offensive sortie. Prevention is better than cure. Intelligent deployment can eliminate the danger. The fullback must first keep an eye on the wing forwards, then cover the center halfback.

Only by experience can he learn the best position to assume. If the opposing wing forward is very slow, he should move up on him, because, even if the ball is passed over his head, his superior speed should enable him to get to the ball first.

If the wing forward goes back halfway into his own territory, and the ball is on the fullback's side of the field, the latter should not hesitate to go up there with him. The fact that he is called a fullback should not prevent him from going well-forward to mark his man when the situation demands it.

The fullback should try to put himself in the best position to intercept passes to his man. If this fails, the next best thing is to arrive simultaneously with the ball. This calls for the development of quick reactions in going to meet the ball, and of good judgment in determining which passes he will be able to reach.

If he cannot get to the ball before the wing forward puts it under control, he should not rush into a hopeless tackle. There is nothing that a good wing forward likes better. The fullback should, rather, approach the winger in a way that either prevents him from cutting in toward the goal or leaves him only one way to pass. He thus presents him with a more difficult problem and may delay the attack long enough to ensure the marking of every forward.

Containing-Jockeying

Just as bad as tackling too soon is backing off too far and allowing the ball-handler to lift his head and look for a receiver. The best position is one that forces the opponent to keep his eyes down on the ball in order to control it. This restricts his vision and makes it harder for him to pass. He has to worry about controlling the ball or he will lose it to the defender. This causes problems to even the best attacker.

Every good fullback will also try to prevent a fast wing from cutting inside of him, and the best way to ensure this is by maintaining a position between the goal and the opponent. Good positioning is the hallmark of the first-class fullback:

1. It always puts him within range of his opponent.
2. It enables him to dart forward and intercept a pass, thus eliminating the necessity of difficult tackles.
3. It helps the defender avoid being caught on the touchline side of his opponent.

This leads to the vital technique of recovery. As soon as the fullback is beaten in a dribble or a tackle, he should realize that a quick recovery back toward his own penalty spot might give him a chance to rectify his mistake. It also could provide cover to a teammate who has temporarily left his opponent to tackle a more dangerously positioned forward.

Understanding with Goalkeeper

The fullback's first duty is to work out a relationship with the goalkeeper. The keeper has a right to expect a certain amount of cover from his fullbacks, especially when leaving his goal to deal with high centers. One or both fullbacks should then fall back to the goal line (Fig. 7.3). Many a dramatic last-second save has been made that way.

One special covering job by the fullback is

backing up the goalkeeper on corner kicks. The standard procedure is to stand inside the post on his (fullback's) side of the field, ready to take the keeper's place when he moves out to intercept a cross. If the keeper is beaten, one of the fullbacks should often be able to head or kick the ball off the line.

The fullback should also develop an understanding with the keeper about passing back to him. When chasing the ball toward his own goal with opponents in hot pursuit, the fullback will find it safest to push the ball back to his keeper. The fullback will often find this advantageous even when unchallenged. The goalkeeper must be ready for the ball and should help the fullback by calling for it. Whereas the keeper can see the whole field and get the ball up to any teammate with a long kick, the fullback is forced to turn with the ball and look. By the time he turns back, a swift opponent could dart in and rob him of the ball.

Offense

The impact accompanying a challenge will often leave the fullback off-balance, and he must recover quickly enough to avoid being victimized. A quick pass to a well-placed teammate is recommended. If the opponent has been dispossessed in a crowded goal area where an immediate challenge is likely, the first thought must be to clear the ball from the danger zone or put it out of play in order to gain time to assume a more favorable position.

However, the cool, resourceful fullback will, whenever possible, clear with a pass that can spark an immediate counterattack. This sort of fullback is a master of the precise setup pass: the chip, the lob, or the drive from a deep defensive position. He will always find one of his teammates and thus immediately convert defense into attack.

Immediately after gaining possession, for example, the fullback may try to feed the wing forward, either through a firm ground pass to his feet or by a chip over the head of the opposing fullback into the area behind him, so that the wing forward can collect the ball on the run.

Fullbacks should move up and down the field with the play and not stand around admiring some brilliant move by the forwards. If the fullbacks advance behind the forwards, as far as and even beyond the halfway line, the opponent is given no

Fig. 7.3 *Fullbacks cover by falling back to the goal line when the keeper has left the goal.*

time to collect the ball and tap it ahead a few yards before being tackled. No large gaps are left between attackers and defenders, and the whole game is speeded up in an effort to sustain the attack.

Overlapping

The fullback is expected to seize every opportunity to advance parallel to his touchline, particularly if his team is playing without clearly defined wing forwards.

In the organization of the 4-3-3 system, there is an attack by a man coming in from behind—an overlap. Since every forward and every halfback (midfield player) is closely marked as a potential attacker, back players—fullbacks—must be used for attacking and scoring, and forwards and midfield players must be used for defensive jobs. The man from behind can produce an effective attack, but it must be carefully prepared. The team must be able to stop a counterattack whenever it loses the ball.

To effect an overlap, a fullback or halfback feeds the wing forward, who drops back and away from the touchline, taking his fullback with him. This creates the necessary space between the touchline and himself so that the fullback can overlap down the flank and receive a pass. A well-timed return pass can enable him to move like a wing forward and finish his run with an accurate center.

This modern overlapping has fullbacks practicing pinpoint centers. They should not lob the ball

a b c d

Fig. 7.4 *Hook volley clearance. A strong leg-swing from the hip at and through the ball, well-coordinated with the necessary pivot, will enable the defender to clear the ball upfield.*

into the goalkeeper's hands, as that would only lead to a quick counterattack while the fullback is out of position.

The overlapping runs provide an excellent means of getting extra men in difficult situations, and, at the same time, obtain a high degree of mobility in attacking play. The success of the move lies in surprise. The opponents do not pay that much attention to supporting players who are behind the man with the ball.

SPECIAL SKILLS AND TECHNIQUES

Hook Volley Clearance

When chasing down a pass to the wing forward or when covering the center halfback, the fullback is often confronted with a high, lobbing ball. A skillful hook volley will enable him to clear it out of touch or, better still, serve it immediately to his own wing forward to set up an attack (Figs. 7.4 and 7.5).

More often than not, the hook volley is attempted off a sprint. But the placement of the supporting foot is essential—it must enable the fullback to check his momentum at least temporarily to ensure the necessary pivot and leg swing. The supporting foot, heel first, must be planted firmly, with the toes already beginning to point in the intended direction. This will allow the fullback to pivot or turn his body fully in the direction in which he intends to play the ball.

He leans sideward and backward away from the ball to ensure that his non-kicking side provides a firm hinge for a sufficiently high and full circular leg swing. A strong leg swing from the hip at and through the ball will produce a full defensive hook volley. The arms are swung wide to help maintain balance and ensure a well-coordinated pivot and leg action. The player concentrates on the ball from start to finish.

The fullback's effort to hook the ball sharply may cause him to fall backward. Some fullbacks achieve the same result by jumping, turning while clearing the ball, and are thus able to avoid the fall.

Overhead Clearance

An overhead clearance is invaluable for the fullback who often finds himself facing his own goal (Fig. 7.6). Under pressure it may be dangerous to control the ball or pass it to the goalie, and he does not want to concede a corner kick—ergo, the overhead clearance. This kick should not, however, be used when close to other players, as it can create a dangerous play situation.

The fullback can either gently lob the ball back over the tackler's head, then wheel around and make the play, or he can put all his weight behind the ball and send it well-upfield.

When making the forceful overhead clearance, the fullback should not neglect direction. He should know the probable disposition of his teammates in order to ensure an accurate and useful kick.

He should never allow the ball to fall lower than chin height, as this makes the clearance exceedingly difficult. Balance is essential to meet the ball at the correct height and lend it both power and direction.

The player should place the supporting foot near the vertical axis of the intended point of impact and lean backward in the direction of the intended clearance. This will ensure a free and powerful leg swing. As the trunk falls back, the hips may be raised (if a powerful clearance kick is required). The lower the hips, the lesser the kicking power.

The knee of the supporting leg should be well-bent to allow the player to fall back freely while simultaneously driving the full instep through the lower part of the ball. The follow through should be as complete as possible, and the fullback should stave off the impact of his fall by reaching back with both hands.

Defensive Heading with Side of Forehead

Heading has great importance in fullback play. Indeed, the fullback is frequently called upon to execute one of the trickiest headers in the game. When running back toward his goal with the ball directly overhead, he must jump and head the ball back in the opposite direction (Fig. 7.7).

Watching the ball over his shoulder out of the corner of his eye imposes a Herculean demand on his eyes and sense of timing. His impression is likely to be limited and slightly distorted in terms of distances and angles.

The takeoff must be with the leg opposite the turning side. A left fullback would prefer to take off with his right leg, after looking over his left shoulder while running back. Most fullbacks prefer to head with the side of the forehead, as it requires a body rotation which the takeoff initiates.

Immediately after takeoff, the fullback swings his body around to face the field. At the peak of his jump, he bends his trunk sideward and backward to unleash the body power. Some fullbacks include a little trunk twist and head swivel for additional power.

The side of the forehead forcefully establishes contact on the lower half of the ball, and the player usually lands on both feet (well-spread) to ensure a soft and safe landing.

Fig. 7.5 *Volley clearance.*

Fig. 7.6 *"Overhead clearance is invaluable for the fullback who often finds himself facing his own goal."*

Back Heading

This is an effective way of dealing with a high ball coming from the opposite wing forward. Instead of heading it back in the same direction, the full-

a   *b*   *c*

d   *e*

Fig. 7.7 *Defensive heading using the side of the forehead to clear the ball. When running back toward his goal with the ball directly over his head, the fullback must jump and head the ball back in the opposite direction.*

back merely allows the ball to ricochet off his forehead in order to clear it over the heads of the oncoming forwards (Fig. 7.8).

As the fullback jumps, he tilts his head well-back and tries to contact the ball with the upper part of his forehead. He merely pushes the ball upward as it glances off his forehead, elevating it enough to clear the heads of hostile forwards.

Sole-of-Foot Trap

This observes the classic wedge principle. The ball is trapped in front of the player between the slop-

| a | b | c |

Fig. 7.8 *Back heading. "The fullback merely allows the ball to ricochet off his forehead in order to clear it over the heads of the oncoming forwards."*

| a | b | c | d |

Fig. 7.9 *Trapping a ball with the sole of the foot while beating an inrushing defender by pushing it through his legs.*

ing sole of the foot and the ground. The placement and timing of the foot must coincide with the impact of the ball on the ground (Fig. 7.9).

The fullback faces in the direction of the approaching ball, with his body across the ball's path. It is imperative to get on top of the ball and watch it right onto the boot. The supporting foot must be placed within comfortable reach of the ball, with the body relaxed and slightly crouched over the ball of the supporting foot, the knee well-bent, and the arms flung wide for stability.

The playing foot is brought into position very much like a regular step, except that the body weight is not transferred forward but withheld completely or just delayed until the trap is completed. In contrast with a natural stride, the leg remains bent at the knee as it is brought forward, while the foot is dorsiflexed to set the trap built by the sloping sole of the foot and the ground.

The space between the foot and the ground should be large enough to accommodate the ball. The angle of the foot will depend on the flight of the ball. Ideally, the ball should strike the sole of the foot at a right angle.

If the ball is descending at a sharp angle, say perpendicularly, the sole of the foot should be

a

b

c

d

e

Fig. 7.10 *Trapping with the sole of the foot with preliminary feint kick. Avoiding a tackle by dragging the ball back to flick it to the side behind the supporting foot and take off.*

parallel with the ground. In the case of a moderate arc, the angle should be oblique. When receiving a low ball, the heel should hardly be raised off the ground so as to prevent the ball from escaping.

The placement of the foot on the ball must coincide with the ball's impact on the ground. It is almost like playing a half-volley. As the ball is wedged between the sole and the ground, a slight pressure will cause the ball to stop dead. A simultaneous straightening of the knee will add a gentle pushing effect to the foot and cause the ball to roll ahead of the fullback, enabling him to get off the mark instantly. Highly skilled fullbacks can cause the ball to spin backward by stroking it back and downward with the sole of the foot in order to keep the ball under close control.

The sole-of-foot trap offers a valuable method of receiving the ball and keeping it close to the feet versus a charging tackler. By keeping the sole of the foot lightly on top of the ball and dragging it back and around the supporting foot, the fullback can turn and screen the ball from the opponent (Fig. 7.10).

A slight modification of this technique can help bring a bouncing ball under control. Whenever the fullback cannot quite beat the attacker to the ball without checking his speed, he can gain possession by smothering the ball with the sole of his foot (Fig. 7.11). He will naturally be forced to take an exaggerated glide step to get close enough to the ball and gain sufficient time to lift his foot above the rising ball.

He must give by flexing his hip and knee at the moment of impact, as he coaxes and pulls the ball to the ground. This will enable him to continue upfield in full stride.

The Sliding Tackle

This is as difficult as it is daring. It should be employed only as a last resort, when nothing else will work—as, for example, against an attacker who is about to shoot after breaking past the defense. The danger is obvious. If the tackle fails, the fullback has taken himself out of the play and has practically no chance of regaining his footing quickly enough to get in another tackle (Fig. 7.12).

The sliding tackle is particularly effective on a wet pitch or in the vicinity of the touchline or goal line. The defender simply prevents the attacker from making the play by sliding the ball to another player or out of play.

Sliding is really controlled falling. When eight or ten feet from the ball, the player drops to the ground and lets the momentum of the approach run do the rest. Since he will lose a second in falling, the fullback should aim ahead of the ball rather than for it (Fig. 7.13).

a   b   c

Fig. 7.11 *Intercepting by smothering a rising ball with the sole of the foot.*

Fig. 7.12 *The sliding tackle. "If the tackle fails, the fullback has taken himself out of the play and has practically no chance of regaining his footing quickly enough to get in another tackle."*

Fig. 7.13 *The fullback must spot-time his slide tackle, aiming ahead rather than for the ball because of the time he will lose when falling.*

Bent-Leg Slide Tackle

This can be used either from a front approach or diagonally from behind after catching up with the opponent. When approaching directly from the rear, the player must veer slightly to the side to obtain the necessary angle. He picks up momentum in the process of catching up with the opponent, and greatly exaggerates his last stride, which ends in a slide. The takeoff is usually from the inside foot, which ultimately receives the full impact of the slide, but it may also be made with the other foot—it depends upon the ability of the player (Fig. 7.14).

When the takeoff is made from the outside foot, the leading (inside) leg is merely used to break the impact of the fall, and the tackling leg is simultaneously brought into position to make the play. When the inside leg is used for the takeoff, the body is allowed to ride over the well-bent inside leg—from heel to toe—in order to lower the center of gravity and ensure a smooth slide. Most of the momentum for either technique must come from the approach run and final thrust of the takeoff; the inside leg is merely used to guide the player gently to the ground.

In both techniques, the player hits the ground on the outer part of the inside foot and shin, and then the thigh, buttocks, near arm, and shoulder follow in sliding comfortably along the ground. The landing and sliding action should be gradual and continuous. It must be timed perfectly; the tackler must be close enough at the critical moment to make the play. As the supporting inside leg doubles up, the outside leg is swung forcefully across, and the instep is driven straight through the center of the ball (Fig. 7.15).

The bent-leg slide permits two different approaches to the opponent with one basic technique. It is also a safe tackle. The studs are not likely to be caught in the ground and the danger of a body burn is minimized by the fact that the initial impact is made with the lower leg. Another advantage is quick recovery. The momentum of the slide enables the player to push himself off the ground with his hands and bent leg.

Hook Slide Tackle

This technique is almost always used when the defender is trying to catch up with the opponent and just cannot get close enough for a bent-leg slide. Since he must hook slide with his inside leg, he greatly increases the danger of ramming the opponent before making contact with the ball (Fig. 7.16).

The takeoff is made from the outside foot,

a   b   c

Fig. 7.14 *Bent-leg slide tackle. The fullback approaches at full speed, times his tackle when he is even with the opponent and after the opponent has played the ball. He tackles with the leg farther away from the opponent. The weight rests on the folding near-side leg and the ball is played away firmly by a powerful leg swing.*

which allows the player to ride heel-to-toe over the well-bent knee, while lowering his center of gravity. The tackling (inside) leg is swung forcefully forward toward the ball, which adds to the momentum of the slide, and the trunk turns slightly toward the opponent.

As the tackling leg completes its kicking action to clear the ball, the other leg drags in a bent position. The inside hand usually drags along the ground with the palm down to break the initial impact of the fall, while the outside hand remains in the air to stabilize the body.

The impact and slide are made on the outer side of the inside (tackling) leg, buttocks, and sometimes even the side of the trunk. If the initial attempt fails, the alert player can have another go at it by swinging the outside leg across to clear the ball—provided, of course, the slide has brought him close enough.

Fig. 7.15 *Bent-leg slide tackle. The fullback makes a last-ditch effort to smother a shot, since the goalkeeper is already beaten.*

REALISTIC PRACTICES

Hook Volley Clearance

The right halfback sets up around midfield and serves high, long, diagonal passes in the direction of the corner flag. The right fullback must clear the ball with a left-footed hook volley, if possible to his right wing forward positioned around midfield near the touchline. The fullback must then immediately support the receiver and get a back pass.

Another technique is the same as above, except

that a goalkeeper and an opposing left wing forward are added. The latter is asked to challenge the right fullback. The fullback now has a decision: whether to clear the ball with a hook volley or play it back to the goalie and then quickly break toward the touchline for a throw from the goalie.

As an alternative, the fullback can feint to play the ball but allow it to go past him toward the corner, then turn quickly and run after it to make the play again to the right wing forward, using a chip pass along the touchline.

While the main task is practicing the hook volley clearance, the fullback is learning when and when not to use it. Once the right wing forward receives the ball, he plays it to the right halfback, and the whole sequence is repeated.

Fig. 7.16 *Hook slide tackle, which is almost always used when the defender is trying to catch up with the opponent and just cannot get close enough for a bent-leg slide tackle. Since he must hook slide with his inside leg, he greatly increases the danger of ramming the opponent before making contact with the ball.*

Tackling—Quick Recovery

The fullback is asked to defend a five-yard square (marked out around the edge of the penalty box) against a number of forwards. Each opponent has a ball and tries, in turn, to dribble past the fullback within the restricted area to get a shot at the goal. The limited area creates a realistic situation. Not only is the fullback first to bid for the ball, he also can use it to advantage in running the forward out of bounds or cornering him and then tackling.

The pressure on the fullback can be regulated by manipulating the intervals between attacks. As soon as a forward leaves the limited area, the next should be allowed to attack.

To make this practice more interesting, a team of, say, three fullbacks are pitted against a team of eight forwards for a given period. The fullbacks are allowed to change on the run when tired or hopelessly out of position for the next tackle. Every successful tackle or shot at the goal is recorded to establish the winner.

Another drill gives two fullbacks practice on chasing back. It involves the left halfback, wing forward, and an opposing right fullback on one side of the field and the identical combination of players plus a goalie on the other side.

The goalie starts by throwing the ball to his right fullback, who immediately starts upfield and then serves to the opposing left halfback, recreating a realistic situation (interception). The latter immediately passes to his left wing forward. The right fullback must quickly turn and chase down the left wing forward to prevent a direct assault on the goal and, if possible, prevent the center.

The goalie should have a number of additional balls at his disposal so that he can quickly feed the left fullback, who repeats the activity on the opposite side of the field.

Offense Against Defense

The fullbacks are best tested in actual matches, of course. A half-field scrimmage, offense against defense, can be arranged so that the fullbacks are repeatedly subjected to a particular style of attack. For example:

1. The long, lofted diagonal pass in the direction of the corner flag, to the wing forward.

2. A two-on-one situation with inside and wing forwards combining to attack.

3. Wandering wing forwards.

4. An attack on the opposite side, testing the fullback's coverage of other defenders.

5. All kinds of dead-ball situations.

6. Initiating the counterattack, playing the ball out of defense.

Each game situation provides a practical lesson that should be analyzed in terms of the abilities of the fullback, his teammates, and the immediate opponent.

Only through such realistic situations will the fullback learn such essential things as how to shepherd the wing forward and force him to the touchline or trap him near the corner of the field.

Attacking-Overlapping

In the initial stage of coaching the overlap, a start may be made with a combination of fullback, midfield player, and right wing forward, against an opposing fullback. The defending fullback has two options: to cover the right wing forward tight (man-to-man) or lay off (zone defense).

In the first instance ("man-on" option), the attacking fullback delivers the pass to the feet of the right wing forward, who drops back to meet the ball. The passer, observing that the defending fullback is staying tight with the right winger, calls "Man on!" The right wing forward must immediately react by wall passing back to the right midfield player.

Meantime the right fullback who delivered the

pass to the right wing forward sprints along the sideline to overlap the right winger. He races into the area behind the defending fullback to collect a pass from the right midfield player (Diag. 7.1).

A second ("turn") option is for the attacking right fullback once again to deliver a pass right to the feet of the wing forward, who is dropping back to collect it. This time the attacking fullback, noting that the defending fullback has decided to lay off and cover a zone, calls "Turn!"

The wing forward immediately eases up on his fast approach and turns to the outside. His prime objective must be to engage the defending fullback in order to allow the right fullback to make his overlap run into position for a timely pass. If the wing forward's pass is made just before the right fullback sprints past the ball, he cannot possibly be running into an offside position.

Once the attacking right fullback breaks away

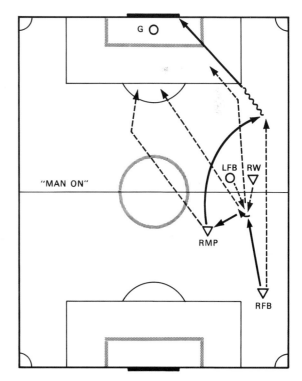

Diag. 7.1 *"The right fullback who delivered the pass to the right wing forward sprints along the sideline to overlap the right winger. He races into the area behind the defending fullback to collect a pass from the right midfield player."*

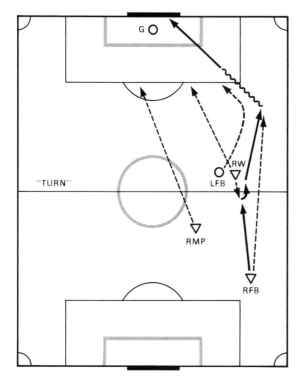

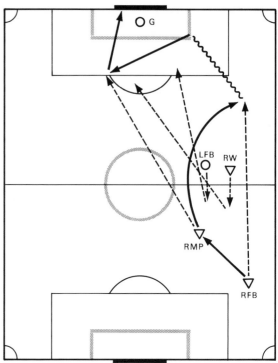

Diag. 7.2 *"Once there is success in breaking past the defending fullback, whether he comes forward to challenge or lays off to cover the wing forward's approach to the goal, we proceed to introduce variations."*

Diag. 7.3 *"The attacking right fullback is racing along the touchline on his overlap run. He collects the pass and proceeds with the ball, taking the shot himself or serving it to the trailing midfield player who has raced toward the goalmouth."*

with the ball, he should be encouraged to sprint toward the near post while the right wing forward simultaneously turns and races toward the goal in an effort to support the ball-handler.

The defending left fullback should be exhorted to try to overhaul the ball. The attacking fullback in possession may either shoot, pass off to the right wing forward, or continue to run toward the goal line and pull the ball back into the path of the trailing right midfield player for a first-time shot.

Once there is success in breaking past the defending fullback, whether he comes forward to challenge or lays off to cover the wing forward's approach to the goal, we proceed to introduce variations (Diag. 7.2). Again start with the overlapping right fullback in possession and assume that he cannot deliver a man-on pass to the wing forward because the defending fullback is sticking

tight and is ready to dash in front of him for the interception. The ball-handler must react by passing to the right midfield player, who must then immediately hit a long ball into the area vacated by the tight-marking defending fullback. Meanwhile, the attacking right fullback is racing along the touchline on his overlap run. He collects the pass and proceeds with the ball, taking the shot himself or serving it to the trailing midfield player who has raced toward the goalmouth (Diag. 7.3).

To obtain variety and flexibility, add another midfield player. This time assume that the right midfield player has possession. He delivers the ball to the right wing forward, who drops back diagonally to meet it. Seeing that the defending fullback is covering tight, the passer calls "Man on!" This tells the right wing forward to wall pass to the center midfield player. Meantime, the right fullback breaks down the sideline on his overlap run and

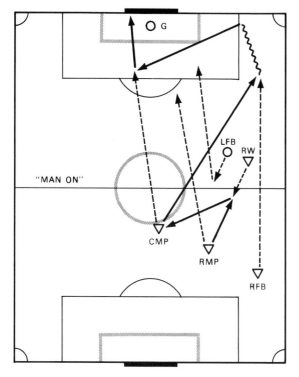

Diag. 7.4 *"To obtain variety and flexibility, add another midfield player."*

Diag. 7.5 *"If the defending fullback accepts the challenge, the wing forward immediately lays the ball back to the center midfield player. The latter chips the ball at once into the open space behind the defending fullback, where the attacking fullback collects it on his overlap run."*

races into the open space behind the defending fullback to collect a pass from the center midfield player (Diag. 7.4).

As a further development, assume that the defending fullback decides to lay back and cover his area, so that the wing forward can turn with the ball. If the defender lays off to the outside to prevent the attacking fullback from overlapping, the wing forward must draw the defender away from the touchline by veering to the inside. If the defending fullback accepts the challenge, the wing forward immediately lays the ball back to the center midfield player. The latter chips the ball at once into the open space behind the defending fullback, where the attacking fullback collects it on his overlap run (Diag. 7.5).

To develop this overlapping pattern a step further, add an additional defender, preferably a centerback, and another attacker, preferably a center forward. Starting with the "turn" option, have the attacking fullback again make the first pass to the right wing forward, who drops back to meet the ball. The defending fullback declines to challenge

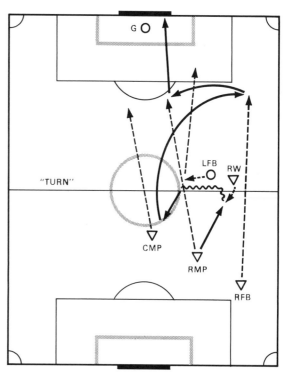

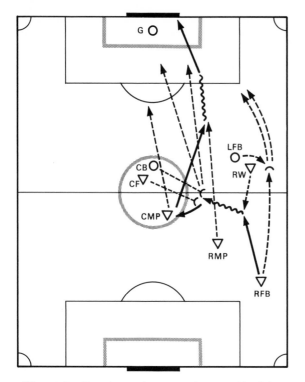

Diag. 7.6 *"Have the overlap prepared on one side of the field and then suddenly switch it to the opposite side, with the overlapping fullback prepared to go all the way and score."*

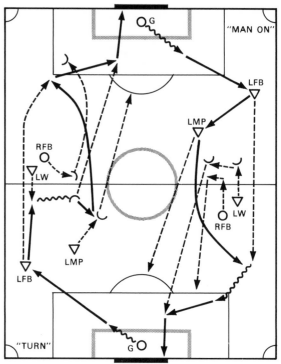

Diag. 7.7 *Method of two-way attacks.*

the wing forward, and lays off to cover space. Upon noticing this response, the fullback verbally signals the right wing forward to turn. The winger does this while the defender is laying off outside in anticipation of the overlap. The right wing forward moves inside with the ball in the hope of engaging the defending fullback.

So far the move is exactly the same as previously described. Now, the right wing forward, instead of playing the ball back to one of his midfield players, passes it to the feet of the oncoming center forward and then sprints to change places with the center forward.

The defending left fullback is left with two options: to mark the wing forward or to continue to lay off and cover the left flank. The centerback is similarly left with the option of staying with the center forward or laying off and covering space. In the event the centerback decides to cover his zone, the midfield player will signal "Turn!" to the center

forward and sprint through the gap on an overlap to get the pass from him. Of course, if both the centerback and defending fullback decide to cover tight, the right wing forward will deliver a man-on pass to the center forward, who will wall pass it back to the right midfield player for a chip to the overlapping right fullback in the space behind the defending fullback.

These moves can form the basis for many other plays. One would be to have the overlap prepared on one side of the field and then suddenly switch it to the opposite side, with the overlapping fullback prepared to go all the way and score (Diag. 7.6).

The final step may be a two-way attack (attacks going both up and down the field) that will make practices even more realistic and save all the time wasted in walking back to starting positions.

In the beginning, the coach may have one team doing man-on and the other doing turn patterns.

Each attack must be completely realistic, being dictated completely by the response of the defenders.

Each attack begins with a throw from the goalkeeper to the right fullback, after which the attacking unit can try any combination previously practiced, based on the reaction of the defending fullback. Since many shots will go wide of the goal, valuable time can be saved by equipping the goalie with a number of balls.

The most obvious disadvantage of the two-way attack lies in the fact that if corrections are necessary, the coach must hold up the practices of both (Diag. 7.7).

8

The Halfback

The great halfbacks of yesterday, called "wing halfs," would be baffled to see the modern halfback—midfield player—at work. The modern halfback is a highly skilled all-around player, and his contributions, whether offensive or defensive, invariably play a key role in the success or failure of his team.

The halfback's chief defensive responsibility is to destroy. He must be resourceful in covering his teammates and determined in his challenge for the ball. Physical strength, authority in tackling, quick recovery, and power on the ball are utterly essential.

The halfback's chief offensive responsibility is initiating and supporting the attacking movements. He must be industrious and imaginative in his use of the ball and have a flair for either spotting or creating an opening.

NATURAL QUALIFICATIONS

High Work Load

Because he is an integral part of the midfield, the heart of the team, the halfback must carry a high work load. His primary job is to control midfield—forestall pressure on his rearguard and initiate and sustain an attack. He also must be ready to help his defense under pressure. Since his position is not rigidly defined, his coverage is limited only by his stamina.

The halfback does not have to be one of the fastest players on the field. In fact, most halfbacks lack something in speed. They are the milers rather than the sprinters. Since it is difficult to maintain a high work load when the game is going poorly, the coach must show the halfback how to increase his output when things are going badly and to avoid overdoing it when the game is going well.

Split Vision

As it is the ability to watch both the ball and the area around it, split vision enables the halfback to read the play and thus control the action (Fig. 8.1).

The common fault on defense is ball-watching. The mesmerized halfback is easily drawn out of position and victimized by attackers who slip by on his blind side into dangerous positions behind him. Quite frequently the movement of opponents is more important than that of the ball. Opponents who are allowed to move into dangerous positions put the team in serious jeopardy.

On offense, the halfback must divide his attention between dealing with the ball and the movement around him. Since his main responsibility is to prepare the attack from midfield, he must be able to see what his forwards are doing. Whenever a forward cuts for a pass, the halfback must spot the best opening and put the ball there instantly. He must be able to visualize the entire field.

Fig. 8.1 *Franz Beckenbauer. Split vision denotes "the ability to watch both the ball and the area around it."*

Fig. 8.2 *"Bobby Moore of West Ham United captained England through the greatest era in her history."*

Reading the Game

The quality that separates the top halfback from the ordinary one, reading the game is the ability to understand what is happening, to anticipate immediate or future developments, and to exploit this knowledge boldly and intelligently. Good players seem to have a natural capacity for it, while others must develop it. Until they can read the flow of the game, they cannot play an authoritative role in directing its course.

The ability to read the game (to think ahead) also enables the player to position himself most advantageously to intercept the pass, cover the dangerous man, and release the harmless opponent.

Above all, the halfback must understand what is required of him on any part of the field and at every stage of the game. Near his own penalty area, he cannot take chances; farther upfield he may take a chance on intercepting a pass or tackling an opponent, since he will have time to recover if he makes a mistake. The calculation of this risk is a matter of skill, judgment, and experience.

Imagination with a Touch of Conservatism

Too many halfbacks get their priorities wrong. They feel that their passes must look spectacular and draw a gasp of admiration from the crowd, and that every move must reflect their skill and imagination.

The halfback must have a built-in safety valve. As the player who feeds those around him, he must have an intuitive knowledge of when to attempt an ambitious pass and when to play safe.

STYLE OF GREAT HALFBACKS

Defensive Halfback

Some halfbacks, because of their particular endowments, coaching, and experience, operate best on defense. They are especially effective when their team is trying to regain possession or working to restrict the attack. They are masters at tracking down the attack from behind and in delivering the outlet pass to exactly the right player to spark the counterattack. And they are also quite capable of supporting the attack from midfield or even going through on a timely overlap to strike at goal themselves.

Bobby Moore of West Ham United, who captained England through the greatest era in her history, is such a halfback (Fig. 8.2). He was a colossus in both the 1966 and 1970 World Cup, not only for his inspirational play but also for his steadying influence on his teammates.

Moore is happiest as a defensive halfback, moving laterally behind his defense to track down dangerous-looking attacks. His natural ability to read the game greatly enhances his anticipation. He exemplifies the English freeback who, eschewing the negative Italian style, serves as a sweeper behind the defense, a screen to blunt the attack at its inception, and an initiator of the counterattack from behind.

Moore is a superb passer-feeder. His coolness under pressure and clever tackling enable him to make the best possible use of the ball. He can be deadly on sudden switches from defense to counterattack and on long, defense-splitting passes to unmarked forwards. Most great halfbacks are exceptional passers, gifted with perception, judgment, and technique.

Franz Beckenbauer of Bayern München, the wonder boy of West German soccer, is a masterful player who is outstanding in both defense and attack (see photo, p. 140). He is Germany's best freeback, best stopper, best midfield schemer, and best forward. Beckenbauer is the modern sweeper personified. His outstanding knowledge, vision, and feel for the game, coupled with his dynamic artistry, make him both a devastating defensive sweeper and creative midfield player as well as occasional finisher. Beckenbauer had no equal in the 1970 World Cup in Mexico, even among the Brazilians.

Offensive Halfback

Martin Peters and Wolfgang Overath have a special flair for innovation. Though they play an important role in setting up the first defensive barrier, they are better qualified to erupt into attack as soon as their team gains possession of the ball.

Fig. 8.3 *Martin Peters "became known as 'The Ghost' because of his uncanny knack of appearing from nowhere to score fantastic goals."*

The test of a searching, offensive halfback lies in his ability to steal into dangerous forward positions and deliver the payoff pass with delicate timing, weight, and accuracy.

Martin Peters of West Ham United and England was one of the first to sense the drift in halfback strategy. With defenses becoming tighter, he knew that many of the best scoring chances would fall to the midfield player who could shoot accurately from outside the box or pounce from the outside to destroy a tangled defense. Peters became known as "The Ghost" because of his uncanny knack of appearing from nowhere to score fantastic goals (Fig. 8.3).

Wolfgang Overath of FC Cologne and West Germany earned his spurs as one of the best midfield players in the world in both the 1966 and 1970 World Cup matches. He is a strong tackler and accurate passer, maintains a high work load, and, above all, is an excellent diagnostician. Since he always seems to be in the right place at the right time, he often is less noticed than his more flamboyant colleagues.

POSITIONAL PLAY

Defense

The halfback has always played a key role in the team operation. In the "offensive system," most popular a half century ago, he was called a "wing half." He played wide, zone covering the flanks but keeping a close eye on the wing and inside forwards.

In the "WM system," the halfback is more specialized. His main responsibility is to shadow the opposing inside forward wherever he goes. Since the inside forwards are the playmakers, the halfbacks must try to shut them off by intercepting the passes to them or tackling them the instant they get the ball.

The modern halfback, more appropriately called "midfield player," has more specific and diversified functions. In the "4-2-4 system," for instance, one halfback will act more as a defender alongside the center halfback, while the other halfback will join the withdrawn inside forward as the playmakers in midfield.

As mentioned previously, the halfbacks are required to serve as the first line of defense, linking defense with attack, and then supporting the entire attacking action. This places great responsibility on the halfback and midfield unit.

Recent strategical developments are encouraging coaches to use three and even four halfbacks (midfield players) as springboards for defense and attack. The primary idea is to produce a heavy concentration of players (numerical superiority) around the ball.

Generally one or more halfbacks will be more defense-conscious. They will deploy in front of the last line of the defense and act as a screen, putting pressure on the ball-carrier and forcing him to part with the ball.

One halfback may also be found alongside the center halfback or stopper, or even behind the last line of defense in the classic sweeper position. From this base, he will track down the opposing attack and speed to the spot of danger.

Offensively, he plays from behind, initiating the counterattack as well as offering himself as a supporting player whenever the situation demands it. The other halfbacks assume greater attacking roles, searching for advanced attacking positions, sustaining the offense, and pressing home the attack themselves on occasion.

Fluidity is essential, however, and these players must interchange and cover for each other. Ideally the offensive midfield player must be able to assume defensive responsibilities when necessary, and the defensive midfield player must be willing to make an offensive contribution when the opportunity presents itself.

In practice, the coach must lay down fairly firm priorities to ensure a strong, cohesive halfback (midfield) unit in which the players know their own roles but can complement each other.

An overly offense-minded midfield unit will leave a great vacuum in which the opposing forwards will be able to initiate and build up their attacks at will. A purely defensive midfield unit will create a large gap between the forward line and the midfield unit, which will diminish the team's ability to build up and sustain the attacking thrust.

The halfback's exact positional responsibilities will depend upon his skill, diagnostic ability, and judgment. He must remember that he can take a good deal of pressure off the fullbacks by blunting the opposing attack before it can get started. When his team has possession, he supports the attack. As soon as it breaks down, he fights back instantly to a position between the ball and the goal.

His primary responsibility, however, is to plague the inside forward, or whoever his immediate opponent may be. The inside forwards, or offensive midfield players, are usually the mainspring of the attack, and it is of great importance to kill the attack at inception. Hence, as soon as the opposition gets the ball, the right halfback must closely mark the opposing left inside forward. Once his side gains possession, he must slip away and join the attack if necessary.

Of course the halfback's defensive responsibilites transcend the mere marking of an opponent. He is also responsible for forming the deflection point of defensive triangles. He must be prepared to challenge any forward who has the ball or is preparing to receive it: Whenever he is close to a ball exchange he must instantly move to the ball and force the opponent into a hurried play or delay him enough for the defense to check back and assume supporting positions.

Good defensive organization reveals itself in a series of interlocking triangles that become tighter as the defense funnels back toward its goal.

The midfield unit must prepare the defense from midfield by forcing the opponent to play the ball in front of them. They cannot give the opposing forwards too much time and space to prepare their attack. They must contain the opponents or present them with poor and flat passing angles. By forcing the opponents to play square across the field in front of them, the midfield players will produce a high pressure area near and around the ball that will force the opponents to hurry their passes.

When forced back to the edge of his own penalty area, the halfback must resort to skintight man-to-man marking. He must pick up a forward and stick with him, especially if the man dives into the penalty area to look for a quick pass.

At the same time, the halfback must have an instinct (cultivated by observation and experience) for knowing when to leave his man and go to a point of greater danger. The focus of greatest danger is almost always a space in front of the goal in which there are more attackers than defenders. The halfback can alleviate the danger by marking the nearest open attacker.

The halfback also has definite responsibilities in dead-ball situations, such as free kicks, corner kicks, and so forth, which are analyzed in Chapter 11.

Offense

Stopping a forward and taking the ball away from him is one thing; making the instant transition from defense to offense is something else. It marks the difference between an ordinary halfback and a good one.

The halfback goes on offense immediately after intercepting a pass to the opposing inside forward or taking the ball from an opponent with a well-executed tackle. If he has sized up the situation ahead of time and checked the location of both opponents and teammates, he should know what to do with the ball.

If he can spot an unguarded forward or an open space in front of a forward, he should pass immediately to him. If an opposing defender comes out to challenge, the halfback should sense that a forward has been left uncovered, and should pass to him. (A basic principle is to draw a defender to you and then hit the open man.)

If the forwards are covered and the halfback decides to keep the ball, he should attack quickly and sharply—preventing the defense from consolidating in front of him. He should really penetrate on his dribble. This kind of power thrust leaves the defenders uncertain, gives them little time in which to assess the situation, and may even induce panic.

If the halfback has a strong shot, he should use it anywhere within his range.

The halfback's chief offensive responsibility is to support his forwards. He will usually find it wiser to support them from behind rather than go in among them. He should form triangles with his inside and wing forwards, and try to create three-on-two situations. Supporting from behind presents an excellent way for him to prepare the attack from midfield and deliver the decisive pass.

Intelligent passing will enable him to bring his inside and wing forwards into the game. At the same time he must be ready to deliver the cross-field pass to the opposite wing forward. Shifting the point of attack is a good tactic.

Since the pass to the wing forward requires great accuracy and strength, especially on heavy pitches, it is seldom attempted, but it can be highly effective. It switches the point of attack, opens up the game, and can catch the opposing defense completely off-balance.

The pass is predicated on the opposing fullback's deployment. If he is covering the wing forward in a tight man-to-man, the pass should be chipped into the space behind him for the wing forward to pick up on the run (after spurting behind the fullback). If the fullback is sagging off in anticipation of the attack, the crossfield pass should be played to the wing forward's feet, allowing him to gain the control and momentum needed to beat the fullback and cut in toward goal.

Last, but not least, the halfback should master the free kick from anywhere on the field and the art of throwing-in short or long.

SPECIAL SKILLS AND TECHNIQUES

The halfback should move quickly and determinedly to meet the ball. Since he will find himself heavily challenged while receiving the ball, he must learn how to bring it under control with one movement and pass it with his next. In many situations he will not even have the time to bring the ball under control, and will then be required to lay off a first-time pass to a supporting player. This means that the halfback must always have two or three possible passes in mind before the ball comes to him.

Every halfback will be required to make many of his controlling movements when moving quickly toward the ball or when being challenged by one or more opponents. He must, hence, be able to relax the receiving part of his body, while working hard with the rest of his body. Once he has the ball, he must regain his balance and composure to effect his next move.

Receiving—Taking the Pace off the Ball

This technique is used primarily in handling firm ground passes, but it is also effective for pulling down a medium-high ball and bringing it under control.

It requires delicacy to take the pace off the ball, to make it stick to the foot, or merely "tame" it

in the air. At the moment of impact, the foot must go limp and "give" with the ball to absorb its pace. This will enable the player to collect the ball from any direction and height with hardly a break in stride.

If, for instance, the ball is met as the right foot strides forward, it is taken to the right with the outside of the (right) foot, or taken to the left with the inside of the (right) foot. The important thing is to make sure to meet the ball with the full surface of the foot.

Pulling a Ball Down from Midair

Whenever a ball comes at an awkward height, the player should, while running, put out his leg to

a   b   c

d   e   f

Fig. 8.4 *Controlling the ball with the inside of the foot. The halfback stands sideward as the ball approaches, establishes balance early, meets the ball, and gives quickly on impact to kill the ball.*

146

coax it to the ground. Some players use the inside or outside of the foot to cushion the impact and stroke the ball to the ground. Others literally catch the ball with the instep and caress it down to the turf. The words "caress" and "stroke" imply gentleness. But it is timing that does the trick, and timing comes only with constant practice.

Inside of the Foot

When the ball is speeding past the player, he can control it by raising his foot sideward and pulling the ball to the ground, taking the pace off it with the inside of the foot. As the player "gives" with (cushions) the impact, he pulls the ball inward and

downward, guiding it gently to the ground in front of him and imparting a spin that will ensure close possession (Figs. 8.4 and 8.5).

Outside of the Foot

This method is especially effective in controlling a ball coming from the side or directly from behind, without slowing up. The player meets the ball with the outside of the foot and takes the pace off it by giving with the ball and simultaneously pulling the foot back across the inside of the ball. Correct timing and touch will cause the ball to come down with proper spin to the player's feet (Fig. 8.6).

a   b   c   d

e   f

Fig. 8.5 *Trapping with the inside of the foot, deflecting the ball behind the supporting foot to avoid the onrushing opponent and to move off quickly to the side.*

a　　　　　*b*　　　　　*c*

d　　　　　*e*

Fig. 8.6   *Pulling a ball down from midair with the outside of the foot while turning.*

Instep

Skillful players can literally catch a falling ball with the middle of the instep and caress it down to the ground or play it off second-touch.

The controlling foot meets the ball, with the leg well-bent, toes pulled up, and the ankle loose. The player catches the ball on the full instep, gives with the ball, and caresses it gently to the ground (Fig. 8.7).

Some players prefer to raise the foot only

148

Fig. 8.7 *Pulling a ball down with the instep while turning in order to avoid a challenge from an onrushing opponent.*

slightly off the ground. This enables them to assume a natural running stride and catch the ball more with the top of the toes than the full instep. The toes are well-pulled up and the leg is slightly bent at the knee. Essentially the ball is "killed" by letting the foot go extremely limp on impact— allowing the ball to slap the foot down (Fig. 8.8). By pulling the foot briskly out from underneath the ball at the moment of impact, the player can impart a controlled top spin to the ball. This prevents a rebound and assures a quick takeoff.

Thigh

The thigh is particularly useful in controlling the ball because of its thick layer of muscles. A relaxed thigh can take the pace off the ball or give the player a controlled rebound. By withdrawing the thigh on impact, the player can kill the ball completely (Fig. 8.9).

The player should, ideally, always deploy behind and across the ball's path and block the ball with the thigh at a right angle. Normally, however, it is sufficient merely to accentuate a natural running

149

Fig. 8.8 *Catching the ball in midair with the instep. The halfback lifts his leg before the ball arrives, catches it with the cup of the instep, and gives on impact to bring the ball to the ground.*

Fig. 8.9 *Killing a ball on the spot with the instep.*

stride, with the body resting momentarily on the supporting foot. Impact is made right above the hip joint. The player absorbs it by lowering the thigh, causing the ball to drop to his feet. He can then check the ball once more or play it off immediately.

Inside of the Thigh

The player often may find himself in a situation where it is more feasible to control the ball with the inside of the thigh. The player can meet a ball coming in from the side by raising his thigh and establishing contact on the broad inside part of the member. He allows the thigh to ride back with the

ball and then draws it away, so that the ball drops to his feet (Fig. 8.10).

Distribution of Passes

Possession and penetration are the name of the game. The ball is precious, often difficult to gain, and it is a crime to turn it back through sheer carelessness. The halfback must be a master of all types of passes: the first-touch pass slotted in delicately; the ball driven hard to a teammate or an open space; the pass to a forward breaking into a dangerous position. The halfback must often ig-

Fig. 8.10 *Controlling the ball in midair with the chest and turning without immediate challenge.*

nore the obvious and have the confidence to seek adventurous avenues (Fig. 8.11).

When to Hold or Pass the Ball

Knowledge of when to hold and when to pass requires much experience. The player must develop an instinct for it. Holding the ball too long can be just as bad as not holding it at all. The halfback should, as a rule, release the ball as quickly as possible. Since the opponents have just been in attacking positions, the halfback's teammates are sure to be unmarked for a split second.

The *timing* of the pass is the most difficult aspect. The halfback should always deliver the ball the moment his teammate arrives in the most comfortable position to receive it.

151

Fig. 8.11 *The halfback feints a push pass in order to commit the opponent to a tackle. Instead he steps over the ball and reverses the play by a crossover heel kick.*

The *quality* of the pass can only be measured by the ease with which the receiver can deal with it. A good pass takes into account the receiver's skill, the situation he is in, and the move he must make.

Passing to Player's Feet or into Space

Whenever a forward is closely marked from behind, the pass can always be made directly to him. This "pass to his feet" can often initiate a promising attack. It is recommended for most tight situations, as it enables the receiver to simultaneously control and screen the ball from the opponent and to move off in any direction.

Passing into an open space offers an effective alternative, provided the space is already there or the forward can create it. The common way to clear a space is by sucking in the defender as if to meet the ball, then abruptly cutting behind him to receive the pass in the vacated area.

Positive Passing

Coaches who are willing to risk passes through, over, or around the defenders must send players into the open spaces behind the defense. The midfield players can develop an attack from apparently negative positions by looking for the forward pass first and then supporting the forwards by running into open attacking space on timely overlaps.

Negative Passing

This term implies unwillingness to take risks or sitting back and waiting for the opponents to make mistakes. The negative team frequently passes square across the field or backward, even when the ball-handler has the time and room in which to advance.

Push Pass

The inside-of-the-foot push pass is the most reliable method of passing because contact is made with the broadest part of the foot (Fig. 8.12).

The approach run should preferably be made in the direction of the pass. Its speed and length are unimportant; it is the last step that counts. It should be timed so that the non-kicking (supporting) foot is placed comfortably alongside and slightly behind the ball, with the knee well-bent

Fig. 8.12 *Push pass. Passing with the inside of the foot while in full stride.*

and the toe pointing toward the receiver. The slightest error in the placement of this foot will throw the player off-balance and off-line and thus diminish the accuracy and range of the pass. The striking foot is brought back naturally during the last stride, as the player begins to turn his near side away from the ball to clear the way for the powerful leg swing.

The eyes are focused on the ball (from start to finish), the ankle is flexed, the upper body is bent slightly forward, and the arms help stabilize and balance the body.

As the leg swing begins, the muscles begin to tighten to ensure the firm impact that produces power. The main source of power is a vigorous leg swing combined with a twisting lower-leg action that culminates in an explosive extension of the knee. The heel is forcefully thrust toward the ball, creating the impression that the player is striking with the heel, and the inside of the foot is driven straight through the dead center of the ball—the sole of the foot clearing the ground by inches.

The body hardly changes position until contact is made. It is allowed to ride forward on the supporting foot, heel to toes, while the trunk falls back slightly to counterbalance the natural follow through of the leg. The long follow through imparts top spin to the ball that keeps it on the ground, ensures greater accuracy, and makes it easier to receive.

The classic striking thrust embodies a long, smooth, firm swing of the entire leg, with the foot maintaining contact with the ball as long as possible.

A common but rather advanced modification of the push pass has the foot stabbing rather than swinging at the ball. The player jabs at the ball with a short, sharp lower-leg action that sharply reduces the back-swing and follow through. It is a more economical kick. Since the leg action is part of the running action, the player can effect the kick with hardly a break in stride.

Warning: When curtailing the back-swing and sweeping follow through of the push pass, the player must stress timing even more to ensure a good delivery—accurate, low, and with sufficient pace.

The inside of the foot must be used like a putter, with the horizontal axis crossing the ball's path perpendicularly. Most errors are caused by an insufficient rotation of the leg, usually due to a straight or stiff knee. The pass thus lacks both accuracy and power. Players with poor balance tend to strike the ball low so that it bounces off the foot as if rebounding off a wall.

Another error is a "hanging" toe. The player fails to dorsiflex the ankle joint and thus finds it almost impossible to establish contact on the metatarsal arch. He hits the ball more around the big toe. As a result the ball is struck off-center and swerves off to the opposite side of the foot used.

Many players try to compensate for their lack of power by turning away from the ball much more than is necessary. They face the ball almost sideward in the hope of gaining power through a pivot. This has a contrary effect, however. It impedes the leg swing and causes the player to drag the ball into the pivot, sending the ball off-target.

Volleying with the Inside of the Foot (Lob Pass)

This is one of the safest methods of passing when the ball is off the ground. The mechanics are much the same as for the push pass except that the foot must be raised to the level of the ball, causing the trunk to fall slightly back and sideward to counter-balance the leg action (Fig. 8.13).

Whenever the ball is above waist level, the player must turn completely sideward in order to raise his foot high enough to play the ball. The leg should be bent at the knee, with the lower leg almost at right angles to the thigh. A short stabbing action with the lower leg will send the ball to its target. Balance and timing are essential to ensure control.

Heavy emphasis must also be placed on the positioning of the inside of the foot at impact. In principle, the ball will rebound in the direction of the approach. Consequently, the horizontal plane of the foot must be adjusted to the angle of the approaching ball and the angle of the intended pass.

A sensitive touch is required to ensure accuracy. In lobbing the ball over the opponents, for example, the player must keep the inside of his foot up and swing the leg upward. In playing the ball to a teammate's feet, it is also advisable to incline the inside of the foot slightly upward to cause the ball to travel in a gentle arc. This kind of pass is much easier to handle than a hard liner around the feet.

Chip Pass

The chip pass offers a useful way of feeding the wing forward from midfield. Since the fullback is usually in a position to intercept a direct ground pass, the only way the halfback can be sure of getting the ball to the wing forward is by chipping it over the fullback's head for the wing forward to take on the run.

Chip Pass with the Full Instep

The approach run must be in line with the direction of the pass and the supporting foot must be close to, almost level with, the ball. Proximity to the ball is the main objective of the approach. The player

must have the ball directly in front of him before he strikes at it. Otherwise, he will have great difficulty getting his foot underneath and chipping the ball crisply with the instep (Fig. 8.14).

The impact must be on the undersurface of the ball, and the line of force must be much nearer the vertical than the horizontal. Backward spin is imparted by keeping the foot in its natural position, rather than extending it, and letting the toe slip underneath the ball. The natural curve of the instep will cause the ball to rise abruptly with backward spin. Very little, if any, follow through is used, as a long follow through will prevent the ball from rising instantly.

The mechanics of chipping with the full instep or the outside of the instep are identical, except that the foot is turned slightly inward. This enables the player to chip and swerve the ball at the same time. The ball is now struck slightly off-center and the follow through is more prominent. This is, however, a most sophisticated skill.

Midfield Tackling

The halfback must be a strong challenger, equally adept on the ground and in the air, though he gets the ball as much through clever interception as hard tackling.

Nowhere is more ball-sense needed than in tackling, as both the opponent and the ball must be considered. The halfback must gauge the precise second the ball comes within reach and momentarily out of the opponent's control. If he tackles too early or too late, he will miss the ball and quite possibly collide with the opponent.

A half-hearted tackle is worthless. It certainly does not win the ball and it causes injuries, as the muscles usually are not tensed enough to absorb the shock. The better the player's ball-sense, the firmer will be his tackle, as he will have more confidence in committing himself. Most tackling techniques are adapted to a particular situation.

Front-Block Tackle

This technique is mostly used by halfbacks in coping with a man coming right at them. The halfback should jockey him, move in, and challenge for the ball when the time advantage is in his favor (Fig. 8.15).

As the attacker approaches with the ball, the halfback should adopt a powerful crouching position with both knees well-bent to lower the center

a
b
c

Fig. 8.13 *Volley passing with the inside of the foot (lob volley).*

a
b
c
d

Fig. 8.14 *Chip pass with the full instep.*

of gravity and absorb the shock of the impact. The more erect the defender, the easier he will be knocked off-balance.

The defender must get as close to the attacker as possible. His aim is to place his supporting foot alongside the ball and shift his center of gravity immediately over this foot while bringing the tackling foot into proper position.

The technique is identical to that of the push pass. The tackling foot is turned at a right angle to the path of the ball to allow the largest part of the foot to contact the ball.

The tackle must be firm and decisive. From his well-balanced position with the leg muscles taut and the toe up, the defender drives the inside of his foot through the dead center of the ball. By moving into the tackle aggressively, he can bring his full weight into the block.

Timing is all-important. It is essential to strike the ball just as the opponent attempts to play it. The follow through must be equally determined in order to brush aside the opponent's foot and take possession of the ball. If close enough, the defender should bend forward and ram his shoulder into the opponent's shoulder (keeping his elbow close to the body) to knock the man off-balance.

a   *b*   *c*

d   *e*

Fig. 8.15 *Front block tackle. The player should try to get his supporting foot as close as possible to the ball. His tackling foot arrives as the opponent plays the ball. It is wedged between the players' feet. The halfback forces the foot through the center of the ball with his weight going through the tackle.*

A well-timed tackle will enable the tackler to break the opponent's resistance and drive the ball straight through him.

If the ball becomes wedged between the tackler and the opponent, the tackler should maintain his balance by keeping his weight on the supporting foot. This will enable him to maintain firm pressure against the ball and use a quick secondary action to free the ball, by dragging it either over the opponent's foot or laterally out of the tackle.

Side-Block Tackle

If the tackler has no chance of confronting the opponent and challenging for the ball, either because the opponent is trying to avoid the challenge or the tackler is trying to catch up from behind, the defender can pivot into a front tackle from the side and use the outer foot to make the actual tackle (Figs. 8.16–8.18).

Fig. 8.16 *The defender uses the side-block technique to block a shot.*

Fig. 8.17 *Side block tackle. The halfback should try to get his supporting foot (near-side foot) level or ahead of the ball. He turns on the heel of the supporting foot to get himself into a tackling position identical to the front block tackle. The knee is well-bent to assure a firm base for resisting the opponent's force. The ball is wedged between the players' feet. If possible, the halfback forces the ball through and out of the tackle in order to keep possession. A well-timed shoulder charge to throw the opponent off-balance might assist in this effort.*

Fig. 8.18 *Side block tackle made with the outside of the foot.*

The principles of the front-block tackle are employed. The major difficulty lies in the timing and coordination of the pivot. As before, the tackler must attempt to get as close to the opponent as possible before committing himself and strive (on his last stride) to bring his supporting foot level with or slightly in front of the ball. He must then pivot quickly and powerfully on this foot while ramming his shoulder against that of the opponent.

He must resist the opponent's momentum while gathering enough momentum of his own to drive the inner part of the outside foot forcefully through the dead center of the ball. With good timing and execution, the tackler should come out with the ball, either by forcing it through the opponent's tackle or by dragging it over or around it.

The common mistake is to commit too early while behind the ball. This will make it impossible to assume the well-balanced, powerful, crouching position that is so essential in placing the weight correctly behind the tackling foot. The result is a stretched, almost split-tackle position that causes

the tackler to fall down or have his tackle easily brushed aside.

Screening and Dribbling

Since the midfield is a heavy traffic center, the halfbacks must learn when to control the flow and make time work for them. That means they must have the ability to hold and work the ball (Fig. 8.19).

Every halfback should learn how to screen the ball with his body. It will enable him to protect the ball, impede the tackle, and gain time for a teammate to move into a supporting position or receive a pass.

It requires courage and confidence to shield the ball from an aggressive tackler. The halfback must learn how to keep the ball close enough to control it and how to adapt his body position to the tackler's thrusts.

Inviting a Tackle

When challenged while advancing the ball, the halfback is inclined to outrace the defender. If he can do so, fine. More often than not, however, it will be wiser to slow down, invite the tackle, and then accelerate as the defender is about to tackle. The surprise will cause the defender to miss the tackle or be late with it and then use up time in regaining his momentum. This stunt is extremely useful in conjunction with a change or reverse of direction, particularly in situations where the challenger approaches from the side.

If the defender rushes in to tackle head on, the halfback may seemingly offer him the ball or force him to commit himself by pretending a kick. He then can check his swing, place the sole of his foot on top of the ball, and draw it back out of the defender's reach. He may follow this by using the inside of the foot to flick the ball either behind the supporting foot or to the side of the controlling foot (Fig. 8.20).

The halfback can turn to either side in edging into a more suitable angle for the next pass. Such quick-turning movements are also useful in switching the attacking thrust from one side of the field to the other.

Throw-In

Though any player may put the ball into play from the touchline, it usually is done by the halfback.

Fig. 8.19 *Body swerve. The attacker feints to his left by using an exaggerated stride as well as a body swerve and quickly reverses direction by pushing the ball with the outside of the foot past the opponent and accelerates, screening the ball while he goes past the defender.*

A long throw to the center of the field can startle the opponent the first time it is used. But once the halfback's power becomes known, the opponents will tend to fall back. This can set them up for the short throw-in.

When a team is attacking near the penalty area, the long throw can be as valuable as a corner kick. The team also should be equipped to handle tight covering. The receiver can signal whether he wants the ball in the air or on the ground; he then can push it back, flick it down the wing, or take it with him. (For more on the throw-in, see Chapter 11.)

REALISTIC PRACTICES

Improving the Delivery of the Long Pass (Crossfield Pass)

Whenever a halfback intercepts a pass or dispossesses an opponent, his immediate objective is to make a pass that will launch an attack. He may have to content himself with a short pass to the other halfback, but he must always be ready to deliver a long pass to forwards upfield in dangerous attacking positions.

The long crossfield pass to the opposite wing forward is a valuable defense-splitting pass, while a firm ground pass offers an effective way for the right halfback to hit the left inside forward.

The ability to read the situation quickly and deliver the correct pass is, as we have stated, one of the most important aspects of a halfback's play. It can and must be developed through constant practice:

1. Five forwards without a ball, plus three halfbacks each with a ball, are set up in a restricted area (half field).

First, the forwards call for a pass by shouting

Fig. 8.20 *The attacker avoids a tackle by quickly drawing the ball back with the sole of the foot in order to flick pass it behind his supporting foot, accelerates, and moves off to the side.*

a halfback's name and running toward him to meet the pass to their feet. Each forward returns the ball by laying off a pass first-time to the halfback.

Next, the forwards again call for a pass, but this time they sprint away so that the halfback must deliver the pass ahead of them and follow up for a return pass.

Third, the same as before except that the forwards work their way toward the goal and finish up with a shot (versus a goalkeeper), while the halfback immediately sprints into a position that will enable him to receive a throw from the keeper.

Fourth, the same as before except that the forward cannot call for the ball. He must, instead, communicate his intention through a sprint, which the halfback must immediately react to with a pass. The halfback who sizes up the situation first will make the pass. The other halfbacks must check, hold the ball, and search for new openings. The forward finishes with a

shot at goal, while the halfback sprints into a position that will enable him to receive the throw from the goalkeeper.

All these drills place special emphasis on the use of the entire area (half-field). Although the passes may initially be restricted to, say, short and low, long and low, or long and high, eventually all sorts of passes will be encouraged, depending upon the situation. If, for example, there is a clear path to the receiver, the halfback must understand that a low, firm pass represents the quickest way to get the ball to him. If there is the slightest danger of an interception, the halfback must react with an air pass.

2. The left wing forward, the right wing forward, and the two inside forwards take up positions across the entire width of the field, with one of them, say the right halfback, assuming a supporting position.

The right wing and inside forwards interpass one-touch in their respective areas on the right flank, while the supporting halfback keeps adjusting his position as he looks for a pass that will enable him to deliver (first-touch) the crossfield pass to the left wing and inside forward. The halfback must immediately follow his pass.

The left wing and inside forwards work the ball just long enough to give the halfback time to sprint across the field, and the activity is then repeated. Since these sprints are rather strenuous, three players may be alternated at halfback.

The purpose of this activity is to perfect a sudden switch of the attacking thrust from one side of the field to the other.

3. Two teams of six players each (three halfbacks, two forwards, and a goalkeeper) scrimmage across the entire width of the field, which is divided into three sections. The midfield section, twenty yards wide, is declared a neutral zone, and must be bridged with a long pass. A five-foot goal is set up at each touchline.

The three halfbacks are backed up by a goalkeeper in the defensive zone, while the two attackers set up in the attacking area. This makes a very realistic two-on-three situation in both zones. The attackers may dribble, but the halfbacks must play two- and later one-touch soccer in moving the ball out of the defensive zone to their forwards in the offensive zone.

The emphasis is on preparing an attack by indirection; that is, drawing the attention to one part of the field through seemingly negative interpassing, while waiting to capitalize on a weakness elsewhere with a timely long pass.

4. Four forwards and two halfbacks (one on either side) set up in an area twenty-five or thirty-five yards wide. Four defenders mark the forwards skintight, as one of the halfbacks starts dribbling the ball. The forwards try to shake their tight-marking defenders to receive the ball from the halfback.

The halfback must, of course, stay alert and deliver the pass to the forward's feet so that the receiver can return the ball first-touch. The halfback must also keep an eye on the halfback on the opposite side. The latter's sprint to his right or left serves as the signal for the ball-handler to deliver the long pass. The forwards then quickly turn around and the activity continues.

5. Same setup as before but with five forwards being marked skintight over half the field. One of the two halfbacks mostly plays a defensive role—he delivers the long pass and is not allowed to cross midfield. The other supports the attack in the role of offensive halfback.

The two halfbacks interpass one-touch, while moving back and forth across the field. The forwards, in turn, try to shake their defenders. The defensive halfback always keeps an eye on the action up front. If a forward creates an opening, he delivers the pass. The attacking halfback then immediately sprints after the ball to support the receiver. The latter tries to play the ball back to the supporting halfback first-touch. The two halfbacks then interpass again, and the activity continues. Eventually the forwards will finish up with a shot at goal. The ball is always brought back to the defensive halfback for the restart.

Modified Games to Improve Halfback Play

A game between teams of five or six players, with a halfback always on the ball side as the odd player, offers effective halfback training. The players use half the field without goals. A team must make ten consecutive passes to score a point; the opponents must not be allowed to touch the ball and the ball cannot leave the area.

The game might also be modified to ensure certain emphases. For example, the receiver may be permitted to touch the ball only thrice, twice, or even once. Or every third pass may have to go to the halfback.

Basketball-style soccer offers an ideal type of lead-up game. The players are permitted to pass the ball only with their hands; dribbling is either forbidden or restricted to one bounce. The coach might also instruct every pass to be made on the ground, below the hip, or above the shoulders, depending upon the players' skill level.

This kind of emphasis is extremely useful in encouraging either a rather deliberate style of play, stressing ball-possession, or a more fluid style, emphasizing mobility, where the players learn to appreciate the importance of supporting the player with the ball.

The coach could then add two miniature-sized goals, one on each touchline, and later on add two more, one at each goal line. Each team can then defend two and attack two. This affords excellent practice on switching the attacking thrust often and quickly.

9

Goalkeeping

The goalkeeper is responsible for the most sensitive area on the field. Whereas the forwards, midfield players, and defenders can rectify a mistake, the goalie's is final. A good team with an unsafe goalkeeper will lack confidence. A poor team with a good goalkeeper will gain confidence with every game.

Goalkeeping has changed drastically through the years. At one time the goalie was a purely defensive player, an acrobat who waited around his goal line to make a last-ditch effort to prevent a goal. Over the years he has had to adapt himself to different styles of play and different techniques.

The modern goalkeeper is an integral part of the defensive unit. He is aware of everything his teammates are doing and the significance of every move. He lets them know that he is with them at all times and blending his skills with theirs. His positional responsibilities are so diversified that he has become an additional fullback, even substituting on occasion for the libero or sweeper.

He has a chance to be a hero in every game by (1) relieving the defense through clever positioning, (2) daring advances from the goal, (3) controlling the immediate goalmouth in the air, or (4) making brilliant dives in desperate situations. By the same token, an error can make him a goat.

It is almost impossible to set any hard and fast rules, as the goalie can never be certain of what is going to happen. Much of his job is predicated on instinct and common sense. Nevertheless, the position demands the mastery of basic skills, a deep understanding of modern defenses, reaction based on this knowledge, and great mobility.

NATURAL QUALIFICATIONS

Physical

No special height is required. The tallest goalies are not always the best. Most top-flight internationalists are about 5'9". Of course a big man will usually have an advantage. An agile six-footer will have an advantage over a smaller man in reaching for the ball, especially on high crosses, and grasping it firmly and more easily. The small man is handicapped in controlling the air in the immediate goalmouth. His limited reach hurts him in fielding the high ball and in diving to make saves. Since he must take great risks to compensate for his size, his positional play will suffer. The tall goalkeepers, on the other hand, are loathe to get down for low shots, are often weak in diving, and are sometimes slow to regain their feet. They also are usually slower than the average-sized player.

It would appear that the ideal height for a goalkeeper is between 5'9" and 6'1", and that he should have proportionate weight and strength.

Mobility and Speed

Speed and quickness are essential. Once the decision is made to go for the ball, the goalie must react

163

instantly. A lightning start is imperative. The goalie does not have to have speed for one hundred yards, but he must be fast for five–ten yards. Speed also comes in handy in his role as an extra defender. A fast sprint from his goal area can cut off any danger from a through ball.

Quick Reaction and Agility

Well-developed reflexes and cat-like agility must be developed through correct training exercises. The goalie cannot afford indecisiveness: Shall I come out or not? Shall I use my feet or dive?

The goalie must come out when the defense is beaten. He must do this decisively and courageously, and he must be ready to jump, dive, or fling himself through the air to make the save. This requires great skill—skill predicated on a full range of body movement on a well-coordinated, supple body.

Psychological (Concentration)

Concentration is particularly important, as goalies sometimes have long periods of inactivity. Yet they must always be ready for a sudden counterattack. The slightest lapse in concentration can be disastrous.

Gordon Banks, a great, used to claim that he was "absolutely exhausted" after a game. This more often than not indicated a mental rather than physical fatigue. A goalkeeper can become physically tired from hurling himself around, but it is the mental stress and concentration that wear him out. Even international goalies are often troubled by nerves and will give away easy goals when their nerves get the better of them.

Anyone who intends to become a good goalie must learn to keep calm during the game and not to let the tension get him down. You can call this the number one requirement.

Anticipation, Positioning, and Imagination

These are the goalie's greatest assets. His ability to anticipate, to predict what the opponent will do in the next few seconds, and to react to the ball a split second before it comes are crowning qualities.

The good goalie is a student of the game; he comes to the game prepared. He seems to attract the ball like a magnet because he is in the right spot at the right time. He displays good judgment and know-how in reducing the angle of the shot. He anticipates through knowledge, rather than relying wholly on instinct.

Where the great goalkeeper makes everything look easy, the flashy goalkeeper is always launching himself at the last moment and making simple shots look difficult.

The "secret" lies in a highly developed sense of positional play. The good goalie often seems to make the save *before* the shot is made. How many times have you seen a forward apparently drive the ball straight into the goalie's stomach for a very simple save? In many of these instances, the goalie should be credited for a wonderful sense of anticipation. By placing himself in position for the expected shot, he is able to make the save look easy. Anticipation stems mainly from the study of tactics and skills, and reading them for an attacking pattern.

Knowledge is thus the key to success, and this can be acquired through observation of the opponents: whether they tend to use the outside or inside of the foot, whether they are stronger with the left or right foot, and which is their favorite shot. Every player has certain habits, which the goalie can observe during midfield play. He should store them in mind for emergency situations, such as when his goal is threatened.

Confidence

The goalkeeper must be sure of himself. He cannot exhibit the slightest uncertainty, as the opponents will instantly exploit it. He must radiate confidence and almost dare the forwards to get the ball past him. He must have that Gordon Banks aura of invincibility about him.

He will often have to react like lightning to make a save, as he has only a split second to make a decision. Once he has made a decision, he must go through with it. It is far better to be decisive and wrong occasionally than to be indecisive all the time. An unsure goalie tends to make fatal mistakes and have an unsettling influence on the team.

Whenever the goalie does make a mistake, even a serious one, he should not stop and dwell on it. He must maintain his concentration, keep cool, resist being rattled. He should transmit confidence to the team either through his safe handling or by shouting instructions and encouragement.

Mistakes are inevitable, of course. Everyone makes them. But the good goalies make the fewest. Experience is the best mistake-eraser there is.

Courage

Whenever the goalie goes for a ball, he must be prepared to move everyone out of the way by the strength and determination of his jump or dive. He must have the nerve to expose himself to hard physical contact where he will have little chance of protection.

It takes courage to launch oneself at the feet of a huge forward bearing down on goal (Fig. 9.1). But, like everything else, it can become second nature and be executed without a second thought.

The goalie who thinks twice about going down is the one who is generally injured. This does not mean that the goalie who takes a courageous dive will never be injured. He occasionally will. But most of the time he will not—and he will be saving sure goals.

STYLE OF GREAT GOALKEEPERS

Some goalies look great diving across the goal to deflect the ball over the crossbar, flinging themselves on the ball to smother a low shot, or turning in midair to make a spectacular save on an unexpectedly deflected shot. They may seem equal to anything that the opposing forwards can unload on them.

Appearances can be deceiving, however. Next week that seemingly unbeatable goalie can let in three goals, each of which could have been prevented by cutting off a cross ball before it reached the scoring forward.

The obvious weakness of this kind of goalie is his positional sense, pronounced through his reluctance to move from his line. This applies to the professional as well as amateur and scholastic goalie. Why does a goalkeeper seem brilliant in one match and unsafe and ordinary in another? The answer is simple—it is a matter of "style."

Showman-Exhibitionist

This is a typical expression of the South American temperament. Gilmar dos Santos Neves of Santos

Fig. 9.1 *"It takes courage to launch oneself at the feet of a huge forward bearing down on goal."*

Fig. 9.2 *Gilmar dos Santos Neves of Santos and Brazil.*

and Brazil played on the world championship teams of 1958 and 1962, and appeared in the 1966 World Cup. All in all he played over a hundred games for Brazil. His play and deportment embodied the best in Brazilian soccer, while showing great restraint in an occasional display of temperament (Fig. 9.2).

Ladislao Mazurkiewicz of Uruguay, though of Polish parentage, represents South American artistry at its very best. He has a rare quality for a South American goalie. He never gets emotionally

165

Fig. 9.3 *Lew Yashin of Moscow-Dynamo and Russia demonstrates his skill as he makes a spectacular diving save.*

Fig. 9.4 *Gordon Banks of Stokes City and England.*

involved in the game and never senses defeat—only danger. Even in moments of crisis, he finds a way of suspending time and motion, making even the most spontaneous save emerge from cool deliberation. Mazurkiewicz is one of the world's finest goalkeepers, perhaps because he tempers the South American predilection for being unnecessarily and dangerously spectacular with the European characteristic of being in the right place at the right time.

These goalkeepers naturally excite the spectators, and very often they prefer to do this rather than safely catch the ball. Their concentration and positional play suffer as a result. By inviting danger, this type of goalie endangers his team. Because of his natural ability, he may be able to cover up and make a breathtaking save. But he will not do as well when subtlety is called for in controlling the immediate goalmouth or simple positional play. He always appears to be at full stretch. Nothing comes easy for him. He seems to be living on his nerves and this tension communicates itself to the rest of the defense, producing the feeling that the next crisis is never far away.

Tactician-Craftsman

The more formidable type, like Lew Yashin of Moscow-Dynamo and Russia, commanded worldwide popularity for over a decade (Fig. 9.3). He

played in three successive world championships (1958, 1962, and 1966) and also for the FIFA team against England in 1963. A former basketball player, he combined great agility with exceptional positional skill. He pioneered command of the penalty area when his team was attacking, and he made a point of almost becoming a fullback in his own right.

Then, of course, there is Gordon Banks of Stokes City and England, who has played more than fifty international matches and is the most capped goalkeeper in English history (Fig. 9.4). His superb anticipation, clean handling, magnificent reflexes, and fine positional sense earned him the reputation, particularly during the 1966 World Cup, of being one of the finest goalkeepers in the world.

Though he must be spectacular at times to make saves that other goalies cannot reach, this sort of goalkeeper not only has natural flair, courage, and agility, but a thoughtful, scientific attitude toward his play. He makes every save look easy and accomplishes everything in a thorough, workmanlike manner. He never goes out of his way to make a play look spectacular. Simplicity and safety are his motto.

POSITIONAL PLAY

Defense

The goalie's situations change quickly and often. He receives few cues from the general development of play. He must adopt positions based upon reasonable probabilities and be prepared to readjust as circumstances change.

The good goalie never loses positional awareness. This is closely allied to anticipation. It is essential in that the goalie must always know where he stands in relation to the goal, the posts, and the other players. And he must have complete control of the goal area plus ninety percent aerial control of the penalty area.

The goalie also must have a deep understanding of defensive tactics, as well as the ability to read the development of the opposing attack. The goalie who always stays on the goal line is giving away his great advantage of using his hands within the whole penalty area.

He must be prepared to act as a cover for his defense, giving depth to the defensive system. As he develops experience in anticipating through passes, he can cut off many dangerous attacking movements on the edge of the penalty area and occasionally outside it.

The great goalkeepers, whenever the ball is in the opponent's half, move out to the edge of the eighteen-yard line, maybe even a few yards beyond it. From there they adjust their position so that they can easily dash forward to kick away a long pass or slip back toward their line.

As the attack approaches, they retreat to avoid being caught by a surprise high shot. Even when the play is in their half of the field, they can deploy near the penalty spot. From there they can go forward, perhaps to the edge of the eighteen-yard line, to catch or punch away a long ball down the middle or one angled in from a wider position on either flank.

Playing the Angle

Whenever an attacking player breaks away, the goalie must present him with the smallest possible target. By changing his position according to the goal behind him and the forward in front, he can

reduce the forward's target. He can make the normally big goalmouth seem very small indeed (Fig. 9.5).

Once in a while one finds a goalie with an intuitive gift for moving into a position that narrows the angle. In most cases, this is learned through trial and error, plus an immense amount of hard work and training.

The largest possible target is presented by a frontal position, wherein the goalkeeper stands in the center of the goal. The simplest way to narrow the angle is, of course, by moving out and reducing the shooting angle. It is good elementary psychology to move out confidently toward the forward who has broken clear. This will distract him, put pressure on him, and prevent him from shooting as calmly and carefully as he would with the goalkeeper on the goal line.

The goalkeeper who leaves his goal indiscriminately, however, is as vulnerable as the one who never gets off the line. He should always be guided by caution and intelligently calculate the risks he is taking. Things he must consider are:

1. If he does not advance, the forward will have the greatest target area at which to aim.
2. If he advances too soon, the forward who has the ball may pass to another.
3. If he advances too far, the forward may attempt to chip or lob the ball over his head. (The farther the goalie advances, the easier this becomes.)
4. If he advances too quickly and without control and balance, he will make it easy for the forward to dribble the ball around him and into goal.
5. If the forward is running very quickly, his ball-control may not be good. A quick advance may enable the goalie to fall on the ball before the forward can regain control.

Whenever the attacker comes from an oblique angle, the goalie should move slightly outward and to the side. He should obtain a central placement that will enable him to save left or right.

The tendency is to get too close to the near post. This of course will sharply diminish the forward's chances of scoring at the near post. It is a cardinal error for the goalie to be beaten there. The intelligent forward knows this, and he could turn the ball back sharply across the goalmouth to an incoming player. Or he can beat the goalie with a delicate lob or inswinger to the far post.

Fig. 9.5 *Narrowing the shooting angle.*

As a rule, the goalie should immediately come out to challenge the attacker who has broken through. He should advance with speed and cat-like agility, then slow down or even come to a complete stop as he nears the attacker. This will enable him to make the play from a firm, well-balanced position. The goalie who rushes forward with reckless abandon will find it extremely difficult to dive or change direction, which will make him vulnerable to a clever attacker. The goalkeeper who comes out of goal quickly is very difficult to beat. He forces the ball-handler to keep control of the ball as well as steady himself for the shot.

The smart goalie will try to determine whether the opponent is so one-footed that he will have to bring the ball onto his good foot before shooting. The goalie can then jockey this kind of forward into a less dangerous position, make him use his weak foot, or force him to momentarily lose control over the ball.

The goalie should try to anticipate the direction of the shot. A close study of the player's style can help on this. For example, the wing forward cutting in toward goal may not be able to shoot at an angle and is thus likely to pass the ball back. If the goalie has spotted this tendency, he can ignore the possibilities of a shot and move off his line to try to smother the center as it comes across. He may also feint to rush forward and then retreat in an effort to slow the attacker down or get him to change his mind.

The goalkeeper must arrive at an absolute understanding with his defenders. He, the fullbacks, and the center halfback must have absolute confidence in one another and play as a unit. The goalie can smother a potentially dangerous situation by coming out intelligently and swiftly as soon as he realizes that none of his defenders can intervene. The defenders, on the other hand, must realize that whenever the goalkeeper advances into the penalty area, he leaves his goal wide open, and that they must then give him immediate cover.

Special Situations

Free Kick, Direct or Indirect, within Scoring Range

The preparation hinges upon the opponent's shooting ability and the confidence and ability of the goalkeeper. Whenever the situation requires the setting up of a wall, the goalkeeper must arrange it, instructing the defenders where and how to line up.

The defensive wall should always cover the near corner of the goal. The goalie should deploy the man at the flank in line with the near post and the placed ball, then add a yard or so to prevent a "banana" shot from swerving by and into the goal. The goalie should then position himself at the end of the wall, giving himself a full view of the ball and enabling him to make the save, whether the ball comes directly at him or floats over the wall.

Corner Kick

The goalie should place his men as he wants them, not as they wish. It is best to put the right fullback on the right-hand post and the left fullback on the left post. These are the only two defenders in his area. The center halfback should deploy on the edge of the goal area in position to counter any ball landing near the penalty spot.

The goalie should set up close to the far post and slightly in front of the goal. From this position he can control the situation. He can see the opponents peripherally while concentrating on the flight of the ball.

He should not commit himself until he is able to judge the flight. If possible he should catch the ball, but when the area is crowded with attackers and he is likely to be challenged, it is wiser to punch the ball out of danger toward the touch lines.

The defenders marking the men who are trying to block the goalie's view should clear out to the edge of the box to give the goalie more maneuverability and more space to attack the inswinging cross. However, the fullback may be called upon to supply cover when the goalie vacates the goal.

Whenever a high cross is floated into the six-yard area, the goalie must call for it and instantly move out to catch it. There are no half measures—he must go. (See also p. 225.)

Penalty Kick

This is perhaps the greatest trial for the goalkeeper. His position is dictated by the rules, which state that he must stand on the goal line with both feet stationary until the penalty-taker has made contact with the ball.

The penalty situation creates psychological warfare between the goalie and the kicker. How should the goalie deal with this situation? Can he induce the opponent to make an error? First and most important, his behavior and positioning should radiate absolute confidence. During the kicker's approach run, the goalie can feint with his trunk, swerving to one side but keeping the feet stationary, to induce the opponent to put the ball to the opposite side—toward which the goalie is prepared to react. Many goalies decide in advance to dive to a particular side. This is taking a fifty-fifty chance on becoming a hero or a goat.

The goalie can deduce the direction and pace of the shot from the kicker's approach run and body and foot positioning. He must make certain that these actions are not ruses, however. That is why it is essential to concentrate completely on the ball. (See also p. 237.)

Directing the Defense

This is imperative on a high ball coming into the goalmouth. The goalie must let his defenders know what he is going to do by shouting instructions and warnings. He must indicate any weakness in marking loudly and forcefully (Fig. 9.6).

If he is going to take the ball himself, he must make his move decisively, without worrying about the people around him. If he calls for a "back" pass, he should not leave the goal until the direction of the pass becomes a certainty. And whenever the goalie leaves the goal for a pass, the defender must take another look to locate him. Any misunderstanding on this play can easily lead to a score.

Fig. 9.6 *Directing the defense.*

That is why it is safer to place the ball to one side of the goal.

Offense

Launching the Attack

All goalkeepers are the last line of defense. The great ones are also the first line of attack. When the ball is in their hands, they think like a super midfield player, taking advantage of any opportunity to initiate an attack. The goalie who can begin an attack with every clearance can be an enormous asset to his team. The goalie who kicks or throws aimlessly is wasting good openings.

Clearance and the Four-Step Rule

The four-step rule has supposedly eliminated time-killing. The goalkeeper who takes more than four steps incurs an indirect free kick at the point of infraction. The goalie may, however, choose to take the steps alternately instead of consecutively and intersperse them with rolling or dribbling the ball. Either way he may be challenged by an opponent.

The goalie must now learn to make space with the ball while staying within the rules. Once he gains possession, his only chance of advancing to the edge of the penalty box is by finding an open route and rolling and/or dribbling the ball toward either of the two corners of the box. Once there he should be composed enough to assess his outlets and deliver a quick throw upfield. He may also kick or, if his defense has been under pressure, he can wait until his defense is well-balanced and prepared for any move.

Problems immediately occur when a forward "stands" on a goalie with the ball. This is where the rule is farcical. If caught on the goal line or by-line and hemmed in by an opponent, the goalie must make a clearance from a ridiculous position.

Tactical Considerations

The problem is when to throw, when to hold, and when to kick. Tactical considerations may delay the clearance. The goalie may want to give his teammates time to move into attacking positions or to relax and regain the composure they need to operate as a unit.

The goalie's use of the ball depends largely on the situation. A throw and a kick can be used to various advantages. As a rule, however, the goalie must know how to use the ball to initiate attacks. Once he has made a save, he should not play the ball aimlessly downfield. He must think of using it to the best advantage.

How and where should he send the ball? Up until this point, we have stressed the importance of speed. How can the goalkeeper satisfy this tactical requirement? Answer: By immediately sending the ball to the teammate who is in the most favorable position.

Many goalies err in unnecessarily bouncing the ball before making the throw or clearance. Others tend to lie on the ground too long after making a diving save. They should regain their feet immediately. Unnecessary movement or slowness in returning to the basic position can lose valuable split seconds that may cost an opportunity for a successful counterattack.

The two commonly used throwing techniques are rolling the ball underhand as in bowling or throwing overhand as in baseball. The throw

170

should never go to a player who is likely to face an immediate challenge, and it should be kept low whenever possible to make it easier for the receiver to control. The goalie should always throw to the side opposite from which the attack was made, as this side will be less congested.

Whenever the goalkeeper is drawn out of the penalty area, he can no longer use his hands. He must then clear the ball or pass it to a teammate with his feet.

Every goalie should be capable of achieving distance with his goal and drop kicks. The goal kick should be his and not the defenders' exclusive responsibility. Why should a fullback not take the goal kick? Because he momentarily takes himself out of the game and thus gives the opposition a numerical advantage.

The goalie who takes the kick himself becomes a more integral part of the team—a psychological factor of some importance. Details on the mechanics of the kick are unnecessary, except to recommend the use of the full instep or inside of the instep for maximum accuracy and distance.

SPECIAL SKILLS AND TECHNIQUES

Goalkeepers use slightly different methods to accommodate their particular physiques. All these methods are the result of long practice and are basically safe.

The first objective is sure possession of the ball. Catching offers the safest method. It takes the edge off a dangerous situation, provided the goalie does not err during or after catching the ball. A safe pair of hands obviously can be an enormous confidence builder.

The goalie's motto must be "safety first," regardless of the technique used to deal with the ball. Carelessness can cause more difficulties around the goal than any other factor.

Since the goalkeeper must, above all, be able to stop the ball safely and surely, he must observe certain fundamental principles. He may not be able to stick to them all the time, but he will become unsafe whenever he deliberately ignores them.

1. Whenever possible, the goalie must place as much of his body behind the ball as possible—whether standing, jumping, falling, or diving. The ball may slip through his hands, but it will not be able to slip through his stomach or chest.

2. He must give with the force of the ball, never meeting it with straight arms, stiff hands, or a rigid body.

3. Quick footwork enables the good goalie to make saves look easy. By using his feet quickly to get himself into the right position, he makes it appear as though every shot is fired straight at him.

4. He must catch the ball rather than punch it.

5. He must keep his eyes and attention exclusively on the ball until he has complete control. He must avoid such pitfalls as trying to catch the ball and move off at the same time, or looking away for a passing opportunity or for an opponent's challenge before he has complete control of the ball.

Any goalkeeper who is apprehensive about being challenged while trying to make the save is going to make frequent mistakes.

The goalkeeper must work on catching or fielding the ball at all heights—from ground level to points that require a full upward or sideward leap. Whenever possible, he should bring his hands behind the ball as it arrives and draw it in as quickly as possible to his midsection.

Catching or fielding the ball cleanly is, thus, the most important basic technique. It puts the goalie in a position of almost unassailable authority.

Going Down on One Knee

This has proven to be the safest method of fielding a ground ball. It lends itself particularly well to situations where the goalie has to move to the side to field the ball, and it also permits him to move in quickly, collect the ball, and move away fairly quickly (Fig. 9.7).

Its basic principle is to keep the legs in a moderate stride position at right angles to the approaching ball. The goalie then bends down on the leading leg, which bears most of the body weight, and slides the trailing leg and knee almost in touch with the heel of the leading foot. This forms an excellent second barrier.

The trunk is pivoted from the hip to face the oncoming ball, with the upper part leaning moderately forward. The elbows are tucked in against the rib cage so that the forearms are parallel, and the hands are almost at ground level, palms upward, fingers comfortably spread, almost touching, ready to scoop the ball off the ground. The ball can then

a	b

Fig. 9.7 *Front and side views of moving to the side to field a ball, going down on one knee.*

a	b

Fig. 9.8 *Front and side views of scooping up a ground ball coming straight at the goalkeeper.*

be channeled snugly into the midsection to prevent any chance of its escaping.

Any kneeling position in which the knee sticks out toward the ball should be avoided to prevent having the ball bounce off the knee and out of control. The goalie should also try to avoid being caught with his full weight on the kneeling leg, as that would immobilize him. Any unexpected bounce could then be disastrous.

Fielding a Ball at Ground Level or Just Above

Most goalies prefer to keep their legs together and straight. They deploy across the ball's path and bend forward from the hips to field the ball. Keeping the palms upward with the fingers comfortably spread, they meet the ball and give on impact to reduce its pace. The velocity will cause the ball to roll up the forearms and, as the trunk straightens, the ball is clutched firmly against the body (Fig. 9.8).

Catching the Ball Directly against the Midsection

This is the safest method. The goalie again positions himself in line with the oncoming ball, and, depending upon the height of the ball, catches it against his waist or chest. Since the secret of goalkeeping is a relaxed, sure pair of hands, backed up by the softest possible surface to absorb the impact of the ball, the stomach obviously is better suited than the chest (Fig. 9.9).

When catching the ball against the lower chest or stomach, the goalie sets his "trap" with a slightly crouched trunk, bent arms, and elbows tightly pressed against the side of the rib cage (Fig. 9.10). He turns his palms upward and spreads his fingers comfortably to allow the forearms and hands to be flung around the ball at the moment of impact. As the ball is trapped and buried, the hip folds simultaneously and the impact is absorbed by the stomach. The goalie folds at the waist and, if necessary, takes a slight hop backward to add to the cushioning effect.

A slight variation is necessary when the ball has to be caught against the chest (Fig. 9.11). The hands are again held palm upward, but this time with the elbows slightly in front of the chest. This provides a deeper chest cavity and an additional impact absorber in the biceps. By simultaneously bending

Fig. 9.9 *Catching the ball against the mid-section.*

the elbows and biceps and shrugging the shoulders, the goalie presents a deep chest cavity that can give on impact. Timing is vital in both methods. If the "trap" collapses too late, the ball will rebound out of control.

A third method exploits the American athlete's natural inclination to catch everything with his hands. The goalie meets the ball with his hands, palms close to each other, with hands and fingers comfortably spread, firm but not rigid. At the moment of impact, the hands give to absorb the pace, the arms bend at the elbow, and the hands slide around the outside of the ball, as the goalie clutches it tightly against his chest. It is essential to catch the ball slightly in front of the head to enable the goalie to judge its flight carefully and watch it right into his hands.

A common error is placing the hands on the outside of the ball instead of behind it. This is particularly dangerous when the ball is slippery, as the ball may go right through his hands.

Another common fault stems from tension: the goalie's failing to have loose hands and wrists as

Fig. 9.10 *Catching a medium-high ball against the lower chest.*

Fig. 9.11 *Catching a high ball against the chest.*

he catches the ball. He will usually fail to kill its pace and will wind up dropping it. Good goalies will catch and hold onto the ball in almost any circumstance.

Catching a High Ball

One of the most difficult saves is the crossed high ball, usually a center from either wing. Perfect balance, positioning, and timing are required to eliminate the danger and make the save in crowded areas (Fig. 9.12).

Knowledge of when and when not to go is provided by experience and constant practice, but the goal area is the goalkeeper's domain. All centers and corners into this area are his responsibility. He must, additionally, always face the direction from which the ball is coming and leap out toward it only when he thinks he has it covered or when it is within range.

"Keep your eye on the ball" is a rule that applies to every sport. In soccer it applies most urgently to the goalkeeper going out to catch a high ball. He has many temptations to take his eyes off the ball, many obstacles in the shape of well-meaning defenders and hostile attackers. He must resist looking at any of them and be prepared for the inevitable physical contact.

As mentioned before, he should call when going out for a ball, and his defenders should get out of his way. They should either mark a man or drop back onto the goal line—always on the alert for a dropped ball and ready to kick clear.

The flight of the ball must be judged precisely, and the goalie must leap with power. This requires good strength. The jump is launched with a single foot takeoff, with the goalie reaching up with both hands behind the ball, fingers outspread. By moving toward the ball, the goalie can pick up momentum and add height to his leap, as this makes for a natural run-up to a single-foot takeoff. The stride before the foot plant is a long one that permits the goalie to swing his free leg powerfully forward

Fig. 9.12 *Catching a high ball.*

and upward. This free-leg swing is most important. It assists in the attainment of height and serves as a fender against onrushing attackers.

If the shot is fierce, the goalie should allow his hands to give and take the pace off the ball, just as on the shot to the stomach. The tendency of young goalies is to let the ball drop until they can clasp it to the chest—enabling the forwards to get up and head the ball. However, the arm-length catch, if timed correctly, should outreach any forward. The ball is watched right into the hands, with the elbows bending to bring the ball quickly down in front of the body, where, if possible, it is clutched to the chest tight and secure.

The goalkeeper should always try to avoid jumping from a standing position. By jumping on the run, he can leap forward and upward. This will not only give him greater height but will force the opponents out of his way and cut down on catching errors, especially those caused by jostling opponents.

He should always bring the ball in quickly and land in a crouched position, ready to dodge and weave his way out of a crowded situation to make his clearance. In overcrowded penalty areas, courage is needed in going out strongly to meet the challenge of physical contact.

One sure mark of a good goalie is the safe fielding of high balls. With his experience and confidence, he can venture beyond the six-yard box and take some weight off his defenders by catching balls as far out as the penalty spot, depending on where the ball is hit.

If possible the high balls should always be taken as the keeper moves forward and upward, although it is possible to save a high ball in a backward angled position.

Balls hit from touchlines or backward positions enable the goalie to get out beyond the penalty spot. Since the ball usually takes a fair amount of time to reach its destination, the goalie has that extra leeway to get out.

He has less of a chance to cut out a ball hit from close range crosses. Since he is dragged toward the near post, he literally has only a fraction of a second to intercept a ball crossed from these positions.

Positioning in Relation to Crosses

For balls hit from the touchline area, the goalie should assume a central position or one slightly farther back to enable him to move either toward the cross or back across to gather the center. Centers closer to the goal tend to drag the keeper farther toward the near post. He must move toward the near post to cover any shot. Passes too are often placed there. At the same time he must be prepared to intercept balls aimed at the far post.

Deflecting and Punching

Goalies catching a high ball should anticipate being charged by a forward as soon as they touch the ground. This especially applies near the goal line. The goalie often knows that a forward is dangerously close and that an element of risk is involved in catching the ball. Since his motto is safety first, the obvious thing to do is turn the ball over the crossbar.

It is extremely unsafe simply to flick the ball over with the back of the hand: The young goalie should use both palms whenever possible. With experience and knowledge he will learn to use a one-handed deflection, enabling him to achieve slightly more height.

In *deflecting* the ball over the crossbar or around the uprights, most goalies use the upper part of the palms, including the fingers, rather than the back of the hand or fist, to eliminate the danger of having the ball slip off the knuckles (Figs. 9.13 and 9.14). The goalie leaps high as though to catch the ball, but, upon contacting it with the palm and fingers, flicks it over the crossbar with the fingers. To avoid any possible error, the goalie should always try to establish contact above the crossbar.

Quite often the goalkeeper will have to play safe on a thunderous shot just below the crossbar. He will have to deflect it over the crossbar. Timing

a   b   c

d   e

Fig. 9.13 *Deflecting (tipping) a ball over the crossbar. Goalkeeper uses the opposite hand and turns with the ball to see it go over the crossbar.*

Fig. 9.14 *Deflecting over the crossbar.*

becomes of vital importance to allow for the upward thrust of the slightly inclined hand.

When the goalie has to dive for a powerful shot, almost beyond the limits of his reach, he again must use his hands to turn the ball safely around the uprights (Fig. 9.15).

Punching becomes strategic on high balls in the penalty area that are being chased by forwards. The likelihood of collisions makes catching unsafe.

Both fists should be used whenever possible, as they make a larger, flatter surface and safer, more accurate contact. The inexperienced keeper should punch the ball in the direction he is facing, positioning himself so that he can punch to the wings. This will give him time to get back to the goal even if the ball goes to an opponent (Fig. 9.16).

The goalie must be decisive. He should make his run early and confidently; hesitation will be fatal. He must concentrate on the flight of the ball at all times, forgetting that anyone else is on the

Fig. 9.15 *Deflecting over the crossbar.*

Fig. 9.16 *Punching. Impact surface when using both fists.*

177

Fig. 9.17 *Goalkeeper intercepts a cross, punching it clear with both fists.*

Fig. 9.18 *Goalkeeper intercepts a cross by diving and punching the ball clear.*

Fig. 9.19 *Goalkeeper, using one-fisted punch, clears the ball from the onrushing attacker.*

field. He should punch through the ball, not at it (Figs. 9.17 and 9.18).

Occasionally, particularly when dealing with high crosses, he will have to punch the ball away with one hand. When he does, he should use the fist and arm farther from the ball, as this allows a more natural arm swing (Fig. 9.19).

When jumping to punch or catch, the goalie often will have to cope with a challenger trying to head the ball. The possibility of collision either in the air or after landing is obvious, and the goalie must protect himself whenever possible.

Most goalies avoid exposing their fully stretched bodies by raising one knee. After a one-footed takeoff, they swing their opposite knee into a right-angled position to obtain greater protection from a knock.

Some goalies raise both knees, but this technique has one drawback—it makes a safe landing rather difficult, as the goalie can be easily knocked off-balance while in the air. The player who tries to completely tuck his body will increase the tendency of his body to turn or spin.

The Diving Save

The goalkeeper in midair, traveling at top speed, is one of the most thrilling sights in soccer. Even when he positions himself correctly, he may still have to make a spectacular dive for the save. The ball can be shot at a speed of seventy-five miles per hour, and this gives the goalie little time to react. His view also may be obstructed until the last fraction of a second, or the shot may be deflected on the way to the goal, so that the goalie will have to change position and react instantly to the new circumstances.

His sense of anticipation and experience will be great assets. But his reaction and agility in flinging himself at the ball, as well as his determination not to be beaten, will prove to be the decisive factors in making the save.

Though the height of the ball and the distance will vary, the technique of diving remains the same. It starts from the anticipatory stance, which varies with the individual. Some stay lower than others, have their feet farther apart, and bring their hands up higher and closer to the body. But the most important thing is to be relaxed physically, with

ankle, knee, and hip joint slightly bent, and the mind vibrantly alert.

Smothering a Low Shot

There is nothing to the dive when the ball is close enough to be fallen upon. In fact the goalie can just drop on it, rather than dive. This will enable

Fig. 9.20 *Smothering a low shot.*

a   b

c

Fig. 9.21 *Diving for a medium-high ball to catch and tuck in tightly to the body.*

d

179

him to cover the ball in the shortest possible time (Fig. 9.20).

If he dives chest first, the ball may slip underneath him. If he dives sideward, presenting the largest possible barrier between the ball and the goal, he is more likely to stop it. The outer shin, knee, thigh, hip, and trunk contact the ground to prevent the ball from passing under the trunk.

The goalie should smother the ball by placing the nearer hand behind it and the other slightly above, then fall on the ball to protect it with the body. He should immediately draw the ball into his midsection and roll over toward the onrushing opponent, drawing up his knees and bringing in his head to protect the ball and himself.

Diving for a High Ball

When the ball cannot be reached with a dive from a standing position, the goalie should step sideward, shuffle, or take a crossover step before launching himself (Fig. 9.21).

In the shuffle (a series of quick, lateral glide steps), the first stride is taken with the foot nearer to the intended line of flight. The other foot follows naturally, and so does the takeoff.

In the crossover step, which may or may not follow the shuffle, depending upon the distance to be covered, the goalie pivots on the foot nearer the direction of the dive and crosses over with the opposite leg. Both feet get a solid purchase, with the greatest force obtained from the crossover leg. When diving to the right, the left foot becomes the take-off member, and vice versa. Although the shuffle and crossover step permit the goalie to cover more ground, they are time-consuming (Fig. 9.22).

The length and speed of the dive obviously will depend upon a powerful and explosive takeoff. The goalie must face the ball on a diagonal before the takeoff to reduce the angle of flight, thus saving distance and facilitating the handling of the situation. The takeoff is actually initiated by both legs. It starts with a push off the far-leg to transfer the body weight to the leg nearer the dive, which is considerably bent at the knee and hip joint. The initial push-off should also cause the body to fall in the direction of the ball.

The takeoff with the near-leg has to be timed in a way that assures a straight body thrust, rather than an arch, to the ball. Time is decisive and the goalie must choose the quickest way to the ball. The takeoff involves a vigorous extension of the ankle, knee, and hip joint, with both arms forcefully swung up toward the ball and the opposite knee thrust toward the chest. While in the air, the hip joint of this leg should be forcefully extended to add another few inches of reach to the dive, and both legs should be well-bent at the knee joint to provide stability and balance, while the trunk is in a full pike position.

The goalkeeper should, on every dive, try to observe the cardinal principle of safety first and put his body behind his hands to form a second barrier in front of the ball. He should catch the ball, but if there is any doubt about making a safe catch and an opponent is challenging, it is wisest to deflect the ball around the uprights.

While still in the air, he must prepare for a safe landing by bringing the ball into the "nest" formed by his arms and tucked-in far-leg. Diving and catching in this spectacular way is often necessary, but it is of no use if, on landing, the goalie drops the ball or allows it to roll out of his grasp.

Many goalkeepers fail to utilize the leg nearer to the ground to break the impact of the fall. The nearer leg contacts the ground with the outside of the foot, shin, thigh, hip, upper arm, trunk, and shoulder, in that order. The rocking action breaks the impact of the fall and the goalie immediately tucks his body, hugging the ball closely to the body, arms, and knees to protect it from jarring loose. The momentum of the dive allows him to roll over toward the onrushing attacker and confront him with his back.

Another daring dive worthy of mention is the one high into the air. Its height will prevent the goalie from establishing initial contact with the near-leg, as he descends headfirst. While descending, he adjusts into a tuck position and uses the outside of the forearm and upper arms nearer the field to break the fall. The shoulder and then the back turn toward the field as he rolls over to break the impact of the fall.

Diving at the Opponent's Feet

Whenever a forward breaks through the defense for an open shot at goal, the keeper must come out to narrow the shooting angle. If quick enough, he occasionally may be able to dive at the opponent's feet and block the shot. This requires courage, confidence, and great skill, as the slightest hesitation can result in either an injury or a goal.

The essential factors are speed, agility, and split-second timing in pouncing on the ball. The experienced goalie can often sense when the forward bearing down on him has lost momentary control of the ball, or he can launch his dive the very moment the forward prepares to shoot, literally taking the ball off his foot.

It is essential to get down quickly because the goalie's vulnerability in such situations is the low shot just alongside his feet. Getting down too early, however, may leave him stranded, since the forward may dribble around him or lob the ball over him. The second most important requisite is for the goalie to use his body as a wall between the goal and the ball in order to block or smother the shot. The third consideration is to concentrate solely on

a

b

c

d

e

Fig. 9.22 *Flat-out dive to turn the ball around the uprights.*

the ball and the opponent's feet. Great goalies become very skillful at "reading" feet.

Tricks and feints can also be used in the goalie's highly specialized position. When diving for a save or at an opponent's feet, the goalie can use a feint to excellent advantage. By swaying in one direction, he may cause the attacker to shoot or move in the other—and be ready and waiting for the man when he does.

If the goalie rushes out toward the oncoming attacker, he can be beaten easily. If he moves out quickly and then slows down, he probably can get the attacker to slow down as well. Almost any kind of movement will tend to confuse the opponent. Since he will be aiming at the goal, the keeper should make this target as difficult as possible to judge. He should never allow an opponent a free shot; he must disconcert him as much as he can.

Head-On Dive

This is so dangerous that it should only be used as a last-ditch effort. The most important thing is to get down to the ball before it is kicked, so that even if the goalie cannot get the forward to stop his kick, the man will hit a firmly held ball and his foot will be stopped dead. It is the follow through that represents the greatest danger (Fig. 9.23).

The goalie should smother the ball with hands and arms, rather than only hands, for two reasons: first, to bury the ball safely, and second, but equally important, to use his near-arm as a fender to absorb some of the force of the kick if the forward goes through with the boot.

Side Dive

This is the most common, most effective, and safest technique. The goalie flings himself, literally shoots out at the forward's feet, and spreads himself as much as possible with the body parallel to the ground and facing the forward (Fig. 9.24).

The positioning of the upper body and hand (left or right) will depend on the anticipated direction of the shot or dribble. The goalie simply tries to put up the largest possible wall between the ball and the goal in order to reduce the forward's shooting angle. He hopes that the ball will be shot against his body, arms, or legs.

Whatever the case might be, he must try to bury the ball under his body and roll over, turning his

Fig. 9.23 *Head-on dive.*

Fig. 9.24 *Side dive.*

back to the forward with knees and head well-tucked-in for greater protection.

Sliding Tackle

This can give the goalie a double chance, yet few keepers exploit it. It is safe in every way. If the initial slide tackle fails, the goalie can still fling himself across to block and bury the ball, and his chances are likely to be improved by the fact that his initial attempt may cause the forward to lose control of the ball, at least momentarily (Figs. 9.25 and 9.26).

Kicking-Throwing

Modern techniques stress accuracy first and distance second. But distance should not be sneered at. The goalie who kicks or throws well can help set up a quick surprise attack.

Fig. 9.25 *Sliding tackle. Goalkeeper attempts to make a desperate save by using a feet-first bent-leg slide tackle.*

Fig. 9.26 *Sliding tackle. Split slide dive.*

a   *b*   *c*

Fig. 9.27 *Punting the ball (drop volley).*

Punting Drop Volley Kick

The ball is held at full arm's length in front of the kicking foot and dropped from about waist level. The goalie contacts the ball at about knee height and gets it off at about a forty-five degree angle. The goalie is, in effect, kicking the ball immediately after it leaves his hand (Fig. 9.27).

By kicking through rather than at the ball with a firm instep, and putting the entire leg and body weight into the kick, the goalie can gain maximum distance and accuracy. A good punt requires a really long, powerful leg swing, with the kicker following through fully in the direction of the kick.

The inexperienced goalie will try to kick the ball high into the air and far upfield in the belief that the farther it goes the safer it will be. If the forwards are prepared to fight for the ball, an occasional booming kick can be of great tactical advantage. Intelligent, aggressive forwards can exploit the enemy defense as it fights for the ball while back-pedaling.

More often than not, however, the opponent will gain possession and the goalie will find that he is back where he started, saving another shot—but sooner rather than later!

a   b   c

Fig. 9.28 *Throwing style: overarm, sling throw, and bowling style.*

The Drop Half-Volley

This ensures a long and relatively low trajectory that enables the goalie to deliver the ball much faster to his intended receiver. Perfect timing and a clean contact with a full, firm instep are vital for accuracy and distance. The half-volley is especially useful when kicking against a strong wind. It keeps the ball much lower where the wind cannot get at it so easily.

Over-Arm Throw

This throw enables the goalie to send the ball almost as far as a kick and more accurately, particularly when he wants to deliver it quickly to a team-mate's feet (Fig. 9.28).

From a well-balanced stance with feet spread and weight evenly distributed, the goalie brings the ball to a point above the throwing shoulder just behind the ear. The ball is held with the fingers well-spread and the palm on the ball. The player turns his body perpendicular to the throw and shifts his weight momentarily onto the rear foot. The goalie then initiates the throw by stepping directly toward the receiver and bringing his arm forward, elbow leading. As the trunk pivots around to the front, the arm whips forward smoothly and full, with the wrist and fingers imparting a final, powerful snapping action.

A good follow through is essential for accuracy and distance. Upon releasing the ball, the throwing hand should come across the body and the goalie should bring the trailing foot forward in a natural, balancing action. The full-arm action and the flow of the weight from back to front necessitate a follow through with the rear leg.

BATTERY OF EXERCISES

Since the goalie's physical and technical requirements are unique, his program must necessarily be specialized and build his body up for the specific skill of goalkeeping.

The goalie must be supple, strong, and quick. His strength must be of the power variety, since he must "lift" or "fling" himself as far as he can and as fast as he can to make saves or interceptions. His program must develop this kind of strength and fitness and at the same time hone his skills and techniques.

For this reason all his exercises should be done with the ball—a medicine ball, if possible. He should devote at least thirty minutes every day to his fitness training, starting with a moderate number and building up to thirty. We repeat—*every day.*

    1. Hop while bouncing the ball rhythmically in front of the body with both hands.
    Variations:

A. Bounce the ball high and jump high, rhythmically.

B. Bounce the ball waist high while in a squat position.

C. Bounce the ball three times, then jump high and bounce the ball through spread legs; turn and continue.

Do thirty successful repetitions.

2. Lie on the back with arms alongside the body and the ball held between the ankles. Roll backward to touch the ground behind the head with the ball and return to starting position.

Variations:

A. From the same position, extend arms above head, in jackknife sit-ups, touch the ball with both hands and immediately return to starting position.

B. From the same position, hold the ball with both hands over the head and do sit-ups while raising and bending the legs, knees to chest. Touch the insteps with the ball and return to starting position.

Do thirty successful repetitions.

3. Stand in straddle position, bend forward, and circle the ball in a figure eight around each leg.

A. Roll the ball on the ground around the feet.

B. Circle the ball around the ankles.

C. Circle the ball around the knees.

D. Circle the ball around the waist while rhythmically circling the hip.

Do thirty repetitions of each in both directions.

4. In straddle position, hold the ball with both hands above the head. Swing forward and toss the ball through the straddled legs high behind the back. Turn and catch the ball before it hits the ground.

Do thirty successful repetitions.

5. In straddle position, hold the ball with both hands above the head. After bending well-back, drop the ball and turn quickly and dive on it.

Do thirty successful repetitions.

6. In straddle position, bend forward and hold the ball between the knees with one hand coming from behind through the straddled legs and the other from the front. Turn from side to side reversing the hands quickly while keeping the ball in the air.

Do thirty successful repetitions.

7. Hold the ball with both hands behind the back and throw it high over the head. Jump after it to catch it.

Do thirty successful repetitions.

8. Sit and throw the ball into the air. Jump up and try to catch it before it hits the ground.

Do thirty successful repetitions.

9. Standing with the ball in both hands, do a forward or backward roll and immediately follow the roll with a very high vertical jump.

Do thirty successful repetitions of each.

10. Kneel, throw the ball forward or sideward, dive on it, bring it quickly in, and clutch it tightly to the body.

Do thirty successful repetitions or go the length of the field, alternating sides.

11. Crawl, bounce the ball forward, dive on it, bring it in quickly, and clutch it tightly to the body.

Variation: Lie on the ground face-down, roll the ball forward and lunge on it.

Go the length of the field, alternating sides.

12. In straddle position, roll the ball through the legs, turn quickly, and dive on the ball.

Do thirty successful repetitions.

13. Place the ball about ten yards to the side, then dive and smother it, burying it under the body.

Go the length of the field, alternating sides.

14. Throw or kick the ball high into the air and do all kinds of exercises before catching it. The ball must be caught before it hits the ground even if a dive has to be made.

A. Touch the toes 1-2-3 times.

B. Do push-ups 1-2-3 times.

C. Sit down quickly 1-2-3 times.

D. Roll forward.

E. Roll backward.

Do fifteen successful repetitions for each exercise.

REALISTIC PRACTICES

The goalkeeper's practice should be set up in a realistic environment—between the goalposts and within the goal or penalty area. Only through hours and hours of practice and moving about the goal can the goalie develop the proper positional sense with relation to the goal.

Ideally, much initial practice should be between the goalkeeper and the coach, with a second goalkeeper chasing the ball and alternating with the first. Or the coach can have two goalkeepers work together, alternating in the task of serving and goalkeeping.

Ball-Handling

The coach stands around the penalty spot and serves the ball toward the center of the goal. He then moves to one side, then the other, giving the goalie a variety of situations. He may start with a well-placed throw or pass and then serve by volleying and half-volleying. He first drives the ball at the goalkeeper and later places it to his right and left.

He should serve with increasing power so that the goalie may practice the various types of saves:

1. Fielding low balls.
2. Catching waist-high balls.
3. Catching chest-high balls.
4. Jumping to catch balls against his chest and over his head.

Making Quick Saves

The ability to make a lightning save of a sure goal is the dream of every goalkeeper, beginner and expert alike. This ability stems from a combination of anticipation, quick reaction, and agility. One of the best ways of developing it is through handling a stream of close shots.

The coach himself should take the firing line. Since he is the only person who knows the limitations of the goalie, he is obviously the only one who can push the player to his limits. The goalie obviously is going to tire quickly from all the bending, stretching, jumping, and diving from side to side to stop each ball. But this is just the time he should be encouraged to fling himself even more determinedly at each shot.

The timing and difficulty involved in handling all this rapid shooting should force the goalie into superlative efforts. The secret is to make each shot just difficult enough to encourage the goalie to go for it, thus extending him the fullest without actually beating him.

The coach should equip himself with several balls and serve from around the penalty spot, if he is skillful enough to place his shots. If he is not, he may move in closer and throw the ball. The alternate goalie should shag the balls.

A realistic situation is created when the goalkeeper's view is distracted momentarily or the ball is deflected by a player; but he is still expected to make the lightning save. A given number of defenders and attackers crowd the goalmouth as they move about. Several attackers, each with a ball, lined up across the edge of the penalty box, are asked to shoot in quick succession at goal.

Diving at Attacker's Feet

The essential timing, courage, and confidence can only be acquired through practice and more practice. The goalie must develop an extremely keen sense of anticipation so that he can begin cutting off the shooting angle almost instinctively.

A forward dribbles at the goal from outside the penalty area, and the goalie moves out to cut off his shooting angle:

1. The forward is initially asked to delay his shot and either keep the ball at his feet until challenged or overkick it slightly, thus giving the goalie a brief chance to capitalize on the mistake. This develops the goalie's confidence in going down at a forward's feet.

2. Since there is nothing more effective than the real thing, several forwards are asked to attack in turn from different angles and try to beat the goalie while he tries to stop them. To keep this activity continuous, a second and even a third goalie may be asked to take over on the fly whenever he feels the tending goalie is momentarily out of position to stop the fast-approaching attacker.

3. Several forwards, each with a ball, approach the goal in turn from about thirty yards out. Instead of dribbling at the goal, they pass to the coach positioned at the edge of the penalty box. He wall passes the ball up for the forward to take in full stride and beat the goalie. The latter tries to intercept the wall pass or dive at the player's feet to block the shot or prevent a dribble.

It is important that the coach make the wall pass because he can stack the odds. As in the second drill, the goalkeepers may take turns on the fly.

Dealing with High Crosses

The safe taking of a high ball requires a lot of practice. The requisite timing and handling can be practiced in several ways:

1. Throw and catch. One player throws the ball overhead with one hand; a second player catches it with upstretched arms at the top of a jump (from a single foot takeoff). The hands should be placed slightly behind the ball and the body leaned forward a little.

2. One player stands in position in goal and then runs out to catch the ball from a long kick. He quickly hugs it to his body and weaves, while bouncing the ball, as though dodging opponents.

3. The high service is varied sometimes with drops near the crossbar. The goalkeeper must

then use the palm of his hand or hands to push or turn the ball over.

4. The ball is kicked from well-downfield or from near the corners, with another player challenging the goalie either by jumping to head the ball or by charging him when he catches the ball.

5. The goalie arranges with his defenders so that they know when to take the ball and when to drop back to cover the goal and leave the high ball to him. The goalie gradually learns when he can safely leave the goal and when he should stay on the line.

Playing the Angle

The goalie now faces a series of situations to which he must react as quickly and as well as he can. He sets up in goal ready to meet the first attack, which comes from a wing forward running in toward him. The goalie obviously must go to the near post and be ready to stop a shot from the right wing forward, dive to cut out a fast low center if near enough to it, or jump high to catch a lobbed ball.

Special Situations

The various types of free kicks, corner kicks, etc., that have been described obviously must be practiced during the training sessions. The defense as a whole must practice and practice until they can automatically react to every possible situation.

10

Team Defense

Good defense depends upon the players covering each other and restricting their opponents' operating room and time. The defenders cannot hope to deny all space, but they must have an understanding of the relative importance of open areas in every situation.

Recent trends indicate that the defense of tomorrow will involve nearly all eleven players without regard to position. The defense will be able to build a sweeper (catennacio), blanket type of defense across their penalty area, and then, as soon as ball-possession changes, break out to attack with all ten men. See photo, opposite, where sweeper Franz Beckenbauer and center forward Gerhard Müller have combined to score a goal.

The simplest consideration is possession. When a team loses the ball, every player must think defensively. Obviously some will be immediately committed to defense, either in (1) marking opponents tightly, (2) withdrawing in order to provide a solid last line of defense, or (3) actually challenging an opponent for possession.

It is essential for the whole team to concentrate on regaining possession, restricting the opponent's use of the ball and space, while at the same time exposing their own goal to the minimum possible danger.

From the tactical point of view, an intelligent defender will realize that it is sometimes better to let an opponent have the ball. As soon as the ball-handler is put under pressure, he is forced to speed up his play and in doing so he may expose momentary defensive weaknesses. Positive action has a better chance of success when it is made from strength.

Withdrawal to a strong base often has an attacking motive. The team can draw opponents forward, wait until their lines of communication are stretched, and then go in to win the ball and launch a sudden counterattack through the gaps the opponents have left.

The ancient motto, "Score more goals than the opposition," has been reversed to "Concede fewer goals than the opposition." Starving out the opposition is not a glorious tactic. It takes the color and spirit out of the game. But such defense need not be all negative; a swift counterattack can be brilliantly effective.

Basically, modern defense is built around an inner shell—a hard core of four or five fulltime defenders and a screen of two, three, or four midfield players. The latter merely present the first challenge so the true defenders are not pulled out of position. When the attack breaks past them, they race back to fill any gaps created in the defense.

PHILOSOPHY OF DEFENSE

Every defensive tactic must be based on each man's ability to handle the triple role of covering a man,

189

providing cover to teammates, and covering space.

If, for example, the two centerbacks do a good job of covering for each other and the fullbacks, and all four backs can cope with the relative manpower of the opponent, then an equal ratio of defenders to attackers should suffice. This assumes that the attackers are doing their share by tackling back instantly or harassing the opponent. The midfield players are thinking principally of delaying, stalling, and retreating in order to complicate through passes and gain time for the immediate defenders to set up a firm bastion and play as a unit.

As soon as the attack passes the first line of defense (the midfield), the defenders must immediately hustle back to add support to the defense.

Every defensive tactic must capitalize upon the ability and intelligence of each man to "read" the game. The players decide when or when not to challenge for the ball, whether to follow their immediate opponent or hold their ground—let their man run free—to keep the whole defense cohesive and in control of the central path to the goal.

The ability of each player and the cohesiveness of the defense will determine whether an extra man (a sweeper) will be needed. A freeback or sweeper must be used on defense, at least temporarily, if (1) the backs have to come out too frequently to challenge for the ball or are drawn out regularly, leaving the vital area uncovered, (2) the defense is caught "square" in a line across the field, neglecting depth cover and are thus being beaten, or (3) the opposition is simply overpowering in man-to-man combat.

The basic framework should be flexible enough for a team to switch to a reinforced defense or attack when the situation calls for it. Defensive organization may be achieved more easily if the players understand the principles of the game.

The coach must realize that his team is a mirror of himself—his philosophy, his convictions, and his confidence. If he adopts a negative approach, he can expect his team to react in like fashion.

Negativism does not make for good team morale nor inspire anyone to attack aggressively. It leads to a dull, sterile, defensive type of game. This sort of coaching sould be avoided. Categoric statements such as "I play sweeper or catennacio" signify a narrow, unimaginative misinterpretation of the objectives. This does not imply that a team should

not be prepared to play sweeper. On the contrary, the coach who understands the sweeper and properly incorporates it will usually wind up with a potent weapon that will reinforce the defense under a sustained attack.

The proper selection of the sweeper player—and all defensive men—is vitally important. Since the play involves a high degree of teamwork, it requires players with all-round ability and a thorough understanding of the game. A defender cannot be expected to support the attack if he lacks the ball-control ability of a forward and if he does not fully understand what is required of him in that position.

The development of the all-round player is an extended process that must begin the first day of practice. The entire training must be streamlined to produce players with the intelligence, poise, and ability to play just about anywhere on the field. They must also be instilled with the will to carry their heavy work load and the driving spirit of attack.

The coaching of defense must be realistic. It must embody full-field scrimmages and the analysis of defensive principles on an individual or collective basis, as the need occurs.

Initially, however, it may be necessary to work in small groups, using both uneven and even numbers—the former when stressing zone defense, support and cover, and even when working on tight man-to-man marking. Certain players can be isolated in a restricted area (on a grid) in order to coordinate this particular segment of the defense.

PRINCIPAL METHODS OF COLLECTIVE DEFENSE

Man-to-Man

This the primary method of defense as play usually comes down to the one-on-one situation.

Each player has a defined position and role. Every attacker must be covered, no matter how the attack shapes itself. The defense must attempt to maintain numerical equality at each stage of the attack. This is particularly important against skilled opponents who can exploit numerical weaknesses.

As soon as the attack develops, the defense must take up positions and mark man-to-man. This is especially important for the defenders near the ball through whom the attack will be launched (Diag. 10.1).

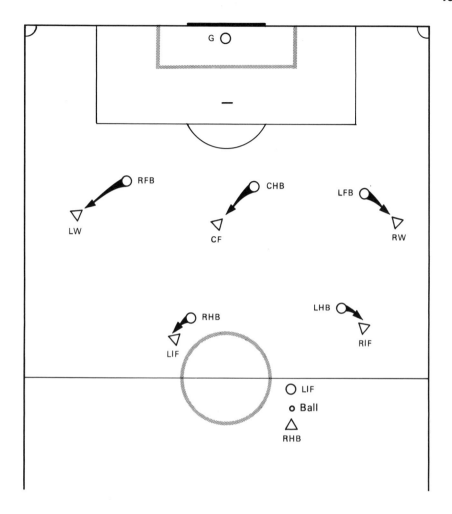

Diag. 10.1 *Man-to-man defense is the key to defensive play. Around the ball and near the goal every attacker must be closely marked by a defender no matter how the attack shapes up.*

The term "man-to-man" is relative. Loose man-to-man cover can be just as effective as the tightest marking—the kind that seeks to deny the opponents even one touch of the ball. The extent to which the defenders can devote themselves to their individual opponents depends on their method of collective defense.

Man-to-man marking was once considered adequate as long as the defender stayed within striking distance of his opponent. This no longer holds true. Such loose man-to-man marking will give the opponents the initiative. The marking must now be

skintight, leaving the forward with little or no scope for expression. The defenders must remain disciplined. The only time they can wage a private battle with their opponent is when there is a free-back.

This means keeping on the goalward side of the opponent and making a quick, vigorous challenge when he receives the ball. The opponent must be followed wherever he goes to prevent him from receiving a pass—ideally by intercepting it—or, if he does receive a pass, to dispossess him before he has complete control of the ball, thus reducing his contribution to a minimum. Skintight marking has a demoralizing effect on the opponent.

The man-to-man defense is advantageous in that it permits the coach to delegate clearcut responsibility to players in every situation, and to match up with the opponents in terms of speed, size, and ability.

Such clear delineation of responsibility should produce better mental and psychological readiness and more determined and aggressive play. Pride in individual defensive achievement will motivate the player to a better team defensive effort.

Should defensive breakdowns occur, which are individual in nature, they can be more easily detected during the course of the game. A team breakdown would require an adaptation by the whole defense. During the game there is not time to explain the principles involved in a switch. In man-to-man defense, a substitution can be made to whom the coach can give instructions.

Man-to-man marking works as long as the forwards remain in position. When they start roaming or when a defender is beaten, some of the weaknesses of man-to-man marking are highlighted.

Man-to-man marking demands superb conditioning. The defensive player can never relax. He must always move with his man in accordance with every movement of the ball.

A common fault of the man-to-man defender is concentrating too much on an opponent *without* the ball and thus contributing nothing to the team defense. It is difficult to play defense on a strictly individual basis. Against skilled attackers, help is needed to assure sufficient manpower around the ball and in front of the goal.

The defense can be wrecked by an attacker who can beat his man. It can also be affected by a midfield player or even a defender coming from behind in an overlap, or by a defender who happens to be off-form (particularly a center halfback).

The more rigid the man-to-man marking, the more likely is the defense to become imbalanced. The expression "skintight marking" must not be taken literally. Only within the immediate vicinity of the ball should the attackers be tightly marked. Without a freeback, or sweeper, one or more players must accept responsibility for providing cover depth. Covering space is sometimes equally or even more important than marking players. The nearer the defense moves toward its goal, the more synonymous the two objectives (space and man) become.

Zone

In a zone defense, each player covers a roughly defined area or zone rather than a man (Diag. 10.2). Any opponent coming into that zone becomes his responsibility—invoking the principle of man-to-man marking.

The main advantage of zone over strict man-to-man marking lies in the fact that the defender remains in his area and consequently is more flexible. In man-to-man, a fullback might have to follow a wing forward who is constantly moving out of position and could thus leave a gap in the defense.

In the early days, zone was the dominating defense. It was a stationary affair. Each man stayed in his assigned area and seldom shifted with the ball. The modern principle of concentration or numerical superiority around the ball was ignored.

The modern zone is highly flexible. The players shift with the ball to get as close to it as they can in their assigned area in order to restrict the opponents' movement and operating room. The zone defender's responsibility differs from that of the man-to-man marker. His responsibility is confined to an area rather than an opponent. His concern is first with the ball and second with the man, whereas it is exactly the opposite in man-to-man marking.

The zone often is preferable for young or beginning players. It gives them more freedom of expression and is easier to learn. It is also a help to slow, heavy, immobile defenders who have difficulty staying with a man, and it is advantageous on small fields, since it reduces the areas of coverage and the width of the attack.

The greatest disadvantage of the zone defense lies in the freedom of movement it permits to the opponent. This often leads to the loss of the initiative. The zone also might encourage the defenders to play too passively. Either fault can be disastrous inside shooting range. Every man must be covered tightly here; there is no room for miscues.

Sliding Zone

Every defender must know when to mark a man closely, when to fall away from him, and when to

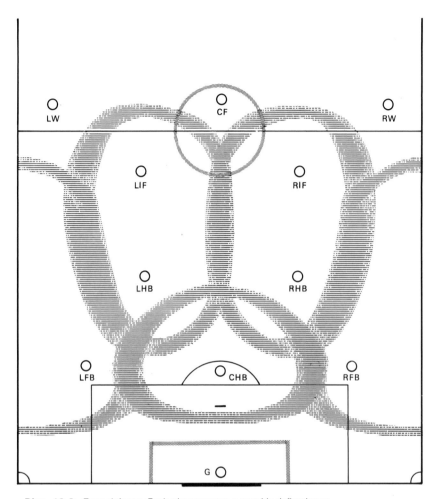

Diag. 10.2 *Zone defense: Each player covers a roughly defined area.*

pass him on to a teammate (as the attackers interchange positions). When the attacker moves into a defender's zone, he must be tightly marked. When he moves from one zone to another, a different defender must accept the responsibility of marking him (Diag. 10.3).

Switching can create problems. A player may have two defenders momentarily covering the same man. If this switch causes difficulty a sliding zone defense may be tried. It is more difficult to learn, but it solves the double-coverage problem.

In a sliding zone, the man who picks up the ball-handler stays with him until he passes. To keep up with his man, the defender may be required to

move into another zone. When this occurs, another defender must slide over to cover the vacated zone.

Compound

The compound defense is basically a fusion of the zone and man-to-man defenses (Diag. 10.4). It affords sensible distribution of players in the danger area to assure depth, cover, and balance. It provides at the same time tight man-to-man marking wherever needed, for example, to a forward who is a good goal shooter or the chief playmaker. This style of defense requires a great deal of visual and oral communication. Each defender must know for whom he is responsible and when a change of

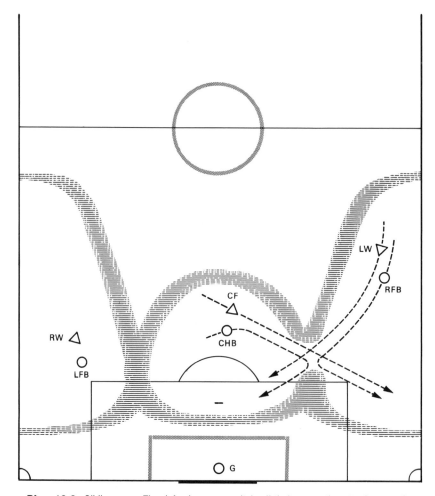

Diag. 10.3 *Sliding zone: The defenders may switch off their respective attackers as the attackers interchange from one zone to another. Or the defender who is covering the ball-handler may stay with him until he makes the play. When this occurs another defender must slide over.*

assignment is required. Lack of communication can disrupt the entire continuity of defense.

The compound defense has the midfield players creating a screen in a zone. Their major role is to challenge anyone attempting to carry the ball up to the second line of fulltime defenders. If the opponent succeeds in breaking through the midfield screen, one back must leave his immediate opponent or the sweeper must come forward to challenge. That means the sweeper is again operating within the principle of the zone.

PRINCIPLES

Depth

Defense in depth offers cover and all-round support. The players support each other and attempt to restrict the gaps through which passes can be made or attackers can safely move. Large gaps between and behind players court danger, sap the players' strength, and offer openings for the opposition. The more compact the defense, the better

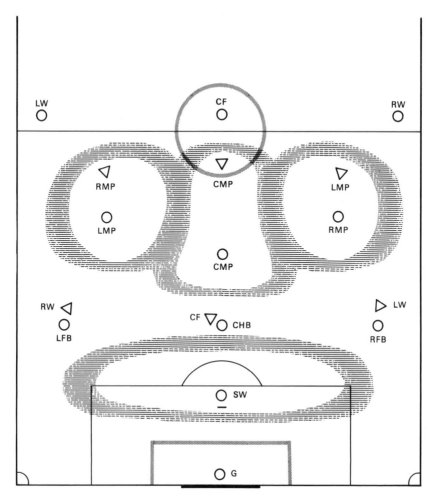

Diag. 10.4 *Compound defense: A flexible fusion of zone and man-to-man or a defined combination of each. For example, the forwards are marked man for man, backed up by a sweeper who covers zone, while three or four midfield players operate as a unit on a zone principle.*

are the chances of intercepting passes. The more widely spread the defense, the greater is the opportunity for offensive exploitation.

Collective defensive patterns consist of a series of interlocking triangular formations, and the farther back they go, the tighter they must become to increase the possibility of interceptions.

The most common situations where depth, cover, and support are neglected are:

1. When defenders are running back toward their goal, they tend to flatten out into a straight-line square across the field. Since they are neglecting to cover each other and guard the more important, vital space behind them, they expose themselves to the through pass (Diag. 10.5).

2. The same principle applies, but in the opposite way, whenever an attacker breaks through on a flank and turns the ball back from the goal line in order to catch the retreating defenders on the wrong foot and flat across the goalmouth. This leaves a midfield player or an attacker coming from behind in an excellent position to score (Diag. 10.6).

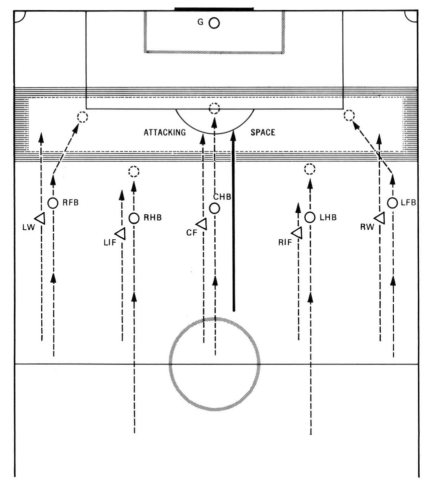

Diag. 10.5 *A most common situation where defenders neglect depth cover support is when running toward their own goal.*

The importance of depth in covering the vital space behind the defenders and supplying cover and support for them at all times is clearly demonstrated by the almost universal acceptance of the sweeper.

Delay

Whenever penetration is a major objective of the attack, delay must be a major principle of the defense. By retarding the buildup of the attack, the defense can gain time to organize: to fill gaps and get into positions of depth, cover, and close support (Diag. 10.7).

The first defensive consideration must be the goal, as it affects every part of the field. Whenever a team loses the ball, it must become aware of the gaps between players and, even more important, behind them. Each defender must mark the immediate attacker, and the nearer the attackers come to the goal, the more closely must they be marked.

The transition from offense to defense must be achieved instantly, fluidly, and effectively. Every player must instantly think and act defensively and speedily put himself between the ball and the goal.

The players nearer the ball must show themselves quickly on the ball, harrying the opponent

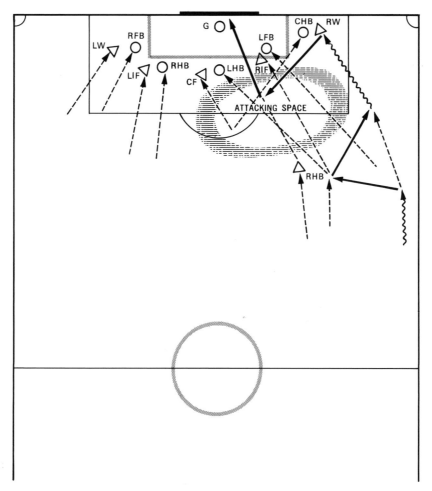

Diag. 10.6 *Defenders frequently neglect depth after the attacking team has succeeded in turning the defense.*

and frustrating his attempt to start a counterattack. If, for example, a forward loses the ball, he must tackle back instantly, not so much to retrieve the ball but (1) to pressure his opponent before the other attackers can take up supporting positions, (2) to hamper him, or (3) to force him into a hurried pass or even a mistake. He must never give the opponent the time and space to make a penetrating pass.

The other forwards also must keep busy. They must harass the players near them and move into the line of any pass toward an advanced and central attacker. They should force the attack to play square across the field. Midfield players must tighten up their marking in their part of the field, while the rearmost defenders must adopt covering positions against through passes.

Every player must have the determination to win the ball back. It cannot be left just for the defensive specialists.

Whenever the opponent threatens to break through the last line of a defense that is momentarily imbalanced or outnumbered, the defender must delay the attack by *retreating* slowly rather than committing himself. The player must *jockey* the ball-handler by moving quickly in front of him

Individual and Team Defense

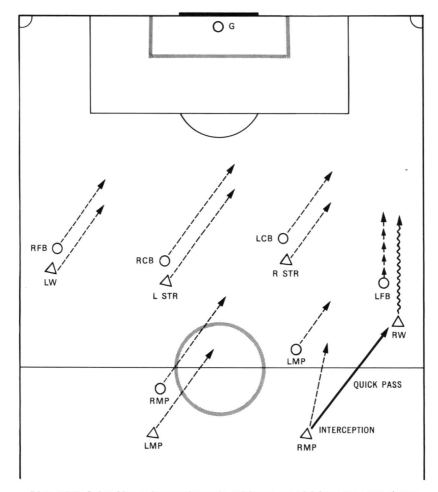

Diag. 10.7 *Delay: After an interception and a quick pass out of defense too many players are caught on the wrong side of the ball. Delaying the attacking thrust is necessary to gain time to allow defenders to take up positions between the goal and the ball and pick up their respective opponents.*

to eliminate his immediate passing angles. At the same time, he should put enough pressure on him to keep him occupied and give ground slowly to avoid evasion.

One defender can delay the progress of two players, or two defenders can delay three or more attackers long enough for the rest of their teammates to assume defensive positions.

Shepherding is a more sophisticated form of jockeying. The defender delays by retreating, giving ground slowly, but he induces his opponent to move in a certain direction. He seeks either to force

him to the outside where the touchline will limit his operating room or to turn him to the inside directly into the hands of a waiting teammate. This "influential" tactic can be a help in assisting a tackle or in an interception.

Concentration

Whenever the defenders are in doubt or are forced to give ground, they retreat, funnel, from their wide midfield positions to converge into central positions at the edge of the penalty box. This concentration of players reduces the space between de-

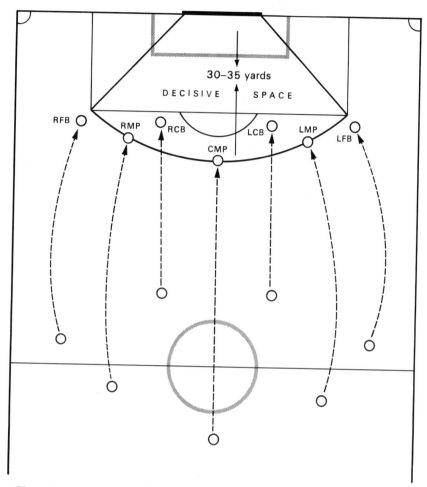

Diag. 10.8 *Concentration: "Whenever defenders are in doubt or are forced to give ground, they retreat, funnel, from their wide midfield positions to converge into central positions at the edge of the penalty box. This concentration of players reduces the space between defenders and keeps the shooters at a reasonably ineffective range."*

fenders and keeps the shooters at a reasonably ineffective range (Diag. 10.8).

Obviously the central path to the goal offers the greatest opportunity for scoring. The defense that moves collectively between the ball and the goal is extremely difficult to penetrate. The players remain in close support of each other, reduce the spaces between themselves, and at the same time provide for depth, cover, and double cover. This makes it almost impossible for the offense to put a ball or a man into the vital area behind the defenders.

Balance

Whenever a defender is beaten and a teammate must leave his position in order to challenge the opponent, the defense becomes unbalanced. If a fullback moves into attack on an overlap, his teammates must balance the defense by covering for him. The halfback must drop back into the fullback's position temporarily, while the inside forward or wing forward must drop back to cover the gap left by the fullback. This reshuffling leaves temporary gaps that can be exploited by a well-organized attack (Diag. 10.9).

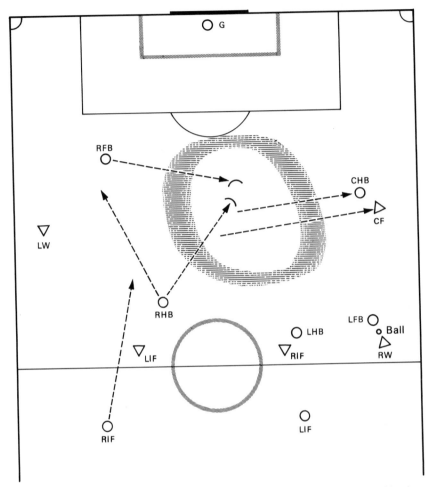

Diag. 10.9 *Balance: Mobility in attack is calculated to draw defenders out of position in order to create attacking space and to destroy the balance of the collective pattern of defense. For example, take a closer look at the three-back diagonal pattern of defense. If the CHB follows the CF out to the wing, man-to-man marking is still intact, but the balance of the collective defensive pattern is immediately destroyed. Balance must be reestablished quickly through either the RFB or RHB filling in momentarily for the CHB, while the created midfield gap can be closed by the RIF.*

One well-known method of unbalancing the classic diagonal defense is by suddenly shifting the attack from one side of the field to the other. The defenders become momentarily unbalanced in their attempt to switch positions and are caught square across the field; their lack of cover and depth can easily be exploited by a sudden through pass.

This weakness has been greatly reduced by the four-back defense, where the centerbacks cover each other and the fullbacks. It has been almost completely eliminated by the sweeper (catennacio) defense, where the sweeper's sole job is to prevent the defense from becoming unbalanced.

The more sophisticated attacking patterns such as the withdrawn center forwards or wing forwards and the spearhead aim at destroying the balance of a rigidly applied stopper, double stopper, or diagonal pattern of defense.

Rigidly applied defensive patterns are effective

only when they are opposed by fairly conventional attacks. As soon as they are asked to cope with interchanges of positions or overlapping defenders, they become unbalanced. Generally speaking, the more rigid the defensive method or man-to-man duties, the more likely the defense will become unbalanced.

Control and Restraint

While attackers are encouraged to express their individuality and aggressiveness, the defenders must often subordinate themselves in a collective effort.

Defense necessitates awareness of risks and priorities, and relative responsibilities. Every player has a function in the collective pattern. Consequently, any miscue can affect the defense as a whole. Since the defense often plays a retreating and waiting game, avoiding any commitment in midfield, a defender must restrain himself from lunging into a midfield tackle. The closer the attack approaches, the more difficult but the more important control and restraint become.

The defender who permits himself to be drawn out of position or lured into an early tackle can unbalance and disrupt the cohesiveness of the collective pattern.

Control and restraint are difficult to teach because they require instantaneous judgment, which comes mainly with experience. For example, a defender must be very cautious when switching from one man to another. Whenever the full defense is not in position to deal with a quick attack, the defender should not leave his man uncovered and rush in to challenge the forward who is trying to break through. He should make every effort to slow down the attack and give the defenders or the halfbacks time to drop back into position.

If the opposing forward is close to or in the penalty area, the defender must leave his man and challenge him. This is where tight formations pay off. Being close to each other, the defenders find it easier to interchange positions in order to cover for each other.

PATTERNS

Pivot or Diagonal

The first successful collective pattern is the pivot or diagonal formation of defense. It combines full field coverage with man-ball-space orientation at all times.

Though evident in the two-back offensive system, it developed into a classic collective defense in the WM period. With slight modifications it appeared in the more recent 4-2-4 system,[12] and some elements of it are retained in the ultra defensive systems.[13]

Though the defense is based on tight man-to-man marking, the principle must not be taken literally. It is only within the immediate vicinity of the ball that the attackers should be tightly marked. Without a freeback or sweeper, the defense must have one or more players accept the responsibility for providing cover and depth. This is, in fact, the essence of the diagonal principle.

Classic Pivot or Diagonal Pattern Based on the Three-Back WM System[14]

The center halfback or stopper represents the pivot of the swivel. The fullbacks are its arms. The challenging and the retreating segments of the defense rotate around the center halfback. The onside fullback challenges for the ball, while the center halfback and the offside fullback sag behind to form the diagonal formation. This affords cover, depth, and, if the need arises, a reasonable amount of balance. Should the attacker escape the fullback or pass through any gaps, the ball will always be covered by another defender (Diag. 10.10).

The halfbacks form their own diagonal and always work in close support of each other. When the opponents obtain possession, the halfbacks retreat to present the first line of defense. The onside halfback offers support to the challenging fullback, while the offside halfback sags back to furnish cover and balance.

The halfbacks also play an important role against quick changes in the attacking thrust. As link men they must stay back to support the defense. The two inside forwards otherwise would have an abundance of room in which to work.

The pivoting movement is rather laborious. Quick changes in the attack can force the three rearmost defenders into a square or almost square alignment for too long. This would leave the defense without cover and depth, badly exposed to the opposing midfield players. The latter could,

[12]See p. 261 for description.

[13]See p. 219 for description.

[14]See p. 258 for description.

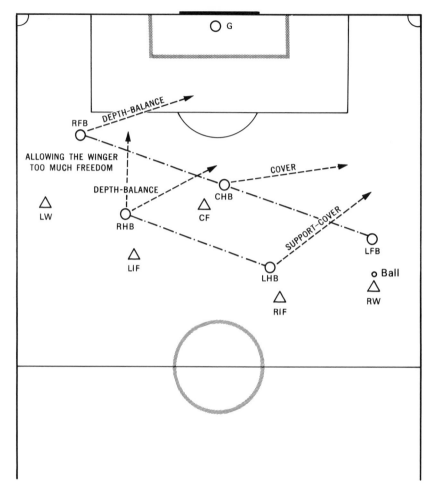

Diag. 10.10 *Classic diagonal pattern of defense based on the three-back WM system when faced with a thrust on the right flank.*

with quick, short interpassing, put the ball into the vital space behind the defenders for their strikers to come in on.

The pivotal defense also can be exploited by a quick switch and crossfield pass to the far wing forward. Since the fullbacks pivot around the center halfback, an opposing winger always has the time and room to control the ball, turn, and prepare to take on his challenger (Diags. 10.11 and 10.12).

This can be counteracted quite effectively by having the near halfback keep an eye on the wing

forward or by even having the winger come back and supply loose coverage to his counterpart.

Whenever a fullback is beaten, he races back to the nearer post. If he is beaten in his own half, he runs toward the penalty spot (twelve yards in front of the goal) or to the position normally occupied by the center halfback. The latter comes across to challenge the opponent, while the offside fullback takes up the position left by the center halfback (Diags. 10.13 and 10.14).

Caution: The diagonal pivot defense based on the three-back WM is inadequate against the

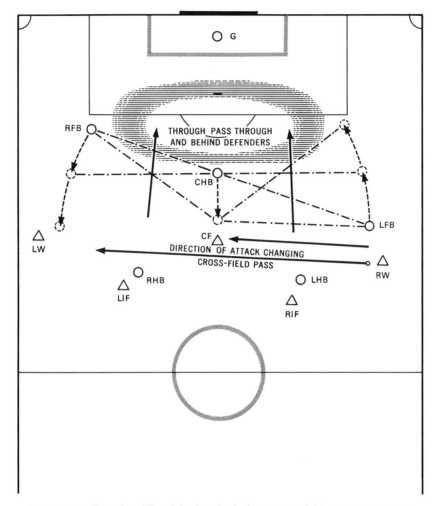

Diag. 10.11 *The vulnerability of the three-back pivot pattern of defense when faced with a crossfield pass.*

four-man attacking formation that automatically throws an extra fulltime attacker against the defense.

Modern Pivot or Diagonal Defense Based on Four-Back Fulltime Defenders

This applies the same basic principles, with the two centerbacks the key. They build a two-man pivot, fulfilling basically the same function as the one-man pivot in the classic pivot pattern based on the three-back system. This form of central cover al-

lows the fullbacks to mark both wing forwards more closely than was possible in the three-back pattern of diagonal cover (Diag. 10.15).

The four-back defense cannot be so easily unbalanced by a change of direction in the attack. It also effects an economy in time and space. This defense greatly reduces the distance covered in the pivot, and the two centerbacks are continually moving to furnish the defense with depth and to cover each other and the fullbacks. Having no cover behind them, they must cover each other as well as the vital space.

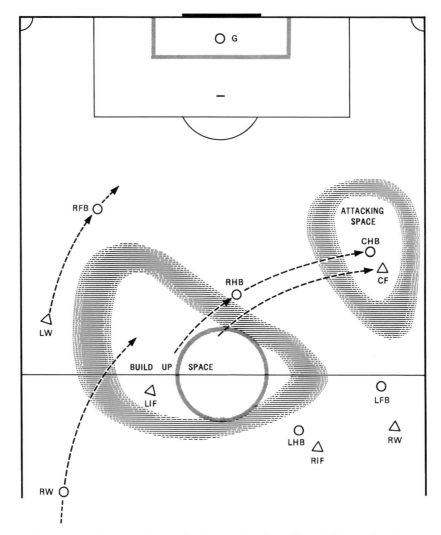

Diag. 10.12 *The vulnerability of the tight-marking pivot pattern of defense when faced by a roving forward and how to cope with it.*

The fullbacks provide only secondary cover in the center and are thus allowed greater freedom of action. When the left centerback is drawn into a duel for the ball, the right centerback will drop to cover him and vice versa. Cover for the right fullback is now provided by the right centerback, while the left fullback is covered by the left centerback (Diag. 10.16).

When the two central defenders follow the flow of play across the field, the defense is left "square" with neither cover nor depth and thus is vulnerable to the fast through pass.

If the thrust threatens the wing or flank, the centerback must slide across the field to supply cover and depth to that side. If a crossfield pass changes the direction of attack, one or both centerbacks must move across the field. Some coaches have one centerback playing deeper than the other; on other teams, the centerbacks are interchangeable (Diag. 10.17).

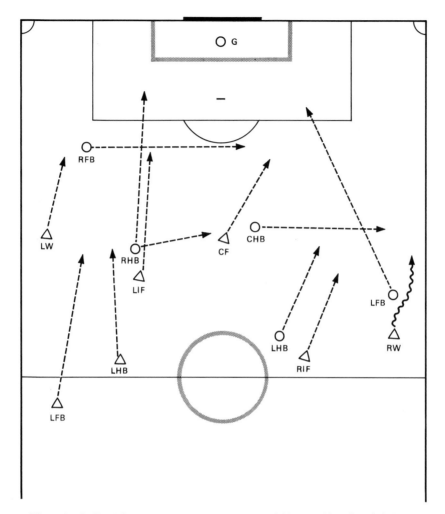

Diag. 10.13 *The fullback when beaten must recover quickly to put himself again between the goal and the ball, while the center halfback comes across to challenge the wing forward.*

If the fullback is beaten, the onside centerback must challenge the opponent while the offside centerback slides across even farther to furnish the necessary cover. The offside fullback—this is the only time he plays an active role in the pivot—must sag to the middle to provide depth. Meantime, the fullback must race back to bolster the defense and give it extra depth and solidity.

As a rule the defender, when beaten by an opponent on a flank, must recover instantly by falling back at an angle to the nearest goal post. When beaten in a central area of the field, he must drop back to the center of the goalmouth.

Many other variations of coverage are possible in the two-man pivot. The deeper of the two centerbacks, for example, often will find himself in an easier position than any other defender to challenge the wing forward. On a long lead pass toward the corner flag for the opposing winger, the centerback can race across to make the play while the fullback again heads for the goalmouth.

Many teams prefer to play the pivot the classical way, using all four defenders at all times.

If the thrust is coming from the right flank, the left fullback will challenge for the ball while the right centerback sags back to provide cover (Diag.

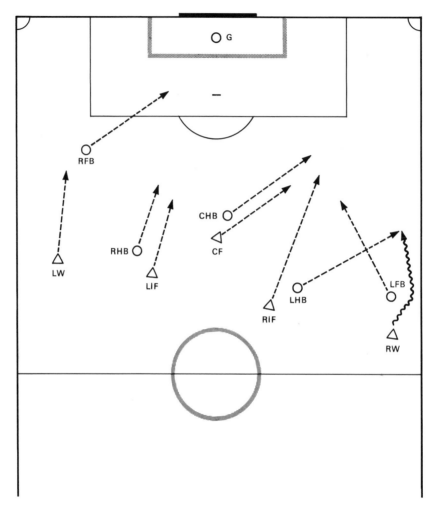

Diag. 10.14 *The fullback when beaten must recover quickly to put himself again between the goal and the ball, while the left halfback challenges the wing forward.*

10.18). At the same time the left centerback and left fullback slide to the center to furnish additional depth, thus completing the classic pivot.

If, however, the thrust comes from one of the interior attackers, then the right striker, the left centerback responsible for covering him, must immediately challenge for the ball while the other defenders sag off their men toward the center just enough to supply a reasonable cover and depth (Diag. 10.19). The left fullback merely drops off about five to six yards, and the right fullback, who is the least threatened defender, sags back to the center to provide cover in front of the goalmouth, if it becomes needed.

Whenever a wing forward with the ball succeeds in penetrating deep, one of the backs must leave his man to challenge (Diags. 10.20 and 10.21). The type of penetration must be considered: whether it is a penetration on the flanks that will lead to a center, or a penetration in the center that will lead to a shot. If an opponent must be left free and the defense has any choice in the matter, it should always pick a wing forward rather than one of the central strikers.

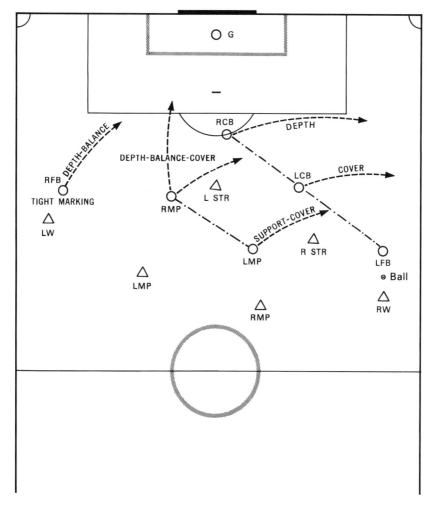

Diag. 10.15 *Contemporary four-back diagonal pattern of defense when faced with a thrust from the right flank.*

A fullback should be elected to challenge the penetrator. When he sees an opponent dribbling forward unopposed, he should step inside to offer a challenge. Note the accent on "step." The fullback should not rush headlong into a tackle, but should cut off the opponent's direct approach to the goal. If he can slow the opponent's advance by jockeying him for two or three seconds, one of the midfield players might catch up and offer a challenge.

The opponent might choose to pass to the unmarked wing forward. That would make the immediate thrust a center or high cross. A slightly inaccurate pass or a miscue by the receiver may well allow the fullback to recover before the center could be delivered. In any case, the defense remains intact with the remaining three backs and the goalkeeper on hand to deal with the center.

The link men play an important role in this type of pivot. They render assistance to the defenders by restricting the open space in front of them and preventing problem situations: whether to stick with their man or switch off to challenge the ball-carrier.

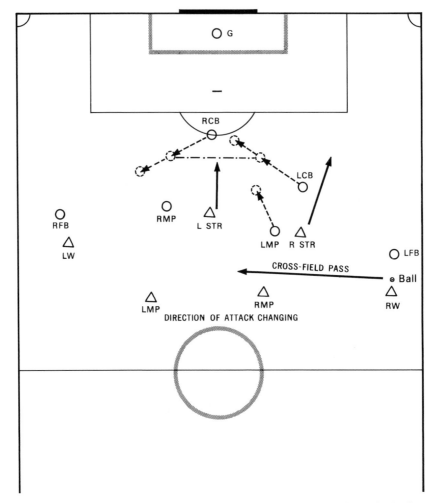

Diag. 10.16 *The four-back diagonal pattern of defense when facing a change in the direction of attack.*

Though the pivot defense gives the opposing forwards more freedom than does strict man-to-man marking, this freedom tempts them to play the ball square. The gaps are in front of the defenders, not behind them, so that the attack invariably has to move toward the defense, thus playing into its hands.

It could be argued that the pivot defense leaves too many players unmarked. Theoretically this may be so, but in practice the link men, midfield players, or halfbacks compensate by filling up the gaps.

The pivot defense mainly concerns the last line of defenders. Its chief purpose is to furnish depth and is not intended as a panacea. A more valid criticism of the defense is its lack of articulation. Players are left with too many doubts, which militate against smooth coordination.

The covering back usually plays everyone onside. Few offsides are called against the pivot or diagonal pattern of defense, therefore. That means the attackers can just put their heads down and run. Against the four-back, based on the two-man

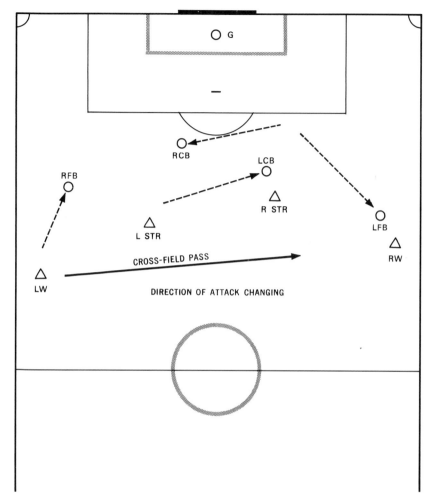

Diag. 10.17 *The four-back diagonal pattern of defense when using the sliding pattern of marking.*

pivot, they will run offside because the diagonal is not so deep and consequently does not offer that much space behind the defensive wall.

The Sweeper

The sweeper, or "extra" defender, has become one of the most effective defensive weapons in soccer. No other tactical development has spread so universally and has been accepted so readily.

Until the introduction of the sweeper, the responsibility for covering was shared collectively.

The weakness of the traditional defense lay in the triple role that the defenders were asked to play. The players were consistently forced to choose between marking their particular opponent and covering an area (in their own defensive zone) while providing the required cover and support to their teammates. The sweeper relieves the backs of their covering responsibility. He supplies cover and patrols the open space, while the backs concentrate on their individual opponents.

One basic principle of the sweeper-type defense

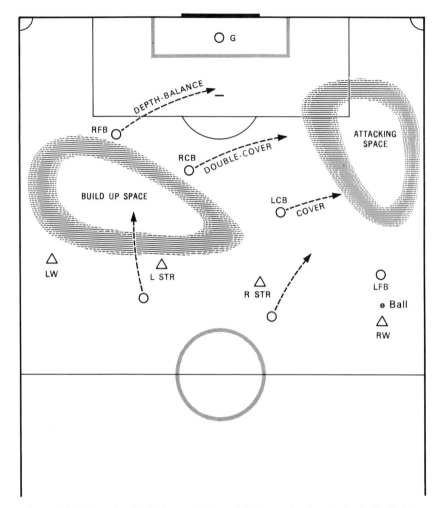

Diag. 10.18 *The four-back diagonal pattern of defense using the classic pivot principle when faced with a thrust from the right flank.*

is to provide a defender for every attacker. If the opposition uses four fulltime attackers, the defense must counter with four fulltime defenders. If the opponents attack with three, the defense need provide only three (in addition, of course, to the sweeper).

It is practically the only defense that provides numerical superiority around the ball. In other words, it assures depth, cover, balance, and concentration at all times. This is a must in modern defense. In theory the extra man can also move up through the defensive line to challenge an advanc-

ing forward or even elect to initiate or assist an attack now and then.

The backbone of the sweeper tactic is tight man-to-man marking. The centerbacks cover the interior attackers or strikers, and the fullbacks closely mark the wing forwards. The defenders stay with their immediate opponent wherever he goes, unless this involves a radical positional change for an extended period of time. In that case, they must switch off with the defensive man who is accustomed to playing in this particular position.

The midfield players must concern themselves

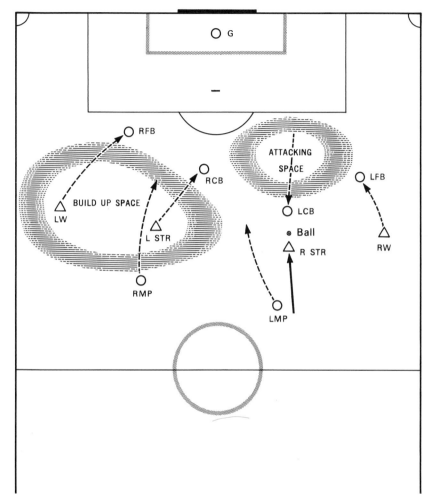

Diag. 10.19 *The four-back diagonal pattern of defense when faced with an interior attack.*

with challenging anyone who attempts to carry the ball up to the second line of close-marking defenders. If the opponent succeeds in breaking through the midfield barrier, one back must leave his immediate opponent or the sweeper must come forward to challenge.

In summary, the sweeper has two primary roles: (1) to cover the vital space behind the last line of defense, floating with the play, and (2) to challenge any unmarked opponent coming from behind. The position is indeed a test of character and ability.

The defense must always mass or concentrate toward the attacking thrust in a staggered formation, with the sweeper covering any possible gap through which the opponents may slip a player or a pass. The sweeper's running pattern is mainly lateral across the field, behind the last line of defense, building triangles behind the defenders challenging for the ball (Diag. 10.22).

While attempting to furnish cover and depth, the sweeper must constantly be aware of the danger of dropping too deep behind the last line of defense. Extreme depth will present the attackers with too much room behind the defensive line,

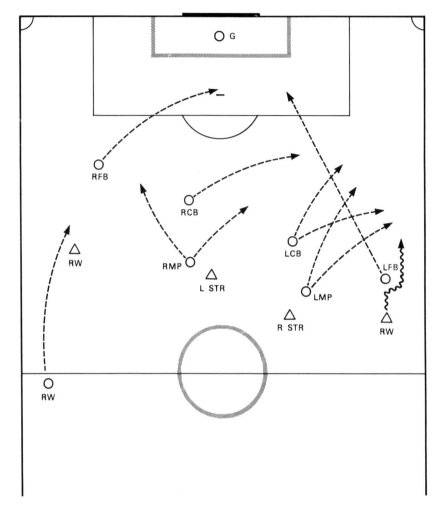

Diag. 10.20 *The four-back diagonal pattern of defense using the classic pivot principle in operation when the fullback is beaten.*

enabling them to drop passes behind the defenders without fear of offside infractions.

The sweeper must avoid dropping back too shallowly, as this is just as bad as dropping back too far. He must get enough depth to prevent any speedy forward from outmaneuvering him.

The sweeper should adjust his position to the style and speed of the opponent. When a defender is beaten, the sweeper will have to challenge the opponent coming through, while the beaten defender must recover as quickly as possible and take

over the sweeper position, bolstering the defense from a central position in front of the goal.

The other defenders will not be required to reestablish defensive balance unless, of course, they are within easy tackling distance. Where players switch positions and responsibilities, they leave attackers unmarked, if only for a fraction of a second. This is one cause of defensive imbalance, which is exactly what the sweeper is trying to prevent (Diags. 10.23 and 10.24).

When the attack comes within shooting range,

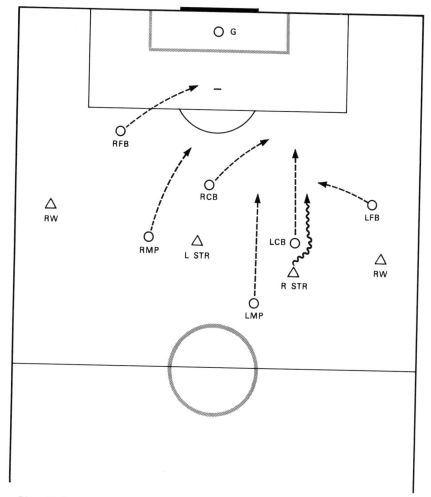

Diag. 10.21 *The four-back diagonal pattern of defense putting the classic pivot in operation when the centerback is beaten.*

somewhere around the edge of the penalty box, neither the last line of defense nor the sweeper can afford to yield. The sweeper must set up so that he becomes almost part of the last line of defense, while still furnishing reasonable depth (Diag. 10.25). The goalie assumes the responsibility of intercepting any pass between the defense and the goal.

With an extra man prepared to cover any immediate break through the defensive line (the sweeper), the attackers can hardly expect to out-number the defenders. This knowledge gives the defenders the confidence to cover their men tighter and challenge for the ball more vigorously. Tight man-to-man marking pressures the opponents and helps prevent them from taking the initiative. This is valuable against opponents of equal or superior ability.

The firmness of the sweeper defense greatly facilitates the counterattack. Secure in the knowledge that an extra man is available to cover him, one defender can exploit an opportunity to break

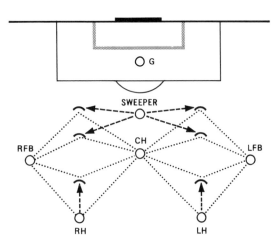

Diag. 10.22 *The relatively new four-back sweeper in operation showing the running patterns of the sweeper covering the vital zone behind the defensive wall, establishing cover depth. One must realize that this form of defense is not as concentrated as in the five-back sweeper as indicated by the wider area to be covered.*

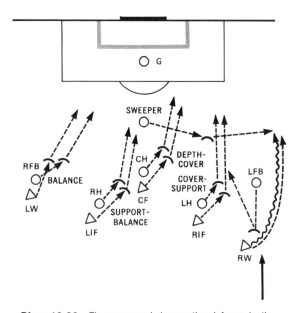

Diag. 10.23 *The sweeper balances the defense in the relatively new four-back sweeper. He moves across to challenge the opposing winger who has broken past the immediate defender.*

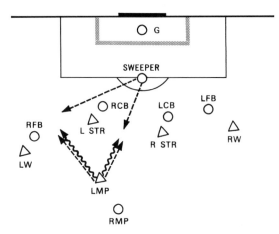

Diag. 10.24 *The sweeper takes the spare man. In some instances he might even have to come out to meet the attacker who is approaching unchallenged toward the last line of defense to prevent another defender from leaving his man.*

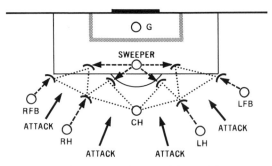

Diag. 10.25 *Near striking distance of the goal the sweeper has to become a part of the last line of defense to avoid giving unnecessary vital space behind the defense for the attackers to run off the ball.*

out into attack. This natural development in the evolutionary process is known as "overlapping."

For example, the left fullback can join the attack while the sweeper temporarily fills in for him (Diag. 10.26). Giacinto Facchetti, the left fullback of Italy's famed Internazionale Milan, has become famous for his bursts along the left flank, and his glamorous goals would make any left winger proud.

Sweeper in a Dual Role

An even more progressive development is having the sweeper double as a surprise attacker on the second wave. The most notable sweeper of this type ("elastic sweeper") is Franz Beckenbauer, the

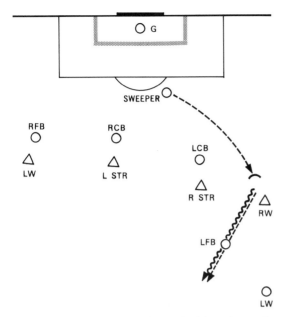

Diag. 10.26 *The sweeper balances the defense by covering momentarily for the left fullback who has joined the attack.*

German internationalist of Bayern München. His sporadic bursts into attack—where he either serves momentarily as the anchor man on the second wave or thrusts through to strike at the goal—have shaken up every opponent he has faced.

Sweeper as a Screen

The latest step in the evolution of the sweeper or freeback is having him operate *in front* of the defensive wall. He now can be described as a "screen."

Among the screen's chief responsibilities are: (1) to threaten any possible through pass and to intercept it in midfield; (2) to challenge any opponent with the ball or at least make it difficult for him to make a penetrating pass; (3) to put pressure on the opponent and force him into hurried, inaccurate, or crossfield passes. This gives the defenders time to set up a well-organized wall as well as to intercept passes more easily.

The essence of the screen's job is to challenge any opponent who has fought through the first line of defense and is progressing within goal range. If left unchallenged, this player sooner or later will draw off one of the tight-marking defenders, who,

in his attempt to challenge, would leave an opponent loose in the penalty box. This would imbalance the defense long enough to be exploited by the opponent.

The screen's first objective is to prevent this from happening. He must not tackle unless he is sure of winning the ball. If uncertain, he must stand off and simply bar any further progress by the opponent, preventing a defender from being drawn out. The rest of the midfield players must, of course, supply support to the screen man. They must restrict the attacker's room to run off the ball, as well as cut off as many passing channels as possible.

Despite the sweeper's sporadic attacks, the nature of his position behind the defensive wall makes him primarily a defensive player. Ordinarily, the key to defense lies in the area of the goalmouth. When the sweeper becomes a screen *in front* of the defensive wall, the key to defense moves to midfield, giving the defense more elasticity for a counterattack.

The screen may play a full part in setting up attacks from midfield, and may even follow up the attack in support. His main job, however, is to sprint back to serve as a screen whenever the attack breaks down.

Considering the screen's large work load, it is advisable to have midfield players alternate as screen every ten to fifteen minutes. A substitution can be made for the screen at given intervals. This is most logical in the scholastic game, and it might also happen in the international game with the adoption of the substitution rule.

Most preferred is a combination of sweeper and screen with stronger emphasis on the screen. The philosophy underlying the sweeper is covering up for weaknesses that have already been exposed. This represents a negative attitude based to a degree on weakness. The idea of the screen is exactly the opposite: to prevent weaknesses from being exposed. This represents a positive attitude based on strength.

A fusion of the two should prove most effective. By pressuring the opponents in midfield, one can hamper their buildup of attack and delay their final thrust, thus giving the last line of defense sufficient time to meet the attack with full strength.

As soon as the attack passes the first line of defense and screen, the principle of the sweeper

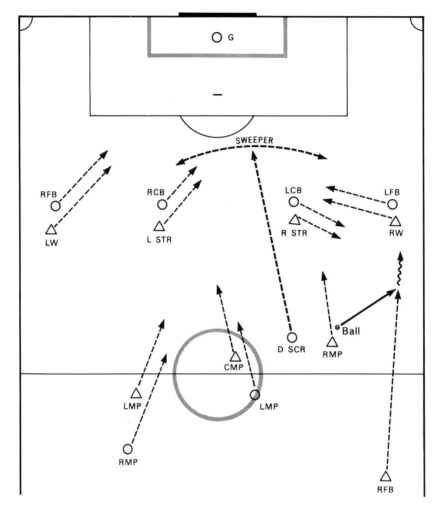

Diag. 10.27 *Ultra defensive five-back sweeper when the dual role of sweeper and screen are handled by one player.*

must come into effect; the prime concern becomes cover for the defenders and the vital space that furnishes depth to the defense.

From a tactical point of view, the defense could operate with a sweeper behind the defensive wall and a screen in front. This would be too restrictive an interpretation of this tactical innovation. A more progressive solution would be to operate initially with a screen, and then, the moment the attack passes him, have him quickly race back to assume the role of sweeper behind the defensive line (Diag. 10.27).

A third variation, better still, is to have the man operate initially as a screen and then, as soon as he is bypassed, have him immediately join the last line of defense by replacing a centerback, who drops back to play as the sweeper. Obviously, this variation requires coordination and experience (Diag. 10.28).

With cover and depth behind them, the midfield players are free to challenge more aggressively for the ball. This marks the return of the midfield tackle, midfield pressure tactics, and superiority in the midfield area. Though it represents only one attempt to enhance the attacking game, it is a step in the right direction.

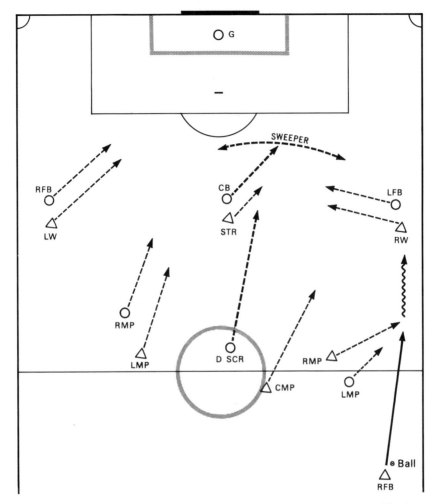

Diag. 10.28 *Dual role of the defensive screen who becomes the centerback while the centerback becomes a sweeper temporarily.*

The coach should regard the sweeper as a *tactic* rather than a *system* of play, and he should employ it aggressively and imaginatively, not negatively or ultraconservatively. (For further discussion of the sweeper, see page 263.)

SPECIAL COLLECTIVE TACTICS

Retreating—Funnel Defense

Retreating, wholesale dropback, and funneling tactics are indigenous to modern defense. They all rely on the principle of delay.

In an extreme instance, the entire team will fall back automatically as soon as the ball is lost. While retreating, the team or a unit of it will form a series of barriers in front of the attack to slow it down and gain time for the defense to organize.

If the ball can be won through a quick tackle or interception in midfield, all well and good. The defense should not risk early penetration, however. They should back-pedal steadily, delaying as they go, and converge to form a strong, compact defense at the edge of the penalty box.

The retreating, funnel defense is largely designed to allow the defenders to retreat *while facing the play* and keeping the attack in full view.

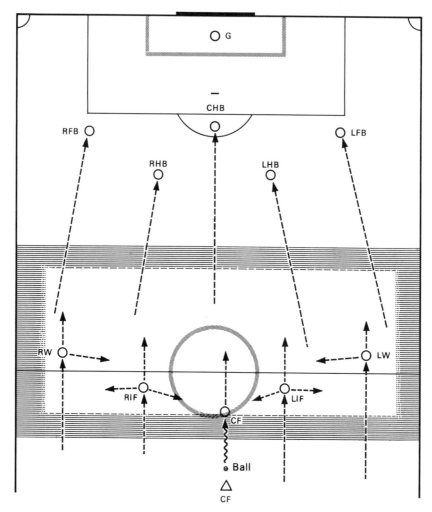

Diag. 10.29 *Retreating defense: From all parts of the field the defense will fall back in the face of an attack. By retreating into a narrow front they have a better chance of intercepting the ball and covering each other. The principle is that the defense must always be massed at the point where the attempt is made to strike at goal.*

This facilitates the players' movement and enables them to assess every situation—which they could never do if they were forced to keep turning around to keep track of the attackers.

In adopting such tactics, the coach should be aware that he is ignoring two very basic aspects of effective team play: (1) a team should try to contain play in the opposing half of the field as long as possible to delay the attack, and it is in this area of the field where chances can be taken

with the least immediate danger, and (2) the player with the ball and his teammates within effective passing range should not be allowed complete freedom to build up the attack.

The defenders are prepared to surrender ground in midfield—seemingly permit the attack to approach unopposed. The fact is that the defenders do not mind their opponents having the ball and are quite pleased to have them interpass to each other in front of them.

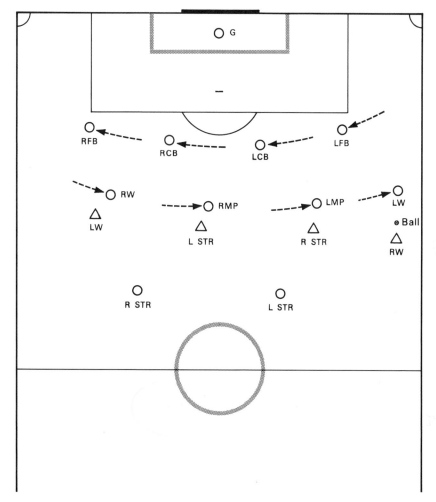

Diag. 10.30 *Blanket defense is designed to ensure numerical superiority and a concentration of players in the vital area. The middle four players are full-time defenders marking tight man-to-man around the ball, creating a high pressure area. The last line of four defenders operate in a sliding zone to provide cover and, if necessary, double cover.*

That defensive barrier is very difficult to cross. If the halfbacks are drawn into the play and the ball is retrieved, the defense can transfer the ball quickly to its own forwards and start an attacking movement in the big open space in midfield (Diag. 10.29). Tackling from the edge of the penalty area is a must if the defense is to prevent the attack from shattering their organization with shots from the edge of the box.

Wholesale dropback tactics are recommended against superior opponents who rarely can be dispossessed in midfield or to lure the opposition into loosening up by giving them the initiative in midfield.

Blanket Defense

The defenders spread over the entire area in front of the goalmouth to confront the attackers with a water-tight defense based on a tight man-to-man and a sliding zone that furnish cover, double cover, and depth. The blanket defense operates as a movable unit between the ball and the goal and is flexible enough to meet the flow of attack.

The blanket defense is designed to assure numerical superiority and a concentration of players in the vital area. The middle four players are full-time defenders marking tight man-to-man around the ball, thus creating a high pressure zone. The last line of four defenders operate in a sliding zone to provide cover and, if necessary, double cover.

Occasionally one of these four men will move behind the line for additional cover depth, playing like a sweeper. This will leave the team with only two or sometimes just one primary attacker, as both wing forwards may be required to challenge their opposing wingers.

For example, if the attack develops against the left flank of the defense, the left winger must challenge the opposing right wing forward while the left fullback assumes a covering role. On the opposite side of the field, the defensive right wing forward must move back toward the opposing left winger to threaten any attack in that direction (Diag. 10.30).

The front curtain of four defenders, covering man-to-man, tend to slide across the field as the direction of attack changes, while the rear curtain, covering in a sliding zone, tends to slide in the opposite direction.

This defense demands high organization and coordination, as any misunderstanding in the vicinity of the goal can be disastrous. The coverage of man and space must be faultless and the tackling instantaneous and decisive. Any mistake can put an attacker behind the defense into the vital area.

The blanket defense is commonly used in a defensive game to keep the score as low as possible or to kill the clock when preserving a lead late in the game.

Pressure Defense

The basic purpose of pressure is to force the opponents into mistakes that will cause loose balls and interceptions, disrupting their game plan. Good forcing tactics will step up the tempo of the game and consequently throw the opponents off their natural rhythm.

Every player must make an instant transition to defense. He must pick up his assigned man and stay with him wherever he goes. The objective is to retrieve the ball as quickly as possible and make

it difficult for the opponent to keep possession and initiate a counterattack.

To assure success, the pressure defense must be based on fairly tight man-to-man marking. The man-to-man assures good match-ups; the zone offers no such assurance. Any mismatch in a zone could adversely affect the whole tactical move.

Pressure defense is a gamble. The team is spread over the entire field and if the tight man-to-man marking breaks down, the opponent is going to inherit the initiative. Whenever this occurs, the players must withdraw to a more compact and less vulnerable defense.

Each player must have a thorough understanding of the mechanics of pressure. The players must complement and help each other at all times. All the basic principles of collective defense apply: the men must be alert, aggressive, and properly positioned and they must be ready to change positions, improvise, anticipate, and forage for loose balls and interceptions.

Pressure can be used in a variety of situations: at the start of the game, late in the half, or late in the game when behind in the score. When sprung at the beginning of the second half, it can catch the opposition by surprise. It also can be used to speed up the game, particularly when the opponents are badly conditioned, poor ball-handlers, weakly organized or slow moving, inexperienced, or tense and excitable.

Pressure can force the patterned team to operate in unfamiliar zones, to change its timing, and to switch to a tempo not to its liking. This is particularly effective in important home games, where the added pressure can induce a demoralizing tenseness.

The pressure defense has weaknesses, of course. Since it is extended over a wide area, it has problems converging on the goal and protecting it against close shots. One poorly conditioned player can ruin the efforts of the others; everyone must be in good condition. Experience also is a must. Being a collective form of defense, it takes time to master. As the individuals learn from their mistakes and learn to function as a group, the pressure defense will begin to pay dividends.

Containing the Superstar

The devastating type of attacker who can take any defense apart requires special handling. Some coaches will put their best man-to-man marker on him, with nearby defenders available to help out. Other coaches will try to control the superstar with two or three defenders in special marking or zoning roles.

One strategy is to force the star to pass the ball. If he is effective both left and right, the defender can overplay him to one side, while a teammate fills the other side. If the dribbler tries to exploit the open side, he will play right into the teammate's hands. A third defender can fill the space behind the attacker. This will force the attacker to put his head down to defend the ball, thereby limiting his view of the area around him. When he sees an opponent in his dribbling area, he may pass the ball.

If the star likes to play on one particular side, a defender can be moved over to support the man marking the attacker. The defender overplays him on one side so that the attacker must play on his weaker side and into the hands of the supporting defender.

Offside Trap

The very nature of the offside trap forces the defense to neglect cover and depth. The positioning is unorthodox in that defenders move back from the goal to let the offenders move ahead of them. If, consequently, timing is not perfect and the trap is evaded by the forwards, and offside is not called by the referee, defenders have little chance of recovering.

If the possibility of human error is eliminated and the trap works nine out of ten times, there will always be the tenth time when the referee will not blow his whistle. There is nothing more demoralizing than the sight of the entire defense floundering halfway up the field while the attackers have a clear path to goal.

Even the ultimate reward for a successful offside tactic—a free kick—is not always that attractive. The kick is almost always delayed, due to the vital seconds lost while the ball is retrieved, and the delay gives the opponents ample time to reform their defense.

There are some advantages to offside tactics, such as:

1. If the opponents rely mainly on the long ball and their speed in going after it, it is wise to use the offside trap to blunt their boldness in putting their heads down and running.

2. In free-kick situations, it is wise to keep the opponent out of the penalty area. It is essential to clear the penalty area after a corner kick or after an attempt at goal.

3. The offside tactic should be used as soon as the ball is cleared out of the goal area, thus forcing the opponents to move back.

The offside trap can be keyed by one man positioned slightly behind the rest of the defenders, or the defense can play in a line and have everyone clear out to put the attacker offside. The timing of the "clear out" is the key factor. If the defenders clear out in front of the most likely pass receiver just before the ball is released, the opponent will be offside. If, however, the defense clears out after the ball is released, the opponent will be onside and in the clear.

The attacker can adjust his position, but more often than not he will be left wondering—provided, of course, the maneuver is perfectly timed and coordinated.

Only skillful and intelligent defenders can effect the offside trap. But these are just the players who do not have to use such negative means of regaining possession! It is primarily a safety first tactic. As effective and safe as it may be, it can be beaten by speedy, quick-thinking opponents, and it is susceptible to human error.

IV

The Game

In restart situations every player must know what is planned and required, even if only two individuals are involved. Suggestions are given for taking advantage of restarts and for defending against them.

Since many circumstances can affect the outcome of a game, hints are given for stalling the game, changing the pace of play, getting the most benefit from substitution, utilizing the rules of the game to advantage, and dealing with external factors, such as the size of the field, field conditions, wind, and sun.

The assignment of areas and responsibilities to players is vital in effecting high team performance. Systems of play, from the offensive system to the contemporary flexible sweeper, historically anecdoted, are analyzed in practical terms so they can become functional tools rather than mere arrangements of players on the field. Recommendations are given for the selection of a system according to the abilities of key players and for adapting the systems to the player material available.

11

Special Game Situations

Both the individual and the team should be equipped with a varied assortment of tactical weapons. The more diversified the team weapons, the more difficult it is for the opposition to anticipate and counter them.

The team arsenal must include methods of exploiting dead-ball situations, such as corner kicks and free kicks. These will depend largely on the level and experience of the players. There are a number of good set plays and variations for every possible game situation.

KICK-OFF

The initial tactical aim of the kick-off is to retain possession. Traditionally, the kick-off man passes to his inside forward, and the team picks up its normal game from there.

Since the entire team must assume positions in its own half of the field and remain there until the kick-off is effected, the attack lacks the depth so vital for penetration. The essential need is time—the time needed to allow the attackers to get downfield. Well-executed plays can enable a team to exploit this situation and even take the opponent by surprise. For example, the center forward can kick off to one of his inside forwards, who in turn passes back to one of the halfbacks. This is a popular pattern because it allows time for the forwards to advance deep into opponent territory

and for the halfbacks to pick out an open receiver (Diag. 11.1).

As the attackers race downfield, they can interchange positions to decoy defenders away from the area that will be attacked. If they are fast and clever, they can exploit any weakness and go in for an immediate assault on the goal (Diag. 11.2).

When designing kick-off plays, coaches should remember that weaknesses—gaps—in the defense are based on the way the players line up. The offense must be versatile and adaptable enough to capitalize on these open areas.

CORNER KICK

The objective of the corner kick is to make things as awkward as possible for the defenders and as convenient as possible for the attackers to score.

The ideal placement of the kick is a moot point. Traditionally, the kicker has aimed between the penalty spot and the goal area. Since the modern goalkeeper will not hesitate to leave the goal to dominate the penalty area, the placement of the corner kick should be predicated upon the abilities of the goalkeeper and attackers plus such external factors as wind and sun.

As a rule, the good corner kick is placed too far out for the goalkeeper yet close enough to tempt him into going for it, in the hope that when he does, he will be caught out of position. The best

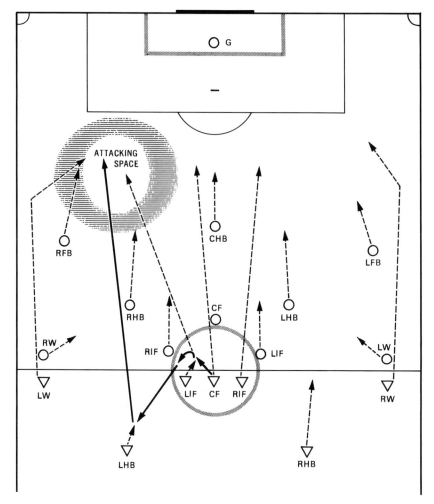

Diag. 11.1 *Taking advantage of any gaps in the opposition's lineup.*

placement is between the edge of the goal area and the penalty spot.

A swerving ball is liable to increase the defense's confusion, but an *outswinger* often is a great advantage to the attackers. The ball swerves away from the goalkeeper right to the incoming forwards, thus providing greater force for the shot or header. It also may tempt the goalkeeper to come out of the goal and thereby give the forwards a chance to shoot before he can get back.

An *inswinger* will not beat a competent goalkeeper unless the swerve is really vicious, but it may deceive the defenders crowding the goal-

mouth so that the ball will drop behind them. This will create a beautiful scoring chance for the oncoming wing forward.

Specific conditions influence the choice of kick. The kicker should make his decision as he places the ball, and then go decisively through with it, unless, of course, a teammate makes an unexpected dash forward to set up a short corner kick. Many mis-kicks are caused by a player changing his mind while in the act of kicking. Uncertainty gives the defense the initiative.

Variety in corner-kick situations is just as important as in free kicks and penalties. An *inswinger*

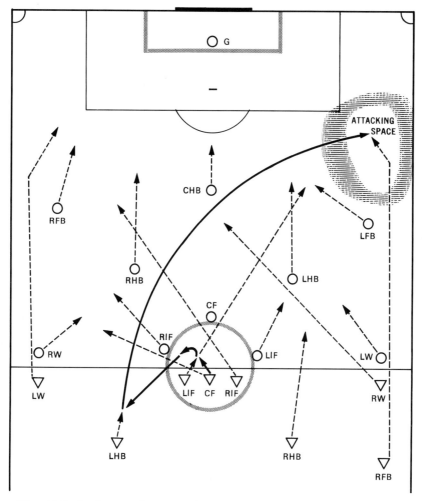

Diag. 11.2 *Creating a scoring opportunity through an overlap.*

is a good choice whenever (1) the goalkeeper is not too happy in a packed goalmouth or apparently lacks confidence and experience, (2) the wind is at the attackers' back, or (3) defenders are not dominating in the air. Even the best professional goalies are unhappy on a wet and windy day to see a high-swirling slippery ball coming across and a tough center forward leaping in to head it (Fig. 11.1).

The *outswinger,* on the other hand, tries to avoid the keeper, the crowded condition in the goal area, and competent defenders in the air. The kick sets up the dangerous header by giving him room to run up and meet the ball (Fig. 11.2). Vital to the success of both inswingers and outswingers is the timing of the attacker coming in to head.

Although there is a definite need for set patterns to coordinate the team reaction to specific situations, a team should not be hidebound by them. The coach may establish a simple pattern of running on the ball by having four or five attackers deploy in an echelon formation (1) just inside the penalty area for an outswinger, (2) further advanced for an inswinger, or (3) according to the most likely path of the ball for a low kick (Diag. 11.3).

Fig. 11.1 *Corner kick, inswinger.*

a   b   c   d   e

Fig. 11.2 *Corner kick, outswinger.*

a   b   c   d

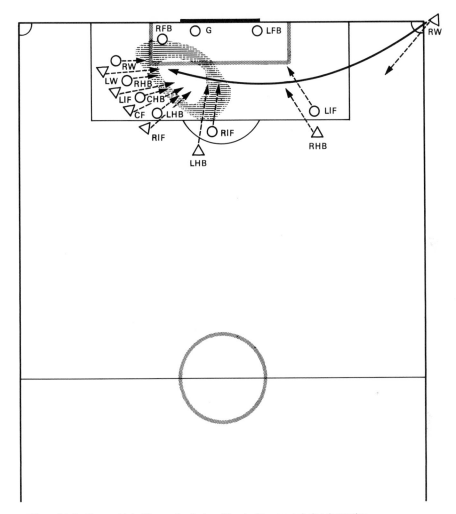

Diag. 11.3 *Corner kick. The method of rushing in from an echelon formation.*

The moment the ball comes across, the attackers move simultaneously on to the ball in the hope of getting a shot or a header by sheer weight of numbers and strength. Perfect timing can give them the advantage, as they are moving in toward the goal.

For variation, the attackers can again deploy in an echelon formation just inside the penalty box and rush toward the incoming ball. This time they only pretend to go for the header. The attackers intentionally let the ball pass in the hope of fooling the defenders and setting up the ball for the incoming halfback or wing forward.

Since the defensive trend on a corner kick is to crowd the goal area, the echelon method may have the immediate effect of drawing the defenders away from the goal to create space for the attackers.

Placement of the Kick

The placement of the kick depends on whether the defense moves out to mark the attackers or holds on to its central position.

If the defenders decide on tight covering, the ball should be placed just inside the goal area to enable the attackers to dash in as the ball comes

229

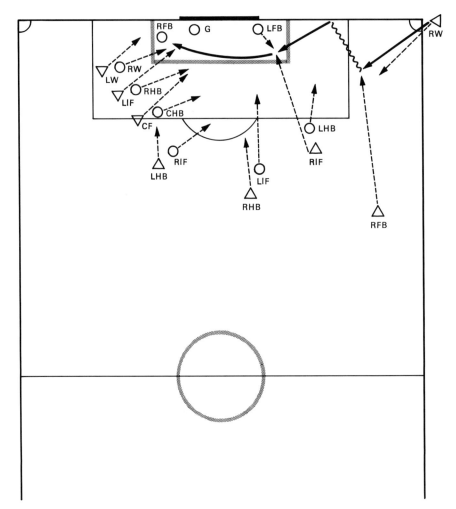

Diag. 11.4 *Short corner kick to draw defenders away from the goal.*

across. If the defenders decide to hold their central positions, the kick should be placed directly to the forwards, although there is always the chance of a deflection or that the goalie will lose sight of the ball.

A short-corner kick offers an effective tactic with which to loosen or spread a tight defense. It forces the defense to clear out of the penalty area in order to check the attackers, while several of them challenge for the ball. As soon as the defenders commit themselves and move out, the ball should be chipped across just behind them to allow the attackers to rush in and knock it in (Diag. 11.4).

Even with set patterns of play, the individual must be given the freedom to do the right thing at the right time. In fact, a certain amount of individual freedom can be incorporated into the planning, such as deploying a player close to the goal line in front of the goalie to distract him and impede his view. This move will draw some defenders into the immediate goal area, and the crowded conditions naturally will complicate the goalie's job. Some teams will bring a tall accomplished header up from the defense—making sure, of course, to have someone cover up for him.

Every corner kick can be enhanced by intelligent

230

decoying moves as the kick is being taken. The initial line-up of the players matters very little, so long as it creates a favorable situation for the final thrust.

In any play utilizing the element of surprise, two things must be kept in mind: the decoy moves must be executed realistically, and the players near the goal must move out immediately. The most beautiful play can be nullified by a slow-thinking attacker who is caught offside after the ball has been played once.

Most inexperienced players move in too soon to head a ball coming across, causing them to miss the ball completely, connect while they are already descending, or take off from a standing position rather than a run and thus lose the advantage of the increased height and force produced by a run-up and single-leg takeoff.

The experienced forward will hold off, seemingly just a split second too long and contact the ball at the top of his jump. This "holding" for perfect timing is the real secret of heading goals.

Defense of a Corner Kick

Coaches are tending to defense the corner kick by packing the goal area and covering either man-to-man, by area, or, if necessary, double cover.

Most goalies set up near the far post, as this makes it easier for them to judge the ball's flight, survey the situation in front of them, and move in toward the ball.

The onside fullback takes the near post and the offside fullback the far one. Both are ready to cover the goal in case the goalie moves out to intercept the ball. If the corner kick comes in low and brisk, the fullback on the near post has a chance to clear it before it curves directly into the goal or passes across the goalmouth where it could be deflected in by anyone. The center halfback and the halfbacks remain on the goalward side of the opponents they are marking. The inside forwards normally set up on the edge of the penalty area. Since they are usually responsible for the halfbacks, however, their positioning hinges upon the deployment of these opponents (Diag. 11.5). It is important to provide double cover for the goalkeeper whenever he leaves the goal, and for each defender to mark an opponent.

Minor variations are possible in the basic defensive setup. Some goalies prefer to take up a more central position. This is particularly advisable whenever an inswinger is expected. It is essential whenever a favoring wind can accentuate the swerve of the ball.

Whenever an inswinger is expected, the defenders should fall back deeper into the immediate goalmouth. As soon as a short-corner kick becomes apparent, the defense must instantly realign itself, with the wing forward falling back to challenge for the ball or cover up for the player who is going to do so.

As a rule, the immediate defenders should not respond to the moves of the attackers, as these are usually designed to draw them out of position. They should leave their positions only after the kick has been taken, but they must do this immediately. They have to clear the penalty area to force the attackers out of this vital area.

DIRECT, INDIRECT FREE KICKS

The referee will indicate a direct free kick with a one-armed forward underarm swing in the direction of the kick. The indirect free kick will be indicated with a two-armed underarm swing in the direction of the kick.

Whether the kick can go directly into the goal or has to be played a second time by another player (indirect free kick), the kicking team must quickly organize to take full advantage of the situation. The more time the defense is given to organize itself, the less will be gained by the award.

For coaching purposes, it is more practical to categorize the free kicks as those within goal range and those out of goal range. For tries out of goal range, the quickly taken kick is by far the most effective. The kicker may find an unmarked teammate in an advantageous position or the defense momentarily showing large gaps and weaknesses. This sort of defense can be split wide open with a penetrating pass. It is thus essential for the nearest player to take the free kick *immediately* rather than wait for a specialist to be brought on the scene.

Occasionally, a team will not be able to kick quickly. That is when a set play will come in handy, as the opponent will have time to bring up reinforcements.

The exploitation of the free kick in midfield requires outstanding skill. A strong-footed player

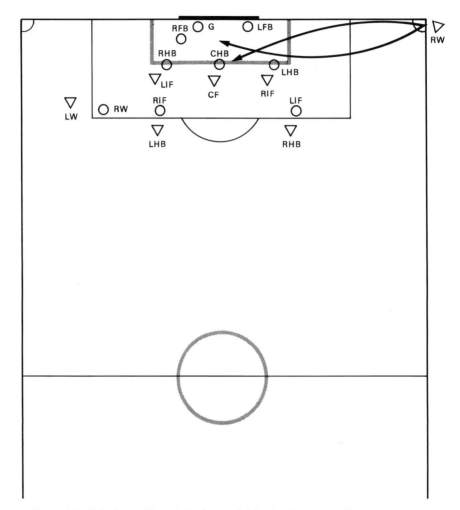

Diag. 11.5 *Orthodox positions of attackers and defenders for a corner kick.*

can lob the ball into the goalmouth from almost anywhere. This is recommended for teams with players who can deal with the ball in the air. If unchecked, the forwards can crowd into the goalmouth and possibly create a dangerous scramble in the penalty area.

The defense usually will check the attacker by forming a line either along the edge of the penalty area or, in special cases, running laterally through the penalty spot, depending upon the distance from which the kick is taken. The attackers must be alert for this to avoid being caught offside. The defense is vulnerable to a ball floated over and behind them for a forward.

For example, the left halfback can lob the ball behind the defense toward the far post, but not far enough for the goalie to collect. The attackers, positioned at the edge or a little outside of the right side of the penalty box, can then sprint toward the goal to meet the lob (Diag. 11.6). The success of this move depends upon the accuracy of the lob and the timing of the onrushing attackers. If their timing is off, they may be called offside. If they are faster than the defenders marking them, they can position themselves farther away or can delay longer before thrusting for the ball.

The strategy behind the free kick within scoring range hinges largely upon the strength and accu-

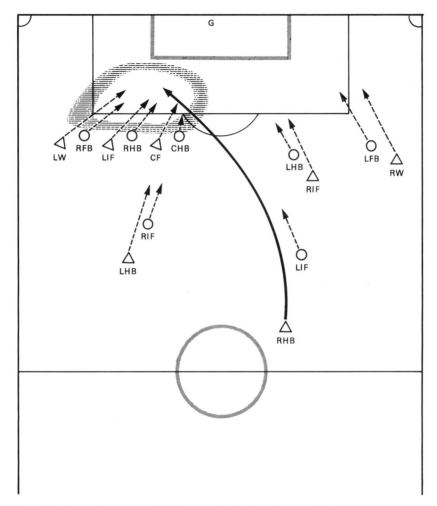

Diag. 11.6 *Free-kick situation in midfield using the lob to the far post.*

racy of the specialist's shot. Even though the specialist can reach the goal from forty yards out, a good goalkeeper will have little difficulty handling it. However, such external factors as field conditions, slippery balls, and the sun can enhance the immediate scoring possibilities and justify a long-range attempt. To further complicate matters for the goalkeeper, the kicker can put a little "english" on the ball to cause it to swerve fiercely.

Under thirty yards it is generally advisable to take a shot at the goal. Naturally, this becomes impossible against a solid wall of defenders. The ball can then (1) be slipped to one side of the wall for another player to shoot, (2) be chipped over

the wall for a player turning into a prearranged position, or (3) one man can fake taking the kick and run over the ball, while a trailing teammate comes in to exploit the defensive confusion.

METHODS OF BEATING THE WALL

Going through the Wall

On the first free kick of a game, it is sometimes psychologically smart to force the ball through the defensive wall, particularly if you have a specialist with a cannon shot. This can intimidate the less courageous defenders, who will bend over or move

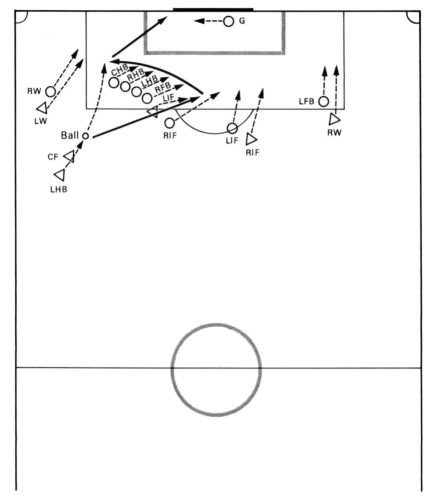

Diag. 11.7 *Beating the wall by going around it.*

aside to avoid getting hit the next time. Such bludgeoning tactics are unwise, however.

Going around the Wall

This involves the difficult, but effective, skill of swerving the ball around the defensive wall into the goal. All free kicks are designed to set up a shot, and to be effective they must be as simple as possible. The most basic form is the aforementioned fake whenever one player runs over the ball and a trailing teammate comes in to make the play. It should be remembered that the player running over the ball will most likely be the only one with any chance of penetrating the penalty area. This can be exploited: he can continue to a position where the ball can be played to him either directly or via another teammate (Diag. 11.7).

Going over the Wall

This presents another effective method. A shot swerving away from the goalkeeper is naturally more effective. Chipping the ball over the wall into the unguarded half of the goal requires great skill, particularly if the free kick is placed on the edge of the penalty area.

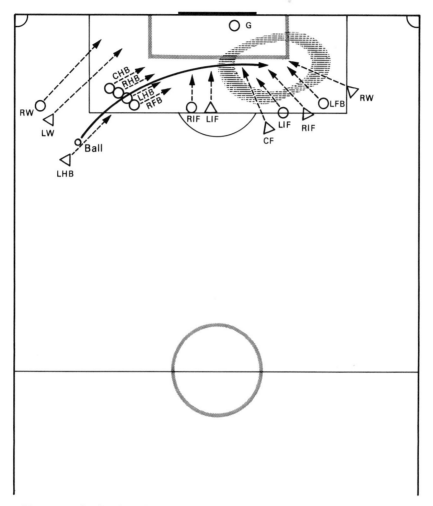

Diag. 11.8 *Beating the wall by going over it.*

There are only eighteen yards to the goal and the wall will be ten yards away from the ball. If the chip is short, it cannot get through. And if it is too strong, it will go over. The best idea is to chip the ball over the wall toward the far post, just out of the goalie's reach. This may give a good-heading forward a chance to run in, outjump the defender, and head for the goal. The timing of the run is vital; if the forward comes in too soon, he will be caught offside (Diag. 11.8).

Various means of confusing and diverting the defense can prove quite effective. When the indirect free kick is less than ten yards from the goal,

the defensive wall must be on the goal line between the goal posts. That leaves the attack with two possibilities: the kicker can shoot at the goal in the hope that the ball will cannon off a defender into the goal, or he can pass to a colleague for the shot at goal.

When these two alternatives are combined with player movement in front of the wall, they may create a temporary weakness in the defense. When the kicker intends to pass off, he should set up a couple of yards behind and to the side of the ball. This will give him enough time and momentum to produce a powerful shot. In certain situations it is advisable to pass the ball back rather than forward to avoid the onrushing defenders.

The stage of the game also will influence the free kick. If the kicking team is ahead in the closing minutes of the game, ball-possession becomes more important than penetration, and it is wiser to pass to a nearby teammate. If a goal is vital, the ball must be lobbed into the opposing goalmouth. This will give the opponents a chance to make a mistake or enable the forwards to create a favorable scoring opportunity.

Defensing a Free Kick

The defensive players take special positions only when the free kicker is likely to go directly for the goal. When a kick is taken from forty to fifty yards

a

b

Fig. 11.3 *Defending a free kick by a human wall. It is important that the goalkeeper has a direct view of the ball.*

out, it is highly unlikely to pose a direct threat at the goal. The defenders should then set up outside the penalty area and concentrate on tight man-to-man marking. They should try to keep the forwards some distance from the goal, preferably outside the penalty box, to prevent the goal area from becoming congested and thus give the goalie the freedom to intercept any ball going behind the defense.

The defenders must depend on speed and mobility, as any ball lobbed into the vital area can become dangerous. Whenever the ball is lobbed well-behind the defenders, the goalkeeper must not hesitate to come out and clear the ball. The defenders can also spring the offside trap by moving forward the moment the free kick is taken.

When the kick is taken from closer range, the defenders must watch for the quick through pass behind them and into the vital area for an attacker coming in for it. Such passes can be intercepted only through alertness and a quick move toward the goal the moment the pass is made.

When the free kick is within striking distance, the defense must form a human barrier. Much will depend upon the angle of the shot and the players' alertness. The wall may be composed of four or more players depending on the ability of Ricker and goalkeeper, guided solely by the goalkeeper. He will have to take most of the blame if things go wrong (Fig. 11.3).

A free kick directly in front of the goalmouth would necessitate more than four players in the wall. The more acute the kicking angle, the fewer the players in the wall. The wall normally should cover the direct path to the goal and the near post, leaving the goalie to protect the far side. The rest of the defenders, except for one or two players who stay upfield, set up in positions that assure everyone is marked. The first player in the wall sets up in direct line with the ball and the near post.

Since the wall can be vulnerable to a ball swerved around it, it is advisable to have the wall overlap the post on that side. Those in the wall must be courageous and unafraid of physical punishment. The remaining players bind tight alongside to cover a portion of the goal.

The goalkeeper deploys in a way that permits him to cover the remainder of the goal and to guard against a shot over the wall. The wall must form quickly to prevent the easy score.

A twin wall can be highly effective against a free

kick taken from directly in front of the goal. A barrier of three players covers each corner of the goal. This permits the goalie to watch the flight of the ball throughout, and to save the ball lobbed over the wall into one of the corners, since he has time to move to either side. The goal is still vulnerable to a well-executed banana shot around the inside of the wall into the upper corner of the goal. If the attacker is known for this ability, it is wiser to block the direct path to the goal.

On indirect free kicks closer than ten yards to the goal line, the rules allow the barrier to be set up within the uprights on the goal line (Fig. 11.4). The goalkeeper stands within the barrier at the most strategic position. Although the ball may be set up less than ten yards directly from the goal, the farthest flank of the wall can be angled toward the ball, since the distance to that part of the barrier, if it remained on the goal line, would probably exceed ten yards.

As soon as the ball is touched, all the players should rush toward the ball *as a unit* to block a possible shot. If any player lags or leaves early, a gap will be created for the ball to go through.

To prevent a quick free kick, the captain should ask the referee to pace off the distance between the ball and the barrier. This will automatically cause the referee to stop play. Quick thinking, good planning, and speed are essential. The opponent can get the most out of the free kick by taking it quickly and catching the defenders off-balance. The defenders must be absolutely sure of their responsibilities, and this can only be achieved through practice.

PENALTY KICK

Theoretically, every penalty kick should produce a goal, as the kicker, shooting unhampered from twelve yards out, has only the goalkeeper to beat (Diag. 11.9). But due to the tension and pressure, one out of every four shots is missed, the ball being kicked high or wide or saved by the goalie.

What is the best way to take this shot? The most natural way usually is the best. This may range from the booming drive that will take the goalkeeper right into the net with it to the fancy shot that tries to hoodwink the goalkeeper.

Two things have to be remembered. The harder a person tries to hit the ball, the less control he

has over it. It is wiser to go for accuracy first and power second. The fancy shot bears the danger of overplacement, which may lead to either missing the goal or hitting the goal post. It is smart to place the ball just about a yard inside the goal post to allow for a possible error.

Another method, although very unusual, also may be considered. The kicker, instead of shooting directly at goal, serves the ball to a teammate coming in from behind. The ball must make at least one complete revolution forward to be considered in play.

Most teams have an acknowledged penalty king, someone with the right psychological makeup as well as skill to convert penalty kicks. The kicker must decide beforehand where to place the ball so that he can concentrate entirely on the shot. The key to success is never to change one's mind once the type of kick and placement have been determined. The ball should travel fast enough to prevent the goalie from leaping across to make the save.

The smart player will vary his run-up. More often than not, a right-footed player running up to the ball in a slight angle from his left will kick the ball to the goalie's right hand. This will be true of younger players who find this technique more natural. Because players tend to kick with the instep at an angle to the ground, the inexperienced player tends to approach the ball from the side rather than from directly behind. This facilitates the goalie's job. The straighter the line of approach, the more difficult it will be for the goalie to read the ball's flight and react to it.

Fig. 11.4 *"On indirect free kicks closer than ten yards to the goal line, the rules allow the barrier to be set up within the uprights on the goal line."*

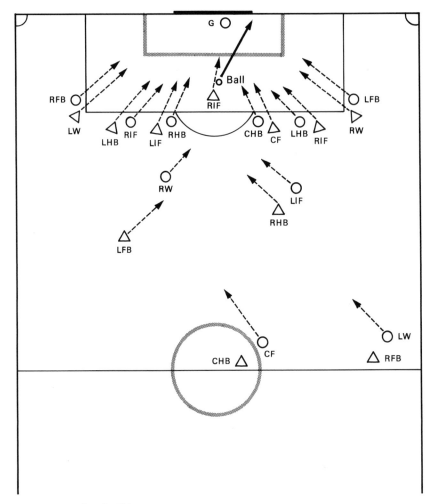

Diag. 11.9 *Penalty kick.*

Every member of the kicking team should stay alert. The forwards should be ready to play any rebound off the post or crossbar. The penalty kicker cannot replay the ball until it is touched by another player. He should follow up his initial attempt in case it rebounds off the goalkeeper.

Since the rules prevent the goalie from moving until the ball is kicked, he is left with very little time to react to the ball. Some goalies set up on one side of the goal, hoping to entice the kicker to aim for the wider side—toward which he has prepared himself to dive. Others guess and then

dive as soon as the ball is kicked. The goalie should watch the run-up and make a snap judgment based upon his knowledge of body-balance and the part of the foot used in kicking.

The other defenders should bid for positions outside the penalty area on both ends of the arc in front and inside the opposing attackers. They look for a possible rebound from the goalie or goalposts. Each side of the penalty box must be covered by a defender. This is as close to the goal as the defense is allowed to get and enables the defenders to move in instantly after the shot.

a *b* *c*

d *e*

Fig. 11.5 *Throwing-in from a straddle position. The player allows himself to fall forward in order to gain more distance. He staves off the fall with both hands.*

THROW-IN

A throw-in is used to restart play after the ball has gone out of bounds. Smart coaches use it as a launching pad for a purposeful attack.

The throwing action must be well-coordinated. The ball is held comfortably in front of the body and the heel is planted on the last step of the approach. The trunk retracts as the ball is brought well-behind the head, and the head sways back with it. The knees are bent to provide balance and impetus to the throw.

The athlete whips the ball forward with a powerful forward thrust of the trunk that transfers his weight from the rear to the front foot. The arms, ankles, and knees straighten out, and a whiplike wrist and finger action propels the ball forward.

The ball is released slightly behind or in front of the head, depending upon the tactical situation, and the body follows through to a completely

239

a   b   c   d

Fig. 11.6 *Throwing-in with the use of a run-up approach and stutter-step in order to gain more distance.*

extended position, braced on the toes. The impetus sometimes will cause the thrower to lose balance and fall forward. The follow through of the arms can be used to cushion the impact of the ball (Figs. 11.5 and 11.6).

Common Technical Faults

The thrower may:

1. Hold the ball incorrectly, making it impossible to put power behind it.

2. Bring his arms forward too early and thereby lose the whip effect.

3. Raise the rear leg off the ground, particularly when using the run-up approach.

4. Fail to lean well-back from the hip before thrusting the trunk forward and thus lose proper trunk action.

5. Make the last stride so late as to prevent the weight transferral from the rear to the front leg, thus losing the support of the trunk action.

Psychological and tactical factors also affect the throw-in. The chief objective of the thrower is to assure his team of possession. He must decide instantly when to release the ball, in what direction, long or short, and at what speed.

Obviously, the throw-in must be geared to the abilities of the players and to the particular situation. Deep in one's own territory, for example, it is wiser to settle for a simple throw-in that assures possession, rather than a dramatic long throw that has small chance of success.

Another factor to consider is the degree of difficulty between throwing toward the opponent's goal and one's own goal. The defense always will pay more attention to a pattern going toward its goal.

A quick decision is vital, and every player must know exactly what to do. He must have intelligent movement to avoid handicapping or paralyzing the thrower, and the latter must be able to decide the best moment of release and throw the ball accurately and with proper pace.

Full tactical advantage should be taken of the fact that the offside rule does not apply to the throw-in. Immediately after the throw, everyone involved in the play other than the receiver should instantly move into position for a return play. The cardinal error is for the thrower to stay put instead of offering himself as a potential receiver.

Crowding the thrower is another common error. It limits his room and his choice of action. The rush can be justified only for the purpose of creating space behind them. The thrower can hardly pass to a tightly marked player. With limited space in which to work, the player will have little chance to take possession. The odds are against a long throw and it is justified only if the thrower can reach the goalmouth.

Most unwise (unless it has a tactical purpose of getting a throw-in farther down the field) is the throw-in at a very acute angle along the touchline, where the receiver is not only hampered by the opponent but also by the narrowness of operating room.

Better use of the throw-in can be assured through planned plays. A throw-in gives the defense a theoretical advantage of one player in the field and can thus afford to double cover the point of attack. This presents difficulties the closer one gets to the goal.

Obviously, the ideal situation is to have a player in an open area with enough time to control the ball and start an attack. This is the advantage of a quick throw: it may create such an ideal situation. The ball also can be thrown into an open area whenever an attacker can beat the defense to the ball. Set throw-in plays can create advantages in the following manners.

Hitting an Unmarked Man in an Open Area

A well-organized team will be able to do this with a quick throw-in that will catch the opponent off-guard. If this is not possible, a throw to a player who can return it is often a good move. The other potential receivers should move away from the receiver to give the thrower enough space in which to work.

Creating an Opening by Speed

The simplest way to do this is to throw the ball into an open area and let the receiver either run after it or go meet the ball. Unfortunately, the opponent can read these moves, so it becomes a matter of explosiveness and perfect timing between thrower and receiver as to when and where to throw the ball (over the receiver's head or directly to his feet).

Creating an Opening by Interchange and Decoy Movements

This is a fairly advanced maneuver, since it involves intelligent and unselfish running on and off the ball. The thrower must be an experienced player in order to time and pace the throw perfectly. If things do not work out as planned, he must be able to improvise instantly. The idea is for one or more players to move in such a way, taking their opponents with them, that space is created for a colleague.

Advantage Situations

For example, the attacking team wishes to gain a ground advantage. The thrower delivers the ball close along the touchline to a heavily guarded wing forward. In most cases, the fullback will play it safe and just put the ball out of touch again. So the next throw-in puts the attackers that much closer to the goal. The long ball right into the goalmouth sets up another situation. The defenders will be anxious to protect this vital area, and the attackers can take advantage of the situation.

STALLING TACTICS

The team that is ahead in the closing stages of a game, particularly in a big match, often will try to run out the clock with a stall. For example, the goalkeeper may delay his goal kick as long as possible. He may pass to a teammate just outside the penalty area, receive a return pass, and take more time to get the ball into play.

A player may steal ground while taking the throw-in, knowing that he will be called back by the referee. This still eats up some of the clock. Or a team will kick the ball out of touch or a defender will intentionally catch the ball.

All these tactics are used to stall for time. Some are recommended with reservation, particularly on the scholastic level, because they are against the spirit of the game. A defense, caught in a territorial or numerical disadvantage may need time to restore the balance. A time-killing stunt may also provide the defense with a breather after it has applied continuous heavy pressure.

Freezing the Ball

This offers a more sophisticated method of stalling that is more in keeping with the spirit of the game. It involves retaining possession without attempting to make any real progress. Three, four, or more players will interpass deep in their own half of the field near the touchline—a relatively safe part of the field, where mistakes can be covered.

If any progress is made, it will be toward their defensive goal, with an occasional pass to the goalkeeper. This eliminates any risk of losing the ball, and if the ball is lost, the defense still has a chance to recover it. This stall prevents the opponent from attacking and runs out the clock.

CHANGING THE PACE

A team with a comfortable lead early in the game may adopt similar tactics in order to *set up a surprise attack.* It will start out by interpassing in front of the defense with apparently no intention of penetrating. The defending team, trailing in score, has to come out and take chances to regain possession. The defenders are thus drawn away from their goal or at least into incorrect positions, opening areas between and behind themselves. That is the time for a sudden switch in attacking emphasis. From a methodical, seemingly purposeless style of play, the attackers can catch the opponent off-balance with a long, accurate, well-timed pass or by changing to a lightning quick, one-touch short passing combination.

The methodical type of attack can be used to control the game, particularly at the start. In an away game versus an unknown opponent, it is good strategy to feel out their strengths and weaknesses and get the feel of the external conditions. It can give a team a psychological boost and the confidence to take the initiative.

It is always a good tactic to *change the pace of play,* to break the opponent's rhythm and establish your own, making the opponent play your game.

One major drawback of the open long-passing and fast-running game is that it tends to become a one-pace game. Rather than move to the ball in supporting positions, the players tend to run away. The opponents can adjust to this style of play quite easily by taking up more defensive positions. This, in turn, will encourage the attackers to begin their runs early in order to get the jump on the defenders.

As a consequence, passes will have to be delivered more quickly and over longer distances. Inaccuracy becomes inevitable, and the more mistakes there are, the earlier the attackers will tend to run, and the faster and more erratic play will become.

A team that plays a long-passing and fast-running type of game consistently quickly attunes the opponents to its speed. Very little surprise becomes possible, since the pace of the game has little variation. Attackers always are in difficulty, as they do not have the time to read the play taking place behind them. The ball will be delivered quickly and powerfully and they must be prepared to run.

The attack can be slowed with safe passes, usually by the midfield players and those behind them. This achieves the following purposes: it gives any player near the ball the time to make a penetration pass in a controlled way, and it can lure the opponents into standing still or even being drawn away from the goal in an effort to regain possession. Since there appears to be no immediate threat, the defensive concentration may lapse, providing the ideal moment to strike.

Other ways to affect the pace of the game are to apply a full-field pressure defense, forcing the opponents to play faster than they are willing, or to use retreating-funneling tactics, giving the opponents all the space and time they wish.

Methodical play for the purpose of stalling, freezing the ball, or changing the pace of play looks simple. It actually requires great teamwork, with everyone running off the ball to create easy passing angles for the man in possession.

SUBSTITUTIONS

Substitution remains a controversial subject. On the international scene, it was practically unheard of until just a few years ago. The United States has allowed substitutions for some time.

Traditionalists claim that substitution destroys the true spirit of the game by softening it up and blunting the great emphasis on stamina, team spirit, and cohesiveness.

When teams were frequently forced to continue playing a prestigious match with only ten players or with one or two badly injured, FIFA experimented with a rule that permitted substitution for the goalkeeper in case an injury prevented him from finishing the match. This proved to be so satisfactory that one additional substitution was approved. The new substitution rule that permitted the replacement of two players any time during the game was introduced into international competition at the 1970 World Cup.

The USSFA has exercised its freedom with respect to substitutions for many years. It allows its member associations to decide policy. As a result, the rule in the United States allows an infinite number of substitutions. Its innovations may have international repercussions, or they may be ignored. Meantime, the United States' substitution rule provides advantages that should be exploited.

The most immediate effect of substitutions is on game tempo. With fresh replacements being available, the tempo of play can be stepped up and maintained throughout the match. As previously mentioned, however, this is advantageous only if the athletes have the skill and maturity to play at the faster pace. By the same token, a faster, more aggressive style of play can compensate for skill deficiencies. For better or worse, this style of play is here to stay in America. It is attuned to the American athlete's penchant for contact and is strongly fostered through platooning.

Frequent substitutions also have a negative side. The soccer player needs time to get the feel of the ball, to adjust to the rhythm of the game, and to gain confidence before he can get into the swing of things and contribute to his team. When thrust suddenly into a game, he will have great difficulty controlling the ball and coordinating with other players. He may throw his whole team off its rhythm, destroying its spirit and cohesiveness.

Substitution is highly effective in making tactical changes in play. Even the substitution of one player with different playing attributes changes the tactics of the game.

LEARNING FROM INTERNATIONAL EXPERIENCE

The site of the game (home or away) has a definite effect on strategy. In European Cup competition, it is the practice to emphasize attack at home and defense away. Famous teams have been known to change their rosters for traveling games. For example, they will replace a high-scoring inside forward with a halfback or scheming inside forward, or insert an extra halfback for a wing forward.

The specialist is still very much part of the game. The all-round player is a rarity, even at the top level. The top teams have, however, a pool of eighteen–twenty players from which to choose, so the coach can field up to seven attackers for home games and up to eight defenders for away games.

This can be related to regular league competition. A coach, after scouting a team thoroughly, will decide on a certain game plan, then choose the right combination of players to effect it. The winning combination for one week may have to be changed the next week for a different type of game against a new opponent.

Numerous other strategies can be effected through substitution. By inserting schemers or a couple of striking speedsters, a coach can change the rhythm or tempo of the game. By constantly moving in and out, he can wear out the defense. Conversely, by freely substituting defensive platoons, he can exert extra pressure on the attackers. He can match his opponents with particular players designed to combat their effectiveness.

If things are not working out well within the tactical framework of the 4-3-3 system and the team is behind by two goals late in the game, to preserve any chance of salvaging the game, more attacking strength is needed. If a striker is substituted for a center halfback—or if substitution is limited, the center halfback can be asked to move out into midfield and a midfield player can move into an attacking role—this will change the system to a 3-3-4 and reinforce the attack while still providing for a solid defense.

The substitution of players, particularly in pressure situations—such as when trying to hold onto a slim lead or trying to even up or win the game in the closing minutes—is more effective than going all-out on defense or attack. There are psychological reasons for this. In an all-out defense, the players tend to become tight and anxious and resort to a completely negative game. As a result, they will clear the ball with a booming kick, only to have it come right back at them. The defense thus remains under constant pressure and is susceptible to vital mistakes.

In the all-out attack, the players also become anxious and waste time and valuable opportunities by taking foolish chances to score. All their teaching seems to go out the window. By substituting an attacker or a defender, according to tactical needs, the coach can assure discipline, organization, and efficiency.

For this sort of sophisticated coaching, it is imperative for the coach, particularly on the amateur level, to explain his thinking to the players so that he may get the fullest cooperation from them.

CORRELATION OF RULES AND TACTICS

Tactics, techniques, and conditioning usually are thought of as self-contained entities. The fact is that they do not exist independently; they are inextricably correlated.

Techniques can be executed without a tactical purpose. A typical example is the juggler in the circus, who exhibits such ball-sense and ball-control that you might expect him to star in soccer. Unless he can combine his extraordinary skill and technique with tactical knowledge and intelligent play, however, he will be humbled.

Since even the simplest tactic is impossible without the help of some technique, the players' skills must be taken into consideration when designing a tactical scheme. The tactics and techniques must be in perfect harmony. It would be foolish, for example, to decide on a short passing game with a relatively inexperienced team. The boys would have neither the ball-control nor tactical maturity to implement this style of play.

Although tactics can partly compensate for technical shortcomings, conditioning is vital for both. When fatigue sets in, every weak skill begins to disintegrate, concentration becomes uncertain, and the team plan or tactic loses its effectiveness. The training program must prepare each player technically and physically to meet specific tactical needs. If an attack is to be employed that has the players interchanging positions, it is necessary to develop the endurance for this sort of game.

The coach must evaluate the technical ability, tactics, and physical condition of the opponents. A shrewd coach can exploit superior condition by forcing the defenders to keep constantly on the move. He can exploit a particular defender known to dislike running by forcing him to run constantly. He should always try to play away from the opponent's strengths. If the opponents are accomplished headers, he will stay away from tactics that require high passes.

Ultimately, then, the coach's choice of tactics must depend upon the skills and maturity of the players. Skill alone is not enough. The players also must have the physical and psychological toughness to execute under stress.

UTILIZING THE RULES

A thorough knowledge of the rules and their practical application can extend the range of tactics.

Free Kicks

Players should be familiar with the kinds of infraction which invoke a *direct free kick,* from which a goal can be scored directly, and an *indirect free kick,* from which a goal cannot be scored until the ball is played or touched by a second player.

The ball has to be stationary when the kick is taken, and the referee must blow his whistle (in scholastic games only) as soon as it is in position to be played. The opposing players cannot be within ten yards of the ball, unless they are standing on their goal line between the goal posts. A player has the right to ask the referee to pace off the distance (to make sure he is in a legal position).

On a free kick award, the nearest player should take it immediately to prevent the opponent from getting organized, thus nullifying the tactical advantage of the kick. If the kick is within goal range, a quick try may catch the goalie or defensive players off-guard.

Penalty Kick

This kick is an exclusive affair between kicker and goalkeeper. Everyone else must stay outside the penalty area, at least ten yards from the penalty mark. The goalkeeper must assume a stationary position on the goal line between the goal posts, until the ball is played.

If the ball rebounds from a post, the kicker cannot play it until it is touched by another player. All supporting players must therefore be ready to move in quickly.

Throw-In

The throw-in should also be taken quickly to prevent the opposition from covering everybody.

The Advantage Rule

This allows a team to go on playing after an infraction. If a fouled player still manages to proceed with the ball, a good referee will wave him to continue. This is known as using the "advantage rule." If the referee stopped play, the advantage would be lost, and the offending team would have gained the time to regroup. That is why the players should be trained to keep playing until the referee blows the whistle, even though they may see an obvious infraction. Many scoring opportunities are never followed up because the forwards, anticipating the referee's whistle, come to a stop after the opponent has committed a foul.

Use of the Body

The judicious use of the body can be an efficient tactical weapon. *Screening* can be used to keep the ball out of reach of a challenging opponent. It merely involves keeping the body between the ball and the opponent. As long as the ball is within playing distance, the player will not be called for illegal obstruction.

A *shoulder charge* can be used to ride an opponent off the play, as long as it is not violent or dangerous.

Charging the goalkeeper is legal whenever the goalie is obstructing or is outside the penalty area. When both players are going for the ball, a collision is not considered an illegal charge.

Offside Law

This rule offers a wide variety of tactical possibilities to both defenders and attackers. The defense can exploit the offside law with the offside trap. The attack can take advantage of situations where the offside rule is not in effect, such as goal kicks, throw-ins, corner kicks, and drop balls.

The rule states that a player is offside if he is nearer the opponent's goal line than the ball at the moment of play unless:

1. He is in his own half of the field of play.
2. Two of the opponents are nearer to their goal line than he is.
3. The ball last touched an opponent or was last played by him.
4. He received the ball direct from a goal kick, corner kick, throw-in, or drop ball.

Defenders can create offside situations by simply clearing out, thus setting the offside trap. It demands close coordination of the whole defense. If just one defender does not clear out on time, the attacker will have a clear path to the goal. A team should resort to offside tactics only when it is well-coordinated and has great speed so that it will always have a slight chance to recover in case the trap fails.

VERSATILITY

The greater the importance of the match, the more effort should be made to study the opponent in advance. Scouting is invaluable, but it seldom can pinpoint all the abilities and eccentricities of the opponents.

Adaptability is the characteristic of good players and championship teams. When an opponent comes up with a surprise tactic, or the ground or weather conditions change, or a team's tactics or countertactics fail to live up to expectations, immediate diagnosis and adaptation are essential.

Reading the game consists of observing and instantly interpreting the actions of the man on the ball and those running off the ball to assist him. This assessment must automatically incorporate the speed and characteristics of the players concerned. For example, some players are more likely than others to take on opponents, or they may prefer short passes to long ones, or they like to set up the play rather than score themselves. A player must be able to instantly size up the opponent and the play in order to counter effectively.

Some players have a natural soccer sense. Others, even experienced players, may have only a shallow intelligence, probably because in their formative years they were merely told what to do and not why it should be done. Until a player can read the game, he cannot play an authoritative part in adapting or directing its course.

Since few coaches have super diagnosticians, it is their responsibility to analyze the strengths and weaknesses of the opponent and suggest means of countering them. A defensive weakness can be exploited with a concentrated attacking thrust. An extremely dangerous attacker may call for special attention either through tight man-to-man marking or more cover and depth in defense.

The goalkeeper can be observed closely for weaknesses or tendencies. He may find it easier to save high balls, and shots can be aimed low accordingly. Players who prefer one foot, one turn, or display idiosyncrasies in feinting, shooting, and so forth, or a team that observes a general pattern of play can be effectively countered or taken advantage of.

When it becomes difficult to spot weaknesses, the coach may elect to go to the opponent's strength. Every team has confidence in the things it can do well. By playing this strength, one can induce overconfidence. If the opponents have a strong attack, they should be encouraged to attack by falling back or retreating to the edge of the penalty area, where the team has a tight defensive structure of seven or eight players.

The idea is to draw more and more opponents into attack and to restrict the amount of open area within the defense and the movement of the attackers behind the defense. Whenever a team becomes heavily committed to attack, it becomes most vulnerable to counterattack, as it leaves the maximum amount of space behind its defense.

EXTERNAL FACTORS

Adaptability is vital, as tactics must constantly be adjusted to a number of external factors. The level of adjustability depends upon the players' experience. Young players usually have to depend upon their coach's guidance to cope with varying circumstances.

The Field of Play

This must obviously be given first consideration. The familiarity of the home environment, the size and quality of the field, and the support from the home crowd can provide great psychological boosts. That is why the home team generally should play boldly, and the visitors usually start more cautiously to get settled and adjust to unfamiliar conditions, though this does not mean adopting a purely defensive game.

Size of the Field

Some fields are too wide compared with their length. In such cases the forwards should exploit the width of the field through clever positioning and interpassing to spread the defense. The defense, on the other hand, dare not follow the attackers too far out to the touchline, as this would leave large gaps in the middle—the central path to the goal.

Other fields are too long in comparison with their width. This gives an extreme advantage to the defense, as everyone is crowded into a relatively small area. Such a field squeezes the attack, particularly when it is operating with a five-man forward line. It is wise to reduce the attack to a four- or even three-man line to assure more space between attackers and also help close the gap in midfield.

It is essential for the attackers to be mobile and to interchange positions frequently to shake off tight marking and create openings. The wing forwards, instead of coming in, should stay close to the touchline to spread the defense.

On a small field the defense is much closer and readier to challenge, and this gives them the edge. The attackers will need great confidence with the ball. Ball-control must be instant and the passing deadly accurate, aimed to the feet of the receivers rather than out ahead of them. Even experienced teams are reluctant to play on small fields because it undoubtedly favors the underdog. The most spectacular approach play can be nullified by a long boot and lead to a lucky breakaway goal by the opponent. This puts a psychological burden on a skillful team. To safeguard against kick-and-rush tactics, the coach should have his defenders stay back rather than move up on attack.

The adjustment to a large field must be made in style of play. A large field is suitable to a more open style of play. The attackers are in a more favorable position because of the greater area in which to work and the fact that the defenders have to cover more space. Obviously, it favors a team in good condition.

Ground and Climatic Conditions

These affect match tactics considerably, as players with only average or poor ball-control do much better on soft ground. They run into trouble on hard, bumpy ground and particularly in strong winds.

Hard, Bumpy Ground

This accentuates each bounce and drastically alters the path of the ball. Players should take possession or make the play before the ball rebounds and make the pass through the air rather than on the ground. The goalkeeper is at a disadvantage. If the ball bounces in front of him, the bumps may deceive him, and he is going to be reluctant to dive on hard ground. The attackers should take advantage of this by keeping their shots low and using every opportunity to test the goalie.

Hard, Loose, or Grassy Ground

Conditions affect the ball differently on this type of ground with regard to liveliness, angle of rebounds, friction in passing, and spin. The differences are exaggerated with the influence of the weather: rain, snow, or ice can make dramatic changes in ground conditions in a relatively short time.

Wet and Slippery but Not Sticky Field

A team can still use a short passing attack, as this ground will have no effect on the direction of the ball. The rebound can be deceptive, however. It will be difficult to deal with fast balls, since they will skid off the grass and slip away if the player fails to judge or watch the ball carefully.

Timing and pacing pose special problems. The ball should be sent directly to the player's feet rather than lead him. Square passes should be avoided as they would force the receiver to slow up and possibly turn back to get the ball or accelerate unduly and thus make it difficult to control the ball.

Wet conditions favor the experienced players who can adjust more easily. The players should try to keep their feet under their bodies and use small strides to prevent sliding. This also will facilitate changes of direction.

The poor footing presents great difficulties for the defenders. They cannot commit themselves in challenging for the ball because they cannot hope to recover and tackle back. They should, therefore, avoid drawing too close to the forwards, as on a slippery field a closely marked attacker can easily outwit them with a body swerve. Shoes with sturdier and longer studs should be used to improve traction, and the soles can be greased to prevent grass or mud from sticking on the studs. Conversely, boots with short rubber cleats should be worn on hard and frozen ground.

Heavily Soaked Fields

Puddles and mud require special tactics (Fig. 11.7). A low, short passing game is out. The ball is bound to stick in the mud or stop suddenly in a puddle, and this style of play also is too fatiguing under

Fig. 11.7 *Muddy fields require tactical adjustments.*

the circumstances. It is more economical to use a long passing game, putting the ball through the air rather than on the ground.

Treacherous ground (mud, snow, etc.) helps the poorly skilled team by enabling it to compensate for technical limitations through aggressiveness, hustle, and stamina. The defenders must be particularly alert around the goal area, as the ball can play unexpected tricks.

The goalkeeper has his work cut out for him. Ball-handling becomes extremely difficult, as the ball gets very slippery. He should catch the ball only if he can do so with safety. Otherwise, he should just punch it clear. Gloves with rough palms that stabilize the grip can prove quite helpful. The attackers should in turn be on the alert for uncertainties by the goalie and be ready to pounce if he makes the slightest mistake.

The Wind

A decisive factor, the wind reduces the flight of any ball coming into it. The ball hangs in the air and descends at a steep angle. The weightlessness of the ball presents control problems, particularly to inexperienced players. The wind also presents psychological and physical disadvantages. More strength and energy is required to pass and to run against the wind.

A short, ground-hugging passing attack is the correct tactical solution to such problems. The defenders should balance each other more carefully and closely to avoid any unexpectancies.

A favoring wind produces the opposite effects. The ball travels much farther than usual, and this naturally allows greater range and speed in passing and shooting, but it presents difficulty in judging and pacing the ball, particularly on lead passes. The wind may pick up the ball and carry it out of the receiver's reach.

Playing the Crosswind

When the wind is blowing from one touchline to the other, it is generally wise to attack into it so that the final pass or center travels downward. This is particularly advisable for younger players whose wing forwards are probably incapable of putting across a center against a strong crosswind.

Conditions such as wind and sun should be exploited at the opening of the game when errors are more likely because players are nervous and tight; there is nothing like a quick goal to boost morale.

12

Systems of Play

A "system of play" is a recognizable order or organization of players on the field for the sole purpose of giving each one a clearly defined function. It must be sufficiently elastic to bring out the best in players, permit them to improvise, and allow tactical changes to be made according to the problems posed by different opposing teams. Great individuals like Pelé (see photo, opposite) must be allowed freedom of expression in any system of play.

ADAPT SYSTEM TO MATERIAL

If the system is chosen according to the experience and talent of the squad, with its design flexible enough to encourage initiative, it is selected only after analyzing each player in match play.

Before making this observation, the players may be allowed to choose their own positions or the coach may ask them to play specific roles. In either case they should be encouraged to express freely their natural ability. The coach may then ask certain players to change their game a little in order to determine whether they can adapt to a game plan or whether they are purely instinctive players.

The maximum capacity for young players may be the offensive or WM systems. These enable the coach to give most players specific offensive or defensive responsibilities. The exceptions are the center halfback in the offensive system and the halfbacks and inside forwards in the WM. These positions demand experienced all-round players who can handle the instantaneous transition from defense to offense and the responsibilities of both.

It is difficult to find the right team combinations of temperament, ability, and experience. For example, scorers and aggressive opportunists are needed in the forward line. Also desirable is a smart, cautious type of player who can hold the ball and set up the other forwards. The same holds true for the midfield or halfback line. An intelligent playmaker with a flair for both the long and short pass is needed to initiate attacking movements. As a balancer, a hustling, indestructible workhorse is required. The halfback line cannot be only offense or defense-minded, because neither by itself can be productive.

SELECTING KEY PLAYERS

The first player to look for is one with the talent to be the key man—the organizer and inspirer of the team. His position will dictate the style and pattern of play. It will become the "schemer" position. Wherever it is, the principle will be the same: the ball should be played to him. That is why almost every schemer operates in the wide midfield gaps. How to organize this is a problem that must be settled by the coach in consultation with his team.

After analyzing the candidates thoroughly and selecting the key players for the system, the coach's first concern must be for the psychological adjustments of the players to it. For them to comprehend it fully and become competent in an entirely new environment, they must be convinced that the system is best for them personally and for the team. The only way to accomplish this acceptance is by frankly discussing the design and the methods of exploiting the various strengths and weaknesses of the players in the system selected.

The system will undoubtedly require changes in basic technique. A variety of new passing patterns will open up. Considerable mental discipline will be required for the extreme positional play in the modern systems. This is particularly difficult for the average American player who likes to move into action with full speed and aggressiveness. He cannot do this on defense, where the objective is massing in the modern style of play. He must funnel—retreat—rather than lunge at the opponent. The idea is to join in the mass defense or stall for time until the other defenders can take up their positions.

The player must adapt psychologically as well as technically to congested conditions. He must accelerate his skill execution when he is under the gun—being threatened by an opponent. In the old style of play, the ball could be stopped or a pass made under relatively unharassed conditions. Not today!

The physical condition of the players is also an important consideration. The players must be prepared physically, intellectually, and technically for the demands of the specific strategy that will be used.

If the task of deep-lying center forward, who is required to cover wide areas, is given to a player who has always been a spearhead attacker, he must be made ready to assume a far greater physical burden. Otherwise he may tire too easily, discourage unduly, and his failure to fulfill his position may affect the performance of the whole team.

The true value of a system is that it gives the players a purpose. It encourages them to think as a team. Some systems demand more practice than others because they are more intricate. The basic principles, however, are the same for all.

It is important to realize that various systems are still being used in this country. In evaluating prospects, then, it is vitally important to know what system of tactical experience they have had. For example, when watching a group of college freshmen it is possible to tell fairly accurately whether a player has been a wing half in the offensive system or a halfback in the WM. This is indeed valuable knowledge as limitations in play may be limitations in the system he has learned and instruction must start with his present understanding.

The ability of the coach to make on-the-spot diagnoses of tactical maneuvers enables him to cope with game situations. If the fullback is confronted with a deep-lying wing forward, it is wise to bring in a halfback. This kind of man can easily cope with the wing forward and help control the midfield, something that the standard fullback could not do.

OFFENSIVE SYSTEM

The term "offensive system" is derived from the offensive role of the center halfback. It was the first tactical arrangement to establish a balance between attackers and defenders. Introduced by Cambridge University in 1863, it represented the first attempt to confront the five forwards with five defenders (Diag. 12.1).

The five forwards were specialized attackers, while four back players were more or less specialized defenders. The center halfback was the dominant personality on the field; he presaged the future in his dual role of attacker and defender.

The basic method of defense had a zonal concept. Every defender was responsible for a particular area. The two fullbacks had to cover the immediate area in front of the goal or, more specifically, the area between the inside forwards and the center forward. One fullback was stationed permanently in the penalty area and became known as the defending fullback. The other fullback roamed freely in front of him, moving quickly into the recurring danger zone; he became known as the attacking fullback.

Both halfbacks, called wing halfbacks, had to cover the area between the wing forward and the inside forward. While not required to mark any particular opponent, they had to keep an eye on the wing forwards as well as the inside forwards.

The defenders tried to delay the attack in midfield in order to give their center halfback time to

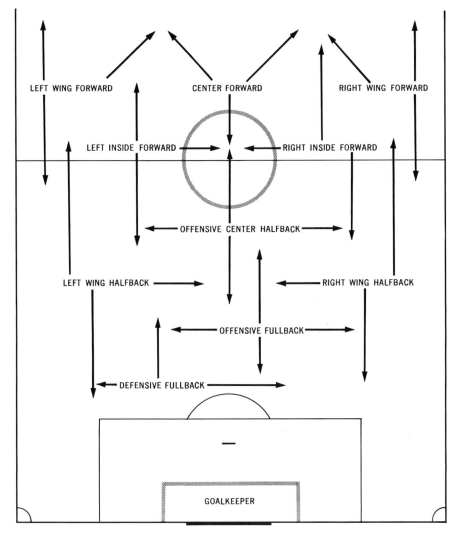

Diag. 12.1 *Offensive system.*

come back. When the numerical relationship achieved parity (five vs. five), the defense marked man-to-man on the ball-side while covering zone on the other side.

The most effective defensive weapon, however, was the offside trap. To be onside prior to 1925, there had to be three defenders (instead of two) between the goal and the attackers during an attack. A clever defense could exploit this rule by staggering the fullbacks while the attack was developing. The defending fullback would play a waiting game, laying back to cover the central path to the goal. The attacking fullback would prepare the offside trap by taking up a position nearer the halfway line, ready to move forward at the slightest sign of danger. This invariably would catch the forwards behind the attacking fullback in an offside position and thus take the sting out of the attack.

The five forwards (two wing forwards, two inside forwards, and a center forward) were forced to attack mostly in one line, supported from behind by the offensive center halfback—primarily an

253

offensive player who served as a playmaker and was pressed into attack at every opportunity.

The offside rule, when effected by both teams, literally smothered the attack in midfield. The forwards hesitated to penetrate, either through running or passing, because of the ever-present fear of being caught offside or having their through passes intercepted by the defenders. The only logical means of attack were short passes, dribbling, and individual play. The heroes of the time were the brilliant individualists.

These defensive tactics decreased scoring and moved the Football Association to modify the offside law in 1925, so that only two defenders were required to be between the offensive player and the goal line.

The change had an immediate effect on goal scoring. The forward formation was immediately adjusted to provide the vitally needed depth and penetration. The two inside forwards were asked to operate slightly behind the wing forwards and center forward in a "W" attacking formation. The inside forwards became the "schemers," and the wing forwards and the center forward were the spearhead of the attack. The spearheads could now thrust deep into enemy territory, as they generally were given ample space in which to work.

The game entered a stage in which the development of passing movements led to a more subtle expression of attacking art. The defense was now vulnerable to the counterattack. Whenever the center halfback and often one or both wing halfbacks were caught upfield, the two fullbacks frequently were confronted by five attackers.

Besides vastly improving the technical and tactical standards of play, the modified offside rule sounded the death knell for the offensive system. Although it was used, with a few modifications borrowed from the three-back game, as late as 1958 by the Uruguayan National Team, it has all but vanished in top-class soccer. It remains quite common on the schoolboy level, however, especially in the primary teaching stages. Since few schoolboy teams have more than one outstanding player, the wise coach will play him as an offensive center halfback to take full advantage of his talents.

Attacking and scoring provide the greatest motivation for beginning players. Since the attack in the offensive system has the numerical advantage, the chances are that inexperienced players will score more frequently. Defensively, the use of the zone concept will prove less restrictive to young players. It will give them the freedom to develop and express their individual styles more naturally.

The obvious weakness of the offensive system is that the defense is frequently outnumbered because the system is numerically and philosophically offense-oriented. When the team is committed heavily in attack (and that often means seven-eight players including the offensive center halfback, plus a wing halfback on the side of the ball) it is most susceptible to a quick counterattack.

Consequently closer attention must be paid to defensive play. The wing halfbacks particularly must be asked to pay closer attention to their wing forwards, still relying on the zone principle. To compensate, the inside forwards must drop back into midfield to pick up the slack and become adjutants to the offensive center halfback in midfield.

The recommended man-to-man assignments when faced with a W offensive formation would be: wing halfbacks cover wing forwards, defensive fullback covers the center forward, offensive fullback covers the advanced inside forward, and offensive center halfback covers the trailing inside forward.

THE SWISS BOLT

The "Swiss bolt" system is based on an equal ratio of defenders to attackers, plus a reserve defender called the "bolt." It was the first system to introduce the idea of a "free" defender covering the defenders in front of him. It was the predecessor of what is known today as catennacio (Italian) or sweeper (English).

Karl Rappan, a Viennese coach who trained club teams in Switzerland, introduced the "bolt," or "verrou" system in the 1930's. It was designed to get an extra man on defense when needed without depleting the attack. Greater safety was provided on defense and weaker teams were enabled to attack from a firm defense.

One inside forward was brought back to mark the opposite inside forward. The former offensive center halfback marked the other inside forward. Both wing halfbacks tightly marked their respective wing forwards, while the former attacking fullback marked the center forward. The former defensive

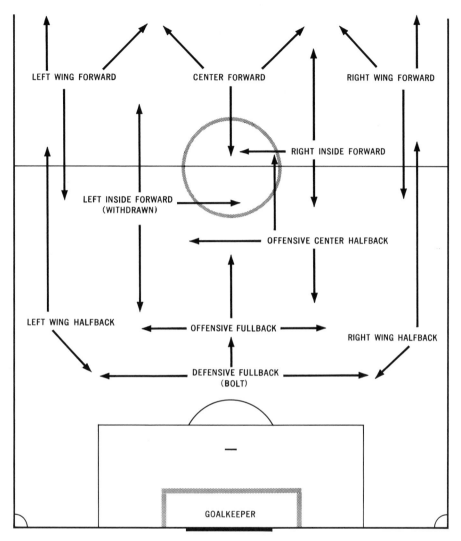

LEFT WING FORWARD   CENTER FORWARD   RIGHT WING FORWARD

RIGHT INSIDE FORWARD

LEFT INSIDE FORWARD
(WITHDRAWN)

OFFENSIVE CENTER HALFBACK

LEFT WING HALFBACK   OFFENSIVE FULLBACK   RIGHT WING HALFBACK

DEFENSIVE FULLBACK
(BOLT)

GOALKEEPER

Diag. 12.2 *The Swiss bolt.*

fullback was left as the free man, the "bolt," behind the defense to cover his teammates. With his experience and tactical knowledge, he was expected to read the flow of the game and keep alert, ready to tackle any attacker who slipped past the outer line of defense. Whenever the extra defender ("bolt") went into action, the teammate beaten by the attacker had to serve as the reserve defender (Diag. 12.2).

The success of this strong defense-oriented system is measured by how well the team can break out to counterattack as soon as it has blunted the opponent's attack. An attacking team that enjoys territorial advantage in midfield frequently will expose its defense and become subject to a quick counterattack.

Once possession is gained, the withdrawn inside forward becomes the target for the initial outlet pass from defense. The center halfback and wing halfback instantly break out into midfield in search of space in which to scheme up service to their forwards.

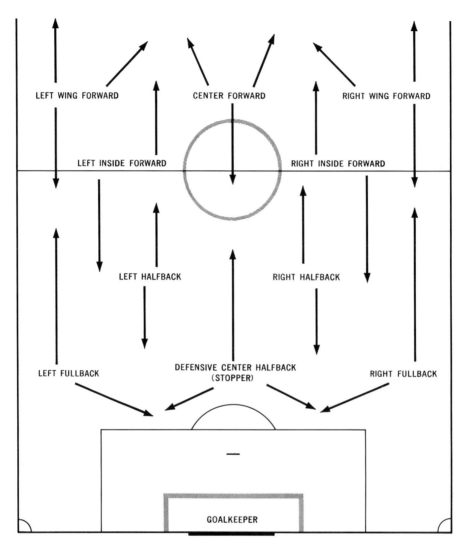

Diag. 12.3 *The WM system.*

With an extra player always ready to cover on defense, the center halfback and wing halfbacks are encouraged to join in the attack. Quite often this gives the attack the numerical superiority over the defense. This method of attack is unexpected and therefore often successful, since the opponent that attacks the Swiss bolt leaves its defense vulnerable.

When possession is lost, six players race back toward the penalty area to take up defensive posi-

tions, while the four forwards attempt to slow down the attack with delaying tactics.

The main advantages of this system are that the defense is extremely hard to beat and the attack relies on the element of surprise: counterattack and defenders joining in the attack. One of its major weaknesses is that it does not have a clearly defined midway stage. When the attack breaks down and possession is lost, the players with defensive duties must race back while four attackers are asked to delay the opponent's progress through tackling back and clever positional play. If the latter are successful in regaining possession, they must then attack on their own. The rather large midfield gap gives the opponent the territorial advantage, time, and space to build up their attacks. More often than not, it leads to frustration and panic. Frequently the opponent does not know what to do with his freedom; he has no answer to the massed defense.

The verrou is a mixture of systems and has never achieved wide acceptance. It has a defensive center halfback and an attacking center halfback, together with two linkmen and four fulltime attackers. The verrou appears to incorporate all the advantages of the contemporary major systems, but it calls for players who are capable of a considerable amount of hard work, are able to adapt to a variety of roles, and can cover ground quickly.

Karl Rappan was probably far ahead of his time. Although the Uruguayans seem to have followed in his footsteps, it took the rest of the soccer world nearly a quarter of a century, until the late 1950's, to catch up with the verrou. That is when the Italians produced the catennacio and convinced many people that it was the only way to play.

The countermeasures against the strengthened defense will be discussed in a section on collective attack (p. 217).

THE "WM" SYSTEM

This is the system of play developed in answer to the difficulties most teams had in adapting their play to the new 1925 offside law, which allowed more scope for offensive play (Diag. 12.3).

Most teams sent their wing forwards and center forward upfield to take up advanced attacking positions, just onside. The offside trap by the clever, but usually older and slower, fullback was risky and often ineffective. The offensive center halfback left open space in the center before his own goal that could be freely exploited by the center forward. Wing forwards were also more frequently free from the marking attention of the wing halfbacks, and therefore space could be found on the flanks for the quick exploitation of attacks.

In consequence, teams began to pay much more attention to defensive organization and particularly

the covering responsibilities of defenders. The offensive system based on zone defense was no longer capable of coping with the fluid, interpassing attack, particularly with the fast spearhead forwards going after through passes.

The defensive formation was reshuffled, and man-to-man defense was introduced on the ball, while the zone principle was retained off the ball. The shorter the distance to the ball, the tighter the man-to-man marking. The farther the distance, the looser the covering could be.

Herbert Chapman of England, generally credited with reorganizing the defense and introducing the third back (known as the "stopper" system in the early 1930's), called the WM system "safety first." His intention was to stop the attack with a well-organized defense, to use the midfield as a buildup area, and to launch promising attacks from this base.

He reasoned that the most dangerous area was immediately in front of the goalmouth, where the opposition had the best shooting angle. Since this was the center forward's milieu, he was considered the most dangerous player and thus had to be marked closely. The offensive center halfback was withdrawn to act as a bodyguard for the center forward, becoming the key player on defense. He was asked to play a purely defensive role, cover the central path to the goal, and give cover to both fullbacks in turn. This "stopper" (center halfback) was a tall, powerfully built player and an excellent header of the ball.

The fullbacks, bulwarks of defense, who traditionally covered the central path to the goal, were moved to the flanks to mark the opposing wing forwards and provide cover to the center halfback stopper. This led to the diagonal pattern of defense with the stopper as the pivot of the three-man line which swung to face the point of danger.

Chapman also realized that the inside forwards had become the playmakers, the initiators of attack. To counter them, he moved the wing halfbacks to the inside where they could more easily control the defensive half of the midfield area and mark the opposing inside forwards man-for-man.

The key to the WM system is the midfield—the halfbacks and the inside forwards—who make up the "magic square." They have to provide the vital link, building up the attack and preparing and organizing the defense from midfield. Since they are the backbone of the team, they have to be all-round players, tactically sound, with good ball-control, innovative interpassing, and great stamina.

The center forward, as the spearhead of the attack, had to be physically dominating in order to succeed against his immediate counterpart, the stopper. Through unselfish running, mostly diagonally toward the touchlines, he had to search for the ball and either penetrate himself or make the stopper follow him, creating opportunities for his teammates.

The wing forwards had to be versatile and talented dribblers. They had to go like the wind and cut in on goal from the flanks. The most promising attacks were carried out over the wing forwards via the cross. The center forward lunged in for the header, or set up a back pass to the trailing inside forwards around the edge of the penalty box.

The WM system theoretically seems to provide an economic distribution of players on the field: three fulltime attackers (spearheads)—the center forward, right and left wing forwards—with both inside forwards and both halfbacks free to join the attack. Also the defense seems to be strong with three fulltime defenders—left and right fullbacks plus the center halfback (stopper)—with the right and left halfbacks in front of them in addition to the right and left inside forwards who also have defensive responsibilities.

Finally, with cooperation by halfbacks and inside forwards, midfield play seems to be well-organized. Four players are occupied in building up the attack and preparing the defense. Any team with four players of an outstanding caliber in the halfback and inside forward positions is certainly extraordinary.

The weakness of the WM system is exposed, however, when it is not well-organized in midfield. Few teams are fortunate enough to have four players skillful and strong enough to play the demanding roles of halfback and inside forward. Consequently they fail to provide the essential link between offense and defense, leaving a big gap in midfield.

Equally important, in the transition period, after a team has been heavily committed to defend, the three fulltime attackers (wing forwards and center forward) are left frequently isolated. On the contrary, when a team is heavily committed to attack, it is most vulnerable to a counterattack because the halfbacks leave a vacuum behind them. With only three fulltime defenders (two fullbacks and center halfback, stopper) strung across the field, with little evidence of cover between them, the fullbacks are overworked by the constant change from man-to-man to zone defense.

A tactical reorganization of the midfield has proven effective. The left halfback was asked to stay back to become primarily a defensive halfback to assure the necessary tightness in defense. The right halfback was now free to become an offensive halfback. The left inside, too, was withdrawn to become essentially a midfield player. In cooperation with the offensive halfback, he was responsible for the midfield organization—more of an innovator, schemer, and initiator of the offense, controlling the buildup of attacking movements (Diag. 12.4).

The right inside forward, now less restricted in midfield, became more of a striker. It is interesting to note the similarities between the adaptation of the WM play and the modern 4-2-4 system.

DEEP CENTER FORWARD

It took nearly a quarter of a century before the famed Hungarians exposed the inherent weaknesses of the stopper in the three-back game with a deep-lying center forward. The rigidity of the WM system, particularly when it is based on strict man-to-man marking, is clearly exposed when consideration is given to the requirements of space.

Withdrawing the center forward to a midfield position, allowing the inside forwards to move forward into positions where they can operate as twin center forwards, sets problems for the defense (Diag. 12.5).

First, and most important, the WM defenders will be put into a state of indecision, in a psychological dilemma, trapped in no man's land, being neither near enough for a decisive tackle nor covering the space behind them. Second, this will offset the M defensive formation that relies on the diagonal pattern of defense to provide cover for the stopper through the fullbacks. Third, by forcing defenders to play out of position, they will be less effective.

The stopper faced with a deep-lying center forward can no longer fulfill his dual role effectively. If he decides to stand his ground and cover space,

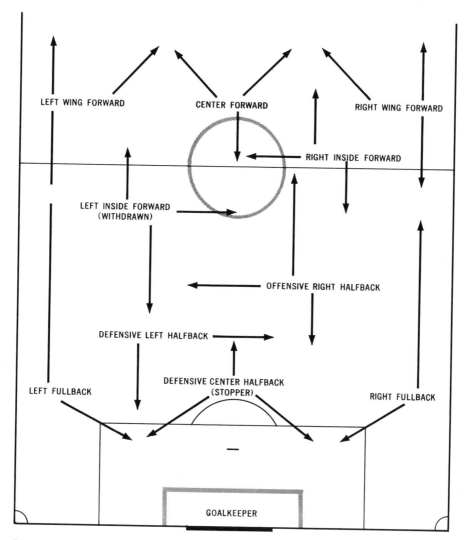

LEFT WING FORWARD CENTER FORWARD RIGHT WING FORWARD

RIGHT INSIDE FORWARD

LEFT INSIDE FORWARD
(WITHDRAWN)

OFFENSIVE RIGHT HALFBACK

DEFENSIVE LEFT HALFBACK

DEFENSIVE CENTER HALFBACK
(STOPPER)

LEFT FULLBACK RIGHT FULLBACK

GOALKEEPER

Diag. 12.4 *Variation of the WM system.*

he allows the center forward freedom to operate at will in midfield. If he decides to challenge the center forward as he withdraws, he will have to leave the central path to the goal exposed, vital space of which the two inside forwards can take advantage.

The halfbacks also are faced with problems. If they cover the inside forwards man-for-man, they clearly can no longer fulfill their responsibilities for organization in midfield. If they do not cover them, the two inside forwards can move into the open

space behind them and beside the stopper, thereby creating a two-on-one situation in front of the goal.

When both wing forwards are withdrawn as well, completing the somersault from a W to an M offensive formation, the fullbacks, too, have indecision as to whether to stay with the wing forwards and cover them man-for-man, leaving attacking space exposed behind them that can be effectively used by the dual spearheads, or to hold their ground, allowing the wingers to run free and take initiative in midfield.

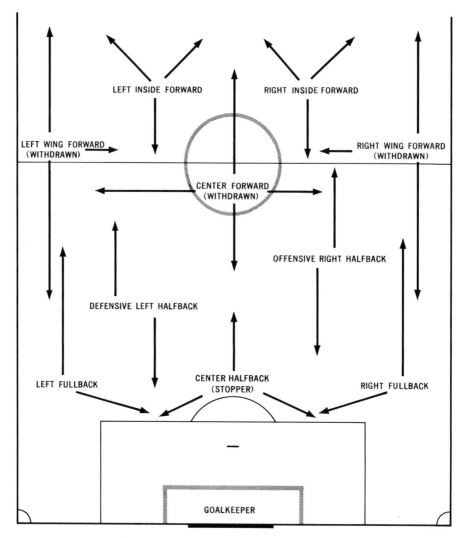

Diag. 12.5 *Withdrawn center forward 3-3-4.*

If the defenders decide to cover their opponents man-for-man and go with them, they will be playing out of position. The stopper and fullbacks will find themselves in midfield faced with more mobile, all-round players than they are accustomed to, as well as having the added responsibility of taking over for the halfbacks the creative work in midfield. The halfbacks are faced with the opposite problem—they find themselves in a strictly defensive role.

The offensive formation with a withdrawn center forward consists of a mobile six-man attack with two shuttling wing forwards, two spearhead inside forwards interchanging positions freely and fluidly, and two scheming midfield players—the deep center forward and offensive halfback. They rely on a controlled buildup and a free interchange of positions to attract the attention of the stopper and provide the possibility of creating an extra-man situation.

A most experienced player in the position of deep center forward as playmaker is essential. Also, the wing forwards must be chosen for their abilities in both initiating and finishing up attacks. The spearhead inside forwards must have the qualities of the traditional center forward (striker).

The midfield is well-organized with the deep center forward as the midfield general and the offensive halfback as his adjutant, assisted by both wing forwards.

The defense of the WM system remains intact when using the deep center forward. The two fullbacks and stopper center halfback can even be reinforced, for in addition to the defensive halfback (who had already become part of the defensive unit), the offensive halfback is now free to pay more attention to defensive responsibilities.

The logical tactical adaptation of the WM system to counter the M attacking formation with a deep center forward is to allow fullbacks and halfbacks to switch roles. The fullbacks cover the inside forwards and the halfbacks the wing forwards. Then an offensive center halfback is inserted in place of the defensive center halfback, stopper, to cover the deep center forward. Such tactical maneuvering should prove satisfactory, since all players, by the nature of their original positions, should be able to cope with their new responsibilities.

THE 4-2-4 SYSTEM

The Hungarians initiated the tactical revolution with a concealed version of the 4-2-4 system by using a withdrawn center forward. The Brazilians brought the 4-2-4 into the open with a second center halfback and a second center forward. It became clear that the defensive left halfback was permanently positioned between the center halfback and the left fullback. It was also evident that one inside forward was operating exclusively in midfield, and that the other inside forward was always up in close support of the center forward (Diag. 12.6).

The aims of the 4-2-4 system are:

1. To negate the defensive center halfback, stopper, by providing two central attackers who can alternate in the final thrust at goal.

2. To provide four fulltime defenders to assure a compact and stable defense. The experience with the M defense had demonstrated that three defenders were not enough to cover the whole width of the field. The fullbacks can mark the opposing wing forwards more closely, since there are two centerbacks to cover them (the fullbacks) and each other.

Four fulltime defenders build the last line of defenders: two fullbacks and two centerbacks, or a defensive center halfback, stopper, and a defensive halfback. The fullbacks must be fast and deft. The two centerbacks must be tall enough and good enough headers to dominate the game in the air. Having no cover behind them, the centerbacks must have the intelligence to read the game and coordinate their efforts in covering each other as well as the fullbacks. When necessary, they also direct the defensive play of the two midfield players.

The link players look after the foraging and purveying necessities in midfield—the left inside forward and offensive halfback. These midfield players must be outstanding, imaginative, all-round players, since they dictate the pattern and pace of play. They are responsible for the smooth transition to offense or defense, for building up the attack and preparing the defense.

Four strikers play in front of them: two wing forwards, and two center forwards who can be further defined as a center forward and a striking inside forward. The wing forwards must be fast enough with the ball to enable them to get around their immediate opponent, as they will be playing near the touchline where they will often lack support. They must be able to cope with crowds and, of course, strike when the occasion arises. The two inside forwards or strikers have to be dynamic opportunists anywhere within range of the goal and they must have the ability to hold the ball until support reaches them.

The idea of the system is to enable a team to have at least six attacking players when in possession and at least seven defensive players when the opposition has the ball.

The 4-2-4 system is based on a compound method of defense: defenders operate within the diagonal pattern of defense with close man-to-man marking on the ball-side and zone cover off the ball. The key players are the two centerbacks who must cover each other and their fullbacks in turn. The four-man defense operating on a zone defense assure enough manpower to outnumber the opposing forwards in the event of a surprise attack. This numerical superiority can be increased when-

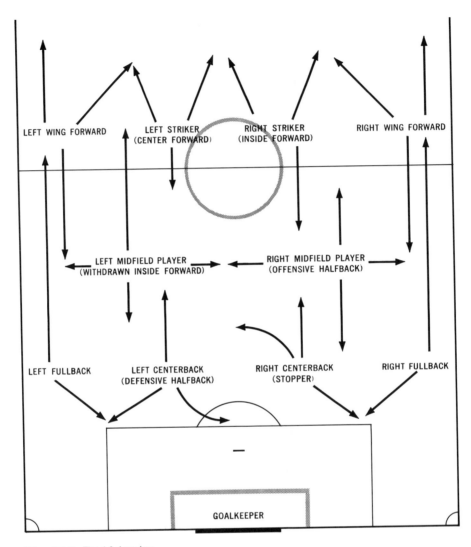

LEFT WING FORWARD   LEFT STRIKER (CENTER FORWARD)   RIGHT STRIKER (INSIDE FORWARD)   RIGHT WING FORWARD

LEFT MIDFIELD PLAYER (WITHDRAWN INSIDE FORWARD)   RIGHT MIDFIELD PLAYER (OFFENSIVE HALFBACK)

LEFT FULLBACK   LEFT CENTERBACK (DEFENSIVE HALFBACK)   RIGHT CENTERBACK (STOPPER)   RIGHT FULLBACK

GOALKEEPER

Diag. 12.6 *The 4-2-4 system.*

ever the opponents are slow in building up their attack or by using delaying tactics in midfield.

The forwards' role on defense consists of showing themselves quickly on the ball as soon as possession is lost and harassing the opponents, while the midfield players, operating on a zone principle, take up supporting positions. The midfielders employ delaying rather than aggressive tactics to enable the immediate defenders to retreat and funnel to the edge of the penalty area to set up a firm defensive wall. This ensures them of close man-

to-man marking around the ball as well as loose cover of the ball for additional support. Whenever the forward line falls back deep into its own territory against an attack, the players wind up in excellent position for an effective counterattack.

The key to the 4-2-4 system is the linkmen. Their task is especially difficult as they are expected to cement the union between attack and defense. When the opposing team has the ball, both linkmen retreat quickly to become halfbacks. When their team has possession, they both become supporting inside forwards. In a rigid form, this system demands a very high work rate from those two linkmen. In all phases of the game, they work in close support of each other.

The 4-2-4 played well must be fluid in order to ease the heavy burden on the linkmen:

1. The defense must move upfield as far as the halfway line, as soon as its own attack is launched.

2. The attackers must fall back when possession is lost to pick up loose balls in midfield rather than wait for the midfielders to reinstitute the attack. This encourages the team to work as a cohesive unit.

3. Both fullbacks must have the skill and natural motivation to assist the attack in midfield or momentarily change positions with the midfield players. Both wing forwards must also be able and willing to assist in midfield.

SWEEPER CENTER HALFBACK SYSTEM

Except for the sweeper center halfback system, all systems of play rely on a collective pattern of defense, based on an equal ratio of defenders to attackers. Thus each defender, in order to ensure an effective defense, has three responsibilities to fulfill: to mark an opponent, cover his defensive zone, and give cover to his teammates.

The sweeper center halfback system was designed to relieve that pressure on defenders by providing an additional defender (freeback or sweeper). It is the sweeper's job, operating behind the last line of defense, to (1) provide depth to the defense by providing cover to his teammates and cover at the same time the vital space behind the defenders, (2) intercept through passes, and (3) challenge any opponent coming through unopposed.

Basic to the sweeper center halfback system is tight man-to-man defense. Defenders, relieved of their collective covering by the sweeper, can now stay with their immediate opponents wherever they go. The centerbacks mark the interior strikers and the fullbacks mark the wing forwards.

The exact disposition of players in midfield and attack depends upon the relative strength of the opposition. It is vital that the team playing the sweeper center halfback system control the midfield in order to ensure effective offense as well as tight defense, not allowing defenders to be drawn out.

Many coaches favor using the system against opponents with outstandingly skilled individuals. Its built-in "insurance," cover by the sweeper in case the tackler fails, enables the backs to make early aggressive challenges for the ball. This puts immediate pressure on the opponents. It is a system designed to take the sting out of the opposing attack and then serve as a launching pad for an effective counterattack.

The success of this strongly defense-oriented system is measured by how well the team can break out to counterattack as soon as it has blunted the opponent's attack. An attacking team that enjoys territorial advantage in midfield frequently will expose its defense and become subject to a quick counterattack.

There are numerous variations, but all have the common denominator of a definite emphasis on defense. The number of fulltime defenders depends on the number of opposing attackers, and the number of midfield players depends on the number and relative strength of the opposing midfield players.

If the opponent is expected to play the 4-2-4 system, the sweeper center half system can be 1-4-2-3 (sweeper, four backs, two midfield players, and three strikers) or 1-4-3-2 (sweeper, four backs, three midfield players, and two strikers). Against a team using the 4-3-3 system, the sweeper formation could be 1-3-3-3 (sweeper, three backs, three midfield players, and three strikers) or 1-3-4-2 (sweeper, three backs, four midfield players, and two strikers) (Diags. 12.7 and 12.8).

The sweeper center halfback system is the result of a hundred years of tactical evolution. Since we know about collective team play, it should be sufficient here to deal only with the system's basic philosophy, but since the innovation of the sweeper is the epitome of modern play, a thorough treatment of how to play it is detailed in Chapter 5 and how to beat it in Chapter 10.

THE 4-3-3 SYSTEM

The 4-3-3 system reflects the contemporary tendency to regard control in midfield as a fundamental necessity. Control of midfield is essential in order to assure a carefully built-up attack. It is equally important for a well-prepared defense, but

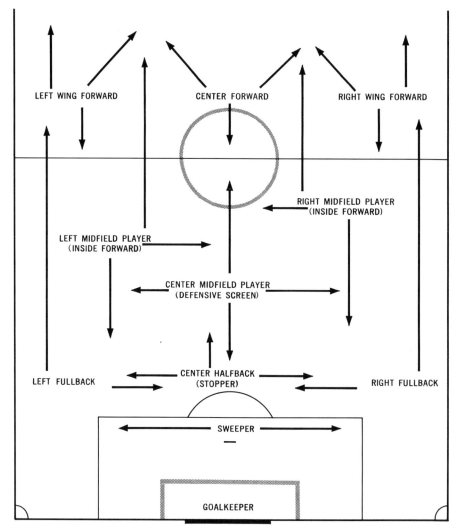

Diag. 12.7 *The 1-3-3-3 system.*

it is difficult to obtain when outnumbered (Diag. 12.9).

The last line of defense consists of two skillful fullbacks, who must be able to attack like traditional wing forwards, and two centerbacks.

If faced with equal attackers to defenders, the defense applies the diagonal principle, close man-to-man marking on the ball-side and zone cover off the ball. Key players are the two centerbacks who must cover each other and their fullbacks.

If confronted by only three fulltime attackers,

the defense is prepared to adopt a sophisticated compound defense. Applying assigned man-to-man marking, the fullbacks mark the wing forwards, the centerback (stopper), playing the traditional role, marks the central striker. The second centerback may be used as an elastic sweeper who tightens up the defense at the point of danger by covering the vital space behind the defenders. At the same time, he gives cover to his teammates who are under defensive pressure.

The advantage of the elastic sweeper over a

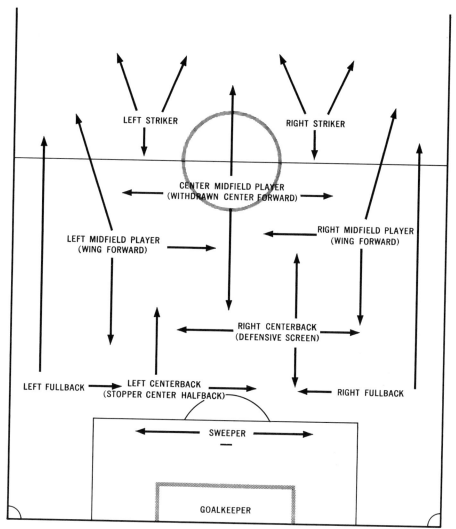

Diag. 12.8 *The 1-3-4-2 system.*

permanent sweeper is that he brings a positive attitude into the game, provided he has the ability. The elastic sweeper usually is the key player in initiating the counterattack. He is also frequently used as a playmaker in midfield and occasionally joins into the attack himself. This is most effective because, coming out of defense, he does not have a permanent opponent. Consequently he can at any time establish numerical superiority in midfield or cause havoc in the opposing defense.

The great advantage of this method of defense is complete flexibility. Defenders are not restricted and can support the attack at will. The elastic sweeper enables the defense to remain compact, with the players pushing up quickly to the halfway line when the attack moves into the opposing half. They must play it "half-half," ready to retreat quickly on defense or to exploit a momentary opening in the opposing defense through a timely overlap.

Such defensive organization requires meticulous planning and preparation, plus match experience.

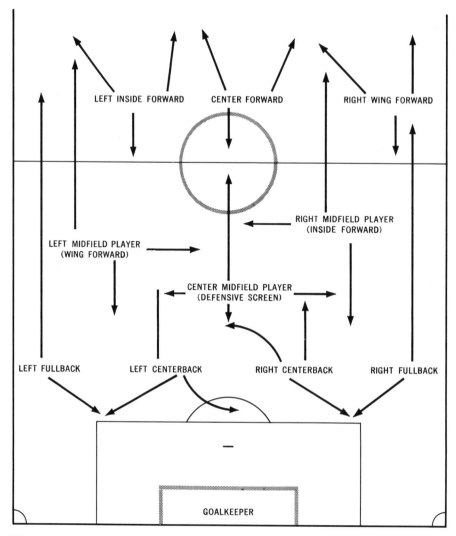

Diag. 12.9 *The 4-3-3 system.*

Many teams do not have the time and experience, which is why they choose to play with a permanent sweeper.

A unit of three midfield players in front of the four backs is expected to present the first line of defense—delay—in order to gain time for the immediate defense to gather its forces. Once beaten they must fight their way back to the goal-side of the ball.

The true defenders are thus allowed to stay home and meet the attack as a unit rather than be absorbed into the action and drawn out of position. Once the attack breaks past the midfield, they race back to fill any gaps.

The midfielders have to ensure numerical superiority around the ball at all times, producing a heavy concentration of defenders at the point of attack and giving opponents little or no time in which to maneuver. Such midfield preparation for defense demands a very high work load from the "heart" of the team, the midfield players. They are equally important in offense and are expected to

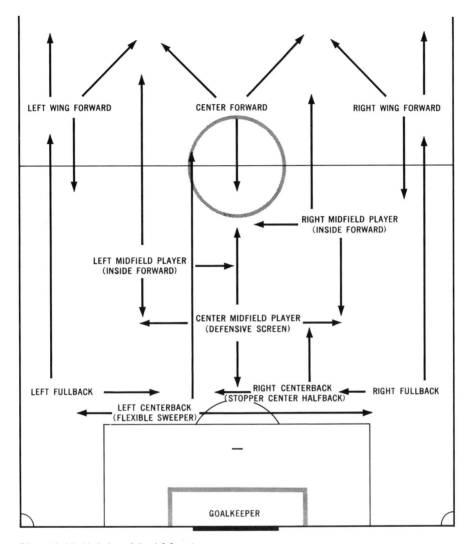

LEFT WING FORWARD   CENTER FORWARD   RIGHT WING FORWARD

RIGHT MIDFIELD PLAYER
(INSIDE FORWARD)

LEFT MIDFIELD PLAYER
(INSIDE FORWARD)

CENTER MIDFIELD PLAYER
(DEFENSIVE SCREEN)

LEFT FULLBACK   RIGHT CENTERBACK   RIGHT FULLBACK
                   (STOPPER CENTER HALFBACK)
LEFT CENTERBACK
(FLEXIBLE SWEEPER)

GOALKEEPER

Diag. 12.10 *Variation of the 4-3-3 system.*

be ready to launch counterattacks and to move quickly and intelligently in support of the strikers. The central midfielder must have the ability to be the general of midfield, pace setter, and schemer of attack. The right and left midfield players must be equal to being creative in midfield and also have the talent of a striking inside forward or wing forward.

The ideal way of effecting the 4-3-3 system offensively is with the center forward as spearhead and the other two strikers as wing forwards. By playing with real wing forwards who stick to the touchlines, attacking on a wide front, it is possible to create big gaps—attacking space—between the central striker and the wing forwards, providing lots of operating room with little restriction for themselves and the central striker (Diag. 12.10).

Just as important, these wide gaps are ideal for midfield players to come through. Consequently this method of attack, whose aim is to get the defenders into positions that cannot be defended with a collective effort, gives the attackers the

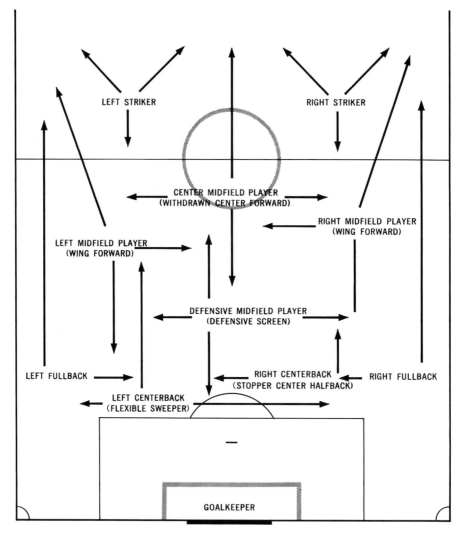

Diag. 12.11 *The 4-4-2 system.*

confidence to take on the defenders knowing that any individual effort has a greater chance of success.

The opponents have to be aware that they can be turned along the touchlines. Forced to spread across the field rather than to concentrate at the point of attack, the defense requires the midfield players and immediate defenders to cover much greater distances.

Attacking play is emphasized by allowing the three midfield players to follow on the second wave of attack. The backs are encouraged to break out from defense in support of attacking play whenever they see the opportunity. An "overlap," the attack from a man coming from behind, is essential.

One cardinal principle of defense is to closely mark every forward and midfield player, as each is a potential attacker. That means a coach must be prepared to use defenders on attack and forwards and midfield players on defense.

The "man from behind" or "overlap" man has

become the most dangerous attacker, since he arrives unexpectedly and unmarked. The whole plan is elastic and players seem to appear bewilderingly in the most unexpected places, to the confusion and surprise of the opposition. The moves must be carefully designed, however. It is nice to get extra help on offense, but a coach must also be thinking of how to stop the opposing counterattack when ball-possession is lost.

CONCLUSION

Tactically the game is now in an all-action phase. Many players are being burdened with heavy work loads on different phases of the game. Teams are using highly integrated covering systems and the midfield is dominated by large units of players. These are not necessarily negative developments. Overlapping tactics wherein fullbacks are thrust forward into wide attacking positions have been part of the game for many years.

Teams are looking for sneak attacking runs from most of the backs and midfield players. The fact that such runs do not occur often in the game shows their difficulty, but it augurs well for soccer that teams are thinking in this direction.

A basic four-back unit, supported or screened by a midfield unit of three or four, means that the main attacking unit will be only two or three players strong. This in turn means that the opposing defensive units can involve themselves in long attacking runs. Since the only way to neutralize a midfield unit of three or four players is by using the same or increased numbers against it, this calls for tight challenging play in all parts of the field, and particularly in the middle.

How can the grip in midfield be loosened? One way might be through committing teams to larger main attacking units without losing strength in the midfield area. The 4-4-2 distribution of players provides that all players are well-supported, particularly when defending or trying to regain possession of the ball, which is, after all, the same thing. In this case, the opponents will present a 4-3-3 distribution in opposition. If the fact is accepted that most teams use a twin spearhead in some way or another, then a look at the following distribution of players is a possibility.

The greater the number of attackers who push deep the defense, particularly toward and beyond the backfield unit, the greater the number of counter measures the defense must take. If a team pushes four main attacking players upfield, the defensive distribution now can become 2-4-4, provided that support is maintained throughout the team (Diag. 12.11).

Contemporary systems are based on hundreds of years of soccer experience. A system has to suit the players. All-round players are needed who can do both jobs, attack and defense, moving from one to the other smoothly and brilliantly. Where does a coach find ten or eleven players of such caliber? Tactics become the stopgaps.

V

Teaching, Coaching, and Scouting

The foundation on which all instruction rests is a philosophy of coaching. From this stems the method of instruction as well as the application of psychology to individual players. The author's philosophy is developed as a sample.

Realizing the importance of the basic skills and techniques, this section includes a progressive teaching unit for the basics. Individual, group, and team tactics are developed in order to effect a smooth coordination between the various team units as well as by the team as a whole. Since this is the most difficult phase of coaching, the greatest amount of time must be devoted to it.

The ultimate goal is to develop a team that can play its own game and retain its poise under severe pressure. This entails the development of an understanding of the game and the ability to improvise in order to achieve a purposeful and instant response to any situation.

Scouting is another important area for effective teaching and coaching. Observing one's own team for a sound program is as important as scouting an upcoming opponent in order to prepare a winning game plan. Recommendations are given for recording data about individual and team performances.

Part V concludes with practical suggestions for teaching and coaching youth soccer in chart form for an immediate overview.

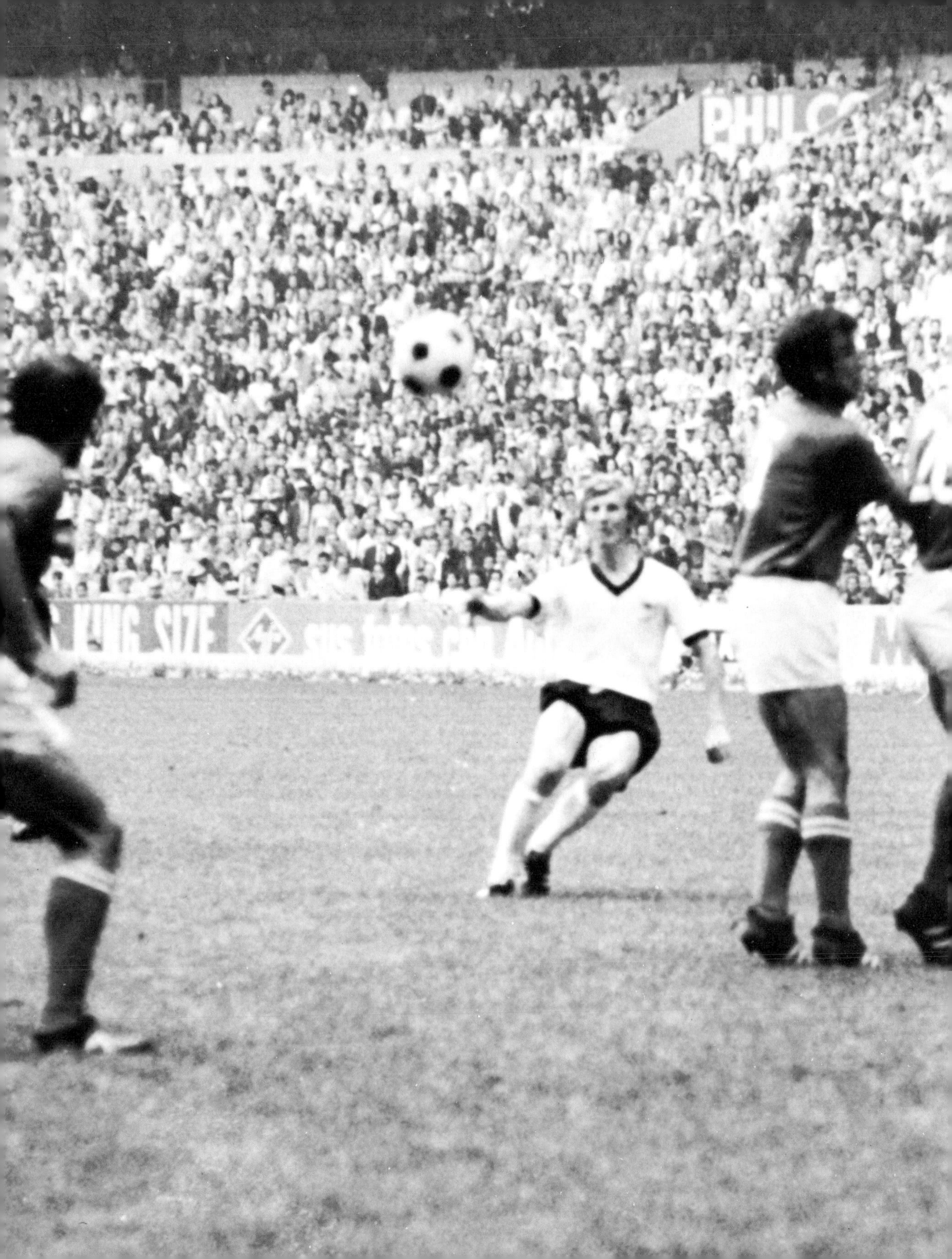
KING SIZE

13

Teaching and Coaching

PHILOSOPHY OF COACHING

Coaching is the ability to resolve human problems, to recognize and develop natural abilities, to motivate and instill a sense of purpose, and to recognize and remove inhibitions so that individual players and the team may realize their potential.

The trademarks of a successful coach, the combination of which make up his coaching style, are human qualities, personal abilities, and professional knowledge. Through these can be created the conditions that foster the desire for and achievement of excellence.

The coach is at once a teacher, leader, psychologist, public relations agent, and professional. In these capacities he has obligations to soccer (and sports in general), to his players, to his fellow coaches, to the opposing team and game officials, to the school or organization he represents, to the press and other news media, and to the community.

Responsibility for a Sound Program

First and foremost, the coach needs a conception of himself in his role as coach within the overall program and the role of soccer in the total picture of his participants. At the high school or college level, he must have a common-sense approach to the game, keeping it within proper perspective and within the institutional and administrative policy.

He is there for the players' sake, not the other way around. If he allows himself to be guided by this, he will not lose objectivity. It is his responsibility to run a program that allows participants to obtain enjoyment and satisfaction. The fact that players come out for the sport because they love the game is the key to all action.

An educationally sound program should provide students with a total picture of soccer. The improvement of personal performance is understandably the main objective, but also of great importance is the players' understanding of the game's history, the evolution of its tactics, and its present state of development in the world. They can then play a more appreciable part in the promotion of the game and have the background needed to take a more imaginative and aggressive part in it. On the basis of this knowledge, players are better prepared to appreciate the coach's decisions about the operation of the program so that it can be run democratically with much give and take between players and the coaching staff.

Everyone May Participate

Since the rewards of the program are in direct relation to the individual's commitment rather than solely to his abilities as a player, cutting players from the squad violates educational principles. The varsity must be limited by the rules of the game. Only eleven men can be fielded at any one time and only eighteen (or whatever number the league decides) can be on the squad, but there is no reason why B, C, or D squads cannot be offered —if that is necessary to accommodate those interested. All players should be equipped and educated with high standards.

Winning Is Not Everything

The coach should use all practical means of winning every contest, since this is the fundamental objective of competitive athletics. He should, nevertheless, play every match within the rules and spirit of the game, urging players (and himself) to accept success with grace and failure with restraint.

A "win at all costs" attitude can propel the scholastic and college game toward an overly aggressive rather than skillful game. If soccer is to establish itself in the United States, as it has in every other country, a highly skillful and tactically fluid game must be developed, which is great fun to play and enjoyable to watch.

All countries have fashioned the game after their own temperaments and national characters. A more rugged game can certainly be tolerated, even encouraged. Because of the basic nature of Americans and their experience with rugged sports, American soccer is definitely more physical, more forthright, less subtle, and with constant movement (the latter a great asset in the modern game). This ruggedness, however, must be a supplement to, rather than a substitute for, the artful skills of the game.

The years ahead are critical for soccer. If the coaches are judged by the traditionalists, they will continue to be graded by their win-loss record. But the modernists will consider their overall contribution to the game: their ability to teach, motivate, and develop desirable attitudes and conduct in their players on and off the field. The attitude and character of the coach is reflected in the actions of his players.

Strong Leadership Is Essential

The team looks to the coach for organization and leadership. It is his responsibility to constantly improve his practical ability so that he can convince his players by demonstration. He should broaden his knowledge in every dimension of the game to stay abreast or in advance, and to be one step ahead of his game opponents.

The growth of soccer depends largely upon its

apostles. Their fire and conviction reflect a love of the game, a pride and pleasure in coaching. This has nothing to do with their background, whether they have had the experience of a Pelé or have just played for fun.

Star players do not necessarily make star coaches. There have been great players who were poor coaches, and poor players who made great coaches. The mediocre player actually is more likely to become an outstanding coach. Since he lacks natural talent, chances are he will be a better student of the game. He will be forced to analyze the techniques and tactics in order to improve himself. The naturally gifted player who does most things by second nature often is unable to transmit the secrets of his success to others.

Enthusiasm is contagious. It will infect the players and everyone else around the coach. No real administrator can fail to be impressed by such vigor, or fail to understand what is needed to improve the game, especially if its goals are well-articulated.

It is up to the coach to see that administrators, spectators, players, and the news media are aware of the demands of this highly skilled, challenging game, and that athletes get the recognition they deserve—even if he has to write the publicity releases himself. A subtle, persistent publicity campaign can foster school and public awareness of soccer and a radical change of perspective.

Coaching demands maximum time and interest. It is impossible to be a clock-watcher and still function effectively as a coach. If a coach is not dedicated to the team, the players will know it and his effectiveness will be diminished. But complete dedication is easy when the coach loves the game and enjoys teaching, and when he considers the discipline and organization, as well as the success and happiness of the team, a direct reflection of his knowledge and ability.

Program Objectives

The basic goal for any coach is to produce a team that plays successful and attractive soccer to defeat opponents of equal experience.

Any player can be coached to improve his individual skills and tactics, depending on the effectiveness of the methods chosen by the coach and the degree of interest and cooperation of the player.

The game itself is the best teacher. Since the ball is the focal point of the game, practices that simulate game conditions, with the ball as the focal point, are the most effective. This means a ball for every player, but it does not demand a top-quality ball—a rubber one will do if budgets are low. If that is still not possible, the higher the ratio of balls to players the better. The idea is educationally sound: then there is no discrimination between the best and the rest, and every minute can be used advantageously.

Preparation for teamwork is done as much off the field as on. An environment is needed that allows a free flow of ideas, friendly cooperation yet individuality from each member. Although in a training program for competition, where there must be a high degree of predicability from participants, players should be encouraged to participate in meaningful decisions concerning their own progress and performance. They need to retain a sense of their own capacity to act as individuals and not repress eccentric conviction or unpopular views. If players are to commit themselves to the best in the team, they need an environment that shows commitment can be made without losing individuality and social or moral responsibility.

Applied Psychology

Much has been said and written about an athlete's technical, tactical, and physical preparation for success. Equally important, an area we know far too little about, is his mental preparation for competition—how to improve his will power, determination to face all odds with maximum talent and effort, and other psychological factors.

Whether or not the players go on the field highly motivated to win is a decision that is more often than not unconsciously made in accordance with the relevance of the contest to them personally. The same team under the same circumstances, handled by two different coaches, will often obtain different results. One coach has the ability to inspire players and team spirit, while the other lacks this vital ability. The ideal would be for the coach to educate players to sustain their own drive, to "psych" themselves up for top performance. But this we can expect only from highly trained professionals whose livelihood depends on their performance on the field. On the amateur level, and particularly the scholastic and college levels, the

player often loses sight of his self-imposed goals. And it becomes the coach's job, game-by-game, to reactivate the players' motivation for playing well.

For most players there is great satisfaction in excelling in soccer. This is the strongest drive. For others it is the social implications of being on a varsity team. Others like the Spartan discipline, the order it puts into their lives. Or they enjoy striving with a group for a common goal, friendships with teammates, traditional rivalries, playing before a home crowd of parents and girl friends. One or more of these factors unconsciously influences the individual's motivation and the degree to which he will extend himself.

Playing the game is not an end in itself. The whole involvement of the player on the athletic field gives sustenance and purpose to his life style. He must be made to understand why he participates, why he should excel, and the relationship of what he does on the field to the rest of his life.

The successful coach is the one who understands each player so well that he can, with the greatest sincerity, motivate each to put out greatest effort in day-to-day practices and in the challenge of competition so that each will feel keenly the relevance of that effort to the success of his performance and be enriched by it.

Every line of communication between coach and players must be open and working in the psychological preparation for each contest. The ideal relationship to achieve such intangible goals (as well as the tangible high performance and victory) is one that promotes friendship, mutual understanding, and respect between the two. The coach should feel affection and responsibility to his players and the players should feel a responsibility, even satisfaction, in pleasing him by their performance.

This is not to imply that the success of the team is then to be attributed to the coach. On the contrary, the players must feel it is their achievement. It is the players' game, and their willingness to give everything is what brings them victory. The more they are made to feel responsible for the decisions involving their whole program, the more they will feel part of the whole process, win or lose. But they can at the same time recognize the investment in time and effort the coach makes, his talent, and be concerned about his reaction to their performance.

For the coach to be dynamic and show some emotion in order to create enthusiasm and psych players up or keep them going is a great asset as long as he is not overbearing and does not lose objectivity. The secret seems to be to push just hard or long enough to keep the individual or team going without feeling that push. The line is thin, but once the coach pushes too much he can be sure of negative results. The players feel the victory is then more important to him personally than their enjoyment; at that point positive effects from his enthusiasm diminish.

Some players have problems, real or imagined, of course, that militate against positive results, even with the best understanding. Most notable are fears of failure that produce tension in tough situations and cause a player to give up when the odds seem to be too great. Players have certain images of themselves and their chances of achieving the goals they have set for themselves, and they unconsciously live up to this image. This is something to which coaches must be very sensitive, distributing responsibility to the team as a whole and not burdening any one player. Each must feel he is an important member of the team without feeling the exclusive responsibility for its success. Seemingly meaningless remarks during the week can have great impact on some players, often adversely, that will cause them to give up when the going gets

tough. Positive reinforcement of their chances to attain high standards is essential.

If winning and losing are put by the coach into proper perspective, after the game everything boils down to whether or not a player has let himself (and the team) down. With maximum effort by each player, the chances of victory are great. The climate of opinion should be such that a player can walk off the field completely satisfied and renewed, even if the team lost, because he gave everything and more during the entire contest. He can be proud of that achievement and so can the coach and his teammates.

THE CAPTAIN

The captain is the liaison between the coach and the players. He does not have to be the best player, but he must certainly be a leader who is extremely knowledgeable about the game and who has the confidence and respect of the squad (Fig. 13.1). If he is a great captain, he can bring out the best in each of his teammates and keep them aggressively oriented toward victory. One real test of leadership is picking up a sagging, apparently beaten, team and giving it new life and hope.

Uwe Seeler, Germany's captain in the 1970 World Cup game against England, provides a classic example. Germany was down 2-0 early in the second half. Seeler, fighting like a tiger himself, went from one player to another with words of encouragement, making spectacular plays one minute and heartening players after mistakes in the next.

During the game the captain is the coach's deputy. He must be kept well-informed of all tactical plans. He sees that tactical assignments are carried out on the field in addition to making the decisions involving sun and wind at the toss of the coin.

Famous captains like Danny Blanchflower, the Irish International from Tottenham, Uwe Seeler of Hamburg and West Germany, and Bobby Moore of West Ham and England, differ very much in style and temperament. Some, like Blanchflower, shout at their players to goad them on, whereas others, like Moore, inspire their teammates by magnificent performances and untiring examples of poise, coolness, and courage. But they all get their message across in whatever way is appropriate for them.

Fig. 13.1 *Bobby Moore and Uwe Seeler going through the ceremonial tradition before an international game. The handshake is more than a gesture of friendship; it symbolizes the spirit of the game, that both teams agree to play according to the rules.*

All great captains seem to be the sort of persons who can be relied upon in a crisis—approachable men whose egos do not get in the way and who can handle their own emotions under stress. Most important, their personalities are such that they can get across their point of view and handle different types of temperament, so players can feel their play and their problems will be understood and handled wisely.

INTRODUCTION TO INSTRUCTION

The objectives of instruction are mastery of basic skills with a minimum amount of effort and the application of these skills in situations where the player is being opposed by one or more men and has an opportunity to work with various teammates. Since these situations require instant decisions, they must be included in the practice activities. Practice must simulate game conditions as closely as possible.

It would be simple to categorize players for practice and play by age groups, but skill does not improve nor can it be estimated by age. More reasonable determinants are physical maturity (strength) and playing experience (skill proficiency).

Attention should be given to learning sequences that will enable players to make immediate game use of each new skill. With only the simplest elements of trapping and kicking with the inside of the foot, players can play soccer. Each skill should be taught with its practical application and tactical implications in the game and, even in the early stages of instruction, linked immediately with other skills, and tested against opponents.

Until the movement has been mastered, players may be allowed to use the foot they prefer and move in the direction of their choice. As soon as it has been mastered, it should be practiced with the other foot and in the opposite direction.

Beginners may focus their eyes entirely on the ball, but players should be urged to use peripheral vision as soon as possible.

INTRODUCTION TO SKILLS

The ability to control the ball in different situations, at maximum speed, and under defensive pressure can be improved by using the following teaching progression:

1. Brief introduction of the skill and its practical uses in game situations.

2. Demonstration of the skill and its practical use in match play.

3. Brief but clear analysis of its execution plus a dramatic demonstration that highlights the crucial points of emphasis.

4. Organization of players to enhance the teaching technique (the group should be easily controlled and observed).

5. Experimentation by players to give them practical experience without interference from the coach (corrections should not be made too early).

6. Correction of errors first on a general level and then on an individual basis (emphasis should always be on the principles that allow individual expression and differences; constructive criticism is particularly effective in the learning process).

7. Progression from the simple to the difficult: from a standing position to slow running, half-speed and power to top speed, from passive resistance by opponents to realistic match situations against pressure.

SKILLS AND TECHNIQUES
Ball-Control—Receiving

It is necessary to develop a broad range of skills to assure ball-control in all situations. Only with excellent ball-control can the player be freed for tactical responsibility.

Juggling—Ball-Familiarity

Juggling is keeping a ball in the air by using the instep, thigh, head, inside or outside of the foot and chest, not allowing it to bounce or using the hands to develop the player's sensitivity (touch) for and coordination with the ball. The ball and the human body have different rhythms—the aim is to harmonize the player and ball.

Teaching Points. The player should be loose and well-balanced, slightly crouched, weight on the ball of the supporting foot. Emphasize good rhythm and harmony with the ball. Contacts should be gentle. Ideally the ball should be played only a yard or so into the air. It is important that the part of the body used is parallel to the ground.

Instep: Foot well-braced, toe pointed for clean contact to avoid back-spin of the ball, contact ball around knee height (Fig. 13.2).

Fig. 13.2 *Juggling with the instep.*

Fig. 13.3 *Juggling with the thigh.*

Fig. 13.4 *Juggling with the forehead.*

Fig. 13.5 *Juggling with the outside of the foot.*

Fig. 13.6 *Juggling with the inside of the foot.*

Fig. 13.7 *"Juggling" with the chest.*

Thigh: Contact is made in the middle of the thigh, rather than at either extremity, with thigh horizontal to the ground (Fig. 13.3).

Forehead: Head tilted well-back, forehead parallel to the ground. Contact ball between the eyes. Player must maintain a position directly underneath the ball (Fig. 13.4).

Outside of foot: With toes raised and knees well-bent, the player should assume a position beside the ball, at least one leg's length away from the ball. In order to play the ball around the height of his hip the player must compensate by bending at the hip and leaning away from the ball (Fig. 13.5).

Inside of foot: Toes raised, knees well-bent and pointed outward. Ball is played closer to the body than usual in order to use the inside of the foot (Figs. 13.6 and 13.7).

Procedure.

1. Ball is played from a hand drop. It is held in front of the player for the instep, thigh, and inside of the foot; to the side for the outside; and tossed into the air for the head. The player gently kicks or heads the ball straight up into the air and catches it.

Variations:

a. Except when using the thigh or head, the player does not catch the ball. Instead he allows it to bounce. Then he kicks it gently straight up into the air, bounce, and so on. Alternate left, right.

b. Contest. The number of contacts is counted: right foot, bounce, left, bounce, and so on until the player loses control.

2. Juggling the ball with right or left foot but without allowing it to bounce between contacts.

Variations:

a. Juggling, alternating left and right feet.

b. Juggling while moving about—forward, backward, sideward.

3. Juggling is begun by picking up the ball from the ground with the foot. By putting the sole of the foot on top of the ball placed about a yard ahead of him, the player withdraws it gently backward and scoops the instep underneath it to lift the ball off the ground. Then he proceeds to juggle as many times as possible with any part of the body—instep, thigh, head, chest, outside or inside of the foot, without the use of hands or allowing the ball to bounce.

4. Consecutive juggling. Players should strive for at least thirty consecutive contacts with each technique.

5. Sequence juggling. Players are asked to start with the instep and juggle the ball for a specific number of repetitions, then proceed to the thigh for the same number, then head, outside of foot, inside of foot, and then repeat.

6. Rhythm juggling and controlling. Players are asked to juggle with the head 1-2-3, and on the third contact, the ball is headed forcefully into the air. They have to time their jumps to meet the ball in midair to control it with the forehead. They continue the 1-2-3-Up.

Variation: The player juggles the ball with the instep 1-2-3-Up, and on the third contact the ball is kicked into the air and the player times a jump to meet the ball in midair to control it with the chest. Then he continues with the instep. The same may be done with the thigh or instep. After the 1-2-3-Up juggling rhythm, player jumps by using a scissors jump to meet the ball in midair to control with the thigh or

instep. Then he continues to juggle the ball with the thigh or instep 1-2-3-Up, and so on.

7. Group juggling: Two or three players to one ball. Each player is allowed to juggle a specific number of contacts, three, five, or more. These may or may not be assigned to a particular technique to be used. Then the juggler plays the ball to the next player who does the same thing.

Variation: Players move about in a given area. The juggler, after finishing his routine, kicks the ball up high into the air and calls the name of the receiver, and possibly even the part of the body with which he must control the ball. For example, "Johnny, chest." The receiver then repeats the assigned routine.

8. Shadow or mirror juggling. Three or five players in a group, each with a ball and one leader whose juggling everyone must copy. Players take turns being leader.

Collecting Ground Balls

To develop a player's ability to take possession with ease of ground balls coming from any direction while moving at speed, turning, or under pressure from opponents is the objective of these exercises.

Teaching Points. The ball is met with the inside or outside of the foot and the player "gives" to absorb the impact in order to take close possession. The ball is met by the player who accelerates after taking possession (Fig. 13.8).

Procedure.

1. In pairs, one ball, players face each other about ten yards apart, pass, and receive the ball with the inside of the foot.

Variations:

a. Player runs to meet the ball, controls with the inside of the foot, and passes to partner to control as he returns to his original position.

b. Player is asked to receive the ball with one foot and pass with the other. The choice of inside or outside of the foot for receiving or passing may be left up to the player.

c. Player goes to meet the ball, controls with either inside or outside of the foot, dribbles the ball to change positions with partner, turns, passes, and follows his pass.

2. In pairs, players move up and down the field about ten yards apart two-touch—passing and receiving the ball. Player receives the ball with the outside of the inner foot and passes it back with the inside of the outside foot.

3. Three players, one ball, triangle formation. Players pass the ball clockwise two-touch, control with inside, pass with outside of the foot.

4. Three players, Indian file, ten yards between each. The middle player is the receiver,

a

b

c

Fig. 13.8 *Receiving a ground ball with the inside of the foot.*

Fig. 13.9 *Trapping with the sole of the foot.*

Fig. 13.10 *Trapping with the inside of the foot.*

Fig. 13.11 *Trapping with the outside of the foot.*

Fig. 13.12 *Trapping with the outside of the instep.*

the other two are servers. The two outside serve firm ground passes to the middle player who goes to meet the ball, controls, and simultaneously turns with it to pass the ball to the server. Servers and receiver alternate.

5. Three or more players move about freely while passing and receiving the ball.

Variations:

a. Touch the ball only twice: control pass.

b. Control the ball, accelerate, and move off in any direction while still dribbling.

Trapping

The classic technique of trapping—killing the ball between some part of the foot and the ground—is the basis of sound ball-control.

Teaching Points. Trap a ball by forming a wedge between some part of the foot (sole, inside, out-

side) or shin and the ground. The angle should be large enough for the ball to fit into the space between the foot and the ground. The foot must be loose in order to give and absorb impact. Timing is essential to allow the player to get on top of the ball to assure good balance and set the trap to coincide with the exact rebound of the ball (Figs. 13.9–13.12).

Procedure.

1. Each player with a ball in line formation along the touchlines moves back and forth across the width of the field tossing the ball into the air and trapping it with the sole of the foot.

Variations:

a. Players move sideward across the width of the field using the inside of the right foot for trapping on the way over. They turn and continue using the right foot as they return.

b. Players move sideward across the field using the inside of the right foot on the way over and the inside of the left foot returning.

c. Players add a preliminary body-feint and then trap the ball with the inside of the foot as they cross the field.

d. Players add a preliminary body-feint and then trap with the outside of the foot as they cross the field.

2. Each player with a ball. They toss the ball high up into the air and then control it in midair with the top of the chest.

Variations:

a. The player jumps to control the ball with the top of the chest in midair.

b. The player drop-kicks the ball, puts it straight up into the air, and jumps to control it with the top of the chest in midair.

c. Player juggles the ball before he kicks it straight into the air, then he jumps to control it with the top of the chest. He continues juggling a number of times, kicks, controls, juggles, and so on.

3. In pairs, one ball. One tosses the ball up high, the partner controls the ball with the top of the chest, then throws it for the first player to control.

Variations:

a. The partner jumps to control with the top of the chest in midair.

b. The partner drop-kicks the ball and puts it straight into the air for the other to jump and control with the top of the chest.

c. The player juggles the ball before he kicks it straight into the air for the partner to jump and control with the top of the chest. He continues juggling a number of times and kicks for the first to control. Repeat.

4. Players move about freely on the field, each with a ball. They drop-kick the ball, trap it with the sole, inside, or outside of the foot.

Variation: Players juggle the ball three or four times and then kick it up into the air to trap it with sole, inside, or outside of the foot.

5. In pairs, one ball. One player juggles, kicks the ball up into the air while the second player has to trap it, then he juggles and kicks it into the air for his partner, and so on.

Variation: The juggler not only kicks the ball up into the air but calls the trapping technique ("inside") his partner has to use. Repeat.

Controlling Ball in Midair

The major objective is to get a ball down on the ground as quickly as possible to make the play; to take the pace off a ball in midair by absorbing the impact to assure a playable rebound for either passing, shooting, or taking close possession by checking the ball again on the ground.

Teaching Points. Use the largest surface of the body, leg, or head possible and meet the ball square. The part used must be loose and give on impact. Player must be in good balance, go to meet the ball, not allow it to touch the ground uncontrolled (Figs. 13.13 and 13.14).

Procedure.

1. Each player with a ball. They toss the balls into the air and smother the rising ball with the whole front surface of the body by running right through it.

Variations:

a. The player drop-kicks the ball straight up into the air and smothers the rising ball.

b. Players juggle the ball a number of times, then kick it up into the air and smother the rising ball.

2. In pairs, one ball. One player juggles the ball a number of times, then kicks it high into the air for the second player to smother the rising ball, then juggle, kick, and so on.

3. Each player with a ball. Players toss the ball high into the air and control the rebound with the top of the chest as the ball descends and immediately check it as it drops to the ground to take close possession.

Variations:

a. The player jumps to control the descending rebound with the chest.

b. Player drop-kicks the ball, jumps to control the descending rebound with the chest, and checks the ball as it drops to the ground.

c. Player juggles the ball before he kicks it into the air and jumps to control the descending rebound with the chest. Then he continues juggling, kicks, controls, and so on.

4. In pairs, one ball. Player juggles the ball, then kicks it up high for the partner to control the descending rebound with the chest.

5. In pairs, one ball. Juggler kicks ball up in air and calls for the trapping technique to be used by partner. Juggler then runs away and keeps running until partner has control of the ball and is thus able to establish eye contact with him. Then he spreads his legs for partner to pass through.

Variations:

a. Juggler kicks ball up in air for himself to control. This is the signal for the partner to move in from prescribed distance (ten–fifteen yards, depending upon technical ability of players) to challenge for the ball. Change roles.

b. In three's, one ball. Now the player who controls gets off a successful pass to third player. Change roles.

a   b

Fig. 13.13 *Controlling a ball in midair. The player's chest expands and then collapses in order to absorb the impact of the ball and deflect it to the ground.*

Fig. 13.14 *Player's chest is expanded and he arches his back to get his chest underneath the ball, bends back in order to give and absorb the impact of the ball to ensure a workable rebound straight in the air off his chest.*

The following stages of instruction are suggested as a continuous progression of ball receiving and ball control:

1. In pairs, one ball, players face each other about twenty–thirty yards apart. They use the throw-in to serve the ball to each other. Player controls the ball with the most appropriate technique.

Variations:

a. The server follows his throw. The receiver moves to meet the ball, controls it, and continues on to change positions with partner.

b. The server follows his throw immediately in order to challenge the receiver as he controls the ball. The receiver must control and continue to beat the challenger as they continue to change positions. The challenge should be realistic, not token. To temper the difficulty, the distance between players is adjusted according to the abilities of the receiver. The more skillful the receiver, the shorter the distance.

2. In three's, one ball, a server, receiver, and challenger. The ball is served by a throw-in from approximately twenty yards from the receiver, who has to control the ball while the challenger is moving in. While the challenger tackles, the receiver may use the server as a teammate, creating a two-on-one situation where the receiver knows that his ball-control skills will be tested by the challenger but also that he has the opportunity of passing to the server to get himself out of difficulty.

Variations:

a. The ball is served by a well-aimed lofted pass.

b. Server and receiver are about thirty yards apart while the challenger, standing directly behind the receiver, marks him tight. The ball may be served by a throw-in or a lofted pass. The receiver's objective is to control the ball quickly and either play it back immediately to the server, or turn with it, beat the challenger, and have a shot at goal. The challenger's objective is to prevent the ball from reaching the receiver or prevent the receiver from getting off the pass or shot.

Kicking

Kicking is a player's most valuable technical asset. Kicking the ball upfield and into the opponent's goal is the basic idea of the game. Clearing the ball out of danger (kicking) is the invaluable weapon in defense.

Almost any part of the surface of the foot can be used for kicking. It would not be difficult to draw up a list of the different ways of kicking and go through them as separate accomplishments. It is better, even in the early stages of teaching and coaching, to think at all times of the purpose behind each technique. For example, the low pass (using the inside of the foot), and the low-driving kick (using the instep) are two vital kicking skills. The low ball takes the shortest time moving from one spot to the other, effective passing is unthinkable without accurate ground passing, and effective shooting is of necessity low trajectory.

The objective in kicking is to develop the player's ability to kick the ball with accuracy and power in the pressure of a game. A quick play at the ball is often the only way of making a sure clearance, an effective pass, or of taking advantage of a brief opportunity of shooting at goal. Therefore a good player must develop his skill at kicking a ball in all circumstances and under any stress the game may demand.

Kicking with the Inside of the Foot (Push Pass)

This is the most common method of short passing and is the most reliable method because the pass is made with the largest part of the foot (Fig. 13.15).

Teaching Points. The body must be balanced by a well-bent supporting leg. The supporting foot is alongside the ball for low passing and behind it for high passing, pointing in the direction of the intended pass. The near-side of the body is turned away from the ball to assist the leg in turning outward from the hip. The kicking leg is well bent at the knee. The striking foot is dorsiflexed, toes up and firm (the most common problem is a "hanging toe"). The inside of the foot is driven straight throught the dead center of the ball. The swing should be a smooth but firm movement of the whole leg, with a long follow through that may become the first step.

Procedure.

1. The player push passes forward gently a swinging pendulum ball with the right foot, then with the left. The suspended ball makes the player aware of the surface of the foot with which the kick is executed. If a pendulum ball is not available, a ball can be suspended from a ceiling, tree, or cross bar, or the player may hold the string himself. The ball should swing slightly; as it swings toward him, the player push passes.

Variations:

a. Alternate left and right foot.

Fig. 13.15 *Classic pass with the inside of the foot (push pass). Front and side views.*

b. Push pass, control. Push pass first with right, then left.

c. Push pass right, control left.

d. Push pass left, control right.

e. Push pass with a change of direction: Push pass forward with right, control with right, push pass with left to the right, control with left foot.

f. Reverse: Push pass forward with the left, control left, push pass with the right to the left, control with the right.

2. In pairs, one ball stationary, players face each other about ten yards apart. Player push passes the ball to partner, who, depending upon his capability, may use his hands to block the ball or stop it with sole or inside of the foot.

Variation: Push pass a stationary ball after a short approach-run. Partner controls the ball and repeats.

3. In pairs, one ball, players face each other about ten yards apart. They serve themselves by rolling the ball gently ahead of them, using hands or push pass, then run after the ball to push pass it to partner, who controls and repeats.

Variation: Players serve each other by rolling the ball (bowling style) gently to each other in order to push pass it back first-touch (without controlling). After ten passes, change roles.

284

a   b   c   d

Fig. 13.16 *Pass with the outside of the foot (flick pass).*

4. In pairs, one ball, players ten yards apart, direct first-touch passing while moving. The player passes to partner who moves forward to meet the ball, push passes it back first-touch and returns to his position.

5. In pairs, one ball, volley passing—inside volley (lob volley). The players face each other ten yards apart. One stands and drops the ball for himself to volley to the partner's chest. Partner catches and repeats.

Variations:

a. Half-volley, players aim for partner's chest.

b. Player tosses the ball head high in order to run forward and volley it after the first bounce.

c. Server tosses ball just short of his partner for him to volley with the inside of the foot on the first bounce.

d. The server tosses ball knee high for his partner to volley directly, first-touch.

e. Players are asked to volley low, aiming at partner's feet, and then lob volley, aiming at partner's head.

f. Players volley the ball first-touch (without catching) after the first bounce back and forth.

g. Players volley the ball back and forth without allowing the ball to touch the ground.

Kicking with the Outside of the Foot (Flick Pass)

This technique is used for diagonal passing in forward and backward directions, for short and medium distances. The advantages of using the outside of the foot are that the movement is very fast and does not interrupt the natural running stride and it is not likely to be anticipated by the opponent (Fig. 13.16).

Teaching Points. The supporting foot is placed comfortably beside the ball (approximately ten inches). It points in the direction the player is running rather than in the direction of the pass. The toes are well-braced and pointing inward, ankle fixed. The kicking action originates more from the knee joint than the hip. There is a short back-swing, quick lower-leg snap, and flick, with a possible long follow through for long distances. The center of gravity may remain on the supporting foot.

Procedure.

1. In pairs, one ball, players face each other at an angle six yards apart and pass the ball back and forth, first with control, then first-touch (direct).

2. In three's, one ball, players stand in a triangle formation ten yards apart and pass the ball clockwise. It is important that players receive with the inside of the left foot and pass with the outside of the right.

Variations:

a. Players move counterclockwise, receiving with inside of right foot and passing with outside of left.

b. Direct (first-touch) passing clockwise, then counterclockwise.

c. While running clockwise, and then counterclockwise, first with control then direct, players pass.

Subsequent activities with the outside of the foot should follow the pattern of combination play recommended at the end of this kicking section. The only peculiarity in passing with the outside of

a   b   c

Fig. 13.17 *Close-ups of kicking with the full instep, inside of the instep, and outside of the instep.*

the foot in zigzag, triangles, or squares is that the pass should be made with the outside of the inner foot. Consequently if the activity goes clockwise, the player may receive the ball with the inside of the outer foot and pass with the outside of the inner foot, or he may control with the outside and pass with the outside of the inner foot.

Kicking with the Instep

The instep is the most powerful part of the foot. When fully braced, it presents a natural extension of the lower leg. It allows great diversity: by slightly varying the impact surface, making contact more with the inside or outside of the instep, it is effective for shooting, passing high and low, and clearing (Fig. 13.17).

Teaching Points. The player must be balanced by a well-bent supporting leg, toes pointed in the direction of the kick. For a low drive, the supporting foot is alongside the ball, kicking knee over the ball on impact (Fig. 13.18). For a lofted drive the supporting foot is behind the ball, and the kicking knee is behind the ball on impact (Figs. 13.19 and 13.20). The kicking leg must be brought well-back in a perfect cocked position, knee bent, heel nearly touching the buttocks (Fig. 13.21). On impact the ankle must be fixed and the instep well-braced. The effectiveness of the kick depends largely on the lower-leg snap. Follow through is in the direction of the kick (run after the ball).

Procedure. Activities with the pendulum ball are an effective way of teaching inexperienced

players the use of the instep for kicking, since the ball is inches off the ground and they need not fear hitting the ground.

1. Ball is just above the ground. Players get the feel for the ball on the full instep by just rebounding the ball with the instep. They should try to keep the ball going straight forward. Alternate left, right.
Variations:
   a. Players go through the full motion of kicking with the instep at half-speed and then receive the ball with the full instep.
   b. Players run at the ball, kick, and run after the ball. First right, then left.

2. In pairs, one ball, players face each other about five yards apart. First from a stationary position, then running, they drop the ball from their hands, held hip height, and, striking it at knee height, volley kick it with the instep to their partner aiming at his chest. Beginners may be allowed to take the foot back before dropping the ball. Emphasize stepping in the direction of the kick following the ball. Partner catches and repeats.
Variations:
   a. Players hit a late half-volley ball to their partner, striking the ball when it rises five–seven inches from the ground.
   b. Players half-volley ball to partner, impact of ball on the ground and the foot coincide.
   c. Players toss ball a little ahead, chest high, in order to take a few steps before volley kicking it to their partner.
   d. Players toss ball chest high and hit a late half-volley to their partner.
   e. Players toss ball chest high and half-volley it to their partner, impact of the ball on ground and foot coincide.
   f. Players toss ball chest high and half-volley it to their partner with specific emphasis: low

Fig. 13.18 *Low drive: The knee is over the ball on impact, supporting foot alongside the ball.*

Fig. 13.19 *Lofted drive: The knee is behind the ball on impact, supporting foot behind the ball.*

half-volley drive (passing, shooting), lofted half-volley drive (passing, clearing).

3. In pairs, one ball, players face each other five–seven yards apart. One player serves in a gentle arc to the other who volleys it back.

Variations:

a. The player volleys after the ball bounces once or twice.

b. The player late half-volleys the ball back to his partner.

c. The player half-volleys the ball back to his partner, with a specified emphasis first on a low half-volley drive (passing, shooting), then on a lofted half-volley drive (passing, clearing).

4. In pairs, one ball, ten yards apart, players face each other. They kick a stationary ball (it is advisable to elevate the ball slightly by placing it on a loose surface—sand, grass, or a piece of cloth, to free the player from inhibitions about hitting the ground and sustaining an injury) from an angle approach with the inside of the instep. They kick, control, kick.

Variations:

a. Player receives ball from his partner,

pushes it slightly to the side, runs after it, and kicks it to his partner in a low drive, then a lofted drive, a short distance (ten yards), then longer distances (twenty-five–thirty yards).

b. The server makes gentle passes to the right or left while the passer kicks the ball first-touch low, then high, back to the server who controls the ball, and repeats.

c. Players pass continually back and forth. They drive high or low at each other with or without first controlling the ball.

5. In pairs, one ball, players thirty yards apart, zigzag passing high and low as they run from one penalty box to the other, ending in a shot at goal.

The following activities are recommended as a methodical progression for all kinds of kicking techniques necessary for passing, interpassing, and scoring. Players may be asked to use only a particular technique—a pass with the inside (push pass), pass with the outside of the foot, inside of instep,

Fig. 13.20 *Chip shot: The foot is used like a golf iron.*

Fig. 13.21 *For power and distance, "the kicking leg must be brought well-back in a perfect cocked position, knee bent, heel nearly touching the buttocks."*

or full instep. Players may be allowed to control the ball before passing or be asked to deliver the ball first-touch (direct).

1. Zigzag passing. In pairs, one ball, players ten yards apart, move about side-by-side passing the ball back and forth. The ball should be passed slightly ahead of the running player so that he does not have to break the rhythm of his stride. They move from penalty box to penalty box, finishing with a shot at goal. They pass with the outside of the foot near partner (the inner foot) and control with the inside of the foot on the far side of partner (the outer foot).
Variations:
a. Control with the outside of the inner foot and pass with the outside of the same foot or push pass with the inside of the outer foot or inside of the instep (chip pass).
b. First-touch (direct) passing with the inside of the outer foot.

2. In three's, one ball, standing (then running) in a triangle formation, players pass clockwise, control left, and pass right.

Variations:
a. Players control with the outside of the right foot and push pass with the inside of the right foot.
b. Players control with the inside of the left foot and pass with the outside of the right foot.
c. The ball is played directly with the right foot and then with the left.
d. All exercises are repeated going counterclockwise.

3. In three's, one ball, two outer players face each other ten yards apart while the third takes up a position between them, always facing the passer. The outer players pass to each other between the legs of the middle man (first with control, then direct). Players change roles at given intervals.
Variations:
a. Players follow their passes to change position with the middle man.
b. They lob pass over the middle man. The middle man gives a token challenge.
c. Players follow their passes and change position with the middle man.
d. Volley passing. The outside man volleys the ball short to the middle man who volleys it back so that the first player must then volley it over his head to the third player long (short-

long), first with control, then first-touch, first without switching positions, then switching.

4. In three's, two balls, two outer players (A and C) with balls face each other about ten yards apart while the third player (B) takes up a position between them. A passes to B, the middle man, and follows his pass to change position with B. B runs to meet the ball, dribbles it to take up the vacated position of A. In the meantime, C passes the ball to A, and follows his pass. A meets the ball and dribbles it to the position vacated by C, and so on.

5. In three's, one ball, same formation as above. A passes to B, the middle man. B runs to meet the ball, controls it while turning and immediately passes to C. C plays the ball back to B first-touch (direct) who meets the ball, controls while turning, and plays to A. Players change roles after a given interval.

Variation: A and C, the outer players, move laterally to force B (the middle man) to look before passing.

6. In four's, one ball, triangle formation with two players at the beginning point. All ten yards apart. Players pass and run clockwise (follow the pass).

Variation: Pass clockwise and run counter-clockwise (away from the pass).

7. In four's, one ball, square formation, passing clockwise and counterclockwise, first with control, then direct (first-touch). Players move to meet the ball, pass, and follow the pass a few paces, then return to their original position.

Variations:

a. Players run in a square. The pass must be placed in the running path of the receiving player so that he does not have to break running stride.

b. Three-on-one within limited space (grid). Count the number of successful passes.

8. In four's, one ball, in circle formation. One stands in the middle (D). Player A with the ball passes to the middle man (D) who passes to B, who returns the ball to him. He then passes to C, and so on. First clockwise, then counter-clockwise.

Variations:

a. Players run in a circle around the middle player and pass the ball to him first with control, then direct (first-touch).

b. A passes to D, the middle man, and follows his pass to change positions with him. The middle man passes to B, and follows his pass to change positions with B, and so on.

9. Zigzag pass combination with ball leading and position switching. In pairs, one ball, players move side-by-side about ten yards apart from penalty box to penalty box and finish with a shot at goal. A dribbles the ball diagonally ahead of B. B in the meantime switches behind A to change sides with him. A plays a well-timed diagonal pass into the running path of B. B then leads the ball diagonally across in front of A, and A switches position with him. B then delivers the diagonal pass. The final pass to serve the player for a shot at goal should be delivered outside the penalty box.

Variations:

a. Player A, instead of dribbling in front of B, delivers a well-weighted diagonal pass and runs after it. B in the meantime switches sides with A, who then delivers a well-timed diagonal pass to B.

b. Zigzag passing—wing forward and inside forward going down the wing and crossing. When players reach the edge of the penalty box, the one dribbling toward goal (preferably the inside forward) delivers a diagonal pass in the direction of the corner flag and continues to cut in toward the goalmouth. In the meantime, the wing forward cuts from inside to the wing to run down the diagonal pass, takes the ball down to the goal line, and then crosses it. The inside forward tries to shoot at goal, first after controlling the ball, then first-touch.

10. Square through pass combination. In pairs, one ball, players run side-by-side about ten yards apart from penalty box to penalty box. Player A plays square to B, and immediately sprints diagonally in front of him. B delivers a through pass and cuts immediately diagonally behind A to change position with him. The final pass may be a through or square pass to serve the player who takes a shot at goal.

Variation: Square and through passing between the wing forward and inside forward down the wing and crossing. When players reach the edge of the penalty box, the wing forward should deliver a square pass to the outside for the inside forward to receive and deliver a long through pass along the touchline. The wing forward cuts to the outside to collect the through pass. The inside forward, after delivering the through pass, cuts toward goal. The wing forward dribbles a few paces to allow sufficient time for the inside forward to reach the goalmouth, then crosses the ball for the inside forward to have a shot at goal.

11. Through through pass combination. In pairs, one ball, players take up positions one beside the other with ten yards between them and move from penalty box to penalty box, finishing with a shot at goal. A delivers a well-timed and well-paced through pass which B has to run down. B delivers the through pass which A has to run down. It is important in this passing combination to change pace, that players in possession of the ball slow up to allow the receiving player sufficient time to sprint ahead.

Overlapping has to be done as follows: the player cuts first to the side three–five yards as if to expect a square pass. Suddenly he cuts diagonally ahead of the passer into the open space to receive the through pass. The passer must sprint immediately after delivering the through pass. Reaching the edge of the penalty box, the player takes a shot at goal.

Variation: Through through pass combination down the flank between the wing forward and inside forward. The inside forward delivers the final through pass and cuts toward goal, while the wing forward runs down the through pass and dribbles the ball all the way down to goal line, giving the inside forward time to reach the goalmouth. Then he crosses to the inside forward to have a shot at goal.

12. Zigzag passing combination in three's. Players run with ten yards between them in a line from one penalty box to the other and finish with a shot at goal. Player A passes to B. B passes to C. C passes to B, B passes to A, and so on. Each player must attempt to deliver a well-timed and paced lead pass into the running path of the receiver so that he does not have to break stride.

Variations:

a. B, the middle man, hangs back about five yards. B begins with a diagonal pass to A. A delivers a square pass to B, then B makes a diagonal pass to C. C again plays the square pass to the middle man, B. B must be sure that he trails the others as they progress to the penalty box and end with a shot at goal.

b. Position switching. B, the middle man, delivers a pass to his left to A, and immediately sprints to his right in front of C, who cuts behind him to switch position with B. A plays a square pass to the new middle man, C. C plays to his right to B, and changes position with A, who now takes up the position of the middle man. They continue to the penalty box and finish with a shot at goal.

c. Zigzag passing combination with dribbling and position switching. Player A delivers a square pass to middle man, B. B dribbles diagonally to his left to switch positions with A. B then delivers a square pass to A. A then dribbles the ball diagonally to his right to switch positions with C and make a square pass to C. C dribbles to his left to switch position with B, and so on, finishing with a shot at goal.

13. Square through pass combination in three's with position switching. B, the middle man, delivers a square pass to C and immediately cuts diagonally in front of him to switch position with C. C delivers a through pass, cuts behind B, and takes up his position. C delivers a square pass to his left to A, and immediately cuts in front of him to switch position. A de-livers a through pass and cuts behind C to take up his position. C delivers a square pass to A. A delivers another square pass to B, who delivers the through pass while they change positions.

The logical progression is to proceed to improvised combination play with various segments of the team against live opposition. (See Diags. 13.1–13.4.)

Dribbling and Feinting

Dribbling and feinting are the actions of advancing with the ball and beating an opposing player. To

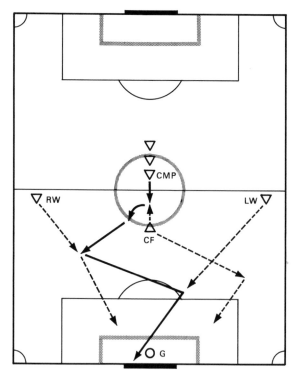

Diag. 13.1 *The attack pattern begins with a pass from the center midfield player to the center forward who drops back to receive the pass and then turns and plays the ball diagonally forward to the right wing forward. While the center forward turns and makes the pass, the wingers must make their diagonal runs. The right wing forward sprints to meet the ball while the center forward, immediately after making the pass, makes his diagonal run to change places with the left winger. The right winger plays the ball first-touch right into the path of the left wing forward as he makes his run toward the goal to shoot first-touch.*

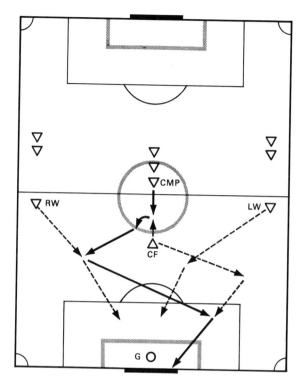

Diag. 13.2 *A variation of the previous pattern can be introduced. By using the left wing forward as a decoy, the right wing forward should be asked to lay the pass right into the path of the center forward as he veers in front of the left winger toward the goal to take the shot.*

Initially the coach would be well-advised to instruct the right wing forward to aim his passes for each of his front colleagues in turn. He should emphasize also to each player running off the ball that whether he receives the pass or not, each run must be realistic and wholehearted. Practices should start without opposition until the players reach the point where they move off after playing the ball without hesitation, then opposition should be introduced.

Even in the three-player combinations, it will be enough to introduce one defender at first and restrict him to a limited role of challenge and interception.

As soon as possible, however, the coach should eliminate all restrictions from the defender but care should be taken that this is not done too early. This will be evident if the defender is too successful; in such circumstances the coach should once again introduce the restrictions on the defender.

When the restrictions on the defender are finally elimi-nated, the attacking players should be encouraged to impro-vise on the basic themes when in possession. It should be clear that the aim here is not to restrict the initiative of the talented player but to ensure that his front colleagues are constantly repositioning in close support.

Diag. 13.3 *The coach should instruct the defender to vary his responses, though in the early stages he should not make feints. With the ball, on his way from the center forward to the right wing forward, the defender must make his decision and move promptly and decisively to cover the player of his choice. If the defender elects to cover the left wing forward, then the pass should go from the right wing forward to the center forward. If the defender moves to pick up the center forward, the pass should go to the left winger.*

Later on, the defender will drop back in deliberation before deciding whom he should challenge, putting greater pressure on the attackers.

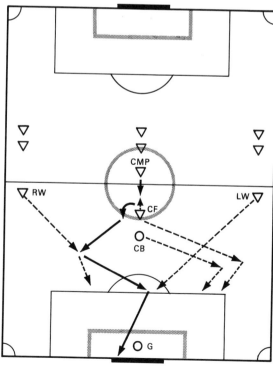

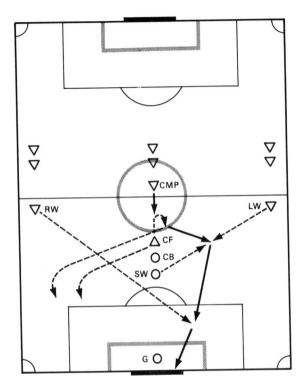

Diag. 13.4 *Going a step further, a second defender can be introduced and he should be asked to present a challenge to the center forward. He should, however, be restrained from tackling and merely show himself at first.*

The center forward, as in the previous practice, receives a pass from the midfield player and turns on the ball to deliver the pass. The centerback covering the center forward will stand off at first to allow the center forward to turn and deliver the pass. Immediately after this the center forward makes his diagonal run to change places with the right wing forward. At first the coach may instruct the centerback to stay with the center forward while the second defender is asked to adopt the position of sweeper. Consequently he must move across to challenge the wing forward who receives a pass from the center forward.

Step-by-step practices should become more realistic. For example, after the center forward delivers the pass he should be free to choose between changing places with the right or left wing forward. He may also be free to feint—to go one way and suddenly check and reverse his direction.

Both defenders should be allowed the same freedom, allowing the centerback to challenge for the pass from the midfield player to the center forward. If he does, the midfield player calls "man on" and the center forward plays the ball back first-touch to the midfield player and again makes his run. The pass is made now by the midfield player and the attack again develops to the reaction of the defenders.

dribble and feint successfully, both speed and ball-control must be augmented with the ability to elude or deceive the opponent.

Teaching Points. The player's center of gravity should be lowered. He should run on his toes, slightly crouched, all joints flexed and loose. This will permit excellent ball-control, balance, shiftiness, and immediate acceleration. When within challenging distance of an opponent, the player should take small, quick steps, stroking the ball gently every, or every other, step to keep the ball close to his feet for instant control. When he can accelerate straight ahead without immediate challenge, he can drive the ball more loosely ahead of him (Fig. 13.22).

Every feint has its specific rhythm. The player should not hurry his feints, but execute them convincingly, watch the reaction of the opponent, and take advantage of the feint's effectiveness by accelerating instantly to beat the opponent.

Peripheral vision will enable the player to control the ball and be aware at the same time of his environment in order to act appropriately; he must avoid being a ball-watcher.

Procedure.

1. Circle formation ten yards in diameter. Player should be allowed to work with his strong foot first. Assuming he is right-footed, the group moves counterclockwise while the player dribbles with the inside of his right foot, stroking it every other step.
Variations:
   a. Moving clockwise, player dribbles with the inside of his left foot, stroking it every other step.
   b. Moving clockwise, player dribbles with the outside of his right foot, stroking it every other step.
   c. Moving counterclockwise, player dribbles with the outside of his left foot, stroking it every other step.
   d. Moving clockwise, the player now alternates, stroking the ball twice with the outside of the right foot and then changing to the inside of the foot, stroking twice, and repeating.
   e. Moving clockwise, player dribbles with the outside of the left foot and inside of the right foot, alternating every two strokes.
   f. Moving clockwise, player strokes the ball with every step, alternating inside, outside, outside of right foot, and inside of left foot.
   g. Counterclockwise, the player dribbles with the outside of the left foot and inside of right

a   b   c

Fig. 13.22 *Dribbling with inside, outside, and sole of the foot.*

foot, alternating every contact, and stroking the ball with every step.

2. Figure eight formation of ten yards. In the first half of the figure eight, the player runs clockwise, stroking the ball with the inside of the left foot. At the intersection, he runs counterclockwise and strokes the ball with the inside of the right foot.

Variations:

a. In the first half of the figure eight the player runs counterclockwise, stroking the ball with the outside of the left foot. At the intersection he runs clockwise and strokes the ball with the outside of the right foot.

b. In the first half of the figure eight player runs clockwise, stroking the ball with the outside of the right foot. At the intersection he does not change feet. Instead he strokes the ball with the inside of the same foot, running counterclockwise for the second half of the figure.

c. In the first half of the figure eight the player runs counterclockwise, stroking the ball with the outside of the left foot. At the intersection he does not change feet. Instead he strokes the ball with the inside of the same foot, running clockwise for the second half of the figure.

d. In the first half of the figure eight the player runs clockwise, stroking the ball with the outside of the right foot. At the intersection he accentuates a change of feet by a lateral stride over the ball in order to continue counterclockwise, leading the ball with the outside of the left foot.

e. In the first half of the figure eight the player runs counterclockwise, stroking the ball with the outside of the left foot. At the intersection he accentuates a change of feet by a lateral stride over the ball in order to continue clockwise and leading the ball with the outside of the right foot.

3. Zigzag dribbling. Player dribbles with the outside of the right foot to go to his right. After two contacts, he uses the inside of the right foot to go to the left. Two contacts and repeat.

Variations:

a. Player dribbles with the outside of the left foot to go to his left. After two contacts he uses the inside of the left foot to go to the right. After two contacts, repeat.

b. Direction changes with each contact of the ball, first with the inside of each foot, right, left, and then with the outside of each foot, right, left.

c. Player first uses the inside of both feet, right foot to cut to left and left foot to cut to right. Next he uses the outside of both feet, right foot to cut to right and left foot to cut to his left. Last, the player uses inside and outside of the same foot to cut left and right.

d. Player dribbles with outside of right foot to his right. Every third time he strides over the ball to drag it along with the inside of his left foot. After two touches with the outside of the left foot to the left, he strides over the ball and drags it along with the inside of the right foot.

4. Slalom dribbling. Flags or cones can be

Fig. 13.23 *"Slalom dribbling—the players have to weave their way in and out of the flags."*

Fig. 13.24 *Live slalom: The player weaves in and out against the stream.*

used as markers for creating a slalom. Players are asked to use only the inside or outside of one foot or the inside and outside of both feet as they move between markers. The markers are placed at *regular intervals,* six feet apart. The player has to weave his way in and out of the flags (dodging the markers is effective for developing a body-swerve) (Fig. 13.23).

Variations:

a. Markers are placed at *irregular intervals* in groups of three markers six feet apart and about ten yards between groups. This is a realistic recreation of dribbling and feinting—the player beats an opponent and then accelerates. The groups of three markers represent the opponent and the ten yards allow the player to accelerate.

b. Markers are placed in a *triangle formation* of three flags every ten yards. This grouping forces the player to make tight turns.

5. Live slalom. Everyone with a ball moves forward in a single line about six feet apart. The first player, moving against the stream, weaves in and out to the end of the line (Fig. 13.24).

6. Shadow dribbling against an imaginary opponent. Players move about in a given area, half the field, and practice all kinds of dribbling and feinting skills against imaginary opponents.

7. Screening. As the player runs with the ball he imagines an opponent approaching from either the right or left. He screens the ball from the opponent by using the foot on the opposite side of the opponent. If the opponent comes

from the left he leads the ball with the right (inside or outside) foot.

8. Change of pace. Just before reaching an opponent he veers off slightly and accelerates in order to dodge him.

9. Stop-and-go, or reverse. Player runs with the ball, stops abruptly, and checks the ball by putting the sole of the foot gently on top of it and either rolls the ball forward and continues on or draws the ball back to turn and reverse direction.

10. Body-swerves. Single swerve. As the dribbler approaches the defender, he swerves to his right, quickly veers to the left, and accelerates to go past the opponent (Figs. 13.25 and 13.26).

Variation: Double swerve. The player swerves first to the left, then to the right, veers to the left and accelerates past the opponent (Fig. 13.27).

11. Feint plays at the ball. Feint kick, stop-and-go, or reverse. Player runs with the ball, shapes in pretense of kicking the ball. Instead he checks the ball by putting the sole of the foot gently on top of it. He either continues on or draws the ball back to turn and reverse direction.

Variations:

a. Player shapes in pretense of kicking the ball. Instead he checks it with the sole of the foot, draws it back and flicks it with the inside of the foot either behind his supporting foot in the opposite direction of the foot used or, with

| a | b | c |

Fig. 13.25 *Dribbling: Changing direction by an exaggerated side-step and body-swerve to one side while pushing the ball with the outside of the foot in the other direction.*

| a | b | c |

Fig. 13.26 *Dribbling option: Instead of pushing the ball with the outside of the right foot to his right, the player steps over the ball and drags it along to his right with the inside of the left foot.*

a slight pivot sidewards, to the same side of the foot used with a push-pass technique.

b. Heel kick with option: player dribbles the ball, steps over it while kicking it gently backward with his heel in order to reverse direction abruptly. Option: As before, but he pretends to back-heel the ball. Instead he swings his leg around to accelerate and drag the ball forward.

12. Players are confined to a grid small enough to create a crowded situation, the size depending upon the number of players. Players should be reminded to keep up their eyes, use

295

a *b* *c*

d *e* *f*

Fig. 13.27 *Double body swerve: The player leads the ball, swerves to his right, then left, and cuts right dragging the ball along with the inside of the left foot.*

the open space, change direction, and practice their feints. They move about with the ball avoiding any body or ball-contact (Figs. 13.28 and 13.29).

Variations:

a. In contest form, except that now there are a few players without balls. They try to kick out of the limited area any ball they can get their foot on. Players who lose their ball must leave

the grid; winners are those still left after a given time.

b. Contest: hunting game. One player is chosen to be a hunter. He tries to hit with his ball one of the other balls. If he succeeds, he switches roles with the owner of the ball hit.

13. Mirror dribbling. Five or more in a group, each with a ball, follow a leader and copy his every move.

Fig. 13.28 *Players dribbling in the confinement of a grid.*

Fig. 13.30 *"The coach, through hand signals, dictates in which direction players have to move."*

Fig. 13.29 *Eyes must be kept up. Only if the player is free of the ball will he be able to accomplish his tactical tasks.*

14. Catch the fugitive. All players with balls. One, possibly the best dribbler, is the fugitive who tries to shake his pursuers in half of the field or the whole field.

15. Players, each with a ball, move freely about in half the field, always keeping the coach in their peripheral view. The coach, through hand signals, dictates in which direction they have to move—forward, backward, lateral (Fig. 13.30).

Shadow dribbling against imaginary opponents or synthetic practices—swerving and twisting around markers—do not teach a player the responses he may encounter from live opponents. The true skills of dribbling and feinting can only be developed against active opponents. The most effective activity is one-on-one where an offensive player pits his wits against a defender, with all its variations. These are thoroughly described on pp. 306–309.

Heading

A well-directed header coupled with adequate speed can be as dangerous as a shot at goal. Any defender detailed to bear the brunt of attack must be a brave and excellent header in order to dominate the goalmouth in the air.

Teaching Points. Head the ball with the forehead, right between the eyes, eyes open. Keep the chin down and tighten the neck muscles. The player may face the ball with his head and chest square to it, bending the body like a bow, or he

297

Fig. 13.31 *Heading the ball between the eyes with the forehead to keep the ball low for passing and scoring.*

Fig. 13.32 *Striking the ball at the hairline to loft the ball (defensive heading) in order to clear it.*

a   b   c

Fig. 13.33 *"Face the ball, head and chest square to it, bending like a bow."*

may stand sideward to the approaching ball, bending sideward for power like a shot putter (Figs. 13.31–13.34). The head should be thrown at the ball, attacking it, and heading through rather than at the ball, with the follow through in the direction of the header. A wide position of the feet, when heading with feet on the ground, provide the base from which power and control develop and allow considerable movement of the trunk backward or forward. When the player jumps to head, timing is the most important factor. He must jump early, hang in the air to head the ball at the peak of his jump. He should use a single-leg takeoff whenever possible. The use of both arms adds momentum to the takeoff and power to the header.

Procedure. The following suggested unit on the

a   b   c   d   e

Fig. 13.34 *Heading: "He may stand sideward to the approaching ball, bending sideward for power like a shot putter."*

pendulum ball should begin with a still ball and progress to one that is moving. The pendulum allows the player to control the speed at which the ball approaches him. It permits aspects of the technique to be isolated and it allows a progressive buildup of confidence and control.

1. Heading from a sitting position is an excellent way to isolate the proper trunk action.
Variations:
a. Head, control, head.
b. Head forward and then sideward at a right angle, alternate right, left.
c. Heading while doing sit-ups.

2. Heading from a kneeling position, follow through by falling forward into a push-up position. The emphasis is on proper trunk action and follow through. The player should land on his hands after every header.

3. Heading from a push-up position. This emphasizes proper head action.

4. Heading from a standing position.
Variations:
a. From a straddle position.
b. From a stride position.
c. Head forward, then sideward at a right angle, alternate right, left.
d. Head forward, control, head forward.
e. Head forward, control, head sideward.
f. Head forward, jump to control with chest, and head forward.

5. Heading, jumping from a double-leg takeoff.
Variations:
a. Jump, head forward, jump, control, and repeat.

b. Jump, head forward, jump, head sideward, alternate right, left.
c. Jump, head forward, jump, control, head sideward, alternate right, left.

6. Heading, jumping from a run-up approach, single-leg takeoff (ball is stationary).
Variations:
a. Ball is moving.
b. Players run, jump, and head the ball, one following the other.
c. Players run, jump, and head in rapid succession, but every other player heads the ball sideward, or controls the ball.

7. While one player moves about in a semicircle, the other tries to head the ball in the direction of the moving player.

8. Partner stands about ten inches in front of the stationary ball with his back to the other player who jumps up and heads the ball without climbing on the back of the "opponent" in front of him.
Variations:
a. Player in front makes it more realistic by also jumping but without attempting to head the ball.
b. Player standing is positioned one yard behind the ball. The player heading the ball has to dodge him to be able to head the ball.
c. Standing partner is under a ball swinging in a semicircle. The player must move from side to side of the "opponent" to head the ball.

9. Heading contest. In pairs players try to jump and head the ball. Player in each pair who heads ten times before the other is the winner.

The next stage involves heading a ball which is

in free flight. The player either serves the ball for himself, uses the aid of a backboard, or has the assistance of a player or coach.

The most important factor in the following activities for the best effect is the nature of the ball service. Generally speaking, the two-handed underhand throw permits the greatest control. The aim of the serve is to produce a certain throw by which the other player is helped to practice a particular technique.

Heading with Feet on the Ground

1. In pairs, one ball, players face each other about ten yards apart. Player tosses up the ball for himself (about three feet above his head) to head to partner. He aims at the chest. Partner catches the ball, tosses it into the air, and heads.
Variations:
   a. Players sit and toss ball for themselves to head to each other.
   b. One player sits. The other stands five yards in front of him and serves the ball to be headed back to him. After a given number of repetitions, roles switch, and the server becomes the header (Fig. 13.35).
   c. The header lies on his back. The server tosses the ball for him to head as he does situps. After ten–twenty repetitions, players change roles.

2. In pairs, players face each other ten yards apart, one ball. The server runs backward across the field and serves the ball to his partner running forward with him to head back to him. On the way back, they change roles.

3. In pairs, one ball, players serve themselves by tossing the ball into the air to head to partner who moves either right or left. Partner catches the ball and repeats.

Fig. 13.35 *Heading from a sitting position.*

Variations:
   a. Player serves the ball and immediately moves off to the right or left. Heading partner must aim the header into the path of the running server, who catches the ball and repeats. After fifteen repetitions, roles change.
   b. Player serves the ball slightly to the left or right of the heading partner to force him to move left or right to head the ball back to him.
   c. Both players run across the field side by side about five yards apart. The server tosses the ball continually for his partner to head back to him as they move. On the way back, partners change roles.

4. Three in triangle formation, one ball, head clockwise. The first player throws to the second, who heads it to the third. He catches the ball in order to serve the ball up for the second, who catches and serves to the first.
Variation: The first and second player run clockwise around the third player, the server. He serves to the first, who heads to second, and the second heads back to server. Then the server throws to the second player, who heads to the first. He heads back to the server, and so on. After a given number of repetitions, players change roles.

5. In three's, one ball, Indian file, five yards apart. The first player faces the other two. He serves the ball to the second, middle man, who heads it back to the server, who then heads it long to the third player, who catches the ball and repeats the procedure.
Variation: The server tosses the ball for himself to head and players are no longer allowed to catch the ball after the long header. The activity continues, heading short, short, long—short, short, long.

6. In three's, two balls, Indian file, five yards apart. The two outside men, the servers, face each other. The middle man, header, must turn quickly from one server to the other in order to head the ball back to the respective server in quick succession. Players change roles in given intervals, time limit, or number or repetitions.

7. In three's, one ball. *A* with the ball, *B* behind him faces *C* who is ten yards away. *A* serves for *C* and follows his throw to exchange positions with *C*. *C* heads the ball to *B*, follows his header to line up behind *B*. *B* in the meantime catches the ball, serves to *A*, and so on.

8. In three's, one ball, players line up five yards apart, facing the same direction across the field. *A* serves the ball by throwing it over *B*, the middle man, to *C*. *B*, the middle man, runs to take up a new position to receive the ball headed by *C*. *B* controls the ball, plays it back

to C, who then serves for A, and so on. They continue across the field, then change roles.

9. In three's, one ball, players run in a triangle across the field. A, the server, runs backward, while C and B run forward. A serves to B, B heads to C, and C heads to A, who catches. A serves to C, C heads to B, B heads to A, who catches, and so on.

Heading with Feet Off the Ground (Double-Leg Takeoff)

1. In pairs, one ball, holder and header. One player holds the ball tight in his hands, arms stretched high above his head. The header jumps from a double-leg takeoff to head the held ball (Fig. 13.36). After fifteen repetitions, roles change.

2. In pairs, one ball, the server throws the ball to his partner so that he must jump from a double-leg takeoff to head the ball back to him. After fifteen repetitions, roles change.
Variation: Server A throws the ball a comfortable jump height to his partner, B, and runs immediately into a new position where B heads to him.

3. In three's, one ball, a server, header, and defender in front of the header, face each other ten yards apart. The server serves the ball to the header over the defender's head. He heads it back to the server without jumping on the defender's back in front of him. Players change roles interval-style, after a half a minute, or after fifteen–twenty repetitions.
Variation: The defender makes it more difficult for the header by also jumping up and down to create a more realistic situation.

Single-Leg Takeoff

1. In pairs, one ball. The ball is served high and short to force the header to run, jump from a single-leg takeoff to head the ball back to the server.

2. In three's, one ball, a server, header, and defender. The server faces the other two. The header takes a position about three–five yards behind the defender to allow a running single-leg takeoff. The ball is served high above the defender's head. The header runs, jumps from a single-leg takeoff to head the ball back to the server. Important: the header must avoid jumping into the defender.
Variations:
a. The defender also moves about and jumps to make the situation more realistic.
b. The ball is served slightly to right or left. Both the defender and header must move accordingly.

Fig. 13.36 *Heading a held ball from a double-leg takeoff.*

3. Single file, any number of players, one ball. The server is positioned ten yards away from the group and five yards to one side of the expected running path. As players run past the server, he tosses the ball for them to jump and head back to him. The headers continue to run another fifteen yards to form a new line single file. When all players have headed, they run in the other direction to head the ball back to the server.
Variation: Two servers, one on either side of the line. It is advisable that the servers take up a staggered position. Players now receive the ball from the left server and head it to the server on the right. Coming back they receive from the right and head to the server on the left.

4. In two groups, headers and servers, each server with a ball, with goalkeeper. The servers line up at the junction of the goal line and penalty box. The headers are positioned at the far post even with the penalty spot. The ball is served by a throw-in for the header to run onto and head at goal. After heading, the header joins the server line and the server joins the header line.
Variation: Ball is served by a center (chip pass).

5. Three groups: servers at the touchline, even with the penalty box; headers about twenty yards away facing them; shooters in front of the goalmouth. Goalkeeper in goal. Ball is served by a throw-in to header, who heads the ball to the shooter, who takes a shot at goal. The server follows his throw to become a header, the header follows his header to become a shooter, and the scorer follows his shot around end line to become a server. Keep practice continuous by having at least two–three players in each position.

Variation: Ball is served by a center (chip pass). The header may take a position around the penalty spot and the shooter positions himself about ten yards outside the penalty box. The shooter indicates where he wants the ball by the way he moves.

Tackling

Tackling is the major technical and tactical skill in defense. A true defender is one who can effectively dispossess an attacker of the ball. Although tactics play a more important role in tackling than in any other technical element, the technical aspects of tackling cannot be ignored.

Teaching Points. The tackler should take a stand-off position, facing the attacker, well-balanced, close enough to put pressure on him, and force the attacker to keep his eyes on the ball,

Fig. 13.37 *"The defender should hold off his tackle until he can jockey the attacker into a position where the odds are in his favor."*

but not be so close that the defender can be easily beaten. The defender should be patient, holding off his tackle until he can jockey the attacker into a position where the odds are in the defense's favor, when the least possible danger can arise if the tackle fails, when other defending players are available to cover him; and the area in which the attacking player can dodge, turn, or avoid the tackle is as small as possible (Fig. 13.37).

The tackle should coincide with the attacker's attempt to play the ball, causing the ball to be wedged between the players' feet. The larger the surface used to block the ball (sole of foot, inside, or outside) the more likely are the chances that the defender will come up wtih the ball (Figs. 13.38 and 13.39).

The force of the tackling foot should be applied through the dead center of the ball. The tackler must move in close enough to put the supporting foot slightly beside and behind the ball, in order to put his full body-weight into the tackle. The whole tackling leg is tensed, driving the ball literally through the opponent's legs or over them, or knocking the opponent momentarily off-balance by a well-timed shoulder charge (Fig. 13.40).

Shoulder Charge

1. Rooster fight. In pairs, partners hop on one foot, arms folded in front of the chest. Players try to knock each other off-balance by charging each other shoulder against shoulder or throw each other off-balance by feinting a shoulder charge. Using elbows or having both feet touch the ground (although hopping foot may be changed at given intervals) is forbidden.

Variations:

a. Contest—interval style, one minute, first half right leg and second half left leg. Every error is counted. Round robin. Player with the fewest total errors is the winner.

b. Knock-out system—winner goes on, loser drops out.

2. In pairs without the ball, players run about and practice shoulder charging. Emphasis is on the legality of a technical execution, timing the charge so that the player being charged has the weight on his outside foot, meeting charge with charge, and feinting and charging.

3. In pairs, shoulder charge while leading the ball. The attacker has to keep control of the ball while meeting charge with charge. To protect himself he can change direction and use feint maneuvers to avoid a shoulder charge.

Fig. 13.38 *Basic front block tackle with the inside of the foot.*

Fig. 13.39 *Basic front block tackle with the sole of the foot.*

a   b   c   d

Fig. 13.40 *"The tackling leg is tensed, driving the ball literally through the opponent's legs or over them, or knocking the opponent momentarily off-balance by a well-timed shoulder charge."*

4. In pairs, charging with individual duels for the ball. The player with the ball defends it through screening (obstructing the ball with his body) and meeting charge with charge. The defender reinforces his challenge for the ball through the use of the shoulder charge.

Variations:

a. Individual duel, one versus one, in a ten yard grid. The idea of the defender is to force the attacker or ball out of the limited playing area. If he is successful, players change roles.

b. Contest—how long can the attacker remain in the grid?

5. In pairs, shoulder charge while running after the ball to one goal with goalkeeper. Players stand on the center line ten yards apart. The coach is positioned in the middle, passes the ball toward goal. Both players sprint after the ball, try to gain possession by using the shoulder charge, continue, and take a shot at goal (Fig. 13.41).

6. Shoulder charge while receiving the ball. In three's, a server, attacker-receiver, and defender, with one ball. Server and attacker-receiver face each other about twenty-five–thirty yards apart. Defender tightly marks the attacking receiver. The server plays the ball with a well-aimed throw or lofted pass to the attacker-receiver who has to control the ball while the defender tries to dispossess him by knocking him off-balance by a well-timed shoulder charge at the moment the attacker is controlling the ball. The ball must be played back to the server. The server follows his serve to become the receiver-attacker, the attacker becomes the server, and the defender becomes the attacker-receiver only if he wins the ball.

Basic Block Tackle with the Inside of the Foot

1. In pairs, one ball, players face each other, one stride from a ball placed between them. The supporting foot of both is placed slightly to the side and behind the ball. The playing foot is back. Players count one-two-three-Go! in order to coordinate their simultaneous striking at the ball with the inside of the foot to make a block

Fig. 13.41 *Shoulder charge while fighting for possession of the ball.*

Fig. 13.42 *Basic block tackle with the inside of the foot.*

tackle. Timed correctly, the ball will be wedged and remain between the inside of the players' feet. This should give them confidence that a powerful block tackle can be made without fear of injury (Fig. 13.42).

Variations:

a. Combine with a shoulder charge as the block tackle is made.

b. Contest: face-off similar to one in lacrosse. Players after blocking try to win the ball by forcing the ball out of the tackle. Player must have control of the ball to be declared a winner.

2. In pairs, one stationary ball, first players jogging, then running. Both are four strides away from the placed ball. Beginning with the non-tackling foot (assuming both players tackle with the right foot), players count one, left, two, right, three, left, planting the supporting foot alongside the ball—Go, tackle right. Players after block tackling try to win the ball by forcing it out of the tackle. Then they place the ball again, step back, and repeat.

3. In pairs, first jogging, then running, players face each other about ten yards apart. Players are asked to move toward each other, one having the ball at his feet. They again try to synchronize their movements by counting: one, start, two, push ball gently ahead, three, plant supporting foot beside the ball, and Go, block tackle. After tackling, players try to win the ball, continue to go past each other, exchange positions, and repeat.

Variation: Defender approaches from different angles.

4. In pairs, attacker with ball. Defender faces him within tackling distance. Attacker runs at defender, defender retreats. Both have to make their moves within a given area. Only after one player has clearly beaten the other, either the attacker getting past the defender, or the defender winning the ball and going past the attacker, are the players asked to square off again.

Sole of the Foot Tackle

1. In pairs, one ball stationary. Player with the ball wedges it between the sole of the foot and the ground while the other player strikes at the ball with the instep. Reverse roles.

Variations:

a. Players one stride from a ball placed between them. The supporting foot is placed within comfortable reach to the side and behind the ball. In order to synchronize their action, players count one-two-three-Go! One wedges the ball between the sole of the foot and the ground. Simultaneously the other strikes it with the instep.

b. Jogging, then running, both players are four strides from a placed ball. Beginning with non-kicking foot (assuming player is right-footed) they step left, right, left, plant the supporting foot, and block tackle right.

2. In pairs, one ball, players face each other ten yards apart. One dribbles and then pushes the ball forward. Tackler traps the ball by wedging it with the sole of the foot and the ground while the attacker strikes at it with the instep. Reverse roles.

Variation: Defender draws the ball out of the tackle with the sole of the foot, either behind him, turning to shield the ball from the challenging player, or he draws it back and flicks it to the side with the inside of the foot behind and to the side of his supporting foot to beat the challenging attacker and continue on to change positions and repeat.

3. In pairs, attacker with ball. Defender faces him within tackling distance. Attacker runs at him, defender retreats. Both have to make their move within a given area. Tackle should be realistic and concluded when one player has clear possession. Whoever has the ball is attacker. Repeat.

Sliding Tackle

A player has to have confidence in his ability to slide without great discomfort. To overcome any fear or to avoid creating it, the coach should be sure that there is a soft surface (ideally a sliding pit) available for early instruction.

In the event that there is no sliding pit available, the coach must be imaginative in using the natural resources as training aids. A rain-soaked field, or an artificially soaked area, can make an excellent sliding pit.

Sneakers instead of soccer shoes will reduce friction as well as danger of injury. And, of course, long pants, padded if possible, would eliminate such minor injuries as strawberries, scrapes, and bruises. These usually heal quickly but some players experience great difficulty in getting a strawberry to heal because each new slide aggravates the injury. A piece of gauze rolled and shaped to a doughnut form and held in place by adhesive can be put over the strawberry. Such a dressing prevents the uniform from coming into contact with the skin and permits new skin to form.

1. Without the ball, player takes up an exaggerated straddle position and twists his trunk right and left, allowing his feet to slide even farther apart. The effectiveness of the slide tackle will depend upon the player's flexibility in spreading his legs without undue strain.

2. Player standing with a ball placed a long stride distance in front of him. He split strides to reach for the ball to kick it away. He allows himself to fall gradually to the ground on the side of the foot used, breaking the impact of the fall by reaching back with the nearer hand.

Variations:

a. Placed ball is within several strides' distance. Player takes a preliminary stride before the split stride to kick the ball away.

b. He jogs from a given point ten yards or so (and later runs) at the placed ball to kick it away.

3. Player serves the ball for himself. He rolls the ball ahead of him and goes after it to make the slide tackle.

Variations:

a. The coach rolls the ball and the player goes after it to execute the slide tackle.

b. Tackle has to be executed before the ball crosses a given restraining line.

4. In pairs, one ball. Tackler and server face each other about five yards apart. The server rolls the ball three-four yards to one side of the tackler, who tries by way of a split-slide tackle to kick the ball away.

Variation: Partner dribbles toward the tackler. Three-four yards in front of the defender he makes his cut to one side. The defender by way of a split-slide tackle, tries to kick the ball out of the attacker's range.

5. In pairs, one ball, players run side-by-side. Player dribbles slowly and pushes the ball ahead, making very little attempt to play the ball again, allowing the defender to come in from the side to execute the slide tackle and kick the ball away before the attacker can regain possession.

Variations:

a. More realistic, the dribbler runs at top speed with the ball while the challenger tries to catch up with him, veering to the side to make a successful tackle.

b. Players practice more realistically, forcing challenging defender to catch up with the attacker, just enough to allow him to make the slide tackle diagonally from behind.

COACHING TACTICS

Coaching methods must be simple. The coach who complicates the game or overloads the players will be hindering the progress of both the individual and the team.

It is essential to effect the transition from offense to defense (and vice versa) quickly and fluidly, avoiding any hesitation or breaks. The team must react offensively or defensively the instant it gains or loses possession of the ball.

The teaching of tactics must be done individually and with small groups, and progress to full-team operation.

Coaching Individual Tactics

Soccer, being a team sport, requires team spirit, team work, and combination plays, but it also needs good individual players. Whenever an individual has possession of the ball or is fighting for it, he must feel that he is the most important player on the team. He knows that if he can win his personal duel and maintain or win possession, his team will be able to attack, score, and win. If he loses the ball, the opponent will get the chance to attack, score, and win.

Individual tactics comprise everything the player requires to maintain or regain possession. The various one-on-one situations offer the most effective method of coaching these tactics. The coach should proceed from a limited area in which the objective should be simply on keeping possession, to one goal, to two goals without keepers, to two goals with keepers.

Coaching Group Tactics

The establishment of numerical superiority around the ball is a sound tactic, which applies to both attack and defense. Whenever one player is drawn into a duel with an opponent, the nearest teammate(s) must assist him.

The first step in implementing this tactic is the formation of pairs. Start with the tactical exercises two-on-one, two-on-two, and two-on-three, and progress from the smallest group of two to a team of eleven, through the following tactical combinations:

3:1	3:2	3:3	3:4	3:5	4:2	4:3
4:4	4:5	4:6	5:4	5:6	7:7	8:8

Play is restricted at first to a limited area without goals, then with one and finally two goals, without a goalkeeper, to one, and then two goalkeepers, maybe even four goals without keepers. Dribbling is allowed or play is restricted to three-, two-, or even one-touch.

Coaching Team Tactics

Coordination of attack and defense can be worked on with the following tactical exercises: six-on-four, six-on-five, and seven-on-five at one goal with keeper, first without a counterattack and then with a counterattack at a miniature goal at midfield. All dead-ball situations are practiced at the same time.

The final stage is a full field eleven vs. eleven practice match.

Having outlined the aims and general methods of coaching tactics, it is possible to proceed to the specific exercises between individuals and groups that lead up to a full-team operation.

Since the game itself is the best teacher, match-like conditions must be considered the best method of coaching everything the players need to prepare them for competition.

INDIVIDUAL TACTICS

One-on-One

This comprises everything a player requires to keep the ball and beat his immediate opponent (attack), or prevent or regain possession when his immediate opponent has possession (defense).

Equally important are the individual duels without the ball, for position—the continuous running off (without) the ball to get open for a pass. Since the sum of the individual duels adds up to victory or defeat, we practice one-on-one situations frequently and intensively. It is our most important tactical exercise.

Objectives

1. Individual duel—players have to retain possession or win possession.
2. Instill the ability and determination to switch from attack to defense easily and instantly when possession is lost from defense to attack the moment possession is won.

Matching Players

The players are first matched according to ability. Later, they are matched realistically, say a wing forward against a fullback, or a halfback against an inside forward.

Fig. 13.43 *Shadow dribbling.*

Fig. 13.44 *Maintaining possession, interval style.*

Procedure

Good coaches minimize their talking and work toward their objective methodically. The first exercise prepares the players for the next exercise, and so on.

First is stressed the individual techniques needed to keep possession or/and beat a defender. Then techniques needed to dispossess a forward are worked on. Then on to game situations where the individual must switch instantly and easily from attack to defense, and vice versa.

1. The players must remain inside the center circle while dribbling about to improve their dribbling and feinting skills. Coaching points: keep your eyes up, look for open space, change speed, change direction, practice tricks and feints.

2. The players pair up without the ball and play tag in half of the field. This exercise incorporates the teaching points in #1 (change of pace and direction, body-feints, etc.) but without preoccupation with the ball and against live opposition.

3. Shadow dribbling in pairs, with the players facing each other. The attacker dribbles and feints while moving laterally from side to side. The defender shadows his movements. This gives the players an excellent opportunity to study reactions and counterreactions (Fig. 13.43).

4. In pairs, interval style, the player with the ball tries to maintain possession and the other tries to gain possession. After one minute, they change roles (Fig. 13.44).

Teaching Points

Player with ball: maintain control by using the body to screen the ball, work on peripheral vision, develop confidence and courage.

Player without ball: set the pace, emphasize mobility, use feints to make ball-handler do what you want him to do, learn what is allowed and what is forbidden, charge shoulder against shoulder—not against chest or spine—and charge only when within playing distance of ball, when tackling, always aim for ball not the player (sole-of-foot tackle, front block tackle, sliding tackle, and so forth), and do not put everything into one tackle, be prepared for a second, even third effort.

1. Players face each other, each with a ball. While dribbling, each has to keep perfect control and, at the same time, try to kick the opponent's ball. Count the number of successful attempts (Fig. 13.45).

2. Each player has his own ball and attempts by means of a well-aimed pass to hit the other's ball (Fig. 13.46). Count the number of successful attempts.

The next step is to achieve competition by including goals. The struggle for possession now develops into a match. Immediately upon winning

Fig. 13.45 *Each player, with a ball, tries to kick the opponent's ball away.*

Fig. 13.46 *Each player, with a ball, tries to alternately hit the opponent's ball.*

Fig. 13.47 *One-on-one with one goal.*

Fig. 13.48 *One-on-one with two goals.*

possession of the ball, the players are urged to go for their opponent's goal and score. A beaten opponent must not be given time to recover and tackle back. The addition of scoring should serve as a constant reminder that possession is not an aim in itself, but only one step on the road toward scoring goals.

1. One-on-one, with one goal (Fig. 13.47). A ball is put down as a goal. The attacker tries to score by attempting to hit the ball with a well-aimed pass. The opponent must defend the ball-goal and also challenge for the ball in an effort to gain possession and try to score.

2. One-on-one, two goals about twenty yards apart (Fig. 13.48). The player's job changes with possession of the ball. One moment he is defending and the next attacking, as each tries to score as often as possible. If the ball goes out of play, it goes to the defending player.

3. One-on-one, interval style, two goals about thirty yards apart. Work with three-man units, such as the two fullbacks and the center halfback against the two wing forwards and the center forward. One player on each side sets up at his respective end line with legs spread wide to represent the goal. One other player from each team shags the ball behind his respective goal to keep the pressure on the two players who are trying to score against each other. Players rotate after one minute—they shag for one minute, represent the goal for a minute, and play for a minute.

4. Two teams compete against each other on half the field—five defenders plus the goalkeeper against five attackers. To make this exercise more relevant, match the fullback against the wing forward, center forward against the center halfback, and so on. The defending team (with goalkeeper) defends the regular goal. The attacking team defends a small goal three yards wide at midfield without a keeper.

Both teams line up in single file alongside

their goal. An attacker starts the exercise by dribbling downfield toward the regular goal (which has the keeper), while the defender and the goalie try to prevent him from scoring. If the defender wins possession or the goalie makes a save, the defender immediately counterattacks toward the small goal at midfield (which has no keeper), while the attacker tries to prevent him from scoring. Play ends only after a goal is scored or the ball goes out of bounds. The objective of this exercise is attack and quick counterattack.

Variation: Same as above, except that both teams line up at midfield, with the defender to the right of the coach and the attacker to his left, about twenty yards apart. The coach passes the ball downfield and both players sprint after the ball. Again the attackers assault the regular goal (with keeper) and the defenders counterattack to the miniature goal at midfield.

GROUP TACTICS

Since ball-possession is always the decisive factor, it is essential to have one player more than the opposition has at the point of danger—where the ball is. In short, a team must have a man advantage around the ball.

The first way to do this is to form pairs in attack and also in defense. When a teammate has possession or is challenging for the ball, a second player should always be ready to assist him. This is the only way of obtaining a two-on-one situation—a vital factor in attacking a reinforced defense or defending against gifted players.

The ultimate objective should be to have as many players as possible team up at some time with the player in possession. The greater the number of pairings, the greater will be the number of possible moves, and the greater the superiority over the opponents. Numerical superiority thus won will enable a player to dictate the next move and increase the chances of achieving the overall objective, the scoring or prevention of goals.

With constant practice, the players will begin learning how to read each other quickly and almost think and react together. The ball-handler assumes the major role, but his teammate's role is still vitally important. The latter must continuously position himself for a pass in a way that will minimize the chance of interception. But it is the man with the ball who must make the decisions and this always takes some doing, as every move by the ball-handler, receiver, or defender effects a rapid situational change.

Two-on-One

These situations call for a great deal of ability to read the setup and react to it correctly and permit the use of almost every game skill to retain possession.

Objectives

1. To work in pairs in trying to establish numerical superiority around the ball.
2. Wall double-pass combination.

Teaching Points

Player with the ball: Direct first-touch passing, pass to teammate's feet or pass into space, learning to time and pace the passes, work the give (pass) and go, hold ball when necessary, dribble when passing is impossible, work on tempo and rhythm, maintain visual control of teammates and defenders.

Player without ball: Continuously search for open space, meet player with the ball, bluff the defender when searching for an open space, always be prepared to receive ball.

Defending players: Attack ball and man, control man without ball, bluff the opponent.

Procedure

Explain, demonstrate, and practice wall double-pass combination. Proceed from the simple maintenance of possession to advancing downfield quickly against the lone defender.

Progression: one goal with keeper without counterattack to two goals with one keeper and defender counterattacking the goal without the keeper. Finally, have the opposition try to play the "offside" game to nullify a breakthough.

1. One-on-one duel for ball: Review one-on-one while introducing a third player as an alternate in a passive-rest position (Fig. 13.49). The attacker tries to maintain possession while the defender tries to wrest the ball from him. As the two players fight for the ball, the alternate rests. As soon as the defender succeeds in winning the ball, the alternate player becomes the defender, the attacker who just lost the ball becomes the alternate, and so on.

2. One-on-one duel without ball: The defender tightly marks the attacker without the ball by facing him, thus turning his back to the ball. This enables him to dog every move of the attacker, who is attempting to gain a split second opening for the ball. If the attacker succeeds, the defender immediately turns to cover the other attacker (passer), and so on.

Fig. 13.49 *One-on-one duel for the ball while the third player rests.*

Fig. 13.50 *One-on-one duel without the ball while the third player passes.*

At first the pass should be delivered only when the attacker clearly outmaneuvers the defender. Mobility and split-second timing and coordination between the attackers are the main objectives. The ball-handler should help his teammate shake off the defender by moving from side to side and backward, if necessary, to avoid crowding his teammate, a common fault (Fig.13.50).

3. Explanation and demonstration of wall double-pass combination (Fig. 13.51).

Teaching Points

Player with ball: Timing is the most important factor—make the first pass bad and the second will be worse, pass to player's feet, and move after it at top speed (pass should be first step). Commit the defender. This is important to enable a player to start off at least level with the defender when a run is made to pick up the ball again. Disguise intention until the last second. Use a teammate as a decoy, pretend a wall pass, but instead go past the defender with the ball.

Player without ball: Go help the ball-handler, maintain acute passing angle, use inside of foot for wall pass.

Defender: Commit yourself, lay off, back-pedal, bluff laying off, then try to intercept the first (square) pass, bluff to commit yourself but instead attempt to intercept second wall pass.

Two-on-One in Limited Area, a Grid

The grid enables the players to become aware of the need for controlled play in a confined area; it simulates the pressure of the game very realistically.

1. The attacker whose pass is intercepted changes roles with the defender who intercepted it.

2. Count successful passes made within a minute.

3. Count only successful wall double-pass combinations within a minute.

4. Count successful interceptions within a minute.

Fig. 13.51 *Give-and-go wall pass combination.*

5. Have the ball-handler fight off a challenge before passing.

6. Two-touch soccer: control, pass.

Two-on-One, Realistic Situation

The right wing forward and right inside forward try to bypass and gain ground quickly against the left fullback.

Note: The defender's initial reaction, when faced with two attackers, must be to delay the approach until his teammates check back to assist him. The attackers must therefore act quickly.

The attacker's instinctive reaction will be to veer away from the defender. He should be taught to do exactly the opposite. He must run directly at the defender, attack him, and force him to commit himself. The idea is to make it difficult for him to prevent a breakthrough no matter what he does.

1. Beating the fullback by committing him. The right inside forward threatens to break through on the inside with the ball to get the left fullback to challenge him. But just before the left fullback can tackle, the forward delivers a simple diagonal lead pass behind the fullback to the right wing forward, who takes it on the run and speeds away.

2. Beating the fullback with a wall through-

pass combination. The right wing forward runs at the left fullback. Just before giving him a chance to tackle, he delivers a square pass to the right inside forward and goes through diagonally behind the fullback, looking for a through pass from the forward (inside the fullback). He takes it on the run and goes for the goal.

3. Beating the fullback by using the right inside forward as a decoy. The right wing forward again runs at the left fullback. But this time the fullback refuses to commit himself. Sensing the possibility of a wall pass, he quickly back-pedals in an attempt to shut it off. The wing forward pretends to deliver the pass, then quickly pushes the ball down the touchline past the fullback and goes after it to attack the goal.

Two-on-One at One Goal with Keeper

Proceed to two goals and one keeper, with the defender counterattacking the goal without the keeper—the defender being permitted to use the serving attacker as a wall pass man.

1. Use of one forward to score goals—he might be a right or left wing forward or center forward.

2. Use of one midfield player as a server who is not allowed to score—he might be a right or left inside forward or halfback.

3. Use of one defender who marks the forward (not the server) man-to-man—he might be a right or left fullback or center halfback.

Beating the Lone Defender with "Setting Up" Passing Combinations

When the ball-handling attacker finds his teammate tightly marked by his opponent, he should deliver the pass right to his teammate's feet, who must make sure to meet the ball to prevent the defender from intercepting it.

The receiver must realize that by drawing the defender with him, he is creating open space behind him. If he returns the ball first-touch and checks out immediately, he will have a good chance of receiving a quick return pass in the open space just vacated by the defender.

The attack can score only after a successful wall pass, through pass, or dribble. Every attack should be finished with a successful shot.

Three-on-One

Quite clearly this is not a realistic situation. But it is ideal for teaching the basic principles of sound positioning (playing without the ball), which is a prerequisite for interpassing.

There are "dead" spaces and "open" spaces on the field. To maintain possession, every player must run out of the dead space into the open. This is what is meant by playing without the ball. The skill serves as preparation for combination play.

Helping the man with the ball becomes the order of the day. This is almost the same as pairing up. Where the three players position themselves correctly, the man in possession will have two targets for passing. A smartly deployed triangle can move the ball so quickly that the lone defender will have no chance to intercept it. With three players against one, we should see first-touch passing moves with teammates of the man in possession constantly moving into open space.

The creation of openings by unselfish and intelligent running off the ball is the life blood of all interpassing movements.

Objectives of Three-on-One Activities

1. Sound positioning: Pair up and play in triangles to assure fluid interpassing.
2. Improve techniques and skills.

Teaching Points

Player with ball: Direct first-touch passing, pass to player's feet or into space, time and pace the pass, pass and quick start to a new position.

Player receiving ball: Look around, meet the ball, feint before receiving ball, control ball quickly, pass quickly and accurately, quick start to new position after pass.

Third player: Continue to move without the ball—run out of the covered space into open space, always being prepared to receive the ball.

Defending player: Attack man and ball; use feints to trap the opponent.

Grouping Players

The first step again is to group players according to ability, while the ultimate is to organize players into game units, say the wing forward, inside forward, and a halfback behind them against a fullback.

Procedure

Start with limited space, a grid, with the attackers simply keeping possession against the lone de-

a

b

c

Fig. 13.52 *Three-on-one.*

fender, and proceed to realistic situations in which the attackers move downfield quickly to beat the defender and score.

The objective is to teach mobility, correct running off the ball, safe angles, what is a safe ball, and when to play it. Soccer is all angles, with an occasional curve thrown in.

Interpassing should be deliberate at first. The ball-handler will be confronted by the lone defender and flanked by his teammates to the right and left, ready to receive the ball. The ball-handler

Fig. 13.53 *Most common fault is players crossing behind the defender's back.*

313

may even help his teammates attain the best position. He may point to the area where he wants them to assume their positions (Fig. 13.52).

Until everyone masters the principles of sound positioning—creating good passing angles—the defender should offer only a token challenge. After that, the play should become realistic with the arm signals being eliminated and the defender offering an actual challenge.

It is vitally important for the attackers to position and reposition themselves continuously and to take the shortest path to the open space. The most common error—crossing behind the defender's back and thus giving the ball-handler momentarily no chance to pass—should be pointed out at the earliest opportunity (Fig. 13.53).

1. Three-on-one within limited space, a grid. Proceed from unlimited to three, two, and one-touch passing. The objective is to keep possession until the lone defender succeeds in intercepting the ball, after which he should change roles with the man who passed the ball.

Variations:

a. Count the successful two or one-touch passes made in one minute.

b. Interval style: Count how many times the defender can intercept the ball within a minute. Every player becomes a defender.

c. Goalkeeper training: He plays as a defender.

2. Three-on-one—realistic situation at one goal with goalkeeper. The setup has a wing forward and an inside forward, plus a halfback behind them, against a fullback at the midfield line. The objective is to advance downfield quickly to beat the lone defender and score.

Variations:

a. The fullback lays back to create a "turn" situation. Play starts with the halfback passing to the wing forward, who drops back to meet the ball. The halfback, seeing that the fullback has decided to lay off, informs the wing forward of this by yelling "Turn!" The initial pass also serves as a signal for the inside forward to run diagonally into a position behind the fullback, close to the touchline. He receives a through pass from the wing forward, who then immediately cuts in toward goal to occupy the position vacated by the inside forward. The inside forward may cross the ball for the wing forward to head at goal, cut for goal and score himself, or turn the ball back for the trailing halfback to have a go at it.

b. The fullback covers the wing forward man-for-man, and the halfback initiates the same exercise (as in a) with a pass to the wing

forward—being covered skintight by the fullback.

The halfback again signals his receiver, yelling "Man on!" The wing forward reacts immediately by wall passing square to the halfback. The initial pass also signals the inside forward to make a diagonal run toward the corner flag, where, in an advanced wing position, he will receive an immediate pass from the halfback. While the halfback assumes the inside forward's position and cuts for goal, the wing forward momentarily takes over the halfback's role.

Variations:

The setup has two inside forwards and the center forward facing a lone defender (center halfback). The exercise again begins with the center halfback in a passive role.

a. The center forward is asked to position himself like a spearhead, allowing the ball-handling inside forward to use him as a wall. From a withdrawn position the inside forward pushes the ball up to the feet of the center forward, who drops back to meet the ball. The inside forward, noticing that the center halfback has elected to lay off in a zone coverage, informs the center forward by yelling "Turn!" so that he can control the ball as he turns to make the play to the other inside forward who immediately first-touches the ball and pushes it across the field behind the center halfback's back. The initial ball-handling inside forward takes it on the run for a shot at goal.

b. The same exercise is initiated, but with the center halfback covering the center forward man-for-man. The right inside forward passes to the feet of the center forward, who drops back to meet the ball. Perceiving the center halfback sticking tightly to the receiver, the inside forward yells, "Man on!" The center forward reacts immediately by wall passing square to the left inside forward. The latter again passes first-touch across the field behind the center halfback's back to the inside forward who takes it on the run for a crack at goal.

These exercises must be repeated until every player understands his role. They can then be used with a different emphasis. The roles may be distributed differently and play may be focused on the inside forward being challenged by the defensive halfback. The emphasis, however, must be concentrated on the interplay between the inside forward and the halfback, and especially on the interchange of positions between the two.

When the halfback moves up to receive a square pass from his inside forward and then carries on to press the attack, the inside forward must fall back to take over the duties of the halfback. When the playing has reached an advanced stage—where everyone understands the possibilities of the situation and is reading the game well—the exercise must be repeated again and again under match-like conditions.

The players, including the defender, must now move on their own initiative. The defender is urged to thwart the trio whenever possible, while the attacker attempts to pull him out of position. The players must learn to glance over their shoulders while dropping back to meet the ball, to see for themselves whether the defender has chosen to follow or hold his ground. The attackers should press the attack and finish off the move with a shot at goal.

In all these exercises we use every opportunity to coach the players individually on all the tactical possibilities. This applies to defenders as well as attackers.

Four-on-Two

Focus heavily on midfield play, as this is the springboard for the offense and the preparation area for the defense. The defense and the offense should be coupled here and trained to effect quick, smooth transitions. Although four-on-two is the normal midfield situation, such drilling can improve the team play in tight situations anywhere.

Objectives:

1. To improve midfield organization as a buildup area for attack and defense.
2. To achieve penetration on attack and prevent penetration on defense.

Teaching Points

Player with ball: Pass to teammate's feet or into space, time and pace the pass, pass and go (quick start to a new position), control tempo and rhythm of play, hold ball when required, dribble when passing is impossible, maintain visual control of teammates and opponents, look for through pass first, make the easy play unhesitantly.

Player receiving ball: Look around, meet ball, feint before receiving ball, control ball quickly, pass quickly and accurately, start quickly to new position after passing.

Players without ball: Always search for open space (mobility), meet player with ball, learn also when to run away, maintain width and depth at all times, bluff defenders when searching for open space, always be prepared to receive ball.

Defending players: Attack ball and player, con-

trol players without ball, cooperation (zone defense), bluff opponent.

Grouping Players

The first step again should be grouping players according to ability, and the final step is always organizing realistic playing groups. The central figures in midfield play are the two halfbacks and the inside forwards against the two halfbacks.

Procedure

Start in limited space, a grid, without opposition and proceed to simple possession against the two defenders; two-touch control pass and then one-touch, with special emphasis on the square and through pass combination.

One defender must attack ball and man, second defender zone covers to prevent through pass, forcing ball-handler to pass square. The first defensive objective is to prevent the through pass, second to allow only the least dangerous pass, and third, of course, to intercept the ball.

At this stage stress must be made on individual defensive play, with special emphasis on zone defense to achieve a smooth coordination between the two defenders. The attacking objectives are to develop poise, control, and patience in waiting for the situation to develop, and then to react instantly.

Progress to game situations in which there is advance downfield quickly against the two defending halfbacks, first to one goal without immediate counterattack and then to two goals with immediate counterattack. Finally, change the emphasis from close passing moves to ground-gaining wing play.

1. Within limited space, a grid without opposition:
   a. Two-touch: control pass, use weak foot only, use inside or outside or instep only.
   b. One touch: direct play.
   c. One-touch: direct play and follow the ball.

Teaching Points

Look around, meet ball, feint, receive, pass, return to original starting position, first follow ball then run away from it, and so on.

1. Within limited space, a grid, with opposition:
   The interpassing should be rather deliberate

a

b

c

d

Fig. 13.54 *Four-on-two. "The player with the ball should be flanked by his teammates, one on the right and another on his left, while the fourth player sets up in front of the ball-handler. This provides the ball-handler with two easy square pass possibilities. The real test of this exercise is to deliver the penetrating through pass between the two defenders."*

316

at first. The player with the ball should be flanked by his teammates, one on his right and another on his left, while the fourth player sets up in front of the ball-handler. This provides the ball-handler with two easy square pass possibilities, but the real test of this exercise is to deliver the penetrating through pass between the two defenders (Fig. 13.54).

The defenders should first be asked to permit the through pass. Soon afterward they must be taught how to prevent the through pass, coordinate their efforts, play zone defense, and attack the man with the ball.

The progression once again is from unlimited three, two, and one-touch passing, with the objective being to keep possession until the defenders intercept the ball. The defender who intercepts then changes roles with the player whose pass he intercepted.

Variations:

a. Count the number of passes.

b. Count only the through passes.

c. Count how many passes are intercepted within a given time limit. Defenders remain constant.

d. Goalkeepers' training: play as defenders.

2. Four-on-two, plus two: Start by counting the number of passes or interceptions within a given time limit. Then change the emphasis from close interpassing to sudden long passes. Also draw the defense's attention away from the final thrust at goal and exploit it through a sudden switch of the attacking thrust.

This enables the team either to emphasize wing play and spread the exercise across the entire width of the field or use surprise long lead passes from deep midfield positions up to the interior forwards, utilizing just about the entire length of the field.

In keeping with these objectives, have two additional players waiting in the limited area on the wing or in the central path to the goal at the edge of the penalty box.

After playing four-on-two in the original area (center circle in midfield), call for a sudden switch to the area on the wing or to the area upfield. The two defenders remain in the original area, while the last two players reaching the new area become defenders.

Variations:

a. The long pass must be made, but not before at least three short passes or after six short passes have been made.

b. The long pass may be delivered only after two through passes.

c. To coordinate the long pass with the forward's run, prepare three grids in a triangle formation. While playing four-on-two in unlimited area, have two additional players waiting, one in each of the second and third grid.

The first activity might be to go to the ball to support the ball-handler. After the pass is delivered, say to the player in the second grid, the player from the third grid sprints across the field to assist the player receiving the ball.

The second activity might have the single player make his run, say the player from the second grid join the player in the third, and have this be the signal for the ball-handler in the four-on-two to deliver the long pass to the third grid.

As above, the two defenders stay back, but one must sprint to cover the momentarily vacated grid. Again the last two players arriving at the grid become defenders.

3. Four-on-two to one goal without counterattack: The setup has two inside forwards with two linkmen (halfbacks) behind them. The two forwards attack the regular goal which is defended by a keeper and two center backs. The linkmen, halfbacks, do not attack. They must play direct, one-touch soccer, hanging back to avoid crowding the forwards.

4. Four-on-two to two goals with counterattack: The regular goal is again defended by a keeper and two center backs. But this time as soon as they gain possession, they counterattack to a miniature-sized goal (without keeper) at midfield.

In doing this, they may use the linkmen halfbacks for an initial outlet pass (wall pass combination). But linkmen must become defenders immediately afterward. The two inside forwards must think and act defensively the instant they lose possession of the ball.

Variations:

a. The attack must play two or one-touch soccer.

b. The defenders are allowed to dribble.

TEAM TACTICS

Six-on-Four

By reinforcing our basic four-on-two with two wing forwards and defensing them with their respective fullbacks, we complete the attack and defense with a very realistic six-on-four plus a goalkeeper.

This new combination of players represents a mixture of the units already used in the previous activities. Both wing segments are coupled by midfield play and by the play that has them switching from one flank to the other.

The four defenders are completely familiar with the problems they have to solve. The only new aspect to learn is how to play together. They now have to cover each other and the dangerous space as the developing situations demand. The objective is to coordinate the attack and defense into an effective collective unit.

Teaching Points

Defense:

1. Man-to-man on ball-side.
2. Zone off ball—marking space.
3. Diagonal pattern.
4. Teaming with goalkeeper.
5. Making instant transition to attack, initiate counterattack.

Offense:

1. Wing play and through passes on ball-side.
2. Wing play with sudden switches to other side.
3. Combination play—double-wall pass combination.
4. Interchanging positions smoothly.
5. Making the instant transition to defense—tackle back.

Grouping Players

This offers an excellent method of matching the first-string offense against the first-string defense.

Procedure

The matching of offense and defense enables the coach to simulate highly intensive match conditions and hence isolate and emphasize various aspects of individual and collective play. In doing this, the coach should make sure to prepare the defense for any new attacking move.

The initial emphasis should be on a flexible combination of man-to-man and zone, allowing for close-marking around the ball as well as for the necessary cover (zone) on the opposite side of the field. The coach must emphasize the importance of sound defensive positioning in marking an offensive player:

1. Keep on goal side of opponent.
2. Always watch opponents and movement of ball.
3. Do not allow any blind-side plays.
4. Always cover teammates and dangerous space.
5. Beat your man to the ball; this encourages anticipation and alertness.

On offense, the coach must strongly emphasize the continuous movement of the ball and the players off the ball. He may now introduce the basic pattern of interchanging positions. First, he may simply ask the passer to follow the ball and change positions with the receiver, setting up the classic scissors move.

The coach must continually point out the great need for maintaining a well-balanced attack, meaning that every position should be occupied at all times.

A sudden switch of the attack from one wing to the other must be carefully prepared on the ball-side. Linkmen must develop the ability to watch the whole field; only then will they be able to spot the exact moment when the switch cross-field pass is on.

Finding the right man and delivering the outlet pass instantly is the key to a successful counterattack.

This is also an excellent time to practice dead-ball situations such as free kicks, corner kicks, and the like.

Eventually add the immediate counterattack to a second goal (without keeper) at midfield.

Six-on-Four without Counterattack

Half-field scrimmage with one regular goal defended by a keeper, two centerbacks, and two fullbacks, and the attack consisting of two interior strikers, two wing forwards, and two linkmen behind them. Linkmen do not attack; they play direct one-touch soccer and avoid crowding the forwards.

The defenders' job, aside from preventing the offense from scoring, is to clear the ball across the midfield line. The linkmen in turn must try to keep the ball in play.

1. Play is continued until either the attack scores or the defense clears the ball across midfield.
2. In either case the ball goes to the attacking team and play resumes at midfield. Next, the defender is asked to try to clear the ball by passing to a specific target. It might be the coach who continually changes his position so that he could be anywhere along the halfway line.

Six-on-Four with Counterattack

As before, the four attackers, plus the two linkmen behind them, attack the regular goal which again is defended by a keeper and four defenders. Play is still restricted to half-field. But this time the defenders, instead of simply clearing the ball across midfield as soon as they gain possession, must counterattack to a miniature-sized goal (without keeper) at midfield. They are permitted to use the linkmen for an initial outlet pass—a wall double-pass combination. But the linkmen must become defenders immediately afterward. The attackers must also think and act defensively the instant they lose possession.

    1. The attackers must play two or one-touch soccer.

    2. The defenders are allowed to dribble.

Six-on-Five

Objectives

    1. To organize a defense with sweeper (center halfback).

    2. To develop an attack against a defense with sweeper.

Teaching Points

Sweeper defense:

    1. He must be the organizer and commander.

    2. He must provide cover and close support to each teammate who is drawn into a duel for the ball.

    3. He must cut off any through pass.

    4. He must anticipate the sudden switch from one side of the field to the other via a long crossfield pass, and he must try to intercept it.

    5. He must challenge anyone coming through unopposed.

    6. He himself must attack by way of timely overlaps.

Offense versus sweeper defense:

    1. Immediate counterattack.

    2. Committing defenders in midfield (mobility).

    3. Attacking the sweeper with a spearhead directly at him.

    4. Beating him via the classic wing play or by turning the defense.

    5. Beating him with the power play—players coming from behind.

Grouping Players

First-string defense with sweeper (center halfback) versus first-string offense.

Procedure

The introduction of the sweeper is the only new aspect of the defense. But because it is rather complex and involves the defense as a whole, a thorough explanation and practical step-by-step demonstration are essential. Not only must the sweeper coordinate his play with the rest of the defenders, but the defenders must also make certain adjustments. They can now cover their immediate opponents skintight, make early tackles, etc., knowing that they are covered by the sweeper.

The offensive problem is to commit the sweeper. Wing play becomes essential, whether by the classic cross, the sudden switch from one side of the field to the other, or by the turning of the defense.

The offense must spread the defense across the field, draw or commit the sweeper, and deliver the decisive pass. Far-range shooting should be encouraged and then double-wall pass combinations in an effort to change the pace and rhythm of play. Last is the introduction of a player coming from behind on an overlap.

Eventually is added an immediate attack at a second goal (without keeper) at midfield. This is an essential step because the real test of a sweeper defense is how well it breaks out into attack.

Six-on-Five without Counterattack

Half-field scrimmage with a regular goal defended by a keeper, two centerbacks, and two fullbacks, plus a sweeper; attacking are two interior strikers, two wing forwards, plus two linkmen behind them. At the beginning, the linkmen are not allowed to attack. They must remain close to the midfield line to avoid crowding the forwards, and they must play direct one-touch soccer.

The defenders' job, aside from preventing the offense from scoring, is to clear the ball across the midfield line. The linkmen in turn must try to keep the ball in play.

    1. Play is continued until either the attackers score or the defenders can clear the ball across midfield. In either case the ball goes to the attacking team and play resumes at midfield.

    2. The defenders are asked to try to clear the ball out of defense to a special target such as the coach himself (positioned anywhere along the midfield line and continually changing position).

3. The defenders are asked to keep possession of the ball, ten consecutive passes counting as a goal.

Six-on-Five with Counterattack

As before, play is restricted to half-field, five defenders plus a keeper defending the regular goal, and four attackers, plus two linkmen behind them, attacking. This time the defenders are asked to counterattack at a miniature-sized goal (without keeper) at midfield. They are permitted to use the linkmen for an initial outlet pass (a wall double-pass combination), but the linkmen must become defenders immediately afterward.

1. The attackers must play two or one-touch soccer.

2. The defenders must try to score with as few passes as possible.

3. The defenders are asked to attack two miniature goals placed at midfield about ten-fifteen yards from either touchline. This encourages quick counterattack, wing play, and frequent switches of the attacking thrust from one side to the other.

As the offense develops efficiency in beating the sweeper defense, the coach should add defenders in order to ensure a realistic confrontation where the defense outnumbers the offense.

Eleven-Man Full-Field Scrimmage

Objectives

1. To play as a cohesive full-team unit—improve teamwork.

2. To develop a system.

3. To work on special tactics—the most important aspect of attack is surprise.

Teaching Points

Offense:

1. Keep ball.
2. Change pace and rhythm of play.
3. Change direction of play.
4. Use ball—let it do the work.
5. Use the open space—run off the ball.
6. Positive running—go through to score.

Counterattack:

1. Prepare the counterattack before opposing attack has slacked off.
2. Instantly break out into open space.

3. Make an immediate outlet pass to open man.

4. Support ball-handler the quickest way possible.

5. Look for most advanced player.

6. Hold ball or dribble only if absolutely necessary.

7. Take quickest way to goal and score.

Defense:

1. Make an instant transition to defense. Tackle back.

2. Fall back—delay. Check back to get on goal-side of ball.

3. Play man-to-man—heavy concentration of players around ball.

4. Zone defense—cover teammates and dangerous space.

5. Attack man and ball.

6. Exercise control—restraint.

Matching Players

Though it may be all right in the beginning to pit the first team against the second or reserve team, this sort of match-up will in the long run produce a false sense of superiority and confidence, thanks to the disparity in strength. The fact that the teams know each other so well also will eliminate the element of surprise.

How about the first-string offense and the second-string defense against the first-string defense and the second-string offense? Obviously, this does not make for any sort of team coordination. The controlled scrimmage against outside competition is more beneficial.

Choice of a Scrimmage Opponent

This plays a vital part in building a positive image and confidence. The closer the season, the tougher such opponents should become. When choosing a scrimmage partner in preparation for a specific opponent, the coach should look for a team that is similar to the scheduled opponent. Another factor to consider is the current disposition of his own team (lack of confidence, losing streak, overconfident because of a winning streak, etc.). He may want easier or tougher opponents as a result. Even the atmosphere of the game field is important—spectators' reactions, whether they sit right on top of the field, the caliber of the playing field, etc.

Procedure

Test different individuals and combinations of players. The final preparation step is the development of a system and a style of play that is adapted to the players. This includes substitute players as well as the upcoming opponent.

Coaching During Practice Games

This is difficult because it has to be done in the middle of all the action. Quick analysis of situations is essential, as the coach must deal with a tactical point the moment it occurs. The coach should not try to referee at the same time, as it is too distracting. He must give the game his full attention. If possible, he should coach one side and have an assistant take the other.

Using the Field as a Chessboard

At some strategic moment in play, the coach can stop the game with a prearranged signal (perhaps successive whistles) and ask the players to freeze in their tracks so that the situation can be studied.

This is a good way to examine positional play, even of those who were not directly involved in the play when it was halted, and to suggest alternative movements. The suggestions can be attempted slowly several times with limited opposition before the game is restarted.

When the coach, as soon as play is resumed, sees an opportunity to use the new tactic, he can urge his players to do so. Such interruptions should be done judiciously, however, to avoid killing interest in the game.

Getting Players to Think Ahead

This may be effected by suggesting tactical moves before the play, in time for the players to readjust their movements. This is also a helpful way to get the players to eliminate poor habits, and to shoot first-time.

But the coach must not overdo this, or he will find the players beginning to await instructions. He should remember that no one can be regarded as

a truly good player until he can think out his play according to the circumstances.

Drawing Attention to Good Play

Praise can give the player a big boost. The coach should also criticize when necessary, as some players require a jolt. But the criticism should be specific and not overdone to avoid discouraging or antagonizing the player.

Focus Play on Specific Themes

Whenever the players seem reluctant to apply a newly taught tactic, the coach may focus on the move for a certain amount of time until it becomes ingrained in the team's play.

Any other techniques or tactics may be emphasized in this fashion, such as quick passing or a rule forbidding a player to touch the ball more than twice before it is played by someone else. There is no better way than one-two to make the players think of what they are going to do with the ball before they play it.

Focus on Specific Individuals

A veteran player alongside a novice in need of attention can feed the beginner passes and advice on when and where to move, how to receive, and so forth. Or the play can be directed toward a particular player, such as having players serve to the left wing forward as often as possible.

The opposition can be told about a player's particular weakness and asked to concentrate on it so that the player can eliminate his weakness. The coach sometimes may find that a player's special skill is not being fully exploited by his teammates and he can suggest that they play up to this player and his special skill.

Learning to Adapt to Special Situations

This can be stimulating where the two teams are told to operate a set tactic for a short period of time. Each team will try to spot the other's tactic and blunt it, while carrying out its own maneuver at the same time.

14

Scouting

Scouting is observing, analyzing, and recording the performance of a team and its individual players. It includes objective data: goals, assists, shots, and subjective observation of offensive and defensive trends, individual playing idiosyncrasies, and similar factors.

Knowing as much as possible about the upcoming opponent is of immeasurable value to the coach when preparing his game plan. His ability to assimilate the information from the scouting report and transmit it to his team is a great determinant to the team success. By being able to give his players an accurate perspective of the opponent's strengths and weaknesses he can eliminate the element of uncertainty and surprise, thereby improving the players' confidence.

OBJECTIVITY

Soccer is full of contrasts in styles and basic ideas of play. The scout may be inclined to form fixed ideas and preferences. His assessment can be dominated by his prejudices and preconceived notions, often to the exclusion of all else. Or his judgment can be profoundly influenced when his emotions are aroused by the atmosphere of the game, by his own partisan spirit, or by a succession of exciting actions, he is less able to give his mind to any calculation of the factors underlying play. Critical assessment of an individual's or a team's

performance requires not only a sound knowledge and perception of the game, but also a mind that can discipline itself to focus on aspects of the game other than the action around the ball.

CONSISTENCY

Scouting should be done by the same person if possible each time in order to have the reports consistent. It should be someone whose philosophy and thinking parallel that of the head coach and who knows the team's personnel, their capabilities, strengths, and weaknesses so that he can compare talent. The check-list type of report, chart, or score book is the most effective instrument because all the reports are then consistent in both content and evaluation.

PREPARATION

The scout should be well-prepared, having acquainted himself with the team ahead of time. He should have reviewed previous scouting reports to recall the salient points and acquainted himself thoroughly with the opposing coach's philosophy and the style of play he represents. He should have read all available newspapers, publicity releases and statistical reports; he should have viewed films with particular attention to individual players (though films must be looked at with some reservation because they focus primarily on the action around the ball, making precise team analysis almost impossible.

The scout should arrive at the field well-ahead of the opening kick-off, and when possible secure a place for himself well-above the field. Some prefer a central, others a corner, position from where they can see clearly the offensive and defensive patterns evolving.

PRE-GAME OBSERVATIONS

For the scouting report to be effective, the maximum amount of accurate information must be obtained. Therefore as much information as possible should be analyzed and summarized in the pre-game period to alert the scout to certain trends. He should pay close attention to a preliminary game. It is reasonable to assume that all teams of the same school will apply basically the same game philosophy, particularly special tactics, free kicks, corner kicks, and throw-ins.

A perusal of a program that lists players' names, numbers, height, weight, and year in school is essential. Local newspapers for information about the team should be checked. If the scout does not reveal his identity, he may also obtain valuable information by talking with spectators before game time. Normally those who are at games early are most interested in the team and are happy to discuss morale, injuries, team conflicts, basic character of players, and other important items.

Quite frequently scouts are seated together in a reserved area. It is an excellent idea to exchange ideas and compare notes with other scouts, some of whom may already have seen the team play; it may help in early organization of notes.

During the pre-game time the scout should observe the physical setup of the field the game will be played on: surface condition—grass, dirt, artificial—dimensions, and any peculiarities. If the crowd sits on top of the touchline or goal line, the lack of approach run would present problems in throwing-in as well as in corner kick situations, or the closeness of the crowd might bother some players.

The team's appearance and behavior during the pre-game warm-up is indicative of morale and unity. The scout should be especially observant of the type of warm-up, whether the team seems to be tight or loose, confident and eager. Though this latter is a subjective observation, it can often be very revealing about the team's morale.

GAME PROCEDURES

These are the most important part of the scouting report. The scout should have a definite method of charting plays, and arranging and taking notes. He must take full advantage of any time the clock has stopped. Time is only stopped if the official gives the time-out signal by raising both arms to cross them over his head. This is usually only for injuries, substitutions, or goals scored.

During the announcement of the starting line-ups it is quite useful to double check the players' numbers and positions. The reception an individual player receives when his name is announced is a clear indication of the crowd's favorites and possibly the stars of the team.

FIRST HALF

Basic system and pattern of play: the experienced scout will jot down the basic alignment of players on the field quickly. For the next few minutes he should try to get a good picture of the game before starting to annotate, chart, and draw conclusions. Concentrated attention in the early part of the game is vital. By making a graph of the initial line-up by position and every player's running patterns, it is easy to determine the basic system of play.

The same should be done for the basic method and pattern of defense and offense. To do this early in the game is important because it is realistic to assume that the team is following strictly the coach's basic instructions and game plan. Later in the game the initial plan may be abandoned for various reasons. Whether or not the team changes or stays with the initial plan will be important to know. It will show whether the team is well-coached, mature, and disciplined enough to follow a game plan, and also it may demonstrate the coach's philosophy and whether he has confidence in his team to play their own game. A change during the game would be indicative of the coach's ability to analyze the game and make necessary adjustments. Whether a system and pattern of play are basically offensive or defensive reveals much about the coach's philosophy and whether they suit the players and bring out the best in them.

Strategic changes often occur in time-out periods. A scout should watch for changes in personnel; he should note the times that substitutions enter, and for whom, and try to determine why the coach made the substitution at that time. Are substitutes merely put in to rest regulars or is the coach trying to vary his tactics? If so, how effective is it? He should also observe whether a change in defense or offense takes place after a time-out, as such changes give an insight into a coach's philosophy.

The best way to keep track of changes is to make slight symbolic notations as they occur and then elaborate on them at a time-out.

Many ideas should be incorporated into the game report, such as the team's physical and mental characteristics. Is it big? Is it fast? Is it aggressive? Is it in good condition? Are the members pulling together? Do they have great competitive spirit? How able are the substitutes?

OFFENSIVE PLAY

Some teams will use more than one offensive formation. The scout should observe the first basic one that the team uses, then concentrate on the variations and how effective they are. Does the offense emphasize the long ball and wing play or the short passing game right down the middle? Who is the principal target man of the offense? Does the offense rely on working the ball in for close-range shooting or do they shoot from outside the penalty box? Does the offense move about freely or do they seem static in their tracks? Is the team using the fast break? If so, how effectively? Who are the key players? Who delivers the outlet pass, who is the receiver, who is the target man? Chart basic plays and special tactics, such as free kicks, corner kicks, throw-ins, and so forth. Are these plays imaginative and well-rehearsed? Does the team have a specialist and how effective is he?

MIDFIELD PLAY

Does the team appear as a unit? Are the defenders prepared to close up when the team is on offense; are the attackers prepared to drop back when the team is on defense? How effective is the midfield preparation in offense? Are they a patient team, moving the ball about in order to prepare a good scoring opportunity? Do they waste a lot of time in midfield when they should not? Are they a one-paced team, not being patient enough or skillful enough to prepare in midfield? Who are the key playmakers and feeders? How effective is their midfield preparation for defense? Are they easily committed, or are they using delaying tactics effectively? Are they able to support the attack well in order to sustain the attack and even join in if the situation arises? Are they too offensive-minded, leaving a vacuum behind them or too defensive-minded, leaving a big gap in front of them? Are they applying special tactics such as delaying, stalling, or wholesale retreating and giving away the midfield willingly?

DEFENSIVE PLAY

Is the basic method of defense man-to-man, zone, or combined? Is the basic pattern of defense diagonal? Does the defense appear as a well-organized and coordinated unit? How quickly and effectively do they concentrate at the point of attack and establish numerical superiority around the goal? Does the defense anticipate well as a unit? Do they appear well-disciplined, knowing when to take a risk and when to be restrained? Who are the outstanding individuals? Who seems to be the organizing force in defense? Are they applying any special defensive tactics, half or whole-field pressure defense, retreating tactics in order to concentrate in the vital space in front of the goalmouth? What is the most susceptible weakness of the defense, their weakest link? Are they well-prepared and organized defending against special game situations, free and corner kicks, or do they have weaknesses?

INDIVIDUAL PLAY

Individual characteristics of each player should be noted, including height, weight, position, number, speed, endurance, reaction, type of player, aggressiveness, competitive ability, temperament, and then, of course, skills and tactical maturity.

Many offensive characteristics should be looked for. Is the player's ball control exceptional? Is he a good dribbler and does he know when and when not to dribble? Is he a good shooter? Where does he prefer to shoot from? Is he able to shoot with both feet? How well does he react when he does not have the ball? Does he move well without it? Does he keep his defensive man occupied when teammates have the ball? Is he a good overall offensive player? (Normally we think of a good overall offensive player as one who reacts well when he has the ball, but intelligent and unselfish running without the ball is often more important, because, if the player is cutting without the ball, either he must be covered and so can create space, or he will be free and become a potential receiver.)

Defensively, the scout is looking for both positive and negative individual characteristics. Naturally the first thing he looks for is the aggressiveness of a player on defense. Is he a good defensive player? Judgment is based more on his position and his defensive attitude than anything else. Does he get back fast enough on defense? Does he react to fakes easily? Is he easy to move out of position? Is he a ball-watcher and consequently drawn easily to it? Does he switch well? Does he talk when a switch is necessary? Does he take unnecessary chances? Is he a good tackler? Can he clear the ball confidently with either foot and is he a good header? Does he know when to tackle or exercise restraint?

GOALKEEPER

Because of his unique positional responsibilities and great influence on defense, the goalkeeper must be observed and analyzed with particular thoroughness. Of great importance are exact height, weight, ability, mobility, and reflexes. Does he have safe hands? Does he catch well? Does he control the immediate goalmouth? Does he play the angles well? Is he courageous? Does he dive equally well for high and low balls? Does he know when to catch, punch, or deflect balls? Does he radiate confidence? Does he direct the defense? Does he overcommit himself easily or is he hesitant in leaving his goal line? Does he have good timing? Does he prefer to throw or kick the ball? How effective is he in finding the open man? Look for weaknesses in general and specifically in special game situations and free and corner kicks.

HALF-TIME

The scout replays the first half mentally and records his impressions, diagramming the pertinent offensive and defensive alignments while they are still fresh in his mind. He should review his notes and jot down doubtful items for checking in the second half. He should also get first-half statistics if they are available and if someone else has kept a shot chart he should check it against his own. He should fill in as many individual personnel observations as he can possibly do at this time.

SECOND HALF

The scout should follow the same procedures in the second half as in the first, writing down impressions, making personal observations of the players, and noting the time that the substitutes enter. All special game situations should be completely diagrammed as soon as possible, noting if they are organized and if they are progressive. Are they trying to score directly or applying deceptive moves?

He should list the starting line-up, making a point to observe which of these players started in the first half and note any defensive or offensive adjustments. As the second half progresses, many changes may take place. One may be the use of reserve players for starters. This may indicate a change in the coach's opinion of the player who has been replaced, and it may change the scout's thinking in regard to the game coming up with his team.

AFTER THE GAME

The turning points of the game must be noted, the method by which the team was able to get the lead and control of the game, and the conditions that may have changed the outcome.

When writing up the game report, the scout should coordinate all the information he has, including statistics and play-by-play summaries that may be available to him, and compare notes by conversing with other scouts who watched the same team.

The final draft should include the individual characteristics of each starting player and each substitute who played—height, weight, relative speed, quickness, overall condition, team playing ability, and individual ability. All positive and negative factors observed should be recorded. Other scouts' comments should be added in parentheses.

The report should be a brief account of the game as he has seen it, the way the game went, why the scouted team won or lost, what tactics were used, and the type of offensive and defensive play, with all special game situations.

The scout should say whether the team he is scouting can be played man-to-man, suggest defensive match-ups for his team, and give reasons for his choices. He should also suggest offensive patterns and maneuvers that he feels will be successful against the scouted team. Included should be a summary of the statistics he has received, and, if possible, clippings of local newspaper accounts of the game.

His observations should be based on fact and objective conclusions, but he should also state any intuitions he may have had, and any opinions he may hold. The relative strength of the team opposing the scouted team should be considered when making such conclusions.

Practical Suggestions for Coaching Youth Soccer

ELEMENTARY SCHOOL

Age	General Information	Subject Guideline	Sessions and Equipment	Competition
6–7	Children have a great joy in movement, but their span of concentration is limited. The purpose is to awaken their interest in soccer, cultivate individual play, and have them learn to adapt to a team. Since they lack a concept of team play and have a tendency to crowd the ball, small groups are better.	No formal instruction, but informal play with known children's games using hands or feet—kick ball, soccer-passing relays, and the like—and advance to small soccer games. They need opportunity to get accustomed to the movement of the ball—to judge its flight and time their approach to it—and learn how to control the body to make effective contact.	Sessions: 2 a week, 40 minutes each, Tues., Thurs. Equipment: Small rubber balls Game ball #3 soccer ball Gymnastic shoes	No. of players: 7 a-side goalkeeper 2 defenders 2 midfield players 2 forwards Duration of game: 2 15-minute halves Size of field: ¼ regulation field, markers for goals set approximately 3 yards apart Opponent: Interclass competition
8–9	The organ and muscle growth is well-balanced and coordination is improving. They have a great eagerness to learn, to increase their experience, and to challenge their skills. Smaller groups are better for development of skills because of the greater ratio of contacts with the ball. The motto should be: ''To play better is more fun.''	Kicking: Inside of foot (push pass) Inside of instep Receiving–Ball-Control: Stopping a rolling ball with sole and inside of foot Smothering a bouncing ball with front surface of body Dribbling and Feinting: Leading with inside and outside of foot Heading: With forehead, feet on the ground	Sessions: 2 a week, 50 minutes each Equipment: Small rubber balls Game ball #3 soccer ball Gymnastic shoes	No. of players: 9 a-side System of play: Preparing for the offensive system goalkeeper 2 defenders (2 fullbacks) 3 midfield players (1 center halfback, 2 wing halfbacks) 3 forwards (2 wing forwards, 1 center forward) No. of games: 8–12 Duration of game: 2 20-minute halves

ELEMENTARY SCHOOL (*Continued*)

Age	General Information	Subject Guideline	Sessions and Equipment	Competition
		Tackling: *Sole of foot*		Size of field: *Half-field (across) markers for goal 3 yards apart* Opponent: *Interclass competition*
10–11	*They are well-balanced physically and mentally. They have a sensitivity for team performance, enjoy competition, and are tough, daring, and ready for action. Power, endurance, speed, and agility can be increased. It is important to provide ample opportunity to improve technique, but not so much as to take the fun out of it.*	Tactics (Encourage attack and the use of the whole field): *Basic positioning of attackers and defenders* *Basic rules of the game* *Basic forms of interpassing* *Individual tactics one-on-one* *Basic tactics of team play* Goalkeeping: *Catching and fielding low and medium-high balls*	Sessions: *School—2 a week, Tuesday, Thursday, 60 minutes each* *Club—(alternate seasons) 2 a week, Tuesday, Thursday, 60 minutes* Equipment: *Small rubber balls* *Game ball #3 or #4 soccer ball* *Gymnastic shoes or soccer shoes with molded sole (rubber studs)*	No. of players: *11 a-side* System: *Offensive system goalkeeper and 2 defenders (fullbacks) 3 midfield (2 halfbacks, 1 offensive center halfback) 2 inside forwards (2 wing forwards and center forward)* Duration of game: *2 25-minute halves* Size of field: *75 yards long, 55 yards wide, 5 yards goal area, 8 yards penalty spot, center circle 7 yards, goal 5 yards by 2* Opponent: *School and town recreation league* No. of games: *8–10 in school and 8–10 in town league*

JUNIOR HIGH SCHOOL

Age	General Information	Subject Guideline	Sessions and Equipment	Competition
12–15	*This is a period of physical puberty that produces difficulty with fine coordination, though technical skills acquired earlier are easy to keep and improve (the best argument for beginning skill training at an early age). This age*	*The emphasis is on techniques and play. Depending upon the experience of the players, the program should proceed with great intensity on refinement of basic skills and techniques and their tactical application in order to*	Sessions: *School team 3 a week, Tuesday, Wednesday, Thursday, 60 minutes each* Club team (alternate seasons)—2 a week, Tuesday, Thursday, 90 minutes each* Equipment: *Soccer ball #4 or regulation size #5*	No. of players: *11 a-side* System of play: *WM goalkeeper 3 defenders (2 fullbacks, 1 defensive center halfback) 4 midfield players (2 halfbacks, 2 inside forwards) 3 forwards (2 wing*

JUNIOR HIGH SCHOOL (*Continued*)

Age	General Information	Subject Guideline	Sessions and Equipment	Competition
	prefers to play as a team rather than to practice technique. Skill practices should be realistic. For example, when practicing centering, the wing forward centers the ball to the center forward to shoot into the goal. Performances will be unsteady. It is important to develop general endurance at this stage (adapted to the participants' development) so that a proper foundation is laid. The more universal this period of training, the better will be the players' later maximum performances.	*ensure good playing habits.* Kicking: *Full instep and outside of foot* *Low drive for passing and shooting* *Lofted drive for passing and clearing* Receiving–Ball-Control: *Trapping with sole, inside, and outside of foot* *Receiving a ball in midair with chest, thigh, instep* Dribbling and Feinting: *Leading with inside and outside of foot, sole of foot with change of direction, keeping up eyesight, using space, change of pace, and simple body-feints (body-swerve or feint kicks)* Heading: *With forehead—feet off the ground* *Side of forehead—feet on and off the ground* Tackling: *Basic block tackle (front and side)* *Shoulder charge* Tactics: *Individual and group: two-on-one, three-on-one, four-on-two* *Basic methods of attack and defense* Goalkeeping: *Catching high balls* *Diving for low balls* *Fundamental positioning* *Drop kick* Throwing-In: *Basic technique*	*Soccer shoes with molded sole (rubber studs)*	forwards, 1 center forward) No. of games: *8–12 in school and 8–12 in town league. Maximum 24–30. This includes all championship play-off games* Duration of game: *2 30-minute halves* Size of field: *Regulation* Opponent: *School and town or regional league, with regional play-offs*

HIGH SCHOOL

Age	General Information	Subject Guideline	Sessions and Equipment	Competition
16–18	Players in this age are keenly interested in individual technique, team strategy, and an individual style of play. They enjoy working out approach play and defensive cover that is suited to their style of play. In instruction, the concern is for economy of motion and the practical application and tactical implication of skills and techniques in the game. Accuracy, speed, strength, and agility are stressed.	Kicking: Volley, half-volley—passing, shooting Unorthodox kicks—overhead and scissors, heel, flicks, kicks with feints, lobs and spins Receiving–Ball-Control: *Trapping while moving and turning with preliminary feints. Killing the ball in the air with any part of the foot, head, or body while moving off to the side or turning (with preliminary feints)* Heading: *Passing and scoring with forehead and side of forehead; dive heading* Dribbling and Feinting: *Feints with the ball Compound feints* Tackling: *Split and slide tackles* Tactics: *Individual, group, and team tactics Collective attack and defense Special game situations* Goalkeeping: *Diving Catching, deflecting, punching Throwing Goal kick Positional play—narrowing the angle and special game situations* Throwing-In: *Run-up Approach Long distance throw*	Sessions: *School team—5 a week, 90 minutes each Club team (alternate seasons)—3 a week, Tuesday, Wednesday, Thursday, 90 minutes each* Equipment: *Regulation soccer ball Soccer shoes with rubber studs for normal weather and screw-in studs for muddy fields*	No. of players: *11 a-side* System of play: *1-3-3-4 goalkeeper 3 defenders (2 fullbacks, 1 center halfback (stopper) 3 midfield players (2 halfbacks, 1 withdrawn center forward) 4 forwards (2 wing forwards, 2 strikers)* or *1-4-2-4 goalkeeper 4 defenders (2 fullbacks, 2 centerbacks) 2 midfield players (2 halfbacks—linkmen) 4 forwards (2 wing forwards, 2 strikers)* No. of games: *14–18 in school and 16–20 in town league. Maximum 38–45. This includes all championship play-off games* Duration of game: *2 40-minute halves* Size of field: *Regulation* Opponent: *School and county league County and state play-offs*

VI

Conditioning and Programming

Physical fitness and conditioning call for improvement in a player's endurance, speed, and power to enable him to sustain a high work rate throughout a game. The various training methods available are described so that this objective can be achieved easily and in a reasonably predictable amount of time. So that as many qualities as possible may be incorporated in one practice activity, including patterns of play with and without the ball, a special soccer interval method is outlined. Generalizations refer to the preparation of top-class adult players; methods should be adapted to suit the age, experience, time, and facilities available.

The essentials of off-season, pre-season, and seasonal programming are identified. Organization and planning are essential for both immediate and future goals: they ensure progression, enable players to assess their performances effectively, and promote their understanding of why the program is necessary for individual and team improvement.

15

Training and Conditioning

ENDURANCE

There are two kinds of endurance: cardiovascular and muscular. Both are primarily involved with circulation and respiration.

Cardiovascular endurance refers to the ability to sustain effort over a long period of time—the ability to withstand the intensity of an entire match without any deterioration in skill.

Muscular endurance refers to the ability of specific muscles to stay intensely active without cramping or impairment of efficiency.

SPEED

Highly essential in soccer, speed involves more than the ability simply to run faster than the next fellow. It entails:

1. A quick start, i.e., quick reflexes, as the first step is the most important; this is a mental (determination) as well as a physical reaction (explosive power).
2. Quick, fluid motions.
3. Agility to change direction quickly, stop suddenly, jump for the ball.
4. Execution of techniques with rhythm, speed, and economy of effort.
5. Ability to make tactical decisions and change course quickly to meet varying situations.

Speed training should be based on these char-

acteristics. Ten to fifteen-yard sprints should be run in small groups with players marking time, kneeling, lying down, leg cycling on their backs, standing on one leg, jumping, and so forth, on the starting line to cause distraction before sprinting, such as they would experience in the game. This should be combined with a variety of "go" signals—a shout, a whisper, a casual order. The same idea should be observed for backward running and turning. By setting up the starting point between a wall and the finish line, you can call on the players to turn and change direction frequently.

Speed reactions should be practiced in pairs short distances, eight to ten yards, with a start and a finish line. On "go," the players sprint the distance and return, meanwhile reacting to the coach's commands: "Turn" and run back, "check" to jump to head an imaginary ball. This is physically demanding when done correctly.

Since most sprinting in a game is done toward the ball or to reach a position in which to receive the ball, the activity should involve reaction to both audial and visual signals and the movements of the players and the ball.

STRENGTH AND POWER

These involve many factors: intense competitive hustle, tackling, holding off a tackle, getting in a shot or pass under pressure, taking knocks, recovering from injuries, reaching the ball first, getting up to the ball in a ruck of players, doing with a wet ball what can be done with a dry one, passing long distances, and lasting the whole ninety minutes.

The coach must condition the players to endure easily the 5,500 yards usually covered in a game. This generally breaks down into 1,500 yards running, 1,000 yards sprinting, and 3,000 yards walking or jogging.

The effectiveness of the conditioning work will depend solely upon the coach's ability to motivate the players to sustain a high work rate and to keep pushing when fatigued or under considerable strain.

The actual work may be broken down as follows:

1. The total sprinting, running, jogging, and walking distances must be organized into standard ten, twenty, or thirty-yard units.

2. Most all-out or nearly all-out runs should be made without the ball under control, although ball contact may precede the initial run or occur during or at the end of a run. Since most sprinting in a game involves attacking the ball, the training should always incorporate this principle.

3. Although most runs will tend to be straight, they should frequently incorporate a quick turn to dodge an opponent, a jump to head the ball, stop-and-go, or acceleration from a stationary or near-stationary position.

4. The player with the ball must, additionally, anticipate or meet a challenge by an opponent. He must develop the ability to improvise, to make instant decisions on technique. Although the coach might have to limit the choice of technique for some reason, the choice of subsequent action must be left open to the individual.

5. Such typical work periods should consist not only of simple running but also of some form of technical or tactical involvement. This involvement should not observe a regular time pattern. It should usually last between thirty-forty seconds and seldom exceed forty-five seconds.

6. The player must be able to withstand stress over a long period of time. But he should not be worked to a state of collapse. The training should be challenging but within the player's capacity. He should always be able to complete the entire period.

7. Rest periods should be interspersed irregularly and be of irregular duration. They should seldom be completely passive. They should involve change of position through jogging or walking, or the mental observation or anticipation of the action.

METHODOLOGY

Most of soccer's training and conditioning methods have been borrowed from track. Soccer has observed the same transition, from running laps at a slow or moderate pace, with only a small segment being run at a fast tempo, to the present interval and repetition methods.

Though such training can develop top physical condition, it is most unrealistic in terms of skill development and individual team play. Yet it was not until the late 1950's that soccer experts began adapting their methods specifically to their sport.

INTERVAL TRAINING

The essence of this method is intensive loading alternated with controlled amounts of rest. The overall distance to be run is broken down into shorter distances and run at a greater pace than in an actual race and interspersed with an easy pace to allow the body to regenerate. The cardiac muscle receives more intensive stress this way than in the continuous form of endurance work. Experience has shown that the prolonged application of the interval method greatly increases endurance and speed capacity.

Through loading and training in stages, we can achieve a high degree of adaptability by the heart, respiration, and muscles. It represents a much more economical use of training time. Hollman[15] determined that interval training can, in less than two months, increase the heart volume by more than 100cc.—an improvement that would take other training methods several months to achieve.

Interval training can be divided into two types.

Slow Interval Training

This consists of repeat runs at a pace slower than the game speed, with a short rest interval and in-

[15]Dr. Med. W. Hollman, "Der Arbeits—und Trainingsinflues auf Kreislauf und Atmung," *in* Wilt, *Run, Run, Run* (Darmstadt: Dr. Dietrich Steinkopf Verlag, 1959), p. 185.

complete recovery of the heart rate. The rest interval is always shorter than the time it takes to run the distance. This type of interval training is used to develop cardiovascular reserve and does not contribute much to speed.

Fast Interval Training

This permits a longer rest interval and consequently greater recovery of the heart rate as well as a faster repeat effort. This type places more emphasis on speed.

Fast interval training may be considered beneficial to both cardiac and skeletal muscle. It improves the endurance of the heart muscle and the resistance of the skeletal muscle, permitting them to withstand the accumulation of fatigue products and to operate with oxygen debt.

Special Soccer Interval

In adapting the interval principle to soccer, researchers sought to combine the development of techniques and tactics with the necessary physical and psychological adaptations. Special problems were posed by the fact that stress appears in irregular stages and intensities. The player must control the ball and carry out tactical tasks—a combination known as "complex activities." Training researchers applied the principle of raising the pulse rate to approximately 180 degrees and then dropping it to approximately 120 degrees through alternating periods of stress and rest.

The results confirmed their belief that the adapted interval method was most effective in the total preparation of the players and was, without reservation, the greatest modern contribution to soccer coaching. As in track, it produced results more easily and could, under near-maximum stress conditions, simultaneously develop speed, stamina, and muscle power. It also allowed the coach to simulate game conditions more easily and more frequently and thus adapt the players better to game stress.

Since players are never allowed to rest completely and must draw on their reserves of will power, this kind of training offers an effective way to improve this vital quality.

The soccer interval consists of the following components:

1. Duration of stress (ideal thirty seconds).
2. Intensity of stress (140–180 pulse rates).
3. Number of repetitions.
4. Length of interval (ideal ninety seconds).
5. The particular activities selected.

By intensifying or lessening any of these components, one can either raise or lower the training stress. The objective of the particular training session will determine the quality and quantity of the various components.

Studies on the soccer interval method revealed some interesting facts. For example, the ratio of stress rose whenever a change of direction was incorporated into a certain distance to be run. Since the length of the rest depended upon the stress, that meant the rest had to be increased about twenty–thirty percent. If the player was involved in leading the ball while running or crossing obstacles, as in the slalom drill, then it was necessary to increase the interval of rest by forty–fifty percent.

The difficulties of the activities had to be carefully calculated. If the interval of rest was too short, fatigue would prevent the proper completion of the subsequent activities. If it was too long, the organism would not be subjected to the necessary stimulus. When the combination of rest and stress was correct, fatigue would come about slowly.

As a general standard, however, we can say that the intervals in Table 1 are suitable:

	Interval (Seconds) Between Sprints	Interval (Seconds) Between Series
5 x 10 yard sprints	10–12	40–45
5 x 20 yard sprints	25–30	45–50
5 x 20 yards running	18–20	50–55
5 x 30 yards running	23–25	65–70

Table 1.

Dangers of the Special Soccer Interval

The choice of activities, duration, and intensity depend wholly on the athletes involved: their level of fitness, the extent of their technical and tactical knowledge, and the effect on them of such outside influences as the weather and hour of training.

Training loads have to be cautiously calculated, especially with adolescents, beginners, or players recovering from illnesses. Poor habits will be formed whenever the players are subjected to complex activities that they cannot perform correctly at the speed required. As soon as the players start failing in execution and precision, the series should terminate.

Research brought out the fact that the series does not require more than eighty to ninety percent of the athlete's energy potential, even with mature players. This percentage is sufficient to improve simultaneously the circulation, the respiration, and the strengthening of the muscular system. The first activities of the series could require only sixty–seventy percent of the energy potential and could be considered a warm-up.

After two, three, or even more series, there should be a large active rest interval of twenty or more minutes. This is the time that the complex activities of the following periods can be worked on at a slower rate to be sure they will be executed flawlessly during the stress period.

The first can be a warm-up period with the prime concern on agility and dexterity, and the second and third should always include activities of a technical and tactical nature, while stressing physical components such as speed-endurance and speed of performance. The last period should always be used for a scrimmage game or a game-simulated activity.

Complex Activities

In the selection of complex activities with a specific intensity of stress, it is important to realize that techniques such as passing, shooting, or dive heading require only a momentary energy output, whereas a technique involving change of direction, dribbling, or ball-leading requires a greater output of energy.

The activities selected must also be directly re-lated to the specific purpose of the training period. If, for example, a coach wants to have the player run four to six yards at least ten–twelve times (an intensity of stress that would raise his pulse beat up to 170–180), he must select a complex activity that does this while the player is employing various techniques.

Two-Man Activities

Following are examples of two-man activities for this purpose:

1. *A* and *B* set up ten yards apart and *A* keeps passing to *B* in a way that forces *B* to run at least five yards to the side to get the ball. *B* passes back to *A*, who then passes to the opposite side of *B*. In short, *A* keeps leading *B* to force him to run continuously after the ball. After a half-minute, the roles are switched, with *B* becoming the server and *A* the receiver. A half-minute of stress follows a half-minute active rest in serving.

The running player is under strong stress. The intensity of the stress can be increased by a constant change of direction and sprinting. The server can do this by passing the ball as soon as he gets it back from the receiver, perhaps in an unexpected direction. The stress is ten–twelve times four to six yards, which would raise the pulse to 170–180 in a half-minute. Under this high stress, such a complex activity repeated four or five times would require two to three minutes active rest. The speed and repetitions would, of course, depend on the participants' fitness.

2. Passing in groups with continuous position switching. Three groups of three members each form triangles eight–ten yards apart. *A* passes to *B* and follows his pass to fall in at the end of *B*'s line. *B* passes to *C* and follows his pass to fall in at the end of *C*'s line. *C*, after passing, lines up at the end of line *A*.

A contest can be made of this activity with two or three teams consisting of nine members. If each of the three groups that make up a team consists of three players, a player would run eight–ten yards every ten seconds. Where the groups are made up of four men, a player would run the same distance every thirteen seconds. The stress then for five minutes is six times eight–ten-yard sprints.

3. Two players face each other eighteen–twenty yards apart. All players have a ball at their right foot, and they approach each other at great speed. Just before they meet, they pass their ball with the left foot to the right side. Each then has to chase the other's ball. Upon reaching the ball, the player has to control it with the sole

of his foot, turn around, return to his original position, and repeat the whole maneuver.

The time of running with the ball is thirty seconds. After the active rest of dribbling the ball back, the exercise is repeated with the other foot. In this half-minute the players are subjected to four pieces of swift action: fifteen yards leading the ball, a pass, a twenty–twenty-five-yard sprint, and a ball reception. The intensity of this complex activity depends, as in any other exercise, upon the speed of execution, repetitions, and distance required.

Complex Activities of a Tactical Nature

The calculation of stress in complex activities of a tactical nature is somewhat more difficult because the stress is contingent upon the energy output of the individual. Consider a tactical pattern that can be practiced with the interval method, such as a passing pattern with position switching.

Two files of three players each set up thirty yards from the penalty area, ten yards apart. *A* passes to *B* who immediately sprints with the ball toward the corner flag, while *A* trots toward the goalmouth. On a signal he sprints and *B* sends him a lead pass, which *A* instantly converts into a shot at the goal. Then the next pair takes its turn.

The players, after performing, must always return to the end of their line. The activity continues until every player has taken five shots and led the ball five times.

The stress is five times two-twenty-five-yard sprints as well as sprinting with the ball twenty-thirty yards. The stress is followed by a minute of active rest, consisting of trotting back to the group, of chasing the ball and trotting back and waiting for the next turn at action. The groups switch roles after a certain amount of time.

A complex activity involving an attack with one halfback has three groups lined up across the field at midfield. *A* and *B*, the wing forwards, are on the flanks, while *C*, the halfbacks, are in the middle. *C* shoots a diagonal lead pass to *B*. *B* dribbles swiftly to the edge of the penalty area, while *C* and *A* go slowly. On a signal, *B* crosses the ball over to *A*, who plays it immediately to *C*, who takes a shot or header at the goal.

All three players run the same distance of about thirty-thirty-five yards with or without the ball. When the activity is repeated four or five times, a twenty-thirty-second interval should be allowed between exercises and a rest period up to two minutes afterward.

Modified Small Group Games or Scrimmage

The game itself, or a simulated game, is probably the most effective form of interval training.

A scrimmage could be held across half the field with five or seven on a side and the goal only two to three yards wide and one and a half yards high.

With five on a side, the players should be given an active rest every two to three minutes, the time being used for technical and tactical activities.

With seven on a side, both the speed and length of the game should be increased, the duration being increased to about five or six minutes. A two to three minute rest should follow for technical activities.

Such games can also have one team attacking for thirty–sixty seconds with full strength and energy, then trying to control the ball (active rest) by interpassing in slow motion. Following this should be another thirty–sixty seconds of aggressive attacking.

Since intensive stress and rest have to alternate consistently, it is important for the coach or an assistant to be on hand to exercise control over the group.

The same system can be observed for a regular practice game. The intensity of stress will depend upon the hustle of the players.

FORTY-FIVE-SECOND INTERVAL METHOD

This is based on the rhythmical interchange of forty-five seconds stress and forty-five seconds rest, with the intensity of stress being irregular in order to simulate the game.

For practical application, with two players working together on a rectangular course twenty yards long and five yards wide, the first player should dribble the ball around the rectangle as fast as he can for forty-five seconds. When the coach signals the end of the forty-five–second interval, the player instantly passes the ball to the second player. The latter repeats the routine, as the first rests. This may be repeated several times, depending upon the objective of the activity and the players' condition.

The activity is quite realistic. Besides simply dribbling the ball, the player must perform six or seven twenty-yard sprints and nine–ten changes of direction. These constitute both maximum and real-istic game stress. The constant sprints between changes of direction and the stop-and-go and con-tinuous shifting create a very realistic work load.

SKILL REPETITION METHOD

This method is predicated on the theory that con-stant repetition of a skill establishes a specific neuronic pattern, and that the greater the number of times that impulses are sent over these path-ways, the more firmly established they become until the skill becomes nearly automatic.

The repetition method must be made an indige-nous part of the daily training program, not just a supplement to it. It is probably the most popular method of developing or sharpening a skill.

Practical Application

It is natural to do things one is good at, but the coach must make sure that everyone spends at least equal time on his weaknesses. He must train the players to spend hours practicing by themselves.

Repetition practice is hard work and can easily develop into a painful bore, as most skills must be repeated hundreds and hundreds of times in practice. Skill practice should always be based on repetitions rather than intervals of time, or on the repetitions that can be done in a given time.

For example, the player who is asked to head two hundred crosses will wind up putting any-where between zero–ten and eight–ten on target. Certainly he will get very tired, but he will perform better with crosses on his mind rather than time.

The coach plays an important role in this type of practice. When the player is doing well, the coach need say very little. But when the player gets tired and his efficiency begins to deteriorate, the coach must squeeze extra effort and concentration out of him by encouraging, goading, bullying, chastising—anything to make him work harder and concentrate more.

In shooting practices, for example, the greater scorers like Pelé and Eusebio hit the ball quickly—not necessarily as hard as they can, but with power. The idea of their repetition shooting is to develop that split-second timing, that explosive power, which will enable them to put the ball home when

it counts. They want to get the shot in first-time.

The inconsistency of the crosses players receive, particularly when the feeders are asked to vary them, will mean that the ball will be coming at the pressured players in an assortment of ways.

The players will pick up the technique instinc-tively—the importance of balance, which foot is best for balls from different sides and angles, how often they can expect results from just hitting the ball without aiming, and so on.

The defenders clearing the ball must also prac-tice doing it first-time. As the crosses are fed to the defender, he must have a target. He must de-velop the accuracy and power to reach a safe area, usually near the touchline.

REPETITION MAZE RUNNING

The idea of this method is to simulate the typical running patterns of match play under controlled loads and intensities. It involves typical distances of fifteen–twenty–thirty yards and includes jumps, turns, stops, and go, and changes of direction. All are simulated through a maze obstacle course with or without a ball.

In preparing the course, the coach must make certain to avoid excessive difficulty. The total dis-tance should not exceed one hundred and twenty yards. The fastest time by any player should never exceed forty-five seconds or go under thirty sec-onds. The trial times should indicate the need to add or eliminate obstacles.

The method lends itself ideally to relay-type competition, and competition permits the reten-tion of interest for prolonged periods. The coach must, however, make sure that the teams are equally matched in speed.

Depending upon the players' condition, the teams may vary from a high of six to a low of two. Where the team is made up of six players, each man should perform in a 1:5 interval—one period of stress to five periods of rest. As the players' condition improves, the teams must be reduced to four, three, or even two players. This means the players will have to work in a 1:3, 1:2, or 1:1 interval, while the number of repetitions remain the same.

In the early stages of training, a run of five hun-dred yards or five repetitions will be suitable for most players who have a low level of fitness. The ultimate number of repetitions should be equivalent to 2,000 yards. That is, when using a one hundred-yard obstacle maze course, each individual should do twenty repetitions.

Whenever this method is used twice a week throughout the five-week pre-season period, the dosage can be increased by three repetitions, three hundred yards each week, or more rapidly, depending upon the response of the players and the length of the pre-season period.

Exact records should be kept and displayed as an incentive. Teams should be given their total course-time. Objectives can be established based on single repetition test-times. Spot checks can be made periodically to determine who and who is not working sufficiently hard. The standard of comparison can be the player's all-out test-time.

Practical Application

1. The following maze obstacle course covers approximately one hundred yards. Starting at the halfway line, there is a ten-yard sprint to obstacle *B*, a vaulting box, or any firm obstacle approximately four feet high.

Obstacle *B* consists of four hurdles three feet high and about two yards apart, the first hurdle being no farther than five yards from the first obstacle. The player must use a double-leg takeoff when jumping over the hurdles, which forces him to jump rather than hurdle.

Obstacle *C* consists of a series of four poles or dummies about a yard apart, through which the player must weave his way.

Activity *D* consists of a ten-yard shuttle run, ending in a shot at the goal, using the penalty restraining circle and the penalty marker as turning points; two balls are placed there for the shot. The player finishes with a straight run back to the starting line to send the next teammate on his way.

2. Starting at the goal line the player weaves his way through a three-pole slalom about a yard apart, toward a ball suspended at a reasonable height. He jumps to head the ball and goes underneath an obstacle (a hurdle or table). This activity is repeated three times. He then weaves his way through another three-pole slalom one yard apart. Then he runs to a ball placed at the restraining circle of the penalty box, picks up a ball, runs to the penalty spot, and takes a drop volley shot at the goal.

He repeats a series of four shuttle runs, ending each time with a drop volley shot at the goal. He finishes the course with a straight run back to the starting line.

PRESSURE TRAINING

This consists of submitting a player to a controlled repetition of various skills through a rapid serving of balls within a given time.

Complicated organization is not recommended. We suggest a series of intensive work periods of not less than thirty-five seconds or more than forty-five seconds. As the player becomes accustomed to practice under pressure, the balls may be served to him more rapidly.

Pressure training offers an excellent method of improving endurance and reinforcing and accelerating the skill learning to the point of automatization. Since the objective is to achieve intensive stress, the quality of performance becomes of secondary importance. Consequently, pressure training is not advisable for poorly skilled players, who might wind up habitizing their faults. To avoid any deterioration in skill, the training should involve only the techniques that the player has mastered.

The training must subject the player to intensive running or jumping over distances of ten–fifteen or thirty yards. Whenever the area is too small, for example, the training is unlikely to have any effect on cardiovascular endurance. The player's legs are likely to give out before any demands can be made on his heart and lungs. An extended practice can make considerable demands on the player's stamina, but the higher his standard of performance, the more economical will be his movements and the longer he will be able to endure the pace and pressure.

Naturally the greater the number of players involved, the greater will be the number of intervals and the less effective the training will become.

Practical Application

1. Three players set up about thirty yards apart. Player *C*, halfway between *A* and *B*, is the man who is put under pressure. Players *A* and *B* each have a ball. *A* passes to *C* who runs to meet it and returns it instantly. He then turns quickly and sprints to meet the ball passed by *B*, and so on.

2. Two players—a server and a retriever—face each other about ten yards apart, with the retriever standing between two markers ten yards apart. The server must pass the ball to the outside of the marker in a way that puts the retriever under great pressure to return the passes in rhythmical succession, left-right, and so on.

Strength and Power

Strength is the ability to overcome resistance without speed or momentum. Power is applied strength; it is the ability to move a resistance with speed, such as a player's own body-weight, the ball, and various resistances produced by different ground or climatic conditions.

A soccer player requires basic muscle strength and the ability to use it in match situations, for example, in running quickly from a stationary position, in changing direction, shooting powerfully, jumping to head, and the like.

Strength and power can be improved only by increasing the resistance or overloading the muscles. There are two basic ways to do this.

Isotonic or Dynamic Training

This calls for the repetition of movement with weights. A fairly heavy weight is needed for improving strength, but the repetitions should not exceed ten. At the beginning, the coach can perhaps seek forty percent of both maximum weight and maximum repetitions. If the player loses form while lifting or repeating, it is obvious that he is doing too much. Later on, the ratio can be increased to sixty percent and then eighty percent (of both weight and repetitions).

Isometric or Static Training

This involves muscle contraction, such as pushing a wall or some immovable object, exerting maximum strength for seven seconds. This form of training achieves quick results, but the effects are quickly lost, so a combination of isometric and isotonic would be best.

THE CIRCUIT METHOD

This method of training, as devised by R. Morgan and G. T. Adamson of Leeds University, is based on the principle of the interval method, except that it does not allow a true interval rest period. The interval consists merely of varying the activities so that one body-part is put under stress while the others are recuperating in an active rest interval. That is why the circuit method is frequently known as the "non-stop method."

Basically, it consists of performing a predetermined number of repetitions of a series of exercises in a set sequence. The exercises are arranged in circular fashion so that the circuit may be repeated several times in the shortest possible time. In setting up his circuit, the coach should select basic exercises that cover all the major muscle groups and arrange them judiciously. He must avoid overlapping the muscle action to the point that premature fatigue can force the athlete to drop out of the circuit. The soccer circuit should naturally show a bias toward legs, hips, trunk, endurance, and speed, and involve the ball wherever possible.

The circuit provides an intensive training process that can be easily adapted to individual needs and controlled progressions, an important aspect of any training procedure. Since the objectives can be easily established, the results can be measured without difficulty.

Training Load and Rate

This must be determined by the player's previous training and his level of physical condition. As a rule, we can say:

1. Number of repetitions: half maximum number of repetitions for each exercise within sixty seconds.

2. Target-time: derived from a trial run. The player uses his own training load for each exercise and tries to complete the circuit as fast as he can. To double his test-time will be his initial target-time, since he will be required to complete two circuits when training.

3. Progression: as the player reduces his circuit-time, he can establish lower time projections. Progression is achieved by periodically retesting and establishing new loads and times. Progression is the most important aim, and the player's goals must be controlled in order to gain the maximum benefit from this method.

The circuit method lends itself ideally to *weight training*. The lighter the weights used, the more repetitions the player can perform and the more muscular endurance he can achieve. This is not likely to increase muscle bulk, however, and certainly will not increase power to any appreciable extent. It is not therefore recommended for soccer players. They require fairly heavy weights to provide effective resistance.

Many laymen believe that weight training always produces muscle bulk and consequently makes the player muscle-bound, stiff, slow, and awkward. Research has proven that a limited number of repetitions with fairly heavy weights will make the player more supple and powerful.

The amount of weight for each exercise hinges on how many repetitions the player can perform with good form. The most common number of repetitions included in strength programs range from eight to twelve, with the ideal being no more than ten.

PRACTICAL HINTS

Warm-Up

The warm-up gradually prepares the body for the great physiological and mental strains to which it soon will be subjected. Considerable evidence supports the theory that increased circulation and metabolism enhance performance. This is the chief reason for warming-up before practices and games.

The increased blood supply to the muscles also prevents injuries, sprains, or ruptures from rapid, unexpected movements, as well as undue fatigue early in the training session or match.

A general warm-up of light running, jumping, and gymnastics helps promote a more economical respiration and increases the metabolism and circulation. The soccer warm-up should also provide for the coordination of limbs and nervous system to prepare the players for the quick starts, changes in direction, special movements with the ball, positioning, quick passing, and so on, that will be needed in the game.

The exercises should, ideally, be done with the ball and should consist of actual techniques, starting with fairly simple movements and gradually increasing the intensity until full muscular and mental readiness are achieved.

Pre-Game Warm-Up

Besides effecting physiological and mental readiness, the warm-up must reduce pre-game tension. A very individualistic type of warm-up is generally recommended for adult players. With inexperienced players it is better to be highly organized. Since pre-game tension might be quite intensive, a loud, large group activity can help combat it. It is especially important to keep an eye on the particularly high-strung player who dislikes warming-up for fear of injury or fatigue. The coach may have to nurse him through this stage.

Start off with exercises stressing flexibility, then proceed to a few ball-control, passing, and shooting drills selected for positional specialization. Or engage in a ten-minute half-field scrimmage, forwards against defenders. This has proven quite effective.

The Daily Warm-Up

This, on the other hand, must set the stage for the training to follow. Besides readying the players physically, it should put them in the right frame of mind and make them more willing to put out one hundred percent. The coach must be sensitively attuned to his players and should choose activities suitable to their disposition and previous regimen. He must observe whether they are down after examinations, unusually exhilarated, and so forth.

For everyday warm-ups, the play concept is preferred, as it can be enjoyed and prevents routine or tediousness. A contest is sought that does not require maximum effort, such as juggling, heading in pairs, or a modified game of German field handball, rugby, or even soccer. The game should start at a moderate pace and then slowly increase in tempo.

Warm-Up Games

Modification of German Field Handball

The game is like soccer insofar as the field, goals, and number of players are concerned, but it is played exclusively with the hands, not the feet.

Variations:

1. A goal can be scored only on a drop volley or half-volley at a signal given by the coach to indicate the appropriate time for a shot.

2. Player determines his own time to shoot a drop or half-volley.

3. The ball must remain on the ground at all times. A goal is scored through a first-touch shot at the coach's signal indicating the appropriate time.

4. Player determines his own time to shoot first-touch.

5. A goal can be scored only by heading the ball into the net.

Passing Game

Players move in a given area. All but a few have their own ball and keep on the move while dribbling, dodging, and feinting. With twelve players on the squad, nine should have balls. The other three players call the name of a dribbler, who must instantly pass to them and call the receiver's name.

Variations:

1. Players without a ball must challenge for the ball.

2. Players without a ball use a visual sign in calling for a pass by a dribbler.

3. The dribbler finds the open man, while the players without balls remain on the alert for a pass.

4. Combinations of any of the above.

5. Coach calls the name of a receiver and indicates by a visual sign from whom the player should expect the pass.

Heading Game

The idea is to advance the ball and score by use of the head. If the ball is not high enough to be headed, it should be tossed up instantly by the nearest player, and play resumed. The toss should not be deliberately directed to a teammate. Any number of players can be used. When a keeper is used, the goal should be made rather large to facilitate scoring.

Circle Soccer Keep-Away

Any number of players stand in any size circle and pass the ball about. A player in the middle tries to intercept. If he gains possession, the last passer must take his place.

Variations:

1. Placing two or three, or even more players in the middle of the circle.

2. Players are allowed to touch the ball only once or twice.

3. Players have to feint before passing off.

4. Circle can be moving.

Dribbling Game

Teams of equal numbers—three-three, four-four, and so on—compete on a limited playing field, such as the penalty box. The idea is to score by dribbling over the boundary lines. Team play consists solely of dribbling; passing is disallowed.

Five A-Side Soccer

Played like soccer except that the field is much smaller and there are fewer players. A small goal may be placed at each end of the field without a keeper, or regular goals can be used with keepers.

Variations:

1. Ball must be kept low, no higher than the knee.

2. Ball can be touched only once or twice.

Walking Scrimmage

Played like soccer except that the players are only allowed to walk. Infractions of this rule invoke an indirect free kick.

Variation: Only the player in possession must walk, but he cannot be tackled. He can, however, touch the ball only three times.

Weak-Foot Scrimmage

Played like soccer except that the player can only use his weaker foot, which is indicated by a rolled-down sock. Infractions of this rule invoke an indirect free kick.

Exercises with the Ball

1. Bounce ball with both hands and jump with rise and fall of ball.

2. Bend trunk sideward while rhythmically tossing ball over head from side to side.

3. Circle trunk while holding ball with arms extended overhead.

4. Bend back and pick up ball lying on ground either directly behind or slightly to side.

5. Circle ball around body while rhythmically circling hips.

6. Move ball in a figure eight around thighs, raising them alternately.

7. Bend slightly forward in straddle position and move ball in a figure eight around ankles.

8. Bounce ball with both hands while bringing an extended leg over ball. Alternate.

9. From straddle position, bend trunk forward and head ball against ground.

10. From straddle position, bend back as far as possible and extend arms with ball overhead. Drop ball, turn, and try to control ball with various ball-control techniques.

11. Stand with arms extended forward, holding ball tightly with both hands, then kick alternately to touch ball.

12. Standing on right leg with knee bent, raise left thigh and extend arms forward with ball. Drop ball and flex lower leg to kick ball up to hands, catch, and repeat while keeping perfect balance. Alternate legs.

13. Throw ball straight up in air. Head it in an arc and catch descending ball with instep.

14. From straddle position, arms extended overhead with ball, swing trunk forward and toss ball in a high arc upward between straddled legs. Turn and control ball instantly.

15. Sitting with ball in hands, toss ball in air, head ball as it descends, then rise without use of hands and control ball instantly.

16. From crouch, bounce ball vigorously on ground and jump up, head it, and go after header and control it instantly.

17. Stand on one foot and bounce ball on ground with sole of other foot.

18. Bounce ball vigorously against ground with both hands and control rising ball instantly with body by pushing hip forward or by bending trunk forward.

Partner Exercises

1. Partners stand facing each other four yards apart. Each tosses a ball into air, heads the rebound straight in air, then changes position to retrieve partner's ball and instantly control it.

2. Partners assume front rest positions facing each other about a yard apart. Only one has a ball, which he tosses slightly up in air and heads it to his partner, who catches it with hands and repeats.

3. One partner lies on back while other stands at his feet with ball in his hands. He throws ball in air so that supine partner can head it while doing a sit-up. Standing partner catches ball with hands and repeats.

4. One partner sits with arms and legs off the ground and tries to keep perfect balance. The other stands three yards away from his feet, facing him. He throws ball so that they can play catch, with seated partner returning ball with an instep punt.

5. Partners stand facing each other, two feet apart. One holds ball over head and slightly forward. Other jumps up to punch ball lightly with head.

6. Players stand facing each other and grab each other by the shoulders. One holds ball tightly between ankles, while other practices lower-leg snap by punching at ball with instep.

7. Players face each other about six yards apart with ball on ground between them. Players dictate their own rhythm, but should strike at ball simultaneously with inside of foot so that ball is blocked.

STALENESS, ITS SYMPTOMS AND CURE

"Staleness" derives from physiological or psychological causes, or a combination of both and culminates in that dread bugaboo called a "slump."

The loss of form is generally the primary external evidence of staleness. Unfortunately, it is generally the best players, the hard-working ones, who are affected. The prevention of this rather mysterious malady is one of the coach's most difficult concerns in devising his training program. Recognition of the minor symptoms is essential, as the longer the player remains "stale" the harder it becomes to cure.

The player's slump in performance is usually accompanied by a slump in morale and a boredom with practice. The athlete may exhibit a drawn or tense look, loss of weight and appetite, irritability, and oversensitivity to remarks and situations. He often becomes afraid of the ball and develops a pessimistic outlook or an unusual concern over his health.

He also experiences unusual fatigue during practice, which does not diminish satisfactorily even after sufficient rest. He loses much of his sparkle and personality and is disinclined to joke and have fun.

Staleness can be produced by many causes. Overexertion is a common one. The victim often is a player who is subjected to a heavy work load without adequate preparation, as when returning to action after a long illness. Outside activities may also account for the overwork, where the athlete begins spending more energy than he can replace by food or rest and starts drawing on his reserves. Poor physical fitness can have the same effect. Inadequate sleep or diet, upsetting events at work, school, or home, or tension between members of the team, are other causes. But the most common one is "overtraining." This can stem from poorly organized practice—monotonous or stereotyped activities, an irrational work load, bad leadership, or a poor synchronization with the match schedule.

The first step in the cure is a complete change of the training routine or environment. If the condition is serious, the player should be given a complete rest from all physical activity or talk of any kind connected with the game. He should be instructed to take frequent hot baths, such as steam baths, get lots of sleep and rest, effect a complete change of activity, and do things he has not been able to do for some time.

Under the guidance of a physician, his diet should be supplemented with a high potency vitamin B complex and additional protein, at least 125–150 grams per day.

Upon the athlete's return to action, the coach should prescribe a complete change of routine. The player should be given frequent short rests and the atmosphere should be made as happy and relaxed for him as possible.

Variety is the most important preventative against staleness. The coach should change his routine as often as possible. He should have some short work days and he should try to inject some humor into practice now and then. A team "clown" is invaluable in this respect. The coach should not crack down too heavily on such "comedians." They help relax the squad. The athlete himself must learn how to relax, balance his life, and learn to live philosophically.

Relaxation is the number one priority. Tension impairs physical and mental efficiency and creates all sorts of problems. Players can be taught how to develop a relaxed state: by tensing the body purposefully and then relaxing one part at a time, and then all together, the state of each body-part can be recognized. This tension relaxing principle can then be applied to the part of the body generally affected. The athlete eventually can apply this principle to all his activities. He will soon learn that a relaxed person has a finer sense of balance, agility, perception, and everything else associated with body motion and feeling.

16

Programming

OFF-SEASON

Research bears out the fact that if players maintain a high level of physical fitness during the off-season, a higher level of performance can be reached faster during the pre-season and early season, and be sustained more consistently over a longer period of time. In addition, players are less injury prone.

The character of off-season activities depends upon the nature and length of the season. On the professional level, where the game is played all year, it is more accurately called a "transition" period. The main objectives of a transition period are to eliminate the physical and nervous fatigue accumulated in the playing season and to maintain a high level of fitness. The nervous system is regenerated through light recreational activities, perhaps of an entirely different nature from soccer.

Work load must be gradually decreased to a light training or complete layoff. Afterwards the process has to be reversed; stress has to be increased to ensure a smooth transition to the intense pre-season training.

In scholastic or college soccer, where the game is almost exclusively played during the fall season, the nature and objectives of the transition period are vastly different. Since a year-round soccer season is unrealistic, the next best thing is to have players participate in other sports, particularly the

spring sports such as lacrosse, rugby, tennis, or baseball. Alternate seasons for varsity play, rather than successive, allow the player to catch up on his studies. Just as important, it permits him to relax socially and do the things he cannot do during the soccer season. The winter sports, such as basketball or hockey, overlap soccer in schedule, often proving to be a distraction for the players toward the end of the season.

The three-sport, or even two-sport athlete, however, on the college level has become a rarity, although still existing on the secondary level. It becomes the responsibility of the soccer coach, then, to maintain the interest of his squad in participating in off-season programs to maintain a reasonable level of fitness.

The main concern in scholastic and college off-season training, particularly with American needs in mind, is to develop and improve individual skills and techniques as well as intellectual understanding of the game through general tactics. Outstanding players have achieved success only after spending vast amounts of time with the ball. In addition, special programs, such as weight lifting, can develop and improve the leg muscles of particular players or can improve flexibility. The coach should keep in mind, however, regardless of the value of organized off-season programs, that he is coaching amateurs and attendance should be voluntary. The player is then much more receptive to

347

suggestions for improvement and development of his skills. There need be no pressure either from the coach or from himself under such optional and relaxed circumstances. When the initiative is left to the player, it also fosters the self-reliance he needs in order to develop into an outstanding player.

The coach's off-season responsibilities do not end there. This is the time to establish close rapport with the players and keep abreast of their scholastic progress and social activities.

The real test of the job the coach has done in educating his players in good habits and self-reliance will show up during the long summer vacation. The coach can write letters (which he should during the summer vacation) encouraging and reminding, even suggesting activities, preferably on an individual basis, but these letters will be effective only if they are the culmination of a clear pattern of progressive training throughout the year.

PRE-SEASON

Coaches are fully aware of the serious decline in general and specific fitness that occurs during the off-season. The extent of this deterioration can be observed in a slower recovery after vigorous activity as measured by post-exercise pulse-rate recovery to normal. For players of certain physical types the deterioration can be seen in considerable weight increase. Therefore, it is of great importance that not only a medical examination precede the pre-season training but also a physical fitness test. With this knowledge, the coach can establish a suitable starting workload, and stress can be increased gradually. He must provide a gradual transition from the off-season to the pre-season training to avoid the detrimental effects of premature heavy training, physiological as well as psychological, that are contrary to a sound progressive training program.

Pre-season training should be looked upon in two phases:

Phase 1, the basic or general conditioning period, with the obvious objective to raise the player's general level of fitness—the development of stamina and endurance, strength, muscle power, speed, agility, and flexibility.

Phase 2, the form-building or special-conditioning period—the development of muscle coordination very closely allied to the skills

and techniques of soccer. The general aim is to develop and improve skills, techniques, and tactics on an individual and collective basis and to coordinate segments of the team as well as the team as a whole into a well-coordinated unit.

Sound training must have a training cycle or rhythm. The most common ratio is 3:1. For example, if pre-season is divided into four parts or weeks, the third part should present maximum stress.

Early pre-season training can use the Fartlek or Speedplay slow interval principle. In the early stages, a slow or moderate pace prevails. This is interspersed with relatively long rest intervals of just walking, exercises of a flexibility or loosening type, or simple activities involving skills and techniques with the ball. Gradually the running pace, intensity, and emphasis is changed by picking up the pace, interspersing more frequent sprints, while shortening the interval of rest and emphasizing the development of speed and speed-endurance.

In accordance with this idea, the coach may start off in the first part of pre-season with a 4,000-yard distance to be covered, which should be raised to 4,500 yards, with a maximum workload of 5,000 yards.

In the second part of pre-season training, the workload should be raised to 5,500 yards, with a maximum workload of 6,000 yards.

In the third part, which is the maximum workload of the whole year, the distance of 6,000 yards is eventually raised to 6,500 yards.

In the fourth part, the overall distance is dropped to 5,000 with a maximum distance of 5,500. This should constitute the maximum workload of the seasonal training. It is also important to establish the training cycle to be used during the season.

These distances are broken down in the following manner: In the first phase of pre-season, the running distances should vary from three hundred–four hundred yards; the second part, two hundred–three hundred yards; and the third, one hundred–two hundred yards to be run at a moderate pace. After this the distances would be cut considerably, to eighty, sixty, fifty, forty yards while the pace is stepped up considerably. These distances must be cut down even further to ten, fifteen, twenty, thirty yards to simulate typical running distances. These should be put into typical running sequences with the ball.

In the first phase of the pre-season period, technical and tactical movements familiar to the player are repeated in their rudimentary stages in order to strengthen his reflex contacts, deepen fundamental movements, encourage newer contacts and coordination, and eliminate faults.

The complexity of the technical and tactical activities is gradually increased. The movements are performed while moving about in unexpected directions or in combinations with other elements. The purpose is to develop through these technical and tactical exercises special fitness for match play by raising the level of individual players.

In the second phase of the pre-season, collective skills, techniques, and tactics are introduced. These overlap into the period of building competitive form or special conditioning, where the main aim is to coordinate segments of the team and the team as a whole into a cohesive unit. There should be full-field scrimmages of thirty–forty minutes, for at the end of the pre-season period, the practicing of technical elements, combined with tactical or conditioning exercises, is done entirely under playing conditions. A pre-season game should be scheduled for Saturday.

A typical pre-season training cycle in the second phase would be:

Sunday: Light training—maximum thirty percent. A picnic, swimming, loosening up activities of a general nature.

Monday: Average—forty–fifty percent. Activities of a technical and tactical nature and development of power.

Tuesday: Heavy—eighty–ninety percent. Combined technical, tactical, and physical activities with special emphasis on speed and endurance.

Wednesday: Average—forty–fifty percent. Activities consisting of a technical and tactical nature and the development of power. Whole-field controlled scrimmage thirty minutes duration.

Thursday: Heavy—eighty–ninety percent. Combined technical, tactical, and physical activities with special emphasis on endurance and speed work.

Friday: Light—thirty–forty percent. Loosening up activities and tactics for special game situations.

Saturday: Scrimmage against outside opponents. Pre-season opponents should be selected in such a way that the early opponents do not present too much difficulty. They become increasingly more challenging as the pre-season period closes.

If two sessions a day are held during this period, each should be no longer than one and a half hours. The morning session would be in the nature of conditioning and improving individual techniques and skills; the afternoon session should consist of individual, group, and team tactics.

In the second phase of the training, the load is reduced in duration of training sessions and in their number while the intensity is increased. In the last weeks, introduce the training schedule to be used throughout the season, having led up to it gradually in terms of load, number of sessions, and duration of practices.

SEASONAL—RETAINING AND TIMING COMPETITIVE FORM

The coach has now established a rhythmic cycle of training that is highly synchronized with the season's schedule of games. The purpose is to enable the player to maintain a high level of performance throughout the season without marked fluctuations. Moreover, without undue intervention in his training rhythm he should be able to play at peak performance at any given time.

The emphasis now is on coordinated teamwork, to preserve and further improve individual and collective skills, and also to acquire new skills. In this way there can be a steadily rising standard of play. Specialization of technical and tactical elements prevail and are geared toward the individual's weaknesses, his sphere of play, and the pending contest.

Seek also to preserve conditioning and further develop speed, mobility, and flexibility. Endurance is no longer a problem because this becomes stabilized through matches. Quantitatively the maximum stress should be no more than eighty to ninety percent of the maximum work load in pre-season training. However, intensity must be highly individual.

Lengthy sessions, though suitable in earlier periods, are not advisable. The duration of the training should be no longer than the duration of match play. The danger of lengthier sessions is that it may develop a lackadaisical or mechanical attitude by the player that would be detrimental to the objective of having complete mental and physical alertness throughout the game. Further, lengthy training sessions become monotonous and enhance the danger of overtraining.

Stress is cumulative. The importance of the game, conditions of the field, weather, and the like have a great effect on the wear and tear of a player. Further, the effects of stress are different with every individual, physically and psychologically. Only the alert and sensitive coach, through knowledge and observation of his players, will be able to estimate the effects of these stresses. Training has to be highly individualized and diversified to ensure peak performance.

Timing Competitive Form

The improvement resulting from a few weeks' training will remain constant if the work load is steady (even if duration is increased). If the work load is increased, after a week or two the athletes reach a new level of efficiency as measured in heart rate, respiratory rate, and decrease of lactic acid in the blood. Consequently we can say that there is a direct relationship between stress and form level of proficiency. By altering the magnitude of the work load, we can influence the form curve.

The effect of increasing the load can be felt only after a certain length of time. The direct reaction of increased stress is a certain decline in form, whereas a reduced strain results in a rising form curve, provided a proper foundation has been established.

Applying this principle in practice we might want to increase the work load during a particular week in the interest of a more long-term objective—an important game or play-off. This must be done carefully, however, because the more immediate game must also be taken into consideration and we must ensure that the decline in form from increasing the strain will not be too great. On the contrary, should our objective be a maximum performance in the next game, then the curve of the weekly load should decline a corresponding extent.

The interdependence of stress and rest, or work loading and regeneration, must prevail even throughout the weekly training program. Stress should not be kept at the same level throughout. After heavy exertion, in a league game, for example, a lighter session should follow so that the player has sufficient time to generate and cope with stimuli of a succeeding heavier session. It has been found that interference with a rhythm, once established, should be avoided. To repeat, this training rhythm evolves around the match schedule and it has within it a fairly consistent pattern of varying intensity of stress.

We can establish by following the interval principle with regard to daily stress the weekly training rhythm in Table 2.

Sunday	Light (L)	Maximum 0–20%
Monday	Average (A)	Maximum 40–50%
Tuesday	Heavy (H)	Maximum 60–80%
Wednesday	Average (A)	Maximum 40–50%
Thursday	Heavy (H)	Maximum 60–80%
Friday	Light (L)	Maximum 0–20%
Saturday	Match Day	100%

Table 2.

According to the game schedule, the most common weekly training cycles are given in Table 3.

Many teams are unable to practice every day. They meet at best three times and more likely two times a week. See Table 4.

WEEKLY PROGRAM

Sunday

The day after a match should be one of physical and emotional relaxation. Since the best method of regenerating is activity, many teams, particularly on the professional level, have gymnastics, sauna bath, and massage. On the amateur, school, and college levels, we often do not have the facilities or that much control over the players on their off-days. The next best thing is to encourage players to take part in recreational activities such as swimming, tennis, or golf to achieve the same purpose.

This is the day for injured players to get proper treatment, because quick action could mean their return to active play in half the time.

It is important to maintain or improve team spirit. This is an ideal day for the coach to have intimate talks with the players about their past performance and the upcoming game. If it is at all possible, individuals should meet with the coach for lunch or supper. Or the coach can telephone players: this is satisfactory, less time-consuming, and it enables him to reach more players. It is

Match on Saturday

Sunday (L)
Monday (A)
Tuesday (H)
Wednesday (A)
Thursday (H)
Friday (L)
Saturday-Match

Matches on Saturday, Wednesday

Sunday (L)
Monday (A)
Tuesday (L)
Wednesday-Match
Thursday (L)
Friday (L)
Saturday-Match

Matches on Saturday, Tuesday

Sunday (L)
Monday (L)
Tuesday-Match
Wednesday (L)
Thursday (A)
Friday (L)
Saturday-Match

Matches on Saturday, Monday

Sunday (L)
Monday-Match
Tuesday (L)
Wednesday (A)
Thursday (H)
Friday (L)
Saturday-Match

Table 3.

Three Practices a Week with Match on Saturday

Sunday-no training
Monday-no training
Tuesday (H)
Wednesday (A)
Thursday (H)
Friday-no training
Saturday-Match

Three Practices a Week with Match on Sunday

Sunday-Match
Monday-no training
Tuesday (H)
Wednesday (A)
Thursday (H)
Friday-no training
Saturday-no training

Table 4.

essential that he talk with those players whom he feels need special attention—those who were injured, had a poor game, made a vital mistake—those with problems that must be resolved as soon as possible. Perhaps he cannot contact all players on this day, but he should be sure that during the week he provides an opportunity for everyone to talk with him. A late Sunday afternoon team meeting is useful, particularly for game film-viewing.

Individual criticism and individual preparation are very necessary for improving team performance. The general mood among the team members and those concerned with the team must be positive and relaxed. Creating such an atmosphere is the sole responsibility of the coach.

Monday

The players should have a solid warm-up stressing mobility and flexibility. This can be followed by fun games to put the squad in a good spirit, a positive frame of mind, and receptive to the team-talk which is to follow.

Match criticism and match evaluation are important ways of evaluating experience and transposing those experiences into future success. They must be constructive. The coach should first analyze the match itself and the manner in which it was played and then follow with detailed criticism of team and individual tactical faults.

In order not to embarrass any player in front of his peers, the coach should have first talked with the players he intended to use as examples in the discussion. He should only mention individuals if it is essential to make his point or so that the whole team may benefit from it. Ideally the theoretical session, which can take place right on the field, is accompanied by or followed up with practical demonstrations to avoid any possible misunderstanding, and also to clarify the reasons why particular errors were detrimental. This should obviously be followed by a special session to improve individual or group technical and tactical shortcomings. In this way the team feels the relevance of the criticism to their future performance. Further, since it has a positive influence because players feel the coach really has their progress at heart, there is nothing better for team morale.

An intersquad scrimmage should finish up the day, because, there is no better morale-booster than the game itself. Players love to play—that is why they take part in the program.

Tuesday

This is a peak day of the week. While at this stage of the season the players should be mentally and physically in top condition, it is necessary for them to maintain that fitness. Consequently the main emphasis is on developing and maintaining endurance, particularly speed work. With a combined method of training, skill and tactical proficiency can be gained while physical conditioning and general or local endurance and speed are emphasized.

A solid warm-up stressing flexibility and mobility should be followed by strenuous stamina, speed, quickness, and possibly power training. The rest of the time is spent on individual, group, and team tactics, with particular emphasis on small-group work to enable the coach to control the pace of the activities.

Players like to be well-organized in their practice sessions, particularly in the work for special emphasis. There is, in fact, a joy in well-organized, tough training sessions; both amateurs and professionals appreciate the fact that haphazard training is of no advantage.

Wednesday

An average day in terms of work load. It is a good day to work on improvement of individual skills and techniques as well as tactics, with the main emphasis on functional practices. Highlights from the scouting report and an expected game plan are put into realistic and practical plans, so that the major points can be worked on by individuals and the team for the upcoming game. When the final game plan is presented, usually the day before the game at a team meeting, the groundwork has been laid and everything is meaningful.

Thursday

Like Tuesday, this is one of the peak work days of the week and should be similar to Tuesday's practice session. The only difference is that there must be great sensitivity to individual needs, starting with a highly individualized warm-up period for flexibility and mobility, followed by speed work (which should not only be individually oriented but also within the framework of functional practices for the upcoming game). For example, if the opponent operates with a long ball to the wing forward, the fullback will frequently be expected to turn and outrace the wing forward for the lead pass. This has to be incorporated into the fullback's speed work. This is true also of individual and group tactics, particularly stressing cooperation and coordination among segments of the team with respect to the upcoming opponent.

Friday

A light day in terms of work load. Whether there is a practice session or not depends upon the kick-off time on match day. If it is an afternoon game, there should most likely be a light practice session. Should the kick-off be in the morning, there should only be an evening team meeting to discuss the final game plan.

A day-before-game practice session should be a short and relaxed one consisting of limbering-up exercises and fun games (not necessarily related to soccer). This is also a good time to work on individual skills, particularly those that relate to special assignments, corner kicks, penalty kicks, free kicks, and throw-ins. Last are special team tactics, concentrating on dead-ball situations, such as restarts, throw-ins, and penalty kicks.

TEAM MEETING

Presenting the Game Plan

The best time for a team meeting is the day before the game because of the immediacy of the match and also because the meeting either takes the place of a practical training session or follows a light session. Consequently the players are well-rested and mentally receptive.

The coach should open the meeting with a brief review of the season to date, the team's general progress, and its standing in the league.

He recalls the season's objectives and individual goals. Appealing to the players' common love of the game and high hopes, he evaluates the team's progress in terms of their objectives on a positive note, if at all possible. This might sometimes require rationalization or special circumstances, such as injuries to key players, to explain why the team or individuals have not been able to live up to their expectations. Whatever has happened so far, he makes clear that this game is the ideal opportunity for the team to get back on the winning track, catch up, or stay on course for its set goals. He leaves the impression that the upcoming game is the most important one of the season.

The pre-match briefing is a time when the coach's tactical judgment is put to the test. The basis for a successful game plan must be the physical and psychological disposition of the team in relation to the opponent. The idea is to make tactical adaptations to counteract the opponent without disrupting the team's customary style of play. The coach must have enough confidence in individual players and in the team to let them play their own game, to force the opponent to play within the framework of their thinking. The idea is not to let the opponents do what they want to do, but rather make them do what they do *not* want to do.

Plans to eliminate dangerous opposing players change every week with different opponents. One week the team will be playing against a big center halfback, who may intercept balls intended for our center forward's head. In that case the coach will impress upon his team the necessity for keeping the ball on the ground where the big fellow does not have the advantage. The next week there may be a small center halfback, and the plans change, with perhaps the best path to goal being via the center forward's head.

During the week the essential points of scouting reports made practices relevant to the match against the upcoming opponent. To give the team a total picture of their opponent, a more detailed and thorough presentation of the reports is presented at this meeting, showing their preferred system of play, basic and special offensive and defensive patterns and tendencies, and the strengths and weaknesses of the team as a group as well as the individual players.

Every possible means of communication is used: blackboard drawings, films, graphic descriptions of every sort, with an open discussion both during and after the presentation to involve intellectually all the players. Experienced players may have already played against this opponent and be able to give helpful suggestions. Others may have heard from friends about particular weaknesses or special tactics used by other teams to contain this opponent. The coach and the staff, with players contributing, talk about what other teams have been doing against this opponent, how effective were these tactics, and the best plan for their own team. This is particularly helpful in order to project opponents' reactions to the tactics so as to prepare countermeasures ahead of time. All this serves to convince players that the final game plan will incorporate what everybody thinks is best under the circumstances. The players must be convinced that through their hard and dedicated work during the week, everything possible has been done to prepare them for the upcoming game.

The difference between winning and losing is often the confidence the coach has in winning the game and the degree to which he can instill that confidence through his game plan into his players.

MATCH DAY PREPARATION AND TACTICS

The most effective match preparation is one that shows great sensitivity by the coach to individuals. Preparation for the upcoming match is made all week, of course, but what a player does twenty-four hours prior to the game is of vital importance, because it will have a direct bearing on his performance and consequently on the outcome of the game.

With the guidance of the coach, the players should have established a routine of proper diet, early retiring the night before the game, and restraining from alcohol, nicotine, and sex. Even in these respects, however, the coach must show understanding for individual differences. Some players may not be accustomed to retiring early; it would be useless, even detrimental, to force them to do so and just toss restlessly. Others may be unduly nervous and a drink might be exactly what they need in order to sleep. If players are used to smoking, it would be harmful if they were forbidden to do so. In short, the evening preparation prior to match day should be similar to the general routine of the individual.

This is particularly important on away games where the coach has to make the necessary arrangements. Hotel rooms must be quiet and comfortable, with customary food available. Regeneration through healthy diet, rest, full sleep, and relaxing recreational activities, are decisive for a good performance. The coach should make room assignments in accordance with the compatability of players in these matters. Assigning players together who have opposite sleeping habits, such as an early bird with a night hawk, would pose difficulties for both.

For any road trip longer than three hours, it is advisable to make it an overnight affair to be sure players are rested for the game. Should this be impossible, it is essential that the coach allow sufficient travel-time to include a brief rest stop every few hours so that the players can stretch their legs and prevent them from tightening up and still arrive two hours before the game. Bus trips are an excellent opportunity for the coach to establish personal contact. By moving about throughout the trip, seizing any chance to chat with players, he can do much to release the anxiety and tension of highly sensitive players.

On the morning of match day, the coach must again show great insight. Some players prefer to sleep late while others rise early. This will influence breakfast and consequently the pre-game meal. The manager may be asked to make the room calls in accordance with the players' individual idiosyncrasies. The coach should make personal room visits, if at all possible. Because of the intimate atmosphere, this is again an ideal opportunity for him to speak with his players. Since this is often quite impossible, a telephone call is the next best thing.

For home games, telephoning personally, particularly to certain individuals who are highly intense, or to players who are making their varsity debut, gives the player the feeling that the coach cares especially about him. A few appropriate remarks will surely be appreciated by the player trying to overcome any unnecessary anxiety or will prepare him for special assignments. This also gives the coach a chance to reassure himself of his players' mental and physical condition.

Breakfast should be made available, particularly

for afternoon games, but attendance should be on a voluntary basis to enable players to sleep late. They should have a substantial meal three–four hours before kick-off time. Most effective is a brunch three–four hours before the game which every player should be urged to have, but even then there are certain individuals who are reluctant to eat anything before a game. This might be especially true with morning games where players would have to get up early, say seven in the morning, to eat brunch for a ten o'clock match. If the coach feels this wish for abstinence is well-founded, he should be willing to tolerate it. Some players are so nervous before a game that they cannot eat or have difficulty digesting, even vomiting. Allowing them not to eat is sometimes the wiser decision. In such cases arrangements for high caloric liquid diets should be made.

For home games the coach and senior manager should meet in the dressing room at least one and a half hours before kick-off time to prepare the uniforms and special needs for each player, most notably gloves and cap for the goalkeeper, and to supervise game arrangements. Hospitable arrangements must also be made for the visiting team, game officials, and the press.

Good locker-room preparation gives the players confidence that everything possible has been done for them. Consequently this ensures the calm and quiet atmosphere essential for pre-game preparation. The players should arrive no later than one hour before kick-off.

In the meantime, the coach should have ascertained the present ground and weather conditions in order to have prepared the right uniforms, such as studs, or at least to be able to advise players of the proper equipment to wear.

On away games, the coach and manager should meet at the point of departure at least one half hour early to make certain that all trip arrangements have been taken care of. On away games, also, since it is probable that the coach and team will travel together to the stadium, both should arrive two hours before kick-off. This allows time for the squad to inspect field conditions. If there is sufficient time on overnight trips, the players should have a chance to look over the field when they arrive in the evening. Eliminating all uncertainties is reassuring to the players.

The trainer should be prepared to take care of

the needs of the players before the game. Those with problems that need special treatment should be asked to arrive early in order not to tie up the trainer. If there is no trainer, the coach should take care of any training duties at this time, assisted by the manager. The squad should be ready to go onto the field forty minutes before game time.

An individualized pre-game warm-up routine (which necessitates at least one ball for every other player) should be established. The team needs a fifteen–twenty minute pre-game warm-up. During this period, the coach, knowing every player's pre-game disposition mentally as well as physically, must be alert to whether things are going normally. He will intuitively know where an encouraging, challenging, or cautious remark is needed. In many instances, particularly with the goalkeeper, it might be wise for him to spend a few minutes with him actually warming him up. By his services he can make the goalkeeper confident and ready to go.

The experienced coach will always have one eye on the opponents' pre-game warm-up in order to get clues that could be of advantage to his team, such as noting injuries or weaknesses of the goalkeeper or other players.

After the warm-up, the team should return to the locker room or a cozy place to gather round the coach for last-minute instruction. The first concern is whether anyone has any physical problems the trainer should take care of. Second is last-minute questions concerning the game plan or individual assignments. Third is the coach's changes in response to any changes in the opposing line-up, because of his observations about their warm-up, or changing weather or field conditions.

The coach then has the final word. He reviews calmly and confidently in a few sentences the major points of the game plan, reminding players of their assignments. He makes an appeal for sportsmanship: "We fear none but respect all opponents, respect and accept the officials' decisions, and if anything out of the ordinary should arise, the only player to voice a complaint should be the captain." Lastly, the players are reminded that the only reason they are out there is because they love the game and enjoy its challenge. This is the time they have been waiting for. They should go out on the field and have fun!

The effect desired from this short pre-game talk is to assure the players that they are prepared for the opponent they are facing. This sometimes will take ingenuity, such as when there has been a sudden downpour creating treacherous ground conditions. The coach must recall some past experience where the team possibly practiced or played under these conditions, reminding them what fun it was, that the idea is to pass the ball to players' feet, recalling some great shot by one of the players and reminding them to shoot from far out because the ball skids.

A match is like graduation day. It is the resolution of the coach's and team's hard week's work. As soon as the team takes the field, they are on their own. There might be isolated instances where the coach's assistance from the sidelines is necessary. Generally it should be his pride and confidence to see his players meet the challenge.

Half-Time

The squad should relax during half-time, preferably in the locker room. Often this is not possible, so a cozy spot apart from everything should be selected beforehand; warm enough on cold days or cool enough and out of the sun on hot days.

The senior manager should have prepared half-time refreshments, towels, and so forth. Some players prefer to sit, others like to keep moving, and others like to lie down and elevate their legs. Individual preferences should be tolerated as long as they do not distract the harmony and calm atmosphere. For the first few minutes everybody tries to collect and relax himself. Some coaches allow their players to discuss quietly and constructively among themselves. Nobody says much. The trainer immediately goes to work taking care of all physical problems. The manager serves refreshments, such as lukewarm tea.

This is a time for adding a personal touch by rubbing players with alcohol on the thighs, chest, or back, all the while making personal remarks, praising one, encouraging another, cautioning some.

Then individual questions or problems regarding play should be brought forward. These questions are valuable for the coach to double-check his first half observations. Some questions have to be answered individually but most should be answered by a brief half-time talk.

The talk can reinforce the general game plan, if it has been effective, or alter it, if necessary, and the same is true for individual assignments. The coach must be prepared for possible changes by the opponent. To be effective this talk must be succinct, discussing not what happened *per se,* but what can be done about it, and how the team can take advantage of the opponent's weaknesses. The essence is positive, showing confidence in the team's ability to handle the opponent.

If the team is ahead, caution is required, for the game is won only after the final whistle is blown. The opponent should be taken seriously so as to avoid lack of concentration. If behind, an appeal to their pride can be made. With all the time and dedication they have invested, they owe it to themselves and to the team to do their best. There is still half a game in which to redeem themselves.

Sometimes it is effective if the coach recalls a particularly memorable game (the choice depending on the circumstances) where the team either lost a game that should have been won, or won where they had been the underdogs and solidly behind at half-time.

An inspirational pep talk is far more valuable at this time than before the game, for most of what is said pertains to what has actually taken place on the field. The coach must see that any momentum achieved in the first half is carried through the second.

Post-Game

The coach has many post-game responsibilities. He should meet on the field briefly with the opposing coach to exchange gracious congratulations or condolences. His foremost concern is that his players return quickly and safely into the dressing room, to prevent tempers from flaring up, outside interference with players or vice versa. Immediately after the match (preferably in the locker room) the coach should gather the entire squad around him, totally excluding outsiders, to give a short resumé of the game. Win or lose, the coach should be in control of himself and be completely impartial. The dressing room should provide a safe and protected atmosphere for the players. In fact it is frequently said that the end of one match is the beginning of the next. The players need encouragement, praise, and positive reinforcement.

An expected victory deserves compliments, with comments relevant to this particular opponent. Unexpected victory reaps congratulations without reservation though also a note of caution to avoid undue overconfidence. Unexpected defeat needs an expression of honest disappointment, though adding quickly that this can happen to the best of teams and the important thing is to recover quickly. After an expected defeat (as controversial as it may sound, there are days when you know your team is in over their heads), the coach can compliment the team for a gallant effort if the defeat was a narrow one. Rationalize by referring to the circumstances if the defeat was lopsided. What is important is that the players leave with a positive attitude, in harmony with the coach and with their teammates, and inspired for the next game.

The smallest injuries should be checked and taken care of by the trainer. There are always a few who do not feel their injury is serious enough to bother with. Prompt and efficient treatment can make all the difference between a player missing one or several games. The coach should later double check to be sure the injured player is completely satisfied and without anxiety about his injury.

As soon as his team responsibilities are over, the coach should meet with the press, being certain that he has control over his game feelings and keeping in mind that the members of the press are just trying to do their job. He should be objective and positive in his comments, never criticizing individual players, opponents, the opposing coach, or officials.

Probably violated most often is what the players do after the game. Since they are usually burned out, any kind of exuberant post-game celebration is highly detrimental to their physical condition. The most sensible thing to do would be to have a long hot bath, followed by a massage, provided the player is injury-free. In the meantime the players sip on a warm drink of tea or lemonade. After an hour or so of relaxing, they should have a healthy meal, high in protein and fruit juices. It is becoming more popular for teams to organize a post-game meal to be sure players get the food so important for a quick regeneration of vital body substances. Ideally, this would be followed by a quiet evening at home and retiring early.

Appendices

Appendix A: Coaching Aids

Coaching aids are useful devices for teaching fundamental skills and techniques. Most provide opportunity for the player to practice by himself, are time-saving in that the ball does not have to be chased, and most important, give variety to the everyday routine.

KICK BOARDS

There are different types of kick boards, but all have the same objective of allowing players to practice their shooting, passing, and ball-control skills against a wall that will cause the ball to rebound back to them (Fig. A.1).

They can be of any size but ordinarily they are larger than goal size. The outline of the goal is frequently painted onto the board, as are various target areas, so that players may aim for specific points to develop accuracy and also to add to the interest of the practice.

The board must be stable, with enough room in front so that players can approach it from any distance. If it is set up wisely, both sides can be used, permitting practice by more players at one time and also eliminate some chasing when the ball misses the board entirely.

PORTABLE GOALS

These aids can be regular size or miniature. They are very helpful in the practice area because they allow the coach to adjust field size or preserve the overused goal areas of the regular game field, and make use of space in other areas. They are extremely useful in small-group games where a number of matches are going on simultaneously or in multiple-goal group games. They can be of any material but ideally they should be of heavy-duty aluminum with steel bases and be completely adjustable and easy to assemble.

PENDULUM BALL

The pendulum ball is an aid of a thousand uses (Fig. A.2). Every team should have one or several. It is especially helpful for heading, volley passing, and shooting. The shape of the extension is unimportant—the purpose is to provide a stable attachment for the pendulum ball, the base of which will not interfere

Fig. A.1 *Kick board.*

Fig. A.2 *Pendulum balls.*

Fig. A.3 *Diving pit used in early training of diving techniques to avoid apprehension and injury.*

with the player's movement. It can be of pipe or wood, though the former is preferable. An eight-foot bar, two or three inches wide, attached to a thirteen–fifteen-foot pole for a T, or an L with a two-foot bar joined to a thirteen–fifteen-foot base can be set into cement or designed to be movable. The ball is suspended in such a way that its height can be adjusted. Strong fishing line is preferable to rope because it interferes less with the ball's movement.

The pendulum ball suspended from such a T bar, L, a tree, or even over the top of the goal, provides a most effective aid. Although the path of the ball travels in almost the reverse of its path in free flight, the pendulum ball allows the player to control the speed and path at which the ball approaches him. Naturally this controlled situation allows the coach and player to isolate and concentrate on the various mechanical aspects of the skill, thus permitting a progressive buildup of confidence and control.

CHALKBOARD OR MAGNETIC BOARD

Used for graphic illustrations in tactical sessions, both boards can be portable to eliminate the necessity for indoor sessions. The magnetic board has an advantage over the chalkboard in that it can be held horizontally, and many players have difficulty transferring tactical plays from a vertical illustration to their horizontal field position. In addition, the figures can be moved around at ease.

Fig. A.4 *Videotaping practices and games.*

OVERHEAD PROJECTOR

One of the better visual aids now available to the coach, it allows him to prepare visual material for tactical sessions, or use pictures, diagrams, or even explanations from books and pamphlets, to throw directly onto the screen.

FILMSTRIPS, VIDEOTAPE, AND FILMS

Filmstrips provide an excellent opportunity for self-instruction (Fig. A.4). Players can look at skill sequences repeatedly and then go out and practice them.

Videotape is unsurpassed as a learning device in that it permits photographing the player performing a particular skill and then providing immediate opportunity for his viewing the performance for possible correction.

Films are most valuable for teaching skills and tactics, providing high-level performance as good examples of play, and in promoting the sport. When the team's games are filmed, countless mistakes can be pointed out, and the players' ball-control, position, or tackling can be corrected. Players thus become increasingly aware of the importance of fundamentals and teamwork.

CONES AND FLAGS

These aids can be used to mark quickly a number of limited areas (grids). The most obvious and most common use is for slaloms for dribbling and feinting skills and techniques. They can be placed in regular or irregular intervals, in straight or triangle formations, to provide obstacles for players to avoid as they advance with the ball.

SHOOTING TEE

This aid serves the same purpose as a golf tee but the elevation for the ball is much higher, though it should be adjustable. It is especially valuable for volley passing and shooting. The advantage of the shooting tee over the pendulum extension is that it can be put directly in front of the goal, making practices most realistic.

SCRIMMAGE VESTS

Variously colored vests make quick organization of teams possible.

COACHING FILMS

The following are available in 16 mm. color with sound:

"Soccer Series" with H. Vogelsinger (3 films), Macmillan Films, Mt. Vernon, New York, 10050.
"Pele, the Master and his Method" (6 films, with wall charts and text), Pepsi Cola Public Relations, Purchase, New York, 10577.
"Football Technique" by Dettmar Cramer (4 films), USSFA, New York.
"Teamwork and Tactics" by English F. A. (11 films), USSFA, New York.

Appendix B: Important Dates in the Evolution of the Game

1848:   The 14 "Cambridge Rules for Association Football" were adopted in England. These rules, except for minor changes, have remained in international effect ever since.

1860:   Soccer was played with eleven men on a team, but with eight forwards and three defenders.

1870:   Forwards generally were reduced to seven, two on each wing and three in the middle. The goalkeeper was allowed to use his hands to protect the goal. Dribbling predominated.

1872:   The size of the ball was determined. Touchlines were marked. Crossbars replaced goal tapes. The first international contest was held between England and Scotland.

1874:   Shinguards were introduced in England. A wooden crossbar was added to the goal posts. Teams changed sides only at half-time instead of after each goal.

1877:   The throw-in was changed to allow the throw to be made in any direction rather than in a straight line.

1879:   England and the rest of the world were greatly influenced by Scottish passing play in which the ball was passed a short distance to an unmarked teammate instead of being dribbled by an individual.

1881:   Referees replaced umpires.

1882:   The one-handed throw-in was replaced by a two-handed throw. Charging from behind was permitted only when a player's opponent was definitely obstructing him from the ball.

1883:   Forwards generally were reduced to six, with the second center forward becoming the center halfback, pivotal player.

1885:   Professional standards were introduced and approved in England.

1890:   Professional soccer became popular. English public school people who had promoted soccer and given it its administration turned their backs on it. (It was to become lower-middle-class until the 1960's, when it became fashionable once more.)

1891:   Goal nets were introduced and the penalty kick was added.

1902:   The penalty and goal areas were marked, as in force today.

1904:   FIFA was organized.

1908:   England beat France in the first Olympic Game.

1912:   The F.A. of Canada was formed. Fuchs of Germany set a record number of goals (ten) for international play in his team's 16-0 win over Russia in the Olympics. Goalkeepers could not use their hands outside the penalty area.

1913:   USSFA was formed to govern both amateur and professional soccer in the U.S. The Football Leagues ruled that the goalkeeper had to play in distinctive colors. The F.A. recommended that opponents be required to stand ten yards from the ball on a free kick.

1914:   The Brazilian F.A. was formed.

1920:   The Football League was extended to forty-four clubs and a second division was formed in England. The International Board ruled that goalkeepers in British championship matches had to wear yellow jerseys. Soccer began to gain popularity in France.

1923:   The First Cup Final at Wembley Stadium (England) recorded an official attendance of 126,047, though it was estimated that 150,000 actually were on hand. The Bolton Wanderers beat West Ham United, 2-0.

1924:   The Scottish F.A. proposed that goals could be scored from corner kicks. Up until then players dribbled the ball in to score. The F.A. altered the law to allow only one kick.

1925:   On the first day of the new offside rule requiring only two defenders instead of three between attackers and goal line, Aston Villa beat Burnley, 10-0.

1927:   Dixie Dean, who had thirty-seven hat tricks in eighteen seasons, set a league record of sixty goals in a season for Everton (England).

1928:   The first appearance, and a most impressive one, of Argentina's team in Europe. Argentina had to go into overtime to win, 2-1, in the Olympics.

1930:   Austria beat Scotland 5-0, Germany 6-0, and lost to the English by only one goal (4-3) with its famous "wunderteam." England lost her first game abroad to Spain, 4-3. Rules were changed to allow a goalkeeper to take four steps instead of two when in possession of the ball. Uruguay won the first World Cup match. The U.S. was third.

1932:   Stanley Matthews made his debut for Stoke City, England. Before he retired in 1964 at the age of fifty, he had made 701 league appearances. He played twenty-nine times for England in wartime internationals and fifty-seven times in peacetime matches. He received a knighthood and was awarded the CBE.

1933:   Herbert Chapman developed the WM system (the "stopper").

1937:   An arc was marked at the edge and in the center of the penalty area, within which no player but the goalkeeper or penalty-taker could advance until after the penalty kick was taken.

1938:   Players were numbered for the Cup Final and then for league matches in England. The league game in England between Glasgow's Rangers and Celtic drew a crowd of 118,567.

1939:   Numbering of players was made mandatory in English leagues.

1950:   The U.S. beat England, 1-0, in World Cup preliminary competition in Brazil.

1953:   The Hungarians introduced the deep-lying center forward to beat the English at Wembley, 6-3.

1955:   Floodlights were accepted for competitive soccer in England.

1958:   The Brazilians won the World Cup with a 4-2-4 system that was adopted the world over.

1965:   Substitutes were allowed for the first time in England. One substitute was allowed for an injured player.

1966:   Two professional leagues began operations in the U.S.: the United Soccer Association (USA) and the National Professional Soccer League (NPSL).

1967:   The two American professional leagues joined to become the North American Soccer League.

1969:   Pelé scored his 1,000th goal. Two substitutes were approved for international competition.

1970:   More than 800 million people watched Brazil beat Italy, 4-1, in the international telecast of the World Cup final in Mexico, played before a capacity crowd of 110,000.

1972:   A FIFA questionnaire, answered by 134 of the 140 affiliated national soccer associations, gives the following figures: number of registered players, 15,667,545; total number of teams, 560,234; and referees, 284,941 (900 in the U.S., 5 of whom are women). A breakdown of the statistics shows that Europe dominates statistically with 73% of all clubs, 69% of the teams, 76% of the players, and 85% of the referees.

Appendix C: Noteworthy Organizations and Competitions

FEDERATION INTERNATIONALE DE FOOTBALL ASSOCIATION (FIFA)
(Hitziweg 11, Zurich 8032, Switzerland.)

In 1902 Sir Frederick Wall, secretary of the English Football Association, presented the Dutch idea of an international soccer union. In May, 1904, the idea was approved. Any nation willing to abide by the rules, laws, and articles of the game as laid down by FIFA was eligible for membership. Though England refused at first to join because of a disagreement with certain technicalities, Belgium, Denmark, Sweden, France, Netherlands, Switzerland, and Spain went ahead. Other countries, including England, soon followed. From seven members in 1904, FIFA had soared to 140 by 1971. No soccer association can now function without official approval of FIFA.

The federation was formed to standardize the rules on an international basis. Its seventeen laws have altered little over the years. FIFA is responsible for policing these laws, the maintenance of discipline, administration and finance, and the organization of international tournaments.

Laws of the game can only be changed at the annual meeting by a special committee of twelve—two each from British associations and four from FIFA. Since this regulation cannot be changed except by unanimous agreement of the board and since any change in the laws must have a three-fourths majority, it can be seen that the laws are controlled by Great Britain.

A FIFA publication of particular interest is a report every four years on the entire World Cup proceedings.

UNITED STATES SOCCER FOOTBALL ASSOCIATION (USSFA)
(4010 Empire State Building, New York, New York 10001.)

This is the national governing body for professional and amateur soccer in the United States. It has direct management and control of soccer in the United States, including international tournaments, and the National Challenge Cup, National Amateur Challenge Cup, and National Junior Cup Competitions. It has been a member of FIFA since 1914.

Among its standing committees are:

International Games Committee, which arranges international games between USSFA and other national associations and supervises and controls the operation of special tournaments involving foreign teams.

Selection Players Committee, charged with the power of selecting players in international competitions under the control of the USSFA.

Olympic Committee, to assist the U.S. Olympic Committee in the preparation for participation of the USSFA in soccer competition at the Olympic Games. It has the duty to determine the place, time, and method of holding tryouts or other competitions for the selection of members of the team for the Olympic or Pan American Games. In addition, the committee nominates the manager and coaches for these teams.

Associate members of the USSFA are:
Amateur Athletic Union of the United States
Intercollegiate Soccer Football Association of America
National Collegiate Athletic Association
National Federation of State High School Athletic Associations
National Soccer Coaches Association of America

Among the USSFA's numerous publications are a monthly newsletter entitled "News From Your USSFA National Commission" and a yearbook with reports from affiliated clubs and results of competition for the various leagues and cups.

NATIONAL SOCCER COACHES ASSOCIATION OF AMERICA
(668 La Vista Rd., Walnut Creek, California, 94598.)

Membership in this association is open to all soccer coaches and anyone interested in the sport. The NSCAA contributes to the growth of the game and the professional improvement of coaches, particularly through its quarterly publication, *Soccer Journal,* and its annual convention. It selects annually an all-American intercollegiate soccer team and operates a film library available to its members.

WORLD CUP GAMES

In 1928, FIFA decided to launch a World Cup competition. It would be held first in 1930 and then every four years (alternating with the Olympic Games), it would be open to all the national associations affiliated with FIFA, and it would be conducted on an elimination basis.

Because Uruguay was to celebrate its 100th anniversary of independence the same year as the World Cup Tournament, the candidates for host nation withdrew in favor of Uruguay. Later on, many European nations violently protested the decision and refused to participate in the games that year. They were held nevertheless with those nations willing to send their teams on the long boat trip to Uruguay. The world contest continued. Now seventy nations enter teams, and there is a long elimination series that generally takes more than a year to complete.

The World Cup trophy, called the Jules Rimet Trophy since 1946, is greatly prized. Any nation winning it for the third time has the right to retain it, which Brazil did in 1970. That statue was created by a Frenchman named Abel Lafleur; it is a figure of victory holding an octagonal vessel in the form of a cup. The cup is of solid gold, based in marble, and weighs a little over nine pounds. The new Rimet trophy (which will remain with FIFA and replicas given to the victorious nation) has been designed by an Italian sculptor, Silvio Gazzaniga. It depicts two athletes, arms upraised in victory, holding aloft a globe of the world. It is made of solid gold and stands fifteen inches high.

Winners of the nine competitions have been (with interruption of the games during World War II):

1930 in Uruguay: Uruguay over Argentina, 4-2, with U.S.A. third.
1934 in Italy: Italy over Czechoslovakia, 2-1, with Germany third.
1938 in France: Italy over Hungary, 4-2, with Brazil third.
1950 in Brazil: Uruguay over Brazil, 2-1, with Sweden third.
1954 in Switzerland: Germany over Hungary, 3-2, with Austria third.
1958 in Sweden: Brazil over Sweden, 5-2, with France third.
1962 in Chile: Brazil over Czechoslovakia, 3-1, with Chile third.

1966 in England: England over West Germany, 4-2, with Portugal third.
1970 in Mexico: Brazil over Italy, 4-1, with West Germany third.

THE OLYMPICS

Soccer was brought into the Olympic program in 1900 and now over eighty nations enter soccer teams in the qualifying rounds. Eliminations are held by zones until the competitors number fourteen, with host countries and defending gold medal winners automatically qualifying. The games are held every four years, alternating with the World Cup games.

Until the World Cup championship was instituted in 1930, the Olympic Games afforded the highest test in soccer. The World Cup diminished the Olympics in international importance, though there have been memorable matches:

England won, 2-0, over Denmark in 1908 and were again victorious in 1912.
Belgium won, 2-0, over Czechoslovakia when the Czechs walked off the field in protest over the expulsion of a player.
Uruguay, spearheaded by stars Nasazzi, Andrade, Scarone, and Cea, won the 1924 Olympics in Paris, and also the 1928 tournament.
Italy won in 1936 with Locatelli, Foni, and Rava.
Sweden won in 1948 with Svensson, Nilsson, and Hordahl.
Hungary won in 1952 with Puskas, Kocsis, and Czibor.
Russia won in 1956 with Yachin, Netto, and Streltsov.
Yugoslavia won in 1960 with Galic, Yusufi, and Soskic.
Hungary won in 1964 with Bene, Farkas, and Novak.
Hungary won again in 1968 with Dunai, Pancsics, and Szves.
Poland won in 1972 with Lubanski, Deyna, and Gadocha.

Appendix D: Glossary

BACK UP.   A player trailing behind a teammate to give assistance when needed.

BLOCKING.   (Legal Obstruction) Moving slowly forward in front of an opponent with the ball within playing distance.

CENTER.   A pass that moves the ball from the flanks to the center of the field.

CENTER BACK.   The old-style "stopper" can still be seen in a 1-3-3-3 team facing opposition that plays with three players up front—two wing forwards and a lone center forward. Here the duties of the center back are confined to a personal duel with the center forward. When a team prepares to gamble on all-out attack, the center back is expected to give cover to either fullback as may be required.

CENTER CIRCLE.   A circle with a ten-yard radius at the center of the field where play is begun.

CENTER FORWARD.   Striker, spearhead of the attack.

CENTER LINE.   A straight line connecting the two sidelines at the midfield, dividing the field into two equal parts.

CHARGING.   Using shoulder against shoulder (each player must have one foot on the ground) to ride an opponent off the ball or to jar him into an unbalanced position.

CHIP PASS.   Lofting the ball over both short and long distances by striking the ball sharply at the lowest point possible.

CLEARANCE.   A kick that sends the ball from one end of the field to the other out of danger. Generally it is a high kick that goes over the opponents' heads.

COMBINATION.   A play involving two or more players on a team or a series of passes and maneuvers.

COMMIT.   To start a movement, either by a player with the ball or against an opponent who has the ball. If the forward can get the defender to commit himself, for example, by a feint move, then the defender will be a second off in following the real move.

CONTAIN.   The technique of keeping an opponent within a given area.

CORNER AREA.   The small arc at each corner of the field from which corner kicks are taken.

CORNER KICK.   A direct free kick from the corner arc. When a defensive player is the last one to touch the ball and it goes over his own goal line, his opponents are awarded a corner kick from the arc closest to the spot where it crossed the goal line.

COUNTERATTACK.   To begin an attack immediately after gaining possession of the ball.

COVER.   To mark, guard, or place oneself so near an opponent that his efforts to play the ball are nullified or at least challenged. To cover for a teammate is to take up his positional responsibilities if he has been called away from them by the play or to give cover to a teammate challenging for the ball.

CROSS.   A pass from one side of the field to the other.

CUSHIONING THE BALL.   Reducing the speed of a ball coming at the player by using the head, body, or feet in order to bring it under control and giving at the moment of impact.

DEAD BALL.   A ball not in play, when it has passed out of the field after a goal, after a called infraction of the rules, or when play is stopped by a referee.

DECOY PLAY.   A play designed to draw an opponent away from a given area, to open up the gap that the opponent was covering. The center forward suddenly leaves the middle of the field and takes the center halfback with him, leaving the way open for a teammate.

DEFENSIVE SCREEN.   A defensive midfield player who is asked to patrol across the front of the defensive wall, intercepting passes intended for the opposition's front players. The screen moves across to challenge the player who has possession regardless of the direction an attack might develop, thus making it more difficult for opponents to pull a tight-marking defender away from his man.

DEPTH.   Extra-man advantage to ensure the player in possession of numerous passing opportunities and support.

DIAGONAL PASS.   A pass made diagonally, say from the right halfback to the left wing forward, relying as much on the surprise element as on the accuracy of the pass.

DIRECT FREE KICK.   Awarded by the referee, generally for a personal foul, the player can kick from the point of infraction directly into the goal.

DRAG.   Pulling a ball in a desired direction (not a kick), usually as part of a trap.

DRAW AN OPPONENT.   To induce an opponent to leave his position or the player he is covering by pulling him toward you and away from a teammate who can then receive a pass.

DRIBBLING.   Using a series of pushes or taps with the feet while moving and keeping the ball under control.

DROP BALL.   A means of putting the ball into play by the referee after a temporary suspension of play not specifically covered in the rules.

FEINT.   A deceptive movement by a player to confuse an opponent.

FIRST-TOUCH or FIRST-TIME.   Passing the ball without first controlling it.

FLICK PASS.   A short, quick kick of the ball to a teammate.

FOULING.   An illegal use of the hands or body that can lead to a direct free kick for the opposition.

FREEBACK.   Sweeper, libero, the freeback is so named because he does not have to mark an opponent. Positioned behind the defenders who are marking men, the freeback covers each defender in turn as his teammates are drawn into a challenge for the ball. In particular he is responsible for covering the central approach to goal when the center back(s) are drawn out of position.

GIVE-AND-GO.   Wall pass. To pass the ball to a teammate who plays it first-touch and immediately runs into a position for a return pass.

GOAL AREA.   The area in front of the nets, twenty yards by six yards. The ball can be placed anywhere in this area for a goal kick.

GOAL KICK.   A kick taken by the defending team from the goal area after the ball has crossed the goal line (but not into the nets) after having been touched last by an attacking player.

GOAL LINE.   The boundary line marking the end of the field.

HALFBACK.   Midfield player, linkman.

HALF-VOLLEY.   A ball played just as it hits the ground or is just starting its ascent after the bounce.

HEADING.   The skill of using the head, usually the flat center of the forehead, to propel the ball intercepted in midair in any direction.

INDIRECT FREE KICK.   A kick awarded for a technical violation that must be touched by another player (teammate or opponent) before a goal can be scored.

INSWINGER.   A corner kick that curves toward the goal.

INTERCEPTION.   Getting the ball before it reaches the intended receiver.

JOCKEY.   Maneuver of a defender to gain time by giving ground.

KICK-OFF.   A place kick from the center of the field as a means of starting play at the beginning of each period or restarting after a goal has been scored.

LATERAL MOVEMENT.   Direction going from touchline to touchline.

LEAD PASS.   A pass aimed ahead of a receiver so the ball will cross his path and can be picked up without causing the player to break stride or lose speed.

LEFT CENTER BACK.   In the dual centerback game of 4-2-4 and 4-3-3, the left center back is expected to mark the right center forward and give cover to the left back and the right center back. With a freeback playing behind, however, he will be free to give all his attention to his immediate opponent.

LOB.   A high kick with no real power behind it. Designed to sail over the head of a defensive player.

MARK.   The defensive action to guard or shadow an opponent. This can be done skintight or loosely, depending on the team tactics.

MIDFIELD PLAYER.   Right midfield: A combination of old WM-type right halfback and inside right forward but with greater freedom of action. He is expected to support his front colleagues but also be in a position to screen the defensive players when required. Center: Best described as the old-style attacking center halfback before the WM system, or later as a withdrawn center forward. He is positioned between right midfield and his duties will be to support the front players and also help in defense when necessary.

   Left: He is expected to challenge for the ball in midfield, support the attack, and help in defense. Any midfield player may be asked to pay particular attention to a key opponent who plays in midfield.

MOBILITY.   Perpetual movement to create and use space and link with the ball-handler in a collective effort to sustain the attack.

OBSTRUCTION.   To impede the movements of an opponent by remaining in his path of movement. It is only legal if the ball is within playing distance.

OFFSIDE.   A player who is nearer to his opponent's goal line than the ball at the moment the ball is played except in specific instances covered in the laws. Or: there must be two opposing players between an offensive player and the opponent's goal unless an opponent or the player himself last touched it. A player cannot be offside in his own half of the field. Or on a goal kick, a corner kick, a dropped ball, if the player is behind the ball when it is last played.

OUTSIDE LEFT.   The left wing forward.

OUTSIDE RIGHT.   The right wing forward.

OUTSWINGER.   A corner kick that swerves away from the goal.

OVERLAPPING.   Sending a back in front of the wing forward into the less heavily guarded area on the wings. When the pass is released at the right moment, performed at speed, this play can turn the entire defense. Or, a fullback or halfback feeds the wing forward who moves forward and away from the touchline, taking his fullback with him, while a player runs round the outside, down the wing to receive a pass. This is the most popular way of beating a packed and retreating defense.

PASSIVE RESISTANCE.   Token or inactive opposition.

PENALTY AREA.   The zone in front of the goal, forty-four yards by eighteen. The goalie is permitted to use his hands in this area.

PENALTY KICK.   If a personal foul is committed by a defending player inside the penalty area, the attacking team gets a direct free kick from a marked spot twelve yards from the goal. No one is allowed to be between the kicker and the nets except the goalkeeper. He must not move his feet until the ball has been touched by the player.

PENETRATION.   To advance the ball accurately and quickly with scoring the immediate objective.

PLACE KICK.   A kick at a stationary ball placed on the ground.

PLAYMAKER.   A player who is concerned primarily with feeding passes to his teammates, setting up the scoring opportunities.

READING THE PLAY.   Interpreting or anticipating what action may take place by watching a player or the situation.

REVERSE PASS.   Plays an important part in overlapping movements. When a wing forward cuts inside (moving with the ball away from the touchline) he creates behind him the chance for a fullback or wing-half teammate to move into an unguarded space. This is an ideal situation to use the reverse pass, for the fullback can become an attacking player with ample room to use the ball. A player dribbles the ball in one direction, draws the defense with him, and suddenly flings the ball in the opposite way.

RIGHT BACK-FULLBACK.   The right back is still responsible for marking the opposing left wing forward. In 4-2-4 and 4-3-3, the right back will also be asked to give cover on the center when the opposition attacks on the other flank or through the center. In any form of catennacio, full responsibility for covering is taken by the freeback and the right back is left to concentrate on the left wing forward.

RUNNING OFF THE BALL.   Getting into position when not in possession of the ball. Continuous movement to escape from the marking opponents into a space where the player can be reached by a pass from the player with the ball.

SAG OFF.   To move away from the opponent being marked.

SAVE.   To prevent the ball from entering the goal. It usually refers to the catch or deflection by the goalkeeper.

SCORE.   A goal. When the ball has passed completely over the goal line between the uprights and under the crossbar.

SCREEN.   To obstruct a player's view of the ball with the body.

SHEPHERD.   Maneuvering the opposition into less dangerous positions while retreating.

SPACE.   Open areas that can be exploited by the offense. The decisive space is in front of the goalmouth and important space is on the flanks.

SQUARE PASS.   One pushed directly acrossfield to a man moving forward. It is often exploited by a wing forward seeking the help of his halfback when he is pinned to the touchline.

STOPPER.   The back who plays at or near the center of the field in the fullback line, usually the center halfback.

STRIKER.   Spearhead of attack, usually the center forward.

STYLE OF PLAY.   Determines the place on the field and the area of movement of each player and the type of game, long or short passing, hustling, aggressive, slow and determined, and the like.

SUPPORT.   Coming from behind to establish numerical superiority around the ball.

TACKLE.   A skill used to take the ball from an opponent, to cause him to lose control of it, or to hasten his play, thus making it ineffective.

THROUGH PASS.   A pass to a point behind the defensive players by kicking the ball between them or over their heads.

THROW-IN.   When the ball goes across a touchline it is put back into play by opponents of the team that touched it last. The ball is thrown with the hands over the head, both hands on the ball and both feet on the ground. This is done outside the field of play at the point the ball crossed the touchline.

TOUCHLINE.   The sideline marking the boundary of the field on each side.

TRAPPING.   The classic technique of trapping—killing the ball between some part of the foot and the ground—is the basis of sound ball-control.

WALL (HUMAN).   A barrier of defenders positioned to assist the goalkeeper in his defense against a free kick near the goal.

WIDTH.   Players holding wide positions so that intelligent passing can be made over the whole width of the field.

WING FORWARDS.   Wingers, outside left and right forwards.

WING HALFBACKS.   The right halfback and left halfback.

Appendix E: Selected Bibliography

Allison, Malcolm, *Soccer For Thinkers*. London: Pelham Book Ltd., 1967.

Batty, Eric, *Soccer Coaching the Modern Way*. London: Faber and Faber, 1969.

Creek, F.N.S., *Teach Yourself Soccer*. London: The English Universities Press Ltd., 1968.

Csanadi, Arpad, *Soccer*. Budapest: Corvina, 1965.

DiClemente, Frank F., *Soccer Illustrated*. New York: Ronald Press Company, 1968.

Finney, Tom, *Instructions to Young Footballers*. London: Museum Press Limited, 1955.

Greaves, Jimmy, *Soccer Techniques and Tactics*. London: Pelham Books Ltd., 1966.

Joy, Bernard, *Soccer Tactics*. London: Phoenix House Ltd., 1962.

Lodziak, Conrad, *Understanding Soccer Tactics*. London: Faber and Faber, 1966.

MacDonald, Roger, and Eric Batty, *Scientific Soccer in the Seventies*. London: Pelham Books Ltd., 1971.

Menendez, Julie, and Matt Boxer, *Soccer*. New York: Ronald Press, 1968.

Moynihan, John, *The Soccer Syndrome*. London: MacGibbon and Kee Ltd., 1966.

Schmid, Irvin R., John L. McKeon, and Melvin R. Schmid, *Skills and Strategies of Successful Soccer*. New York: Prentice-Hall, Inc., 1968.

Smith, Stratton, and Eric Batty, eds., *International Coaching Book*. London: Souvenir Press, 1966.

Vogelsinger, Hubert, *How to Star in Soccer*. New York: Four Winds Press, 1967.

Vogelsinger, Hubert, *Winning Soccer Skills and Techniques*. New York: Parker Publishing Company, Inc., 1970.

Wade, Alan, *Coach Yourself Association Football*. London: Educational Productions Limited, 1970.

Wade, Alan, *The FA Guide to Training and Coaching*. London: William Heinemann Ltd., 1967.

Wilson, Bob, *Goalkeeping*. London: Pelham Books Ltd., 1970.

Winterbottom, Walter, *Coach Yourself Series*. London: Educational Productions Limited.

Winterbottom, Walter, *Modern Soccer*. London: Educational Productions Ltd., 1958.

Winterbottom, Walter, *Soccer Coaching*. Kingswood, Surrey: Naldrett Press Ltd., 1952.

Winterbottom, Walter, *Training for Soccer*. London: William Heinemann Ltd., 1960.

Index

SPECIAL SKILLS AND TECHNIQUES ORIENTATION CHART